C86 AND ALL THAT

by the same author

DOCUMENT & EYEWITNESS:
An Intimate History Of Rough Trade

C86 & ALL THAT:
Artefacts & Ephemera From The Creation Of Indie

With many thanks and much respect!!!

C86 AND ALL THAT

THE CREATION OF INDIE IN DIFFICULT TIMES

NEIL TAYLOR

Ink Monkey
EDITIONS

First published in 2017 by
Inkmonkey Books
www.inkmonkeybooks.com

Typeset by Megan Sheer
www.sheerdesignandtypesetting.com

Cover Design by Karen Morgan at Morgan Radcliffe
Photographs courtesy of Paul Groovy

A CIP record for this book is available from the British Library
ISBN 978 1 909502 32 1 (HB)
ISBN 978 1 909502 33 8 (TPB)

2 4 6 8 10 9 7 5 3 1

For

John Reed

'Young people ought not to be idle. It's very bad for them…'
Margaret Thatcher, 1984

'It's not what you give, it's what you can take – and in what amounts'
'Another Side To Mrs Quill', Yeah Yeah Noh, 1985

THE SECOND CHAPTER OF THIS book, 'Familiarity Breeds Bananas', first appeared as an extended essay in the CD box set *Another Splash Of Colour: New Psychedelia 1980-85*. Small parts of other sections of the book appeared in prototype as long-form sleeve notes for *C86 and Artifact*. The support of Cherry Red is gratefully recognised. A greater debt is owed to the following whose generous support enabled the writing of the book: Maris Kreizman, Yancey Strickler, Benedikt Koehler, John Andrew Massey, Joanna Woodward, Sam Adams, Henning Korsgaard Christensen, Eli J Kasan, Co Co, Connie Churcher, Michael J Madsen, Neil Hendry, Jenni Armstrong, David Wilson, Adam Orton, Knut Tore Breivik, David M Smith, Chris Tighe, Iain Sellers, Jo Brooks, JL, Simon Cobb, David Todd, Catherine Palgrave, Albee, Nick Hall, Jon Johnson, Charlie Panayiotou, Guyda Armstrong, Robey Callahan, Christopher Harris, Jonathan, Adam Lopardo, Sam Matheson, Lindsay Huber, Ralph Brandi, Michael Branch, Carsten, Lubos Mokras, Stefano Cremonsi, John Morrow, Lucy Mediratta, Rémy Rékaj, Mark Johnson, Rachel Thian, Alyssa Marie Steffani, John Ford, Matthew Towles, Tom Meyer, Salvatore Patti, Michael Prince, Thomas Zimmerman, Christer Nilsson, Philippe Tacon, Graham Wiggins, Ian Hartley, Robert Bruce, Nicholas Wroe, Tim Naylor, Terry Hook, Richard Boon, Dylan Cascio, Susan Broyles, Giacommo Pucci, Kirsten Borchardt, Jeremy Rose, Simon Heath, Peter Johnston, Andrew Roach, John Quarmby, Ben Lawley, David Cinabro, Ulrich Hoffmann, Danny Lee Garrett, Steve Antill, Karina Santos, Gareth Kay, Amy Sammartino, Neil Dingwall, Mark Dowman, Keri Mackley, Giskard, Rob F, Martin Hand, Alastair Furnival, Patchouli Knowledge, Robert Helmering, Tim Harper, Alastair Dickson, Mike Bowen, Kim, Jamie Manley, Jim McAllstr, Uta Bretsch, David Kennedy, Joseph Partridge, Bryan McConachie, Simon Trigwell, The High Frontier, Kai Talonpoika, Mark Atkinson, Jon Smmns,

Rob Glander, Gareth Barker, Maxine Knight, David Fryer, Shaun Charman, The Vapid Wench, Jenny, William McAlpine, Stuart Hugget, Melitta Dennett, Susannah Gallacher, Jeremy Paige, Eric Damon Walters, Thomas Reinke, Dave Wilkinson, Claire Cannings, Etienne Le Campion, David Callahan, Simon Norfolk, Harvey Williams, Alfred Armstrong, Wayne Woodward, Ian Davis, Bing Broderick, Charlie Waterhouse, Kieron Flaherty, Frank Burge, Derek Vosskuhler, Delta7, Julian Browne, Jon Leach, Richard Culver, David Jones, Jonathan Meacock, Neil Guthrie, Zoë Howe, Lee Thacker, Graham Sellors, John Hibberd, Harry Koniditsiotis, David & Joanna Nash, Simon Hayes Budgen, Emma House, Glory, Benjamin Howarth, Michael Edwards, Adrian Westfield, Gerry Millar, Sergi Coma, Johannes Schneider, Zatapathique, James McNally, Cord Altes, Kim Harten, Gavin Morgan, Simon Dipple, Lane Dunlop, Mike Noble, Jon Pruett, Dr Maz, YY, Henry Ahner, Mike Schulman, Stewart Anderson, Steve Cameron, Phil Slavin, Mike Higgott, Paul Marijetic, Patrick Federli, Danny Le, Laurel Berry, Dan Granata, Jyun-Ao Lin, Phil Andrews, Scott Arnold, Norm Waz, Kris Fernandez-Everett, Andrew Turner, Donald Chin, Martin Bentley, Tony Bacic, Ian Wells, Asako Koguma, Thibault Narbalatz, Steve Watts, Michael Tiley-Evill, Steve Jones, Jarmo Savinainen, Craig Thomas Chin GuoLang, Clint Barnes, Stephanie Mireille Halser, Kieran Lamb, Heinz Brossolat, AHD, Mark Hynds, Julian Humphreys.

CONTENTS

INTRODUCTION

THE COOL UNIVERSE

ON 1 MAY 1997 THE Labour Party returned to power after eighteen years out of office. A mood of great optimism greeted it. The economy was buoyant – as it had been for most of the 1990s – and a cultural renaissance was taking place, with both British pop and British art blazing a trail in terms of sales and exposure. Successes in film, fashion and design followed close behind. Seeking to capitalise on the good fortune, the Government introduced a policy to promote economic growth through creativity, and to help publicise it the Prime Minister threw a party.

The 'Cool Britannia' reception was held in Downing Street on the 30th July and many of the great and the good attended. Designers Paul Smith and Vivienne Westwood lent their support, as did comedians Tony Robinson and Lenny Henry. The film director David Puttnam was present, and the writers Melvyn Bragg and Margaret Drabble. But the next day when the news editors began assembling their obligatory 250-word photo story, it wasn't any of the above they chose to write about, but Oasis star Noel Gallagher, who had attended the party with his wife Meg and record company boss Alan McGee. McGee had donated £50,000 to the Scottish Labour Party and was a worthy invitee in his own right. The pictures in the papers showed Noel, Meg, Alan and Tony: all beaming smiles and bonhomie.

The picture was a measure of how far so-called 'indie' music had come since the monochromatic days of the early 1980s. I'd not met Noel Gallagher, but was an old friend of Alan McGee, although I hadn't seen him since the late 1980s when I'd stopped writing music journalism and the success of his Creation Records label was starting to take him to a place where our paths were unlikely to cross. When we'd first met, in the early 1980s, he was working as a stores clerk for British Rail, and moonlighting as a concert promoter. In August 1983, he began putting on shows in the tiny upstairs bar of a pub in central London. He christened the venue the Living Room.

The bands that appeared at the Living Room – including Primal Scream, the June Brides, the Jesus & Mary Chain, Shop Assistants, the Pastels, the Jasmine Minks, the Loft and scores of others – were part of a new wave of indie music that laid the groundwork for what in the 1990s would be called Indie (note the capital letter). The story of old indie was less about garden parties with centre right prime ministers and more about grit and determination against the odds. It was story not without its successes, and there were a few spectacular, *cause célèbre* moments, but the successes, at least commercially speaking, were not quite like those that followed, including the one enjoyed by Oasis whose career trajectory, like the title of one of their singles, went supersonic.

In the 1980s, indie was still to be turned into a brand. The economy was stagnant not buoyant. The gulf between the have-s and have-nots was almost as great as it is at the time of writing. Politics was deeply divided. Music was also deeply divided: at times, indie felt like the barricades, the last line of defence against a mainstream pop culture that had become increasingly slick and commercially-focused, as befitted the times. The mainstream sound of the age was synthetic: synthesizers, syn-drums, syn-sincerity.

Alan McGee's club was just one of the clubs (and later labels) that set about changing things. Various Government-funded schemes and a more generous dole culture enabled many to play in bands in lieu of the jobs that in any event were not out there for them anyway. Some of the less lucky unemployed were on the Youth Training Scheme or the Youth Training Programme, the Government's method of artificially keeping young people out of the unemployment statistics. The schemes were a free market licence for exploitation by unscrupulous (and largely unregulated) employers – in 1982, seventeen youths were killed on the schemes that according to *The Times* amounted to 'industrial conscription', or 'back up the chimney for all those who fail their 11-Plus', as Julie Burchill more colourfully put it at the time.

The threat of nuclear annihilation was another concern. The Cold War got considerably warmer at the start of the 1980s when around 100 US nuclear weapons bases were located on UK soil. Youth CND membership rose dramatically and 70,000 turned up for a 1983 CND concert in Brockwell Park (featuring the Style Council, Madness, the Damned and others). That same year, the mass-market edition of Raymond Briggs graphic novel, *When The Wind Blows*, imagined a nuclear attack on Britain by Russia and in the process became a runaway best seller. It was particularly popular with young people. Penguin took adverts out in the music press, drawn by Briggs and offering a simple message: 'READ IT'. One of the two principal characters, Hilda, asks the question, 'Nuclear War? Who wants to read about that?' 'Well, it could affect us all, Hilda,' comes husband Jim's reply. '*Look!* I think you *ought* to read it – *SOON!*' he adds. '*Soon?* Why? What's the hurry?' says Hilda. 'Well…' says a crestfallen Jim as the strip ends.

This then was a backdrop, but it wasn't just politics and the threat to continued life on earth that agitated: even indie itself was a cause for concern for some. In summer 1982, a 'Statement' had appeared in *Jamming!*, railing against the lethargy and apathy that the fanzine saw all about it. There was disquiet in the music press as well, commentators regularly damning the indie status quo and, in the words of one writer, 'baying for anything with a hint of guts'. Events came to a head in February 1983 when the *Melody Maker*'s ever-passionate Mick Mercer accused its readers of 'lethargic, anti-social practises' and slammed a number of indie grandees, including Siouxsie & The Banshees, the Cure, Echo & The Bunnymen and Scritti Politti. These and other bands had proved the lie to 1977: what people had settled for was safety and conformity. Mercer's article was followed, almost immediately, by an *NME* cover story in which Richard North set out the arguments for a more 'Positive Punk'. Not for the last time, the paper was pilloried for supposedly attempting to create a genre.

Gothic Rock, as positive (or progressive) punk became more broadly known, was, mercifully, a short-lived phenomenon, but highlighted the tendency for those with the critical crystal ball to look back to punk for a way forward rather than to the future. That punk was unlikely to provide a solution had been most dramatically underlined at the end of 1982, when the Jam had called it a day. At the start of 1983, the *NME* (re)reviewed *all* 23 Jam singles in the same week's singles column: the critics were as shocked as the fans by Paul Weller's decision to split the band.

Punk had rounded on the 1960s – 'no Beatles, no Stones', etc – but many indie bands began looking back to the period for inspiration. Some attempted to fuse the bubble-wheel optimism of that decade with the energy of the punk explosion that followed later. On television, re-runs of cult television programmes from the mid-1960s, such as *The Prisoner* and *The Avengers* proved popular, although, as the critic Brian Case astutely pointed out in a *Melody Maker* review at the time: 'Economics determine social nightmares, and our decade seems set on a grittier pillow-tosser'. In other words, the nightmare of the fantasy – giant plastic balls rolling around the beach at Portmeirion, a benign and rather fatherly captor – was no match for reality.

In 1984 there were new clubs, new bands and new labels. Sometimes the clubs were short-lived, popping up for a month or two in pubs like the Pindar of Wakefield in London's Kings Cross; in other instances, they were more substantial, such as the club the enterprising Leigh Goorney put on at Thames Polytechnic in Woolwich where he staged a staggering 55 gigs during the 1984/85 academic year, introducing hundreds of new indie bands to new fans. Significant label start-ups included Pink and Ron Johnson. The many new bands found mouthpieces in the new fanzines that began to emerge, publications such as *Trout Fishing In Leytonstone*, *Hungry Beat*, *Debris*, the *Legend!* and *Adventure In Bereznik*.

Overshadowing everything in 1984, of course, was the miners' strike. This was no make-believe Orwellian dystopia but a surreal interjection when 'civil war without guns' was played out across the village greens and pitheads of small communities. The strike stirred up a considerable amount of anger, and many indie bands and artists put their shoulders to the wheel, playing benefits and recording in support of the miners' cause. By Christmas, mainstream pop had found its own cause – Band Aid. Many in the indie camp, while sympathising with the plight of the Ethiopians, questioned the motives of the bourgeoisie pop stars involved, accusing them, in some instances, of shameless self-promotion.

The frustration and anger found one channel of release in the music of the Jesus & Mary Chain who notoriously appeared as the year drew to a close, a foul-mouthed ball of energy and shock to the system not seen since the days of punk. At a time when all were being asked to be caring, *they* wanted us to believe that they didn't care about *anything*, not even themselves, as the opening lines to their classic single 'Never Understand' pointed out:

The sun comes up another day begins
And I don't even worry 'bout the state I'm in

The Jesus & Mary Chain were at the forefront of a mini revolution and where they led, in 1985 many followed. Of the 22 bands that were brought together on the *NME*'s *C86* cassette, sixteen either formed or released their first single that year, including Primal Scream, the Wedding Present, the Shop Assistants, Miaow, Age of Chance and We've Got A Fuzzzbox And We're Gonna Use It. It was as if every week there was a new band to go and see, or read about, or write about, or a new fanzine was being published, or a new club was being opened up, such as Dan Treacy and Emily Brown's Room at The Top club that opened at the start of the year, or Bay 63, which began life at the end of the year.

The aim of this book is to tell one story about independent music roughly between the years 1983 and 1986. It is not a book specifically about *C86*, the albatross that hangs wearily around the neck of mid-1980s indie. Almost all of the events discussed occur before 1986 and many of the bands involved weren't even included on the *NME*'s cassette. Neither is it a book about *all* independent music created during that period – such an undertaking would run to many volumes. It goes where the author's eye roams and only fleetingly deals with the music created by some of the more stylised labels, such as Factory, Mute or 4AD. The legacy of those fine labels, and of Rough Trade also, has largely been covered elsewhere.

It is, however, a story that deserves and needs to be told. The story opens with a tracing of the early influencers and pioneers that emerged in the late 1970s and early 1980s, deviates to some important byways such as that of the new psychedelic revival, before locking on to the development of the guitar-based independent music that is at the book's core. It has been important to contextualise the story – reflecting how background events such as the miners' strike and the Stop the City Marches fed into indie – hopefully giving a flavour of the harshly-divided politics of the 1980s, which very much played its part in the music that was created.

Somewhere between the end of the 1980s and Tony Blair's garden party seven years later, indie stopped being a means of expression regardless of commerce and became a brand to be exploited. Even purported serious histories of the period tend nowadays to assess the music purely in terms of its commercial reach.

It feels like it's been that way for ever now, but it wasn't always like that, as I hope this book shows.

CHAPTER 1

PILLOWS, PRAYERS, PIONEERS

ON 25 DECEMBER 1982 CHERRY Red Records gave the world a Christmas present. It was an unusual day to be formally releasing a record, but then *Pillows & Prayers* was no ordinary album. A compilation of songs intended to shop-window the wares of the record label, it featured tracks from a modish lists of bands of the time, including the Monochrome Set, Eyeless In Gaza, the Passage and Thomas Leer. The record's eye-catching cover depicted the sentimental image of a Victorian child blowing bubbles borrowed from an old encyclopaedia and its title was lifted from a children's book of a similar vintage. But perhaps most seductive of all was the instruction printed in the top right corner to 'Pay No More Than 99p', or roughly the price of a single. Many did as they were instructed, and the album quickly found its way to the top of the independent charts, selling, in the process, a staggering 120,000 copies.

By the start of 1983 budget compilation albums were hardly a novelty. Packaging companies like K-Tel and Ronco TV-advertised them. Ever since punk and new wave the market had been awash with them. They were often botched-together, major label releases that *just about* reflected the zeitgeist they were seeking to exploit. Their corny titles plastically reflected the corporate marketing man's concept of the ground attempting to be covered – *We Do 'Em Our Way*, *20 Of Another Kind*, etc.

Throughout the 1970s and earlier, major record labels had used the compilation album to brand promote. CBS had launched an excellent series called The Rock Machine Turns On and Island had started a folk series, You Can All Join In. Sometimes bands got in on the act – the Who's *Odds And Sods* compilation from 1973 is widely regarded as one of the group's best albums, and was the model looked to eleven years later when Rough Trade released the budget price album by the Smiths, *Hatful Of Hollow*, an album similarly regarded by many as one of that band's best.

Cherry Red itself had been down the route before, releasing *Business Unusual (The Other Record Collection)*, a collection of '*not hits*', in 1978. The album had featured artists both on and off the label, including Throbbing Gristle, the Vice Creems, Cabaret Voltaire, UK Subs, Robert Rental and the Leighton Buzzards. The album was respectably successful though the tills but no match for *Pillows & Prayers* which, by the standards of any compilation, was something of a runaway success.

The 99p retail price undoubtedly drove the phenomenal sales of *Pillows & Prayers*, but, once purchased, what many listeners found alluring was the skilful way in which the album had been curated. A&R man Mike Alway's taste was almost the wilful opposite of the doom-laden times, veering towards the baroque and the esoteric and favouring the classic song structure. Peering into the furious white heat of punk and its aftermath – 'the explosion in the edifice', as he called it – the things that had impressed him had been contrary, as he later explained: '"Ambition" by Vic Goddard, the first Durutti Column album on Factory and the Young Marble Giants album on Rough Trade. All those things said to me that "light" music has a place in this revolution.'

Pillows & Prayers mixed the light *and* the dark, and added in a healthy dose of the esoteric. The music ranged from the unadorned lo-fi beauty pop of the Marine Girls to the textural guitar sounds of Felt and the abrasive squall of the Nightingales, from the semi-operatic Piero Mileso to the rantings of Attila the Stockbroker, and on to the psychedelia of the Misunderstood and the musings of national treasure Quentin Crisp. Also included was the Monochrome Set, the 'ultimate purveyors of light music' (according to Alway) who were led by the irrepressible Bid – 'pop's Mel Torme'. Along with Eyeless In Gaza and the Passage, the Monochrome Set was, on paper, one of the key bands on the compilation. Yet when the record was released, many listeners were more impressed by the talents of some of the more relatively unknown artists, including Felt, the Nightingales and, in particular, the Marine Girls.

The Marine Girls had formed in August 1980 and were part of a loose coterie of like-minded artists who, whether for reasons of self-consciousness, lack of technical ability or a desire to foster the cottage industry mentality, took a more stripped-down approach to music making and had a big influence on the new indie. The aesthetic grouping included Young Marble Giants, one of the earliest proponents of the quiet-as-the-new-loud approach, whose most well known single was 'Final Day' and based on an Ian Fleming short story about nuclear annihilation. Swell Maps might also be gathered in – they performed regularly with the Marine Girls and had been going since 1972, pushing out the DIY boundaries with their blend of abstract noise and quiet acoustics. They did little after the advent of punk to change their experimental sound, Nikki Sudden told *Breach Of The Peace* fanzine in 1981, save for speeding it up. Shortly after Swell Maps formed in the early-1970s, another maverick got going as Patrik Fitzgerald began reciting his poetry with plain acoustic guitar or simple keyboard backing. Fitzgerald was canned off stage for his troubles at the start of punk but remains a key influence on the *C86* generation.

The Marine Girls recorded first for a 1980 compilation album *Rupert Preaching At A Picnic*, contributing a track called 'Hate The Girl' that heavily borrowed off the Delta 5 song 'You'. In December 1980, Tracey Thorn, Gina Hartman, Jane Fox and Alice Fox recorded ten tracks in Tracey Thorn's bedroom on a borrowed portable four-track recorder. In the end, twelve tracks appeared on a cassette release, *A Day By The Sea*. 'We pooled the money we earned from our Saturday jobs to pay for 50 copies to be made,' recalls Gina Hartman today. 'Tracey had a job in the local post office, Jane worked in a funny, space-themed café in a department store and I worked in a shoe shop. I think Alice may have contributed some birthday or pocket money.' The songs had charm and were 'as melodic and engaging as the playing is haphazard', claimed Tracey Thorn in her autobiography, before, in self-deprecating fashion, noting that the material 'had all the sophistication of a class of Year Five children let loose in a music room'.

Beach Party, the Marine Girls' first proper album came out on cassette in the spring of 1981, initially released on producer Pat Bermingham's In Phaze label. A crane driver by training, Bermingham had a four-track studio in a shed in the back garden of his parent's suburban house in Ilford (records were credited to 'Shed Sounds' productions). Reviewing *Beach Party* in August 1981, an early critic set the tone for the seaside jokes the Marine Girls would have to endure whenever being written about, describing the tape as 'a seaside special' before adding that '… [o]ver a sparse guitar and bass the all-girl four-piece croon of things both romantic and coastal, like a modern day Shangri-Las equipped with buckets and spades'.

'Pat's shed was at the bottom of the garden, remembers Gina. 'It was quite small, like a little shack. He had a reverb tube behind the door that we loved to make a noise with. He was very patient and sweet and made it easy for us. His mum would bring us cups of tea and sometimes we'd sit on the front wall of the house. Goodness knows what his neighbours must have thought. Originally, he'd wanted to release a version with a dub B-side but for some reason that didn't happen. He *loved* dub, he was really into it.'

The echoes of dub that are all over the 'spacey sound' of *Beach Party* unified it. The material shows the Marine Girls to have been far more barbed wits than many of the critics took them to be, when sometimes writing off the songs as little more than diary entries set to music. The songs are treachery and spite, *and* all things nice, at times, as on 'Friday' which ends with: 'You said I broke your heart/ But I said I told the truth/ So I win, yeah?', that last sub-clause reinforcing the important point, or, 'Honey', one of the album's very best songs, where Tracey Thorn sings 'I know I'll love him forever' before landing the killer punch: '… or at least until I find another boy'. Delta 5, the Au Pairs and the Raincoats are clear influences, but its Buzzcocks that provide one of the most integral parallels.

By March 1982, the Marine Girls were the 'glorious exception to the general standard of garageland grunge' according to Adrian Thrills reviewing their first single, 'On My Mind' in the *NME*. Pop was, he declared, in 'a strange sort of limbo', with 'too many of its observers looking a little too keenly at the charts'. A month later the band found itself on the front cover of *Melody Maker* as Dan Treacy's Whaam! label reissued *Beach Party*. In the article, Tracey Thorn pointed out that it's 'really hard to respect people if they're not good musicians and I'd like to be good enough to be respected' whilst at the same time recognised the value of the amateur approach, citing a love of Orange Juice whose occasional mistakes and sometimes out of tune guitars were all part of their appeal.

In fact, by the time of the *Melody Maker* front cover, Gina Hartman had left and Tracey Thorn had gone off to do a degree at Hull University. The band had also signed to Cherry Red publishing and when Tracey Thorn had returned at one point during the academic year, she'd recorded some further demos in Pat Bermingham's shed and sent them off to Mike Alway at Cherry Red, believing that they might form the basis of some future Marine Girls songs. In time, however, she judged that the new material was 'so intensely personal' that it needed to be sung by her alone and so she returned to Pat Bermingham's to complete the job. Once again, it was a relatively cheap and quick process and after two days Tracey Thorn emerged with a bill for £167 and a minor masterpiece.

With a running time of around 24 minutes, there isn't an ounce of fat on *A Distant Shore*, just seven sparse originals and one cover (the Velvet Underground's 'Femme Fatale') all drenched in reverb. Once again, it is far from the entirely angst-free experience that on a superficial listen the surface texture might suggest. It is heart-breaking listening in some places and scarcely less uncomfortable in others: that it is a soul bared is clear immediately the album opens when Tracey Thorn's sings: 'This is all too much for such a small-town girl….'. The album takes its title from the track 'Seascape', which continues the troubled theme and finds the song's subject 'watching tides… to take me away to a distant shore/ And I don't want to be saved'. But, like all the very best tragedies, everything is redeemed by fortune and Tracey Thorn has never sounded better.

A final album by the Marine Girls, *Lazy Ways*, appeared in spring 1983, but by then, Tracey Thorn had joined forces with Ben Watt in Everything But The Girl and released a reworking of the Cole Porter classic, 'Night & Day'. The Marine Girls were over in all but name, although Alice and Jane Fox would later go on to form the more esoteric Grab Grab The Haddock.

Artists like the Marine Girls, Patrik Fitzgerald, Swell Maps, the Television Personalities and the Pastels (of which more later) bequeathed the new indie scene an *approach*, one that in essence could be traced back to the access and enablement philosophy of punk when *un*pop bands like Vic Godard's Subway Sect had, by choice, only half-heartedly bothered to learn their instruments (before, in the case of Subway Sect, being fired by manager Bernie Rhodes for 'poor musicianship'). Since then, there had been creeping conformity, and a growing belief that in order to advance a more sophisticated approach was required.

Postcard Records – 'the Sound of Young Scotland' as it termed itself – wasn't particularly sophisticated but it was ringing and confident. Founder Alan Horne claimed that setting up the label had been easy since all he'd done was sign the only good bands in Scotland (in Orange Juice and Josef K). A stream of perfectly-realised singles followed, becoming another major influence on the new indie. The Postcard bands, like many before and since, had been influenced by the Velvet Underground (whose reputation was reanimated in 1984 with the release of their 'long lost' album *VU*) but it was groups like Josef K that were the link, drawing in the interest of the new bands through what Paul Haig in 1982 described in *Melody Maker* as 'our jangly little sound'.

Whilst Tracey Thorn when starting out had famously been too shy to perform except in a wardrobe, Postcard founder Alan Horne, a former botany student, was the exact opposite, a man who appeared to take a perverse delight in anything that shocked. When Postcard started in 1979, Horne was sharing a flat with Brian Taylor (or Brian Superstar, as he unassumingly liked to be known) who would later co-form the Pastels. Between them they had an encyclopaedic knowledge of hip and arcane pop music. They also owned a video player and one tape on continual rotation was a *History Of Rock* programme about the Byrds, a band that had fallen out of popularity since the 1960s but whose influence would massively reassert itself in the years to come.

Orange Juice's 'Falling & Laughing' was the first Postcard release, its cost funded partly by Horne and various members of the band. Being a non-musician didn't stop Horne from also assuming a role within the structure of the group, and, as he grandly claimed in the self-penned *Brochure*, published in 1981, he 'became, by turns Orange Juice's friend, fan, patron, manager, record label leader, guru, corruptor and ultimate confidante'. 'Falling & Laughing' was followed by another Orange Juice release, the plangent 'Blue Boy', another lovesick, laughter-and-tears ode that came out in late summer 1981. By then, Horne had convinced Josef K to sign with the label. Whereas Orange Juice brimmed over with the promise of a pop sensibility that married the sound of the Velvet Underground with the choppy poundings of disco, Josef K was an altogether more dense and abstract proposition, although not one without moments of iridescence that could give a more instantly giddy rush than Orange Juice.

Josef K were, as their name suggests, well versed in literature and philosophy. In Paul Haig they possessed a songwriter with a voice as equally as robust and distinct as that of Edwyn Collins, but someone whose focus of attention could be less romantic and sometimes downright bleak. For instance, 'It's Kinda Funny', which became the fifth Postcard release was Paul Haig's response to the death of Joy Division's Ian Curtis. The song's title is ironic, in a work which sees the narrator, who might be Ian Curtis, 'disappear through the crack in the wall/ And the memories I leave will be nothing at all'. Before releasing 'It's Kinda Funny', 'Radio Drill Time' had appeared, Postcard's third single and the band's second (after 'Chance Meeting', which had been released in 1979 on Absolute Records, a label run by Stephen Daly from Orange Juice.)

In February 1980, Alan Horne and Edwyn Collins had driven down to Rough Trade to deliver Orange Juice's first single and to hopefully strike up some sort of distribution deal with the company. While they were in the legendary shop at 202 Kensington Park Road, their eyes fell upon a single by the Go-Betweens – 'Lee Remick' – that had been released on the Brisbane-based Able label. 'We'd both heard this when it came out in 1978 but had forgotten about it until we were considering starting a record label,' Horne later recounted. Thus began a manhunt.

By the time Horne and Collins had tracked down the two members of the Go-Betweens – Robert Forster and Grant MacLennan (Lindy Morrison joining in the autumn of 1980) – the band had already signed to Berserkley, the home of Jonathan Richman's music. But fortune intervened when the American label went bust the following week and Postcard was able to record 'I Need Two Heads', using the money recouped from 'Falling & Laughing' which, for the time being, the label had decided to delete. At the time of the recording of the single in April 1980, the Go-Betweens played their first UK date, with Orange Juice and Josef K. It was a joyous occasion, according to Alan Horne, with members of the audience getting up on the stage to perform between the band's sets, and videos being made of the night's proceedings. 'A Glasgow audience for once managed to dance to a group,' Horne later remembered: 'Warhol on a Clydeside level. The start and finish of any Glasgow "scene".'

In spring 1981, with the label scarcely a year old, Postcard unearthed yet another gem. Malcolm Ross, the guitarist in Josef K had talked Alan Horne and Edwyn Collins into going with him to see a band supporting the Rezillos called Aztec Camera. Aztec Camera was fronted by the teenage songwriter Roddy Frame, but didn't disappoint. The experience was almost cathartic for Horne, as he noted in *Brochure*: 'Aztec Camera were a revelation, like stumbling into Max's to find the Velvet Underground, but this Lou Reed was sixteen and the audience was sixty-one. We had all been proven wrong, there *was* another group in Glasgow apart from the Orange Juice.' The two singles that Aztec Camera subsequently released on Postcard – 'Just Like Gold' and 'A Mattress Of Wire' – were peerless, the first, claimed Horne, a candidate for 'single of the millennium'. Roddy Frame was no scenester, either, and, like Horne and Brian Superstar, was open minded in his appreciation of music – as likely to find inspiration in the work of Wes Montgomery or Django Reinhardt as he was in that of Magazine or the Clash.

In a short space of time, Postcard had built up a boutique label of formidable quality. It didn't take long for either the press or the major record labels to take notice. The epicentre of independent music had shifted considerably since the eruption of punk, from London to other major cities, including Liverpool, Manchester, Leeds and Birmingham in quick succession. Now it was Scotland's turn, as it would again be four or five years later.

Although in interviews with fanzines and the music press, both Horne and the bands argued that there was no point in moving labels unless there was a material advantage, it was inevitable that Orange Juice and Aztec Camera would be leaving the label. The lure of money for recording and the wearing thin of patience with Alan Horne's increasingly dictatorial style would see to that. If Orange Juice and Aztec Camera really were the best bands in Scotland (and by extension, therefore, in the UK), what did that make Alan Horne? Would Postcard have survived longer if it had stayed regional, as Richard Scott, head of Distribution at Rough Trade, later argued?

In the end Postcard could not withstand the weight of its own structure. An inevitable amount of bickering crept in. Issue 1 of the fanzine *Born To Lose*, published in summer 1981, ran an extensive interview with Orange Juice (and a shorter one with Alan Horne) and took stock of the band's situation in the face of increasing recording offers from elsewhere. No, Postcard wasn't Alan Horne's label, the band claimed – it was meant to be a co-operative. Referring to the label's drumming feline logo, Edwyn Collins commented: 'I thought up the cats and a friend of mine thought up the name and James [Kirk] did a lot of the artwork to begin with…' In what was termed an Orange Juice/Josef K 'bandzine' published at the same time, Alan Horne peered at the thought horizon and offered the following: 'Sometimes I think it would be great to just finish what we started out to do, releasing both the Orange Juice and the Josef K albums, then just pack it all in, keeping your integrity intact. It would be great to go out when you're on top, before it all gets stale…'

Josef K began recording their *Sorry For Laughing* album in November 1980, according to *Brochure*, but the project was aborted following a trip to Brussels, where they were invited to perform at Plan K, a converted sugar refinery with 'five floors of magic shows, transvestites, boxing, silent films and silent freaks'. In

Brussels, they recorded a couple of tracks – 'Sorry For Laughing' and 'Revelation' – for release on Les Disques du Crépuscule. In so doing, they achieved, said Horne at the time, 'the sound Josef K had been looking for all along'. *Sorry For Laughing* was scrapped and a new album, *The Only Fun In Town* released instead. *The Only Fun In Town* – 'the band's second debut LP', as one fanzine dubbed it – attempted to capture the band's live sound and was hastily recorded. As a result, it was not well received by the music press, *Sounds* being particularly unimpressed and awarding it one star (out of five) in its review.

Aztec Camera moved on to Rough Trade and Orange Juice signed a deal with Polydor and by the autumn of 1981, barely eighteen months after it had started, Postcard (in its first incarnation) was no more. In the end, it was, arguably, the malfunctioning Josef K that became the most influential of all of the Postcard bands, in terms of effect on those that followed, but none of the groups (with the possible exception of the Go-Betweens) ever again creatively matched the work they delivered on Postcard.

By self-destructing before it had barely got going, Postcard, ironically, became the perfect label, leaving behind a miniature trail of gems and a reputation unsullied by failure.

Less, in its case, really was more.

For Mark E Smith, less has never equalled more. In a career spanning forty years his band the Fall have released close to 100 albums (counting live releases and compilations) and the number of band members consigned to the wayside – 'the Fallen' – is legion. Smith's impact has been colossal and even rock superstars aren't immune to the charms of a Fall song: in the 1980s, Rod Stewart chose 'Totally Wired' as the backing song to enter the stage to during his stadium tours.

Mark E Smith was also, of course, one of the original pullover wearers – and has handed-down more than just a sound to those that have followed. But it was in the music that the Fall's influence is most clearly obvious, and in particular in its adherence to the value of repetition. The early, almost motoric, bass driven sound of the band was pre-punk, and lifted much of its inspiration from the drug-scorched wasteland of the Manchester streets where the band was based, causing some commentators to label it 'northern rockabilly' or 'modern folk'. When the songs aren't dealing with urban blight or pharmaceuticals they espouse a form of stateless and creedless politics, lifting superficially on occasions from punk's idiotic fascination with certain aspects of German nationalism. It was the raw guitar work and the rumbling bass that future indie bands – those Mark E Smith in 1984 disdainfully referred to as 'my bitches' – took from the sound of the Fall.

Smith's dislocated vocal delivery and sawn-off lyrical style was also much copied, often by those who ended up sounding nothing like him. The classic Fall lyric is a kaleidoscope of ideas and broken fragments, an acid blot of a work, durable but pointless to overanalyse. Not many strayed close too close to the Fall, but lots who did and adopted a similar kind of urban folk approach got tarred with the copyist brush. Some bands, such as Yeah Yeah Noh, openly admit a debt to the Fall in the early work but moved away as they developed, in their case adopting a more surrealistic and psychedelically warped approach in their all too short career.

The Birthday Party was another similarly combustible band of equal influence. Wilfully scabrous and more limited in scope, Nick Cave's band were never really able to top the brilliance of the early singles, in particular 'Mr Clarinet' and 'The Friend Catcher' that made such an enormous impact. It was the shock value that – well, shocked. Some saw the band as rock's final resting place or limit (in a pre-Swans, etc, age), whilst others questioned the Barnum & Bailey onstage antics of Cave and compared the band's style to the fabricated trash aesthetic of the Cramps. Live shows could be good for a bit of tasty audience participation. Nick Cave responded to the critics by complaining that the Birthday Party didn't set out to provoke the audiences, it was the audiences that provoked them.

For a seemingly whirlwind moment the Birthday Party were the most thrilling band in town, but by the time of the release of 1982's *Junkyard* album, the ideas were beginning to look a bit routeless and staged. The album plundered the gothic imagery of the southern states of America but tipped over easily into 'cartoon horror show' (or so claimed the *NME*), as was apparent from the lyrics to the otherwise frighteningly turbid title track: 'Hatchets sweetly swinging/ American heads roll in Texas/ Those skinny girls, they're so quick to murder…. Get stiff in your crypt'. Fittingly, an almost certainly, the band's finest act was a Gothic one, delivering up the earlier and extraordinarily frenetic 'Release The Bats' single, an initiating rite in the passage of the forthcoming gothic rock. 'DIRTINESS IS NEXT TO ANTIGODLINESS' claimed the record company adverts accompanying the release of the single.

The Birthday Party shuddered to a halt at the start of 1983, around about the same time that Rough Trade signed the Smiths. The Smiths were simultaneously part of the new indie but also a big influence on it, through not just the towering wit and intellect of Morrissey and the extraordinary guitar playing of Johnny Marr, but also in the tightness of the rhythm section of Mike Joyce and Andy Rourke. Shortly after they emerged, Alan McGee, in a typical moment of abandon writing in the fanzine *Groovy Black Shades*, called them 'the catalyst we've all been waiting for' and Johnny Marr 'a man with a marvellous haircut, a 12-string Rickenbacker… 14 harmonicas who loves the Byrds.' In dealing with the sheer volume of demand for the Smiths records, Rough Trade, by far the independent sector's most ethically focused and culturally important structure of dissemination, ended up hiring a major record label's strike force, thus compromising, for some, the company's independent ideals. Hybrid record labels started up, financed by major record label money but still able (for a while) to register in the independent charts, much to the chagrin of wholly independent labels such as Chiswick.

Cherry Red *was* wholly independent and a year on from the album's release, *Pillows & Prayers* was still going strong in the independent charts. One track that sat easy on the ear was 'I Unseen' by the Misunderstood, the Californian garage band inspired to form in the mid-1960s having witnessed the British Invasion. The Misunderstood only ever recorded a handful of tracks during their mid-1960s prime, but, based for a time in London, they became favourites of John Peel and were pioneers of a primitive form of acid rock. Back in 1966, they had soldered a guitar jack onto a car light bulb and created an early lightshow (a 'visual sound' experience) whereby the light reacted directly to the playing of the guitarist.

In fact, the garage rock and psychedelic sounds of the 1960s appealed to and inspired some of the creators of the new indie every bit as much as Punk, or DIY, or the Fall, or Buzzcocks, or the Postcard label, or other innovators and outliers, such as Mark Perry and his band ATV. One key moment was the publication in the *NME* in December 1983 of Julian Cope's *Tales From The Drug Attic* essay that introduced many indie kids to the obscurer delights of psychedelic and garage rock for the first time. Names like the Seeds, the Chocolate Watch Band and the Thirteenth Floor Elevators got added to a list that already included the Velvet Underground and the Byrds. Cope's essay was an eye-opener, but for the cognoscenti the first indication that the decade meant to have been rolled over by punk was back had already occurred in the spring of 1981 when a small club in central London opened at Samantha's nightclub and psychedelia was added to the then ever-growing list of revivals.

CHAPTER 2

'FAMILIARITY
BREEDS BANANAS'

NEW PSYCHEDELIA EMERGED IN THE summer of 1981, bringing a much-needed splash of colour to an otherwise dreary music scene and brightening up a drab Britain marred by recession and inner city rioting. Initially the plaything of a group of bored Mods looking for something with a bit more novelty than the staple diet of Tamla Motown and the Who, it quickly assumed an identity all of its own, drawing in closet '60s revivalists and the first stirrings of a scene.

The story had really started in May, when the Groovy Cellar had opened in a basement club in London's Piccadilly. Every Friday night a small group of Dandies dressed up in far-out glad-rags and Roger McGuinn glasses frugged away to the psychedelic sounds of bands like the Herd, the Move, the Smoke, the Rolling Stones, Shocking Blue, and other *Revolver*-era music. The boys wore striped hipster slacks, regency jackets and silk cravats, paisley shirts and suede Chelsea boots, the girls wore Mary Quant mini-skirts and sported Peggy Moffatt bobs, modelling their look on the 1968 underground sci-fi flick *Barbarella* and that of *Avengers* star Emma Peel. There was nowhere else quite like it in London – at least for a very short time.

But it wasn't just the clothes and the music of the 1960s that the scene appropriated, it was the social idealism as well: part of the appeal of the Groovy Cellar was as subterranean oasis away from humdrum reality. It opened shortly after the time of the Oi! movement when inter-tribal youth culture friction was as rife as it had been during the dark days of the 1970s. Its escapist, underground liquid-light optimism was in sharp contrast to and an escape from what was happening above ground, where the governments of Thatcher and Reagan, the riots and the Cold War prevailed. It made for a curious contrast, as the inimitable Dan Treacy (an early devotee) was to later point out on 'She Was Only A Grocer's Daughter': 'Relax your mind and float downstream/ Pretend it's all a very bad dream'.

Alexis Bienkov, a postman at the time and vocalist with the Marble Staircase, underlined the re-interpretive nature of the early scene when interviewed for the *Observer* who ran a piece on the club and emerging scene in September 1981. 'Love and peace is really what we believe in,' he is quoted as saying. 'I despise the older generation. They accept violence, in the street and on the football terraces. They've forgotten about Toxteth already… We'd rather stand on the streets and give out flowers.' Over thirty years later, Bienkov's comments read like parody and time has distorted what were very genuinely held views in a scene that was, at least initially, bereft of cynicism.

Almost hot on the heels of the opening of the Groovy Cellar, and closely linked to it, came a second club. The Clinic was a Wednesday night happening at Gossips nightclub in Soho's Dean Street and was presided over by the scene's pre-eminent DJ, the Doctor. In the same *Observer* article, the Doctor (aka Clive Jackson) – a six-foot-five tall former scout patrol leader who dressed up in a cape and wore a shocking, jet black wig – confirmed Bienkov's nobly pacifistic view but underlined the (at least for him) novelty aspect of the scene: 'We're a reaction against the violence of London,' he told the magazine, before adding: 'Here you can be what you want to be. We're carrying on where the 1960s left off. We put jelly on the floor and ask people to eat it. The fact that they do shows there's still hope for the world. The cool eat jelly, have fun.'

They certainly did, as *NME* journalist Paul Du Noyer had already discovered when visiting shortly after the club had opened, finding the resident Doctor 'preparing his alter for the night's initiation rituals' with 'some candles, some flowers, "communion hosts" of dried banana and a dish of wine, or strawberry jam, or red jelly'. Indeed, the fun was such that come the summer a handful of other clubs decided to get in on the act – a rival Wednesday night psychedelic happening started up at Le Kilt (in the process ruffling a few feathers), and even the Bridge House at Canning Town, legendary mod venue, got in on the act, running a prominent ad for an 'experience' night by the Bumpers in August. 'ATTENTION ALL MODS,' the ad shouted. 'Sick and bored with so-called "FUTURISTIC ROCK BANDS" & dance groups that leave you cold? If you are, here's something that will interest you… PSYCHEDELIA (is just beginning) – Don't be left behind – See the action, feel the beat'. A second ad assured that the Bumpers 'ARE NOT AN OLD IDEA RENEWED' but 'AN EXCITING, UNIQUE NEW EXPERIENCE', before adding: 'PSYCHEDELIC DANCE MUSIC HAS BEGUN!'

A full-on 1960s revival had been threatening for some. In 1980, the Jam had released *Sound Affects* and taken from the album a number of singles that were, putting it mildly, Beatles copyist in construction, such as 'Start'. That same year, garage rock band the Barracudas had released 'Summer Fun', a surf/ punk anthem that saw them sporting white denim and stripy T-shirts on the cover. Unashamedly nostalgic, the record hit a spot with the buying public and the band ended up on Top Of The Pops. By the time that their debut album *Drop Out* appeared later in the year, though, the summer outfits had been replaced by frills and patterns of a more psychedelic hue, a look that caught the eye of the Neo Mods out there, especially when they heard the band sing lyrics like 'I wish it could be 1965 again'.

That the New Psychedelia had at least part slipped out from between the Parka fishtails of mod was further apparent from the genesis of the scene's prime band. Mood Six were a six-piece combo formed in the heat of the moment from assorted bands such as the VIPs, the Merton Parkas, and bands that regularly played at the home turf location of the Castle pub in glamorous Tooting Broadway. But they, like others, were looking for something new. Paul Shurey (keyboards), Tony Conway (guitar) and Clive Soloman, the band's manager, had helped set up the

Groovy Cellar and shared a love for the kind of 1960s culture that was celebrated in isolated pockets of youth culture such as the Regal clothing stall on the first floor of Kensington Market. Very quickly, the band became the scene's chief promoters, but the apprenticeship on the sweaty pub circuit had taught them a more imaginative approach was required, and they didn't take too long before putting some grand ideas into action.

The band's first notable public foray – and an impressive one – took place on Thursday, 6 August, when (for their seventh or so gig) they booked out the cruise ship Royal Princess and sailed up and down the Thames from Westminster Pier. Tickets, for the lucky river-faring few that got them, cost the princely sum of £4, and sailing commenced at '7.45 sharp'. The audacious move served its purpose in ensuring that the band got noticed, and a week or so later the music press duly went overboard, a large news story appearing in the *NME* with the predictable but highly appropriate headline, 'Granny Takes A Boat Trip'.

It was, as Paul Shurey told *NME* in the band's first substantial music paper interview ('FAMILIARITY BREEDS BANANAS', *NME*, 12 September 1981), 'a matter of giving people a whole evening's entertainment, which I don't think we can do at the Marquee. We don't just want the band: we want a great DJ like the Doctor, we want loads of little happenings, little plays, light shows, dancers…' The bells-and-all approach brought in extended band members, and the line-up of six Moods was often supplemented by the appearance of Tin Tin and Melody who were 'go-go dancers and flower distributors'. Playing up the showbiz aspect of the band did them no harm, at least initially, and on one occasion Mood Six's antics even caught the eye of *Nationwide*, the BBC's prestigious news and current affairs programme.

That the early New Psychedelic bands aimed to put on a full-blown performance reflected the depressing state of the real world, but also was a conscious attempt to do something different from the 'futuristic rock scene' that they were often lazily lumped in with. But whereas the New Romantic scene had been elite and discriminatory, New Psychedelia was inclusive and welcoming. The New Romantics had given dressing up (something Londoners in particular had liked to do since time immemorial) a bad name, and in the process created a scene that was deeply snobby: clubs like the Groovy Cellar and especially the Clinic counterbalanced such snobbery by making a virtue out of the practise of having nonsensical fun.

The cinematic approach wasn't entirely followed by all – forefathers of the scene the Barracudas, for instance, had been though a number of flamboyantly-attired phases but had reverted back to a more conventional pose by the end of 1982, and High Tide, who were at that time fronted by Simon Le Bon-lookalike Grant Bolt (replacing former vocalists Chris and Anne-Marie Newland) had been wary of the clothes-horse approach from the start, of what guitarist Martin O'Neill described as 'the Swinging London idea… fictitious dancing on tables and all that crap', possibly seeing the whole thing as something half-baked and foisted upon the public by a press caught slumbering during the Blitz Club boom.

Miles Over Matter, one of the very best bands on the scene, had no such concerns, taking the flamboyant in their stride with what one journalist described as their 'winning enthusiasm and lunatic glee'. Formed out of the ashes of the Electric Kool Aids in 1980, the band initially included Babel Wallace (vocals), Miles Landesman (guitar) and Steve Counsel, whose guitar work and song-writing prowess immediately set the band apart. They played the 1981 Daze Of Future Haze Festival in Leeds, along with Echo & The Bunnymen, the Cramps and Bauhaus before gigging on the London circuit at such notable venues as Islington's Pied Bull. Their music was a cross between Traffic and Tomorrow and the dirtier sounds of bands like the Electric Prunes and

Blues Magoos, with a valid touch of their own ideas thrown in for good measure. The humour in their work showed through in such gloriously-titled songs as 'Fly Like A Fly In The Sky' and 'Father's Name Was Dad (Mother's Name was Mum)' – a cover of Fire's freakbeat classic – and their commitment to the cause was such that *Melody Maker*'s Steve Sutherland described them as 'the greatest pop group to pass this way in years', one with 'more energy and riot potential than any band since the Sex Pistols'. He recognised in the early performances the 'first frenzied symptoms of a mass epidemic'. Alas, it never came to pass.

Like all those involved in the scene, Miles Over Matter took their fashion seriously (their manager Jade designed many of their clothes), and just as punk had had its look shaped by a couple of designer/ clothiers (in the form of Malcolm McClaren and Vivienne Westwood), so too did New Psychedelia. The Regal had started out life as a first floor stall in the fashionable Kensington High Street Market, before a shop proper was opened in Newburgh Street, just off Carnaby Street (and just down from the skinhead shop, Well Hung). The Regal was the prominent example of New Psychedelia tailoring, but there were others, such as the Fantastic stall in Carnaby Street's flea market. At the centre of operations at the Regal was an extraordinary tailor who had been around during the original Psychedelia's heyday.

Andrew Yanniakou found design inspiration in the look of the Dandies of the Eighteenth Century and used original fabric from the 1960s to create a neo-psychedelic range of clothes that became part of the scene's cultural highpoints. There hadn't been so much colour, zest and flamboyance in serious men's fashion since the days of Swinging London and emporiums like Granny Takes A Trip and Hung On You. At the same time, Yiannakou's partner Anne-Marie Newland (part of the original High Tide), set up the boutique Sweet Charity to cater for the girls, with designs inspired by the work of Mary Quant, the

Op Art patterns of Bridget Riley, and the glamour of such TV characters as Emma Peel.

The Regal became a focal point for the scene, somewhere to hang out – all day long, if a customer felt so inclined. Although only a tiny shop, it managed to pack in not just clothes but some fanzines as well, including, importantly, Paul Groovy's *Groovy Black Shades* (which documented the scene in early editions), as well a small number of records that included, in time, the releases on Whaam!, a label set up by Dan Treacy and Ed Ball of the Television Personalities. Treacy and Ball had been enthusiastic adherents of the scene – indeed, Ed Ball's group the Times was one of the movement's most important bands – and had started their label the same year New Psychedelia got going, in 1981, releasing the Marine Girls album (*Beach Party*) and singles by the Gifted Children ('Painting By Numbers') and by the Times ('Red With Purple Flashes'). The label was most productive during 1982, though, releasing a number of records by those involved with the scene, such as Clive Jackson's band Doctor And The Medics ('The Druids Are Here'), Le Mat ('Waltz Of The Fool'), and the Times ('Art Goes Pop'), along with releases by Small World, the Pastels, Direct Hits, the Television Personalities and Jed Dmochowski (formerly of The VIPs) all of whom at least skirted the movement if not always involving themselves directly with it.

As summer passed into autumn, so Mood Six continued their series of offbeat gigs, performing at the London Dungeons at the start of October and later putting on a surprisingly well attended show (given the venue) at Regent Street's salubrious Café Royal, an upmarket Toff spot whose previous patrons included Oscar Wilde, Aleister Crowley and Brigitte Bardot. The London Dungeon show, which featured a more restrained High Tide as support, received a huge write up in *NME*, complete with evocative Peter Anderson photograph of Regally-clad fan clearly having the time of his life. The razzamataz served its purpose in garnering column inches, but reviewer Barney Hoskyns was less impressed with the sound, seeing in the music (at least in the case of Mood Six) the noise of old Mod dressed up in the Emperor's New Clothes, nothing much beyond a 'straight mixture of Speak-easy-style r'n'b and nostalgic *Smashing Time* cine-pop'.

The London Dungeon review showed a music press eager to give considerable space to New Psychedelia, and where the press led so generously, the major record labels inevitably followed. In fact, there had quickly emerged a small cluster of bands for the A&R men to pursue, all playing regularly on the circuit that stretched from the Bridge House in east London, across to the Windsor Castle in west London, and up from Clapham's 101 Club to Hampstead's Moonlight Club.

Many of the 'new' bands were seemingly put together on the spot in an attempt to not miss the moment, and as such the influences were sometimes all too apparent, from the Mod/Jam strains of the Marble Staircase across to the punk-influenced the Earwigs (who went on to appear on *Granada Reports* during the Falklands War, where presenter Tony Wilson pronounced their song 'War Games' to be 'psychedelia as a post-punk phenomenon', whatever that meant). The Earwigs had been formed by Mark Standley, a man whose previous groups included V2 and the Drones. As if to reinforce that slender boundary between punk/post punk and the New Psychedelia, the Silence, who also toured the circuit regularly, played New Wave, but with a slightly perverse edge.

In some cases, the influence was obvious, in others it wasn't. For instance, the Barracudas, fronted by the inimitable and erudite Jeremy Gluck, confused everyone, ultimately arriving at a garage rock sound via Psychedelia, although as Gluck lamented (in 1984), not enough people seemed to get what he called the band's 'basic rock 'n' roll' approach. 'We've come to be patient,' he confessed, in a Karmic way. 'Our belief in a law of compensation that will visit us acts as fuel.' In the case of other bands active on the London scene, the paisley shirts metaphorically peeped out of the Parka hoods, such had been the rush to switch styles. Le Mat had grown out of Mod band the Leepers, who sadly never left any vinyl legacy, whilst Soldiers Are Dreamers had also been Mod, the Killimeters reincarnated, perhaps a little too hastily: punk frontman Vic Szczesnowicz had been through a few rapid change transformations – from Vic Vomit to Vic Vespa and back to to Vic Szczesnowicz. The band added a 12-string guitar element and had reputedly switched their drug of preference from speed to acid, but many remained unconvinced….

Ed Ball's the Times were, perhaps, a case apart. Some said that the original motivation for the scene had not been Psychedelia but Swinging London, something that at its height pre-dated Psychedelia by a couple of years, although for most people the two movements are indistinguishable. The real difference arguably lay in motive: Swinging London was unashamed about conspicuously displaying affluence at a time of economic growth (as was Brit Pop); Psychedelia and the counter culture was a deliberate move away from that, a retreat into what William S Burroughs called Inner (rather than outer, ie material) Space.

If the original motivation had been Swinging London, then the Times, with the bubblegum epic 'I Helped Patrick McGoohan Escape' hit the nail on the head. Although the cult TV series *The Prisoner* hadn't appeared until September 1967, and with its surreal settings and plotlines amplified the counter culture it was birthed in, it was styled very much in the period before that, with McGoohan dressed in pipe-edged tailoring that was suggestive of early boutiques such as Rupert Lycett-Green's Blades rather than Michel Rainey's Hung On You or Nigel Waymouth's Granny Takes A Trip. The show's use of such props as the Penny Farthing bicycle only added to that.

The Times (along with the Television Personalities and the Whaam! label) took a Pop Art line, as referenced by the title of the Times' first album (*Art Into Pop*), a flat, bold approach to the business of reinterpretation that for some strayed just a little too close to parody. A visual analogy might be the bright, emphatic work of Patrick Caulfield rather than the fluid, intermingling lines of psychedelic poster designers Hapshash & The Coloured Coat or Martin Sharp. The approach reflected the humour and the formidable intelligence of Ball, to say nothing of his musical skill in mimicking the period. But what was at the centre?

This was the question the major record labels were asking. In 1981 they were hyper cautious in signing acts, a number having had their fingers burned during the Neo Rockabilly revival when investment was sunk into acts that fell commercially far short of the success enjoyed by the scene's most successful band, the Stray Cats. The major record companies were initially seeking a band that would transcend the scene (or 'fad'), or, failing even that, just looking for a decent song.

EMI thought that they'd found both in Nick Nicely whose 'Hilly Fields (1892)' single they released in 1982. Nicely was an experimental artist who worked across the electronic/psychedelic divide and had previously released 'D.C.T. Dreams', a record that showcased both styles, on Ariola/Hansa. 'Hilly Fields (1892)' followed the more psychedelic path, using cellos and even an early form of scratching by rotating backwards and forwards tape spools. The record made Single of the Week in *NME* ('the best psychedelic record since the 1960s') but was poorly promoted. Even so, for many it remains to this day the crowning glory of New Psychedelia.

With the exception of Mood Six, the major record labels didn't see *any* band as having the potential for the kind of exploitation that was usually engaged in. So, although Mood Six were courted, as were to a lesser extent some of the other bands, the solution that presented itself was to package the movement, *en masse*. This had the distinct effect of emphasising that somebody somewhere thought there *was* a movement – something that had the potential to backfire horribly on the bands involved (many of whom were being given the irresistible opportunity to record for the first time). At the same time the approach benefitted any label that took on the project since it could be undertaken relatively cheaply on a suck-it-and-see basis.

The compilation album *A Splash Of Colour* was announced in December and released in the first week of January 1982. The first thing to note was its visual impact – David Hines' striking cover was fluid and vibrantly psychedelic, and did a good job of unifying what was quite disparate content. The thirteen tracks featured the work of nine artists and the album opened with a spoken word 'Prelude' by the Doctor, whose suitably cod-American accent inadvertently set a tone that proved hard to match. The scene's more marquee names, each contributed two tracks, Mood Six offering up 'Plastic Flowers' and 'Just Like A Dream', Miles Over Matter bequeathing 'Something's Happening Here' and 'Park My Car' and High Tide contributing 'Dancing In My Mind' and 'Electric Blue'. Elsewhere, there were tracks by the Times ('I Helped Patrick McGoohan Escape'), the Barracudas ('Watching The World Go By'), the Silence ('Love Letters'), the Marble Staircase ('Long Weekend'), and the Earwigs ('Keep Your Voice Down'). There was a further contribution by the Doctor, as well, the eerily gothic 'Mortal Dreams'.

Spanning, in truth, a number of genres pushed hastily together to try to create a new one, the overall effect of *A Splash Of Colour* is in part a mix of Neo Mod, Bubblegum kitsch, old school New Wave, Power Pop recreation, and Psychedelia filtered through the Mobius Strip conjuring of the more outre elements of the Beatles' *Revolver* and the Oedipus-fixated dramatics of the Doors' 'The End'. As with any compilation, the individual qualities of the bands are homogenised. If a unified scene did exist and a new style was emerging, then it's clarion call was in the lyric to Miles

Over Matter's 'Something's Happening Here'. Part prophecy and part hostage to fortune, it set down a challenge: 'We've gotta get on and do it/ It's up to you!'

There were various showcase gigs for A Splash Of Colour, including one at Heaven under the arches in Charing Cross and another at the Moonlight Club in west Hampstead. A number of bands, including the Times, played solo gigs advertised under the banner of the album's title. The reviews were respectful and suspicious, and the record was dogged by the fact that many critics still saw the whole thing as little more than hype. Journalist Paul Tickell, witnessing Miles Over Matter live, found that the 'Mysterioso organ and biscuit tin drum-rolls fall rather short of an attempted synthesis of the Small Faces telling us it's all too beautiful and Deep Purple saying "Hush" Billy Joe Royal style', observing overall that 'Revived wardrobes are really coffins demanding media overkill then instant burial'.

And then almost as quickly as it had started it appeared to be over. A new club, the Fantasy Attic opened at Samanthas, but the enthusiasm had gone. It wasn't quite the usual scenario of bandwagon, bickering, break-up, and disillusion, but scarcely had the album hit the shelves than a post mortem started. Promised record company marketing support allegedly evaporated and the bands were left like soap stars momentarily 'rested', conducting the follow-on publicity but struggling to justify something that they appeared to realise was already passed. EMI stepped in and picked up Mood Six, released 'Hanging Around' (a song later covered by Toni Basil!) and then promptly dropped them. A second Mood Six single ('She's Too Far (Out)') reached test-pressing stage but was never released.

From a distance, it seems that the amount of effort and imagination required in getting the period detail accurate ultimately left little spare energy for the act of creating a substantial body of original work. There was the further problem that from the initial flicker to fading out, the first phase of New Psychedelia was over in almost an instant. A number of high profile contemporary indie bands, such as Echo & The Bunnymen, the Teardrop Explodes, the Psychedelic Furs, the Cure, Bauhaus and Siouxsie & The Banshees, flirted with New Psychedelia but declined to pin their colours to the specific mast. Had they done so (and there was no direct reason why they should have), the 'movement', as some of the bands involved ultimately started calling it, might have got more traction. But Psychedelia for them was an interesting stopping off point on a journey, not a final destination.

Immediately prior to Christmas 1981, the *NME* ran a news story, 'Psychedelia Hits Celluloid', trailing what was pitched as 'a fantastical documentary' cataloguing the scene. *The Groovy Movie* ended up as the movement's memorial. It remains a brilliant piece of work, a crazy paving composition, in the spirit of the time. Described as not being a 'documentary of any "scene" nor purely a promo for any of the bands involved' it sits curiously in between.

The film opens with homage to *The Prisoner*, as Ed Ball drives a kit car to the Houses of Parliament miming 'I Helped Patrick McGoohan Escape', before the action segues to a village that looks like Portmeirion, the setting for the cult TV show. There's footage of the Groovy Cellar, shots of the Regal and an interview with Andrew Yiannakou whose sincerity and modesty is largely reflective of most of those featured. But it is left to the Doctor, somewhat less of a wallflower, to spell out a philosophy which also unwittingly serves as obituary:

'Well, as you can see, the mass medication centres were taking place, people were reacting, the children were becoming colourful and bright, the treatment was working. If I describe it, it was as if the sky was clearing the haze of the last ten years, the dark haze was going aside, and looking to the sky I could see like a bright beam of sun hitting the ground, things were being done, people were beginning to move, it was a beautiful time.'

By the time that the film was completed, alas, many had moved on, some distracted towards the sounds of Northern Soul, echoes of which were turning up in the music of bands like the Jam and Dexys Midnight Runners. Sadly, for many of the bands involved, there was no such escape – they were drawn like a paisley Icarus towards the 'bright beam of sun' the Doctor referred to, and perished accordingly.

Revivals tend to be short-lived or short-sighted – Power Pop did little more than rehash the brief moment that was Merseybeat, and the Mod revival revolved around no more than two or three key songs, or so said some. This, perhaps predictably, was the fate of the early neo-psychedelic pioneers. Dan Treacy picked up and ran with a number of their playful themes shortly afterwards with a series of 'Spontaneous Happening' events, where live bands, film projections, poetry, and action painting all jumbled into one in a way that Mood Six would have approved of.

But this kind of astute playfulness wasn't lazy revivalism, as he was quick to point out, sympathising with those brave souls involved just after *A Splash Of Colour* was released. 'The Sixties were about music, literature, television, ways of thinking', and it was a time when 'you were free to say what you wanted to say and free to express yourself. Free to BE yourself!' Criticising those influenced by the 1960s was as pointless as castigating people for still liking Shakespeare. There had never been such a thing as a Shakespeare revival, and, just like the Bard, London, the Swinging Sixties and Pyschedelia was every bit as immortal.

By the end of spring 1982, the mainstream music press had turned against New Psychedelia and went on to do a far more comprehensive job in knocking the genre down than it ever had done in building it up. In any event, the music papers found a new sartorial fad, one equally as blinding, as during the course of the next 18 months or so Boy George and Culture Club dominated. Psychedelia disappeared *Alice In Wonderland*-style down a rabbit hole, and most declared it lost forever. In its first phase, it had appealed to disaffected Neo Mods, but ex punks had also been involved, together with the supposedly 'lone wolf' '60s obsessives who had suddenly made the pleasing discovery that they weren't alone. Whereas the Mods were younger, and lured into the scene more by its style trappings, the punks were older and in some cases revisiting a music that they'd first discovered just before punk happened, when publications like *Zig Zag*, *Bam Balam*, *Dark Star* and others had been representing and writing about the psychedelic sounds of the 1960s, usually celebrating American psychedelic groups like Love, the Charlatans, Quicksilver Messenger Service, Kaleidoscope, the Doors, and the Thirteenth Floor Elevators.

This music, whose scene (like its English counterpart of 1967) had none of the bad connotations of the 1981 recreation, had been gradually in the process of rediscovery for some time. By 1983 it was more popular than ever at an underground level, the faithful supplicated through devoted magazines like *Bucketfull Of Brains*, which had been first published in 1979, and shrines such as the Zippo record shop in Clapham and Rock On in Camden that did so much to keep the spirit alive and re-energise it.

Both Zippo and Rock On had labels associated with them. The Zippo label was home to the new US psychedelia of the Paisley Underground (Rain Parade, Green On Red, Opal, etc) and its back-catalogue label, Five Hours Back, released work by Roky Erikson, the UK Kaleidoscope and Julian Jay Savarin. Rock On was run by Ted Carroll, who had co-founded Chiswick with Roger Armstrong (and released important punk singles by the Hammersmith Gorillas, the Count Bishops and others) and also Big Beat, which released a string of garage punk and trash and had bands like the Sting-Rays and thee Milkshakes on its books. In time, Big Beat began reissuing 1960s garage punk classics by bands such as the Chocolate Watch Band, the Standells and the Seeds. Arguably, the most important reissue label was Edsel, part of the Demon Group. In 1978 and 1979, Demon's sister company Radar reissued a select choice of Psychedelia, including the Thirteenth Floor Elevators *Psychedelic Sounds Of* and the Electric Prunes' *I Had To Much To Dream Last Night*. A bespoke reissue label was quickly set up, called Edsel. Edsel reissued hundreds of out of print psychedelic albums during the 1980s, including key releases by the Creation, the Pretty Things, Move, and Kaleidoscope (US). Bam Caruso, run by the energetic Phil Smee, followed hot on Edsel's heels, reissuing work by the Left Banke, the Eyes and others, and putting out a series of important compilations that gathered together psychedelic obscurities on sets such as *Circus Days*, *Garagelands* and *Rubble*. Another early psychedelic reissue label was Psycho Records in Margate, home to all manner of wonderful treasures, including albums by Electric Toilet, Fapardokly and C.A. Quintet. French label Eva also was active, reissuing important lost works by the Charlatans, Josefus, and the Remains, amongst others.

Alan Duffy's excellent Acid Tapes must be added to this list. It began in 1983 with the express intention of bringing psychedelic bands before the public eye. Acid tapes released material in cassette form, tapping in to the then burgeoning cassette culture that the Home Taping Is Killing Music industry campaign of the time did nothing to halt. Acid Tapes put out a number of important releases between 1983 and 1995, including fine work by the Cleaners From Venus, Paul Roland and the Mixers.

Some of those shopping for the above artists first found out about them through Julian Cope's passionate, double-page love letter to Psychedelia ('Tales From The Drug Attic'). Just as the Barracudas would bemoan the British public's failure to get 'basic rock 'n' roll', so Cope (in typically breathless style) praised Psychedelia's rudimentary and more genuinely worthy legacy of 'Garage-music overproduced in four-track studios'. The pioneers of this sound sometimes led stultified, 'dry-wank' real lives: they were often social misfits; they 'couldn't play well, and the singer didn't know the words' to the classics they were interpreting. But theirs was a genius that had gone criminally uncelebrated, as Cope pointed out. The heroes included 'Ed Cobb, Sky Saxon, Keith Relf, Eddie Phillips, Arthur Lee... Mouse, Dave Agular'. Whilst the Cope article confirmed that the essential listening inevitably amounted to key titles by more obvious artists such as Pink Floyd, the Doors, the Beatles and Traffic *et al*, and the lesser well-known work of Love and the Thirteenth Floor Elevators, it also included Lenny Kaye's seminal 1972 compilation *Nuggets* – a bolt from outer space which had introduced for the first time to many such acts as the Standells, the Chocolate Watch Band, the Remains, the Seeds and the Electric Prunes.

Thus, the appreciation of Psychedelia broadened out and began including the less stylised and more ragged or vagabond aspects of garage rock that owed as much to the pose of Keith Richards as it did to the music of Syd Barrett and others. Reflecting this was Alice In Wonderland, a club that opened in the early part of October 1983 at Gossips, the 400-capacity former home of the Clinic. By the second week the place was nearing full – no mean feat for a club held on a Monday night. The enterprising Christian Paris had hooked up with Clive Jackson in the summer, concocting a plan to present punters with music that drew together '60s Pyschedelia and '70s sleeze glam. The Doctor added some appropriately wacky features that eventually became a trademark of the club, such as hanging streams of single-ply toilet tissue from the ceiling, initially designed to confuse early punters into thinking that the club wasn't empty.

The Doctor acted as DJ, occasionally making way for Paris to have a stint at the turntable, and Jackson's band the Medics played from the second night onwards, effectively becoming the 'house' group, treating their growing band of followers to their inimitable set, which included original songs such as 'The Goats Are Trying To Kill Me', 'Love, Peace & Bananas', and 'The Molecatcher's Boot' mixed in with covers of such classics as 'Blockbuster', 'Motorhead', 'These Boots Are Made For Walking', 'Gloria' and 'Silver Machine'. In the words of Christian Paris, those that came were a broad mix, 'psyches, punks, goths, surfers, glam rockers, hippies, bikers, and just ordinary people who were there to … have a good time' and to experience The Doctor's echo-box treated 'psycho babble' as his between-song banter soon became known.

Alice proved that the borders of the New Psychedelia had never been as regimented as the music press had wanted them to be back in 1981. For one thing, ever since 1967 and Haight Ashbury, nobody had really come up with an adequate definition of Psychedelia, although most felt comfortable using the term. In January 1982, High Tide's Jon Helmer, verbally tussling with *Melody Maker*'s Steve Sutherland, argued that its vagueness was positive, and that 'in that sense, it is a good label because without a definition it doesn't really mean anything'. Alice's use of psychedelic imagery on such things as its early flyers advertising the club were clearly intended to be psychedelic in flavour, crude representations that mimicked the work of such American graphic pioneers as Wes Wilson, Stanley Mouse and Rick Griffin. But by the end of 1983, the few groups that had played Alice could scarcely be described as mind-trippingly psychedelic: if all had been stacked together on one bill, there would be little danger of mistaking it for the second coming of the 14 Hour Technicolour Dream, for instance. The bands included Scarlet Party, Persian Flowers, Billy London, Jeremy's Secret and Ring Of Roses.

As was noted at the time, the sound of Psychedelia rippled through the music of a number of post-punk bands, including Siouxsie & The Banshees, whose lycergic take on The Beatles' 'Dear Prudence' (featuring Robert Smith of the Cure on guitar) made it all the way to the top three in the charts. Many artists dabbled, some setting up alter egos or side projects to demarcate or otherwise accommodate their interest, bands like Elvis Costello's backing band the Attractions, XTC, who began a parallel career as the Dukes of Stratosphere with the 1984 release of *25 O'Clock*, and the Damned, who donned wigs and tongue-in-cheek presented themselves as Naz Nomad & The Nightmares, convincing some that they were a Swedish psychedelic band presenting a 'lost' classic soundtrack album to a (fictitious) low-budget horror flick called *Give Daddy The Knife, Cindy*. The record came packaged to look like authentic underground '60s film soundtracks, such as *The Trip* and *Psych-Out*.

The Damned were regular punters at Alice and played there as Naz Nomad on 30 January 1984, in the process recruiting a number of the club's regulars to appear as cover stars on the Naz Nomad sleeve. The band also gave support slots to Doctor & The Medics wherever they could and plugged Alice In Wonderland incessantly in interviews at the time. Shortly after they'd played at Alice, Naz Nomad made it to the cover of *Sounds* where the paper's readership would have to have been very gullible indeed to believe that Naz (looking suspiciously like Dave Vanian) owned 'an antique store in Bergen, and also a partnership in a travel agency'.

The article in *Sounds* was part of a psychedelic edition that also featured the rise of the Paisley Underground, psychedelic fanzines, three 'psychedelectable indies' (Rhino, Bam Caruso and Demon/Edsel) as well as interviews with the Unclaimed, the Chesterfield Kings, the Playn Jayn, the Green Telescope and, somewhat confusingly, the Nomads (a real Swedish psychedelic band). The issue was mainly devoted to the rise of US neo-psych (Rain Parade, Green On Red, Long Ryders, etc) but ran a full page appraisal of Alice In Wonderland written by fervent supporter Tibet, where Christian Paris, joining the queue of those struggling to define Psychedelia, offered up the following gnomic comment: 'psychedelic is something that happens which is conjured up by the word itself. The *colour* of the word sums it up. Something could be really psychedelic and have *nothing* to do with the '60s, and *nothing* to do with music'.

The Psychedelia-as-state-of-mind approach, not unduly fettered by sartorial accoutrements, was one adopted by others during 1984, including Alan McGee whose Creation record label, taking inspiration from Dan Treacy, launched in February. McGee's own club, the Living Room which had opened in the autumn of 1983 at the Adams Arms pub and later became a Pop-Up club at various venues. Creation act the Jasmine Minks played at Alice in 1984 and McGee then managed to get the the Jesus & Mary Chain an early gig there as support to Green on Red on 17 September. It was to be the first of many aborted performances as the East Kilbride band, somewhat tired and emotional, were forcibly ejected from the stage for fear of damage they might inflict on the PA being loaned them. According to Paris, McGee had been suitably impressed with the venue, booking it out one Wednesday night with the possibility of setting up a long-term club to be called 'The Trip'. But Paris was having none of it. 'I spoke to the management and told them there was room for only one psychedelic club, so they closed him down after just one week,' he later recounted in his entertaining autobiography, *A Pretty Smart Way To Catch A Lobster*.

Just as Mood Six had in 1981 set out to inject novelty into the live circuit by deliberately playing more unexpected venues, so too did Alice. The idea of a Magical Mystery Tour was scarcely novel, but there hadn't been too many between 1967 and 1984 when Paris and Jackson decided to give their customers a slightly more alternative experience. Doctor & The Medics performed at Chiselhurst Caves – which sprawled over 23 miles and had previously played host to Jimi Hendrix and the Rolling Stones. Eight coaches were booked to ferry people there from central London (one poor soul left Chiselhurst in excitement for the mystery tour only to be returned to her home town). The day involved the music of the Medics as well as video entertainment in the form of the children's television programme *The Magic Roundabout* and the original *Batman* movie. The fact that the primitive power supply inevitably tripped, plunging 525 revellers into claustrophobic darkness, seemed to make the experience more rather than less enjoyable.

There were further mystery trips, including to the deserted Decca Records factory in Battersea (billed as *The Alice In Wonderland Trip To Fairyland*) and to the former Butlins Holiday Camp in Clacton, where a staggering 2000 people attended and special trains had to be laid on to transport them all. There were Alice In Wonderland film festivals, all night affairs, the first at the legendary Scala Cinema in Kings Cross, where appropriate cult classics such as *Head, Barbarella, The Trip, Blow Up* and *Wonderwall* were shown, along with Doctor & The Medics own film, the snappily-titled *I Keep Thinking It's Tuesday (Two Pieces Of Cloth Carefully Stitched Together)*. In time there were Planet Alice shops and a clothing line – the whole thing lasted in excess of ten years – in what must rank as one of the most commercially successful exploitations of Psychedelia ever.

But this is to jump forward, and in truth by the end of 1985, the scene's creativeness had gone beyond its tipping point. By now, much of what was attractive – the homespun inventiveness, the random creativity – had evaporated: bands like the Cult and the Mission and their major record labels, with their cartoonish borrowing from the movement, turned it into another marketing gimmick, to be dropped at the appropriate moment. And then in spring 1986, Doctor & The Medics reached number one in the charts with their cover of Norman Greenbaum's classic 'Spirit In The Sky', drawing some sort of line under all that had happened since the Groovy Cellar had opened back in May 1981. The success was fitting and Clive Jackson had done more than anyone to keep the spirit alive during the previous five or so years.

Jackson himself was himself once asked to define the term Psychedelia and decided that although it was 'everything', 'the first thing that hits your mind is LSD'. Those who had taken the drug knew instantly the secret; for those who hadn't, an explanation was hard to fathom.

In the end, it was better not to worry about it. Instead, turn off your mind, relax and float down stream…

CHAPTER 3

THEY COULD HAVE BEEN BIGGER THAN THE BEATLES

LIKE OTHER *UN*POP PIONEERS SUCH as the Marine Girls, Patrik Fitzgerald and Swell Maps, the Television Personalities followed the DIY tradition when it came to the process of music making. This approach applauded the amateur (as in its true meaning, to be a 'lover of'), and recognised that experimentation, trial and error was every bit as valid an approach, if not one more so, than the rigorous quest for a more formal standard of musicianship. 'Like boffins tinkering in the garden shed,' is how Geoff Travis once aptly summed up the maverick genius and methodology of Swell Maps at the end of the 1970s and the Television Personalities were the same.

In fact, Dan Treacy has, over the years, taken the 'tinkering' approach to its ultimate. His method of working is maximal with very little seemingly filtered out in a body of work that is ever expanding. For some, he is about as close at it comes to an enigmatic indie genius – a sort of Pop Art Pynchon. The work he creates tends to be bold, flat and colourful, like the paintings of those pop artists of the 1960s, summing up a mood or a period in a bright and simplistic, almost functional way. During his most productive early period, his output was prodigious, with seemingly little time spent fine tuning the work he created.

Treacy's songs tend to be either anonymous and observational, where they are often at their most perceptive (*a la* Isherwood and *I The Camera*), or else they are self-enclosed mini-worlds, created or re-created from Treacy's richly-remembered childhood experiencies. Most of those who jumped on to the '60s-revival bandwagon, did so as an act of homage, with little or no directly meaningful experience of the culture they were attempting to mimic. But Treacy was right in the thick of it, as a child growing up in Chelsea during the whole Swinging London period and beyond. The family flat was in a block next to Nigel Waymouth's Granny Takes A Trip boutique on the Kings Road (and opposite the shop that became Seditionaries, which was handy when punk came along). Treacy's father was an asphalter (and part-time poet on the side) and his mother did dry cleaning, which is how, as a child, he came to rub shoulders with some of the Chelsea bohemians, including John Hurt, and David Bowie, who he says he met at the age of five. When punk took off, he looked down from the flat at the foot traffic flowing in and out of McClaren and Westwood's shop; it was an odd mix of the fascinating and the fascinated and included not just the emerging punks but also characters like Rolling Stones drummer Charlie Watts, actress Diana Dors and news reader Reggie Bosanquet. The experience was put to good use when looking about for inspiration for the first Television Personalities single, '14th Floor', a part-observational ('I'm looking down on London…') tale of the de-humanising alienation of living in a council high-rise, where the song's narrator 'think(s) the bloke next door is a Jamaican/ But he could be an Irishman'.

Dan Treacy has said that he was taught to play guitar by nuns, when attending the Servite RC Primary School in the Fulham Road. It was whilst at his secondary school, the London Oratory School in Fulham, that he formed the Television Personalities, along with Ed Ball, Joe Foster and John and Gerrard Bennett. Writing in the debut issue of the Television Personalities Fan Club magazine (in 1985) he whimsically outlined how in 1974 Ed Ball had shown him a guitar and set him off on the path that led to the Television Personalities.

'It was then I knew what had to be done,' wrote Treacy. 'I ran all the way to the bank and withdrew my life's savings from my Midlands Young Savers account…. I ran like I had never run before… I could feel my face, taut as every sinew strained, the wind hurting my eyes. But I made it, 5.29 pm. The shoppers stared as I ran through the Woolworth's haberdashery, through the confectionary, left at the gardening display… and suddenly it caught my eye. I stood, frozen to the spot, money clenched in my fist. The glittering prize awaited me, a magnificent Wingfield Jetstar guitar, cherry and metallic blue, hand-crafted in Hong Kong and only £19.99 complete with tremolo arm. I clutched it to my chest all the way home on the number 11 bus. I went into my bedroom and … strapped it around my neck and gazed into the full-length mirror. A new world waited for me, I was a man now…'

At first, the Bennets and Ed Ball had shut Dan Treacy out, playing a couple of the school dances in a band they called O Level. Treacy continued writing songs alone, leaving school in 1976. A short while later he bumped into Joe Foster at the Roundhouse and the idea of all of them getting together again in a band was reanimated. According to Treacy, 'We had often talked about putting out a record. Ed had suggested that O Level were going to make a single but it did not look like they ever would. By this time, I had been working and saving money. I figured that if Eddie would come and play drums in the studio, I could record a single. He agreed he would.'

Treacy was suspicious when Ed Ball turned up with the others, but pressed on with the plan anyway. 'We were very unsure what to do. The studio engineer was not that helpful. We knew nothing about studio techniques. We assumed we had to record it live… It was all very spontaneous. The two tracks we recorded were '14th Floor/ Oxford Street'. I went away feeling very pleased. It took four hours recording and cost the huge amount of £18. This was August 1977.'

Having recorded the single, Dan Treacy had no idea how to go about getting it pressed up, but on a Butlins holiday met the resident cabaret band, Jasper. Jasper had just self-released an album which they told Dan they'd had pressed up at the pressing plant SRT. Problem solved. Or at least, part-solved, in that Dan knew now how to go about things but had no money left to actually press up the single. A couple of white labels were made, one of which found its way to John Peel, who played the single with a plea that someone help fund its release. After a couple of further plays, Treacy's parents took pity on him, agreeing to lend him the money to press up the single so long as he found work. 500 copies (475 delivered) were pressed up, followed by a further 387, the maximum number that Treacy could afford.

In keeping with the times, Dan Treacy also started a fanzine (along with Ed Ball). The aptly-named *Kings Road* detailed further the whole rigmarole of releasing '14th Floor' in a poem by 'Nicholas Parsons', entitled 'What Nicholas Did Today'.

It begins,

I've made a record and it's DIY
They asked me why I did it but I didn't know why
We only ordered 500, we couldn't afford more
It's by The Television Personalities, it's called 14th Floor

before going on to detail the various setbacks – missed deadlines and ridiculous delays, added expenses and the fact that only 475 of the 500 records reached them. Dan also discovered that having the sleeves printed properly was a financial bridge too far.

We couldn't afford picture sleeves from Delga Press
So we made them and stapled them, they looked a mess
Then we found we were 100 short
So I drew some with pencil, I was very distraught

But all is well that ends well as John Peel comes to the rescue:

He played it on the radio when I was ill
And it did far more for me than any doctor's pills

On the copy of the white label that Dan had sent to the DJ he had decided to list the names of the Television Personalities as those of real television personalities: Dan became Nicholas Parsons and Ed Ball became Russell Harty. Other names chosen for band members at various times included Bruce Forsyth, Hughie Green, Melvyn Bragg and Bamber Gascoigne. The whole thing was a joke (one taken very seriously by some), but the hiding behind a persona was an early indication of how Dan Treacy sometimes preferred to work. And in the light of his often outspoken comments, it has probably also been a useful tool for covering over any insecurity. 'I'm not worried about being taken seriously… I'm worried about NOT being taken seriously, which is a different thing, really,' Dan Treacy told *Melody Maker* later, at the start of 1982, putting his finger on an itch that would need constant scratching in the future.

Ed Ball had gone back into the studio following the recording of '14th Floor' and made the first O Level single, 'East Sheen'/'Psuedo Punks' which he released on a label he called Psycho Records. Shortly after, the Bennetts left O Level and Treacy and Ball decided to pool their resources and start a label, also called Kings Road. 'In August 1978, we went into IPS studio in Shepherds Bush,' recalled Treacy in the fanzine newsletter, 'and recorded the "Where's Bill Grundy Now?" EP. A week later, Eddie recorded the second O Level single, "We Love Malcolm"… playing all the instruments himself. Both were released in November 1978.'

The title track 'Where's Bill Grundy Now? told a wistful tale about the real life disgraced television presenter who had famously clashed swords with the Sex Pistols on live TV and lived to regret it. It was a very strong song, but largely overlooked once the brilliance of one of the EP's other songs, 'Part Time Punks', was discovered. 'Part Time Punks', with its status-deflating story of poseur punks remains to this day one of *the* songs of its era. It has an absolutely brilliant lyric, yet does little really other than paint a picture of what Dan Treacy observed from the window of his tower block flat on the Kings Road. Funny and catchy, it is not quite the parody that has painted the band into corner ever since its release (when *Sounds*, for instance, in crowning it Single of the Week, described the Television Personalities as 'the Gang of Four meets Barron Knights'.)

'Peel again went potty,' Treacy later recalled, 'and played the single every night for a month. It topped the indie charts for months and sold well enough to be a Top 20 hit. It sold about 20,000 on Kings Road. I did little for the next six months except making and gluing self-made sleeves for the record. Only 1,500 appeared in a proper sleeve. I made myself very ill and became something of a recluse. Rough Trade kept pestering for more [copies] and eventually suggested re-releasing it on Rough Trade. They repressed it with a label designed by Swell Maps and sold another 15,000 copies!'

'Dan used to come into the Rough Trade shop,' recalls Geoff Travis. 'He'd been in to sell us copies of the first single and on one occasion I'd gone around to his parent's flat on the fourteenth floor in a block on the Kings Road. He was shy and unsassuming but he had a talent. I loved the satire in the work: he was sharp-witted and a keen social commentator, rather like Ray Davies.'

By 1980, both Dan Treacy and Ed Ball were writing prolifically, enough for them to have material left over for various side-projects that were on the go. '[We] write so much and are open to so many influences that we thought it was poor idea to be stuck in a band together, so we decided to do separate projects,' explained Dan, at the time. Around about the time of the Rough Trade re-release of 'Where's Bill Grundy Now?' Ed Ball, helped out by Dan and Joe Foster, recorded a single as the Teenage Filmstars ('Clouds Over Liverpool', complete with mock Liverpuddlian accents) and released it on his own Clockwork label. A second followed ('The Odd Man Out') which appeared as an 'experiment' after Ball got a deal with the Pye subsidiary label, Blueprint, in 1980 – taking a course of action he described as 'the alternative to the alternative'. A third Teenage Filmstars single, 'I Helped Patrick McGoohan Escape' appeared on Fab Listening in November the same year.

The stress of the 'Where's Bill Grundy Now?' EP sent Treacy into a depression and he began suffering with bad nerves. The band, though, was getting more and more of a cult following without seemingly existing in any kind of tangible way. Treacy wanted to have a band but didn't feel well enough to take the steps necessary to make that happen. Joe Foster was in touch, however, and suggested that people were waiting for The Television Personalities to play live. Treacy asked Foster to join him and Foster told Treacy that 'he knew a kid called Mark who had a drum kit'. Treacy realised that he needed to put the band together or, as he told *Nag Nag Nog* fanzine, forever be 'carrying to an extreme the idea of the imaginary school band where people rehearse together occasionally and fancifully call themselves a band'.

Treacy, Foster and Mark 'Empire' Sheppard *did* begin rehearsing together. 'We knew about five numbers, mostly Mod and soul stuff and my own handful of songs,' Treacy later wrote, 'but we took a risk and fixed a performance at the Central School of Art in London. It was the first "PSYCHO-DELIC" happening since the sixties. The early Sex Pistols gigs were no comparison. I got to play two numbers before I started hallucinating. Someone had spiked my drink with LSD!'

Jowe Head was one of those who got up on stage to help finish the performance. 'I arrived at the place a bit late,' he presently remembers. 'Joe Foster and Mark Sheppard were struggling to do a set on their own, without Dan. Bemused, Nikki, Epic and I stepped up to help them play a few songs. I recall us doing "14th Floor", "Part Time Punks" and a few Yardbirds songs. Later, Dan claimed that someone had spiked his drink, and he dashed out in a state of disorientation.

'We'd come across The Television Personalities on the radio – *Top Gear*, of course! John Peel had played "14th Floor" at the same time as he played our first single, "Read About Seymour". We felt a kinship immediately; we even recorded a primitive cover version of "14th Floor", and also an improvised tribute to them on our second single's B-side. We realised Dan was making the identical responses to the record industry – he was ignoring it. He, like us, was devising the same processes of recording/ design/ manufacturing/ distribution independently and with the same minimal resources. There were precious few of us doing that back then.'

Dan Treacy got his act back together for the band's second performance that took place a week or so later at the Clarendon Hotel in Hammersmith, with the Television Personalities supporting fellow Rough Trade artists, This Heat and Essential Logic: 'As we were first band on we decided to make the most of our chance and ... organised an elaborate film and light show. We had two huge screens erected at either side of the hall and we projected a collage of oil wheels and "arty" slides along with films of the Royal Family and the Supremes, amongst others,' Treacy later recalled. 'We would often rummage through the dustbins in Dean Street in London where all the film studios are. Anyway, the gig was a great success. I had not seen a genuine hippy since I was a child in the 1960s. Well here in the hall were 400 of them, all sitting cross-legged on the floor. We came on dressed in the most outrageous Mod Pop Art clothes – all RAF flying jackets and cravats – and they thought we were weird. Everyone told us we were "super", and of course we were.'

The success of 'Part Time Punks' had, curiously, not spurred Treacy on creatively. Decisions to record always seemed to be taken at random. Indeed, between the release of '14th Floor' and the recording of the 'Where's Bill Grundy Now?' EP, Treacy had gone back into the studio just once, alone and to record four tracks solo – 'Seditionaries', 'Chelsea To Battersea', 'Sometimes I'm Sorry I Am A Boy', and an early version of 'Where's Bill Grundy Now?' It wasn't until January 1980, though, that he felt comfortable going into the studio again to record some new Television Personalities material. The experience was not a comfortable one.

'I went into a 24-track studio with very little idea of what I was going to do. I intended going in on my own but at the very last minute I asked Eddie to play the drums again,' Treacy told readers of the second issue of the Television Personalities fan club magazine. 'The studio hadn't booked a drum kit and so we had to play along with a drum machine first and attempt to overdub the drums later. This nearly gave poor Ed a nervous breakdown.'

The songs recorded over the seven-day session were 'Smashing Time', 'King & Country', Anxiety Block', 'Favourite Films, 'Games For Boys', 'Jackanory Stories', 'Once Upon A Time' and 'Three Cheers For Simon'. Upon hearing the recordings, Rough Trade offered to release 'Smashing Time' and 'King & Country' as a single, the follow-up to the 'hit' that had been 'Part Time Punks'. For such an accomplished artist, the song is thin gruel in truth – a primitive, simplistic tune underpins the story of a day out in London spent by the narrator and his cousin Jill who is taken to the various tourist haunts (Madam Tussauds, Tower of London, etc, as well as, crucially, and perhaps inevitably, Carnaby Street and the Kings Road.) Borrowing its title from the 1967 film *Smashing Time*, starring Rita Tushingham and Lynn Redgrave, the song, like the movie, is partly a satire on the mores of 'Swinging London'. When it was released, the *NME* criticised its 'studied naivety', causing Dan Treacy, not for the last time, to have to respond to such criticism. 'We are the least naïve people in the world,' he told *Nag Nag Nog* when the subject came up in an interview the fanzine did with the band.

In August, the Television Personalities one and only John Peel Session was broadcast and shortly after they went off to Germany to play a residency at the Excess Club in Berlin. The band proved enormously popular in spite of the fact that most of those in the audience only knew the song 'Part Time Punks'. They played two sets a night, and were on stage for around four hours each evening – 'Just like The Beatles!' as Treacy later recalled. Mark Empire returned home to England but Treacy and Foster got delayed as a result of a German rail strike, meaning that they were unable to fulfil an obligation to play at the Rock Garden, so Ed Ball and his pal John East stood in for them. The promoter never realised and neither did most of the audience. In fact, the *ad hoc* performance earned two encores.

Upon returning from Europe, Dan Treacy and Empire went into Mount Pleasant Studios in London and over the course of three days recorded the songs that would make up the first album, *And Don't The Kids Just Love It*, which was released in January 1981. Studded with real gems, such as 'Geoffrey Ingham', 'Look Back In Anger' and 'A Picture of Dorian Gray', once again the combination of Treacy's winsome vocals and deeply incisive lyrics proved a winner. Part of the charm was the utter Englishness of the sound of the voice, which took the listener on a journey back through the more obvious intersections of punk and the garage rock of the 1960s and beyond to the early vocal stylings of David Bowie's Deram-period recordings and even to the 1950s proto-sound of Tommy Steele. At the same time, it was an overall sound that would itself be hugely influential, and, as *Record Collector* noted in July 2002, '*And Don't The Kids Just Love It* was the entire '80s indie scene before it happened. Andy Gill, writing in the *NME* at the time of the record's release, called the record 'the best overtly *amateur* album I've heard in a long time', praising its 'bluff, gruff, social realism', 'wry, comedic undertones' and commenting on the natural unforced beauty and emotional awareness of Dan Treacy's song writing.

The Television Personalities released 'I Know Where Syd Barrett Lives', Dan's ode to his hero Syd Barrett, before returning to Europe for a tour of Holland where the single was proving to be a big hit. Alas, the experience turned to nightmare, with hotels for the band allegedly not booked properly and a badly planned itinerary in place. Halfway through, the group walked out and returned to England, where Rough Trade demanded compensation for the aborted venture, which had been funded by them. The experience severely damaged the band's relationship with Rough Trade. Future albums, at least for the time being, would be released on the new label that Dan and Ed set up, Whaam!

As the new label got under way, Ed Ball (who had fleetingly re-joined the Television Personalities, playing bass on the aborted Dutch tour) once more concentrated on his own projects and started to go under the banner the Times. Dan Treacy, not wanting to draft in a replacement for Ed Ball, also decided to make a clean break and decided to change the name of the band to the Gifted Children. The first two Whaam releases, in late spring, were 'Red With Purple Flashes' by the Times (a line lifted from a promotional ad for 1960s garage band the Creation) and 'Painting By Numbers' by the Gifted Children, which was Dan, Empire and bassist Bernie Cooper.

The Gifted Children was short lived. An offer for the Television Personalities to play a couple of dates in Germany (one supporting legendary chanteuse Nico) was gratefully accepted and when the band returned Treacy decided to stick with the original name. Prior to the German dates, he had gone into the studio with Empire and Bernie (who later vanished) to record some tracks for a proposed Gifted Children album. The project now became a Television Personalities one, with Ed Ball drafted back in temporarily to handle bass on some new tracks that were recorded.

Mummy, You're Not Watching Me was released in February 1982, the third Whaam! album, after *Beach Party* by Marine Girls (autumn 1981) and *Pop Goes Art* by The Times, which came out a month earlier in January. Ed Ball had experienced a few problems getting the album the way he wanted it and Dan Treacy had helped him out, as well as playing a handful of Times gigs. 'Ed had spray painted the first 1000 sleeves [of *Pop Goes Art*] in his bedroom,' Treacy recalled in 1985. 'The smell was mind blowing! By this time the psychedelic revival had spawned a number of groups so at last we thought we had some new playmates. It was fun going to the Groovy Cellar club on a Friday. It really was like being transported back in time. Naturally some bright entrepreneur had to try and cash in…'

The reviews for *Mummy, You're Not Watching Me* were satisfyingly positive, many noting the growing maturity of Dan Treacy's writing, apparent in songs like 'Magnificent Dreams' and 'If I Could Write Poetry'. Johnny Waller in *Sounds* picked up on the 'little diamonds lurking undiscovered, just waiting to be polished and made into hit singles'. In fact, the lack of polish, as ever, was partly what gave the music of the Television Personalities its charm, creating 'an awkward mixture of early Floyd and ugly Pistols' according to Steve Sutherland, an ever keen and loyal champion of the band's work.

With an album and a single to promote, Ed Ball focused wholly on the Times and set up yet another record label, Artpop!, as a vehicle for future releases. Whaam! issued the Television Personalities 'Three Wishes' and then Dan settled down to concentrate on running Whaam! and to sort out the substantial amount of material that had been recorded but never used, usually due to the limitations of space. There were further Whaam! singles released in 1982 by Small World, the Pastels, Doctor & The Medics, Direct Hits, Le Mat and Jed Dmochowski. Dmochoswki, a former member of the VIPs, also had an album released, *Stallions Of My Heart*. 'Dan offered to hear my songs, and I went around his place and played virtually a whole album of songs acoustically, which he immediately agreed to release,' recalls Jed Dmochowsky. 'He was very down to earth about it, very unpretentious about what he did at that time. All he lived for was writing his songs and putting his low-fi band out onto a lo-fi stage with low-fi music. And he did it with such integrity that people saw its value.'

Jed Dmochoswky's album was released in the autumn along with the third Television Personalities album, *They Could Have Been Bigger Than The Beatles*, which drew together the recording odds-and-sods that Treacy had been sorting. Clocking in with over 50-minutes worth of material, it was an impressive statement, one that pulled together variant takes, instrumentals,

B-sides, unreleased material and interesting oddities, such as Dan Treacy's ode to the Groovy Cellar scene, 'The Boy In The Paisley Shirt' ('The girls all dressed like Kathy McGowan…/ The boys all dressed in velvet hipsters…'). Like those budget albums by the Kinks, the Who and others in the 1960s, *They Could Have Been Bigger Than The Beatles* assumed an identity greater than the sum of the parts, Dan Treacy receiving fan mail from a listener saying the album 'reminded them of their scrapbooks they made as a child and still kept and looked at fondly from time to time'.

Following the burst of label activity, by the end of 1982, Treacy was keen to both begin writing again for the Television Personalities and play a few more gigs. Mark Flunder joined the band on bass and the group played a 'comeback' concert at the Dive, London (at the end of which Dan spray-painted a Ban The Bomb sign onto a makeshift sheet backdrop). Reviewing the show for *Melody Maker*, Steve Sutherland put his finger on the enigma that was Treacy: 'Some see Dan as a Sixties pop plagiarist, pilfering from his heroes for his own whimsical ends. Others treat him as some expert mimic, Mike Yarwood-ing the vital concerns of youth's last coherent rebellion, but listen close and the paisley shirt hides a terrible hurt, an aching insecurity, a dangerous instability.'

Aspects of the instability of the band rose up at the end of the year when the Television Personalities played at the Moonlight on one of the nights in December when across London at Wembley the Jam were playing one of their farewell concerts. Intending to jokily mimic Paul Weller's band, Dan Treacy announced on stage (not for the last time) that the Television Personalities were ceasing to exist. Unfortunately, nobody made the connection and the joke fell somewhat flat, sending Treacy into a guilty spin from which, he later claimed, it took time to recover.

The Television Personalities then expanded into a five-piece group, partly as a result of an offer to play a large indoor festival in Italy. Dave Musker joined on keyboards, drummer Jeff Bloom came in (replacing Empire who had gone off to work with Robyn Hitchcock) and Joe Foster came back into the fold. This was more or less the line-up that would go on to record *The Painted Word* album in June 1983. But there were problems. 'To be honest, the new TVP's sound was losing its appeal for me,' Treacy later said. 'I was writing simple songs which were often brutalised by having too many different ideas from other band members. I delayed recording for as long as I could. I tried to be subtle and let the others know that I was only asking them to help on the LP, but at the time I felt very removed from the situation.'

At the same time, Treacy was also growing bored of recording using a traditional bass/ drums/ guitar format and decided (in the face of much scepticism) to try recording without using a drummer. The drums that appear on *The Painted Word* were done when some demos were made earlier when Empire was still in the band. One of those demos was 'A Sense Of Belonging' which Geoff Travis at Rough Trade heard and offered to release.

'A Sense of Belonging' saw the Television Personalities moving creatively in an altogether different direction, with the darker side to Treacy's writing being allowed to show through. Ostensibly a song in tune with the 'Ban the Bomb' movement, Treacy was telling *NME* in February 1984 that it was as much about the hopelessness of being unable to change things as it was about waking up to the reality of nuclear annihilation. 'Once there was laughter … now only tears', the message on the back cover proclaimed, while the front cover showed, uneasily, a picture of a beaten child's face.

According to Treacy, the violence of nuclear holocaust was mirrored by the cover, its image just another example of violence manifesting itself. It proved a step too far for Rough Trade, and even long time supporter John Peel considered it 'harrowing'. Rough Trade released the single, and then failed (according to Treacy) to promote it in quite the way they had promised. They also declined to release *The Painted Word*, since Geoff Travis, according to Dan Treacy, considered the album 'really insecure'. Whaam! owed its manufacturers money and got taken to court – consequently, there was little chance of the record appearing on Treacy's own label. It was eventually released on Illuminated Records (home of Portion Control, 400 Blows and others) in February 1984.

The Painted Word carried through the politics of 'A Sense of Belonging' with Treacy casting his formidable eye over such subject matter as the fashionable cynicism of the anti-nuclear movement and the horrors of the Vietnam War, dark observations leavened slightly by the more expected fare of self-analysis: the stark, bleeding-heart honesty of 'Someone To Share My Life With' and 'Stop And Smell The Roses' are wistful and regretful without being over-egged.

The delay between the release of the single and the album didn't help, but, in any event, the critics remained predictably confused. Jack Barron in *Sounds*, open as ever to the ambitions of this kind of music, praised it, while long-time supporter Steve Sutherland in the *Melody Maker* found it frustrating, 'one of the most wanton and wilful cases of self-immolation you're ever likely to hear inside one LP, a deliberate mess of fragments from every emotional and stylistic which-a-way'. The *NME*'s Cath Carroll reviewed the album in parody, comparing Treacy to the wet fictional character Fotherington-Thomas from the Nigel Molesworth series of books and comparing the songs to cast-offs from the children's TV series, *Sesame Street*. 'This opus even made the cat cringe,' she witheringly confessed.

The reviews were disappointing, but a month or so later events took a distinct turn for the worse. Dave Gilmour, Pink Floyd's guitarist, whose solo album *About Face* had been released at the same time as *The Painted Word*, booked the Television Personalities to support him on a promotional tour. Gilmour had been impressed by Dan Treacy's quaint ode to Gilmour's former Pink

Floyd band-mate, 'I Know Where Syd Barrett Lives', which ventured to answer, Dan-style, the question that had been troubling a number of Syd-botherers for some time. The answer was – 'in a little house/ with a little pet dog/ and a little pet mouse…'. Unfortunately, Dan not only *knew* where Syd lived but also chose to read the address out live on stage at the Hammersmith Odeon and the band was consequently thrown off the tour.

Whaam! didn't survive long. Singles in 1983 by the Page Boys, the Marble Staircase, 1000 Mexicans and Kartomb proved to be the label's last. Two albums appeared in 1984, the Direct Hits' *Blow Up* and a label compilation, *All For Art*. Interestingly, *All For Art* had a couple of tracks featuring the involvement of Alan McGee who Treacy had got to know a couple of years earlier. The Television Personalities soldiered on, after a fashion, although there wouldn't be another album proper until 1989's *Privilege*.

The releases slowed up but the songs continued to pour out, as they always have done. Some say that over the years he has squandered a formidable talent, but Dan Treacy's muse was never going to fit neatly into that bottle by which most people measure pop success. The fact that people seem to mostly judge him on what he *might* have produced is, in a way, a form of flattery. It shows that in spite of a prodigious body of work, he still remains an enigma.

CHAPTER 4

HA! HA! HEE! HEE!

IN JUNE 1982 THE FANZINE *Jamming!* published its editorial railing against the sorry state of the UK music scene. Couched in the form of a 'STATEMENT' and printed in eye-catching red, black and white, the article mourned the gradual demise of pop music as a unifying force and damned the current status quo. The music scene, it said, had regressed and was '…somewhere around '74 heading for the horrible greyness of 1975'. It bemoaned the lack of adequate venues for independent music to flourish in and noted that some of the new musicians involved resembled the old ones that punk was meant to have made obsolete. Music moved in cycles and what was need was another 1976, or 1968, or even 1956, something that would inject excitement into a scene that was in torpor.

But it wasn't all doom and gloom, as the article went on to note. There was 'Optimism!'. There was 'Hope!'. More importantly, 'there [was] a generation of youngsters about who were affected by punk, but were either too young to get out there and do something at the time or were living in the country and, again, couldn't get involved. These people have learnt over the years what punk meant; they haven't fallen for quick fashions… or punk revivals, but have taken their time and are ready to start being noticed.'

The statement had been written by Tony Fletcher, *Jamming!*'s editor, and although he had yet to meet Alan McGee, Fletcher's words might have been written with McGee in mind. When the article was published, in June 1982, McGee had by then spent two years in London attempting to make it as a pop musician, but his enthusiasm was on the wane. A couple of week's before reading the article he had experienced his first taste of promoting and more or less given up on the idea of trying to make a success of the band he was in, the Laughing Apple. The article in *Jamming!* re-energised him, but also alerted him to the fact that what was needed was a broader strategy of attack if he was to succeed.

Sometime in 1977, McGee had met Andrew Innes after guitarist Innes and a drummer called Pete Buchanan had advertised for a bass player to join their group the Drains on Radio Clyde's *Streets Sounds* programme. Innes was a highly-talented musician and McGee an inexperienced bassist. Innes encouraged McGee, helping to develop McGee's technique and teaching him how to play the instrument in a rudimentary, punk style. Very quickly, Innes and McGee kicked out Buchanan and, later that same year, McGee introduced Innes to his old friend Bobby Gillespie. The three of them would get together and act as if they were a band – Innes playing a cherry red Les Paul copy, McGee a Gibson SG copy and Gillespie banging on cardboard boxes and aping around like he was Iggy Pop. They dreamed up a name for their imaginary bedroom band – Captain Scarlet & The Mysterons – but spent most of the time listening to the Sex Pistols, Clash and Sham 69. 'We never played a gig,' McGee later recalled. 'We were the audience *and* the band.'

The following year, McGee became bassist with H20, a five-piece synth-pop group that incorporated sax and keyboards and was led by an ambitious singer called Ian Donaldson. Donaldson was an old school punk who saw which way the wind was blowing and was attempting to create a band that was a little more sophisticated. McGee played with the group at its first gig at a local Campaign for Nuclear Disarmament festival, banging away competently on bass like a wannabe Jean Jacques Burnell. He later drafted Innes in to the band when one of H20's guitarists left. Then Innes and McGee quit the group, taking with them guitarist Neil Clark (later of Lloyd Cole & The Commotions). They found a good-looking singer called Jack Riley and a drummer and in 1979, shortly after McGee had first read George Orwell's *1984*, formed Newspeak.

According to the local fanzine, *Fumes*, Newspeak sounded like a cross between XTC and Gang of Four with 'lots of full-blooded grunts and screams in the songs'. But as the first proper band that

McGee had been involved with, it was the dream, it was what kept him hopeful as he toiled away at an electrician's apprenticeship. Newspeak made a demo and McGee ran off thirty-five cassette copies and sent them out to record companies. He didn't get a reply.

For McGee, as for so many before him, music was an escape. As he later revealed in his autobiography, his working class background involved a troubled home environment and the prospect of a life that would remain crushingly unfulfilled: 'Maybe, I'd have become a taxi driver… had fifty conversations a day about Rangers. When the heart attack arrived, I'd have probably been glad.'

Sometime towards the early summer of 1980, part of the escape route involved Innes convincing McGee that to succeed the band needed to be in London. In June, the two of them, along with Jack Riley, headed south, ending up in a flat in Tooting. By that point, McGee had begun working for British Rail. 'I quit my job and caught the train down with Andrew Innes,' McGee later recalled in his autobiography. 'I took nothing with me except a new Yamaha bass guitar bought on credit and a very small bag of clothes. We had no plan except that we would arrive in London and become pop stars'

Living in London pursuing the dream tested the trio's resolve. As the singer in the band, Riley was confident and expected naturally all the attention while Innes and McGee festered, frustrated at the music world's evident disinterest in their plight. Innes and McGee took out their frustrations on Riley. 'We were cruel and we were nasty and we loved it,' McGee later sorrowfully recounted. 'There was a bitterness in me, a rage at those who had had it so much easier than me. When you think the world doesn't want to let you into its club, you can either give up trying or make yourself sharp like a knife and try to stab yourself through.' Within a few short months, Riley was retracing his journey back to Glasgow and McGee and Innes had thought up a new name for their band: the Laughing Apple.

For the Laughing Apple to proceed, at the very least they needed a drummer. They found one in the most coincidental of ways when McGee ran into a flamboyant punk at a phone box and asked her if she knew any drummers. The girl led McGee to St Alphonsus Road in Clapham, then one of the most notorious drug den squat areas in London, and introduced him to Mark Jardim who subsequently became the third member of the Laughing Apple.

The band used the squat to rehearse in and began picking up gigs in local pubs such as the Stockwell Arms and the Wheatsheaf in Tooting Bec. At one point they supported the UK Subs on a tour. At first it was Andrew Innes who wrote the songs, McGee observing and learning the ropes as Innes took inspiration from what he saw around him and immortalising it in lost offerings such as 'Wandsworth Common Northside'.

McGee and Innes took Jardim with them when they returned to Scotland in December, travelling to Sirocco Studios in Kilmarnock to make their first record. McGee played bass and doubled up as producer. The four-track 'Ha! Ha! Hee! Hee!' EP was financed through a £500 loan from Govern CND, McGee and Innes having met the anti-nuclear group the first time when H20 played the CND festival in 1978. In return for the loan, CND asked for a credit on the sleeve designed by Bobby Gillespie who had begun working at a printshop. The record was released on a label they called Autonomy, named after a Buzzcocks song. Part 1960s garage band recreation and part pop confection of the kind being then churned out by bands like the Teardrop Explodes, the EP was an oddity, its more emotionally mature qualities (in songs like 'Sometimes I Wish') counterbalanced by some kitchen-sink inspiration, as in the more literal 'Chips For Tea'.

Shortly after the EP was released in the spring of 1981, the band were, unusually, written about at length by Dave McCulloch in *Sounds* who was on the trail of groups who looked like they might measure up to being the new Jam. McCulloch considered the Laughing Apple EP to be one of the three best releases of the year (the other two were records by Orange Juice and Aztec Camera, both still on Postcard). He praised the band's 'superb neo-Cope-esque love songs' and also their optimism. The band themselves were quoted briefly, McGee venting some of his pent up frustration in a sharp comment on the current music scene: 'They are all hippies in London, their attitudes belong to ten years ago. They don't really care about music, it's just the fashion they care about now.'

A few months after Dave McCulloch's article, Mark Jardim left the band and was replaced by Ken Popple, a drummer who previously had been playing music similar to that of Nine Below Zero in an R 'n' B outfit called the Results along with comedian Ronnie Barker's son, Larry. When the Results fizzled out, Popple went to work for Brent Council and spent time scouring the Situations Vacant column in the *Melody Maker* looking for a new band to join. One day his luck was in.

'The advert read: "DRUMMER WANTED FOR BAND INTO TEARDROP EXPLODES, ECHO & THE BUNNYMEN AND THE NIPS",' remembers Popple. 'I rang the number listed and Alan answered. We had a bit of a chat and then he asked me which bands I was into. I thought about it for a moment, and then said, "Mainly the Teardrop Explodes, Echo & The Bunnymen and the Nips". "That's fantastic!" he said, and I was in.

'Alan asked me to meet him on Clapham Common and he turned up with Andrew Innes, who was wearing a Parka coat which was buttoned all the way up to the top. Andrew looked like a Dickensian urchin. It was the middle of a boiling hot summer. Alan was incredibly striking, with his shock of bright red hair that he was growing out. He was wearing a tank top and red drainpipe jeans. They took me to their "rehearsal rooms", which turned out to be in a squat that we entered by climbing through a back window. In the rooms was an amp, half a drum kit and a microphone that was attached to a bare wire hanging down from the ceiling.'

In the *Sounds* article, the band had vowed to ensure that 'Participate!', one of their very best songs, would be released as their follow-up record. Shortly after Popple joined, they therefore returned to Kilmarnock to make good on the promise. The very title of the record, with its cajoling exclamation mark and punk directness, anticipates the kind of breathless language ('Direct!' 'Action!', 'Create!', etc) that would surface in the fanzine McGee's would start in 1983 and also matches the hyperbole of the statement in *Jamming!*, with its promises of 'Optimism!' and 'Hope!'. A clean, bright, rush of a record, it was, musically speaking, a progression, even if the obvious debt to the Jam was never going to be repaid given the band's capabilities.

Returning south and back to his hometown of Boston in Lincolnshire, Popple immediately began spray-painting the band's name on various bits of street hardware, the impetus of 'Participate!' carrying through in some sort of after-burner effect. 'I was good friends with Dick Green and one day we went out and wrote the words Laughing Apple all over the local road signs,' Popple recalls. 'Unfortunately, just as we were finishing work on one sign – I think Dick might have been balanced precariously on my shoulders, it was all less than discrete – a police car turned up. They arrested us but agreed to not press charges so long as we went back and cleaned everything up. When I got back to London and told Alan, he couldn't believe it. Getting a criminal record for the sake of the Laughing Apple – how brilliant!'

When Popple lost his job at the Council and could no longer afford to pay the rent on the place he had in Wembley, he moved into the squat in St Alphonsus Road in Clapham that McGee and Innes by then also shared, and was introduced to a world of drug addicts, dealers, army deserters, petty criminals and thieves. 'People came and went in the middle of the night, unnamed people arriving off boats from unspecified locations, much coming and going, and everyone, of course, entered their squat through back windows,' says Popple. The premises were, however, virtually next door to the squat where the Laughing Apple rehearsed – which was an advantage, at least until the moment when Popple's drum kit got stolen and he had to buy it back, bit by bit, from the local second-hand shop, at which point the short-lived novelty of living in the squat wore off and he moved out.

But living and rehearsing together 24/7 made the Laughing Apple a better band and they began picking up further gigs at more prestigious venues, like the Moonlight Club in Hampstead, the legendary venue run by Dave Kitson who went on to set up Red Flame. Very gradually they were starting to gain a modest following. One person who had read the Dave McCullogh article was Jerry Thackray, who would later reinvent himself as the Legend!, and he began going to see the Laughing Apple whenever he could, very quickly becoming one of the band's (two) most loyal fans.

'There would be twenty people in the audience on average at one of our gigs,' remembers Popple, 'and most of those people would be standing around not doing a great deal. Then down the front there would be Jerry hurling himself around as if we were the best band in the world. It was all a bit unusual and I found that rather strange, to be honest.'

Like most, Jerry Thackray picked up his tips for music from the weekly papers and from occasionally listening to John Peel: 'I took all my recommendations from my favourite writers in the music press. I was into a lot of the Scottish bands at the time – the Scars, all the Postcard Records groups, and I went to see the Laughing Apple for the first time when they supported the Sound in April 1981. I thought that they were great and I danced down the front, because that is what I did if I liked a band. It never bothered me that nobody else was dancing. Looking back, I think a lot of it was repressed sexuality – I needed to let all that energy out. I didn't really care what anybody else thought.'

Life in the St Alphonsus squats was, to put it mildly, insalubrious and after Innes contracted a serious bout of Hepatitis B he returned to convalesce in Scotland. Ken Popple suggested as a replacement Dick Green, his friend from Boston, a guitarist whose natural style wasn't entirely dissimilar to that of Will Seargant in Echo & The Bunnymen. Green joined, and another guitarist, Dennis Pooley, also occasionally helped out.

Another member of the Boston contingent was Dave Evans, who ended up playing in a number of Creation bands and went on to work for the Jesus & Mary Chain for a period around the time of *Psychocandy*. 'I came on to scene after I'd gone to see a gig by the Laughing Apple in Brixton that I heard was happening,' he remembers. 'I was in the same year at school as Ken Popple and Dick Green was in the year below. My brother went to the same school as Simon Down who set up Pink. I stayed chatting and ended up going back to Alan's place. A little later, after Simon had moved to London and moved in with me, we would regularly go around Alan's with a bottle of Merrydown cider to chat and listen to records.'

Around about this time, McGee signed a publishing deal with Cherry Red, which may account for the Laughing Apple being taken on as a support on a tour Cherry Red band Eyeless In Gaza did of the university circuit. 'It wasn't all fun in those days being in the Laughing Apple. Well, almost none of it was fun,' McGee admitted in his autobiography. One particularly unpleasant moment occurred when the band was on the tour travelling between gigs at Edinburgh and Glasgow and the van Dick Green was driving hit a patch of black ice. 'We were doing about 70mph,' recalls Ken Popple, 'and suddenly it was like being in a tumble dryer – the amps, the guitars, the drums: everything was flying around. The van was completely wrecked, the windscreen smashed out. We walked away relatively unscathed. I found my glasses, completely in tact, in the middle of the motorway.'

Innes' departure and Green's arrival changed the sound and placed the onus for song writing on the shoulders of McGee. McGee also found himself responsible for any promotion that needed doing. To his surprise, he found he was rather good at it, on one occasion sufficiently enough badgering a reluctant John Peel to play the Laughing Apple records until the DJ relented. There was something infectious, as well, about how he went about selling himself and the band. 'He always claimed to have a master plan,' says Popple. 'It wasn't necessarily that you believed him, but his self-confidence was always high and that ended up having a great influence and a great effect upon a lot of people.'

In the interests of promotion, it was occasionally necessary to stretch the truth a little. To ensure that the band's name was kept, however modestly, before the eye of those reading the music press, McGee would sometimes make up fictitious gigs and send them in to the news desks. He'd invent the name of the venue. There was a listing for a non-existent gig at the wonderfully-named Southend Reaction Club one time, and another at the Cedar Club in Cambridge. Popple read that they were playing a venue in Croydon that he'd not come across and questioned McGee about it: 'He replied that there was no gig but that he'd just decided to list one anyway,' says Popple. 'Someone actually wrote in and complained about it, some poor soul wandering around Croydon late at night trying to find the venue. Fictitious gigs at fictitious venues – I think it was Alan's attempt at a bit of Situationist fun.'

A year or so after having seen them at the Rock Garden, Jerry Thackray went to see the Laughing Apple again at the Greyhound pub in west London. 'This time around I thought they were awful. They'd changed their sound and gone from a kind of Scars/

Jam-influenced band to more of a New Order-influenced one. I'd travelled from the other side of London, otherwise I might not have stayed, so I carried on down to the front and did my usual dancing thing. At one point during the set, as I was dancing, the singer jumped off the stage and ran up to me and started talking to me. I was super excited. Talking to somebody who had been written about in the music press – it couldn't get any better than that.' It was the start of McGee and Thackray's friendship.

The same snowy winter of 1981 that the van accident had happened, Ken Popple was living back in Boston. The call came to go into the studio to record the third and final Laughing Apple single, 'Precious Feeling'. This time the venue was London and Simon Down drove Popple to the studios in his bright yellow Vauxhall Viva car, meeting McGee for the first time. A couple of days later, the recording was done, Simon Down driving Popple back to Boston through a six-hour blizzard. 'Whatever the sound was that we were aiming for, we never quite found it,' says Popple of the eventual single. 'We ended up sounding like a cross between Echo & The Bunnymen and Joy Division and it just didn't work.'

Reviews for the single were thin on the ground, the most significant one in the *NME* where a kindly Adrian Thrills compared the sound of the band to that of the Fire Engines and the Famous Flames, although Thrills spent most of the short review trying to fathom out the accompanying press release which claimed the song was about 'the valuation of love and the individual's conscious realisation of being able to give and receive love'. But in 2000, McGee was undoubtedly the single's most severe critic, calling it a '…really terrible version of Joy Division… absolutely like one of those things that you hope people will never hear.' The record came out. 'And then the band broke up.'

As soon as 'Precious Feeling' came out, McGee must have had serious doubts about the viability of making the Laughing Apple a success – the band was certainly not the knife that was going to enable McGee to cut through and make people sit up and take notice of him. But the experience of organising things and possibly even manipulating them in a positive way was rewarding. Perhaps there was more than one way of getting into that club that kept denying him access?

He took his first, faltering steps as a promoter when he booked out the Africa Centre in London's Covent Garden for a gig he promoted there on 16 May 1982. The timing could not have been worse – the Falklands War had just begun, the first conflict to be directly experienced remotely, as meta-war on television – and very few people were about, many glued to a television screen watching reporters like Brian Hanrahan as he famously 'counted them all out and counted them all in' (the soldiers).

In a way, the choice of venue was ideal – a relatively small concert hall (originally opened in 1964 to cater for the African diaspora) with a track record of putting on bands like the Birthday Party. McGee asked the Nightingales and Skat (formerly the Chefs) to play and also some friends of his from Glasgow called Buroo Ha Ha, a name that roughly translates from Glaswegian to Unemployment Bureau, Ha Ha. Outside an A-board listed a further band, the Car Crashes, which turned out to be Alan McGee and Andrew Innes, according to the Laughing Apple's second and equally loyal fan, Geoff Stoddart, who went along on the night.

Alas, only about 30 or so people turned up to watch a performance in a venue that comfortably held 250. The night had been promoted, according to the flyer, under the auspices of the 'Soul Organisation', a name that suggests a nod to the Jam, who at the time were playing their 'Trans Global Unity' tour. For those present, the Nightingales with their twin guitar attack put in a predictable and blistering performance, as did Skat, Helen McCookerybook delivering her perfectly pitched songs to a gleefully receptive audience. The night ended, and McGee went home and licked his wounds.

But when the statement in *Jamming!* appeared, less than a couple of weeks later, McGee's spirits were lifted again. There had been enough of a good reaction from the show at the Africa Centre to suggest that the venture hadn't been an unmitigated disaster and now Tony Fletcher's editorial was encouraging him to not just keep going but open up attacks on all fronts. Be in a band, put on shows, publish fanzines, etc. Even if he would have to keep working the day job he had (retaken on) at British Rail, things were headed in the right direction.

In October, he booked out the London Musicians Collective building in Camden and put on a series of Sunday shows that ran for a couple of months under the umbrella of 'the Communication Club'. The LMC had been set up in 1975, essentially, one large and basic performance area that came without any extra trimmings, such as toilets for the bands or audience. Anyone caught short would have to troop over to the Engineer pub across the road, or brave the snooty glares of near neighbours the Film Co-Op, who were blessed with such amenities. The property was an old British Rail canteen and sometimes the noise from the passing trains made more noise than the performers on stage.

McGee had been able to book the venue at an extremely competitive rate by becoming a member. The LMC needed its membership numbers up in order to receive the funding it got from the Arts Council. This meant that although it had originally been opened primarily as a space for free jazz and avant-garde musicians coming from mainland Europe, anyone could walk in off the street and take advantage of the rudimentary facilities. On one occasion, the Dead Kennedys showed up and played an impromptu set, causing queues around the block as word got out, and complaints from the neighbours who bore the brunt of the rather enormous PA system that the band brought in for the occasion.

Earlier in the year, McGee had experienced a road to Damascus moment, when he'd gone to see the Nightingales at the Venue in Victoria and come away overawed by the band sharing the bill with them, the Television Personalities. The visual high-point of a notorious performance had been the moment when Joe Foster ran across the stage and sawed in half Dan Treacy's Rickenbacker guitar, an instrument that quite possibly had been worth around twenty times what the band were being paid for the gig. But it wasn't the Metzger-like, auto-destructive aspect of the performance that opened up McGee eyes and was filed away for future reference but the fact that the band's performance – part punk urgency, part homage to the icons of Swinging London – was 'racing with the speed rush of the 1960s Mod scene'. Forget Joy Division, forget Echo & The Bunnymen, the future had already happened. 'I watched that show and thought, "Hmm, I could do that…",' recalls McGee.

Unsurprisingly then, the Television Personalities were one of the first acts booked to play the Communication Club. McGee turned to his trusty pals the Nightingales as well. Also welcome, were Apocalypse, the band formed by Tony Fletcher, whose *Jamming!* editorial had made such an impression on McGee. Skat played, as did Patrik Fitzgerald, Eyeless In Gaza, the Go-Betweens and Whaam! artists, the Marble Staircase, reflecting McGee's newfound interest in that label and Dan Treacy. There were always plenty of supports, in keeping with how McGee's later club, the Living Room, would run, including Andrew Innes' band the Formica Tops, 12 Cubic Feet, Jerry Thackray's bands Futile Hurling and Fixed Grin, and Richard No Soup For Me, which was Dick Green 'playing solo, Sterling Morrison-style guitar and singing over it, a bit like Josef K with just Paul Haig singing and Malcolm Ross playing guitar, with not as good songs', according to Geoff Stoddart. Compere for all of the events was 'the Legendary Jerry Thackray'.

'Alan asked Jerry to compere the shows because Jerry was basically the least appropriate person for the job,' remembers

Stoddart. 'He wasn't exactly Mr Showbiz. Alan would also have a bit of fun with the gullible as well, telling them that Jerry was actually Syd Barrett's son.'

The Communication Club ran for two months and there was the same sort of atmosphere of fun that would later characterise the early nights at the Living Room. Thackray's band, Futile Hurling, for instance, did a song version of Dr Seuss' famous story *Green Eggs And Ham* and the same sort of policy of people wandering in and out of each other's performances was in place. Andrew Innes had his band Formica Tops ('like the best bits of the Laughing Apple combined with Revolving Paint Dream,' according to Thackray) but also appeared with Thackray's other band, Fixed Grin on occasion.

In terms of paying guests, the residency at the London Musician's Collective was a failure in much the same way that the show at the Africa Centre had been, with too few people showing up to make the club sustainable. 'I was earning £70 a week as a British Rail clerk and I was losing £70-100 a week', McGee later said. But there was, at least, one redeeming feature – he was building up a bank of contacts that would serve him well in the future. And perhaps the real problem with the Communication Club had been its location and the fact that for many it was just too far off the beaten track. Something more central would work better, and something more intimate.

'UNMANIPULATED INDEPENDENCE' proclaimed an early fanzine advert for the Communication Club. For McGee, independence would be a little while coming, but at least, he had found his metier.

There would be no going back, and next time things would be different.

CHAPTER 5
FEROCIOUS APACHES

THE SAME MONTH ALAN MCGEE began putting on gigs at the London Musicians Collective, one of his favourite bands announced that they were quitting. Such was their popularity that the Jam made clear their intention in October 1982 but carried on right through to the start of December when a week of farewell concerts were held. The outpouring of public grief caused Paul Weller to have to write a personal note of explanation, published in the music press at the end of the year, and the critics, for once, seemed as unsettled by the news as the fans. Weller justified the decision by saying that no band ought to face the moment when they are too scared to quit and therefore 'carry on until they become meaningless'.

The Jam were the most commercially successful band to have emerged out of the punk era and had pulled off the trick of *just about* retaining punk credibility at the same time as selling records in the kind of quantities that put them in the big league. An indication of how successfully they'd achieved this difficult balancing act came a month after the farewell shows when the *NME* ran a 23-gun salute in its singles column, reappraising every one of the band's singles since 1977's 'In The City'. It was as if nobody wanted to believe that they were gone.

The Jam's demise created a lacuna. The problem was less to do with the absence of the band or its music – in truth, the Jam had for many already reached the point Weller feared reaching – and more to do with the fact that the intense mourning symbolised the subconscious fear of many that punk, the last great youth cultural uprising, really was well and truly over.

Many feared a creeping grandeur that seemed to have seeped back into music, made worse by the fact that many of those involved justified their approach by claiming to be building upon their punk ethics. Both New Pop and New Romanticism celebrated excess whilst claiming the credibility of the more Spartan movement that had inspired them in the first place. New Romanticism was, creatively speaking, a spent force by the middle of 1982 but banner bands like Spandau Ballet, Visage and Ultravox had yet to enjoy their most successful periods in commercial terms, which occurred long after the New Romantics had supposedly died off.

Two weeks before Alan McGee had put on his show at the Africa Centre, Steve Strange had re-opened the old Music Machine in Camden which he renamed the Camden Palace. It was a club, wrote the *Melody Maker* that week, for 'plebs, debs and celebs'. Strange, a man with a phenomenal work ethic, had made his way up from cleaning the toilets at the punk dive the Roxy to handling more clubs than a professional golfer, starting with Billy's in Soho and moving on to the Blitz club on the northern edge of Covent Garden which rapidly became the focal point for an outrageous group of fashion-oriented misfits who liked to refer to themselves – in classical fashion – as the Movement, although others often called them Blitz Kids and the label that eventually stuck was New Romantics.

By the middle of 1982, there were still plenty of people getting dressed up as Mary Magdalen, or Gestapo officers, or gangsters or pierrots, or even Boadicea and braving the streets of central London to go and listen to a re-running of the music of mid-period Bowie before returning home, copy of Christopher Isherwood's *Goodbye To Berlin* tucked in their pockets, to watch Liliana Cavani's *The Night Porter*, the Nazisploitation film starring Dirk Bogarde. Weimar Berlin and its attendant decadence (or the idea of it) was largely experienced through watching Bob Fosse's enormously popular film *Cabaret*, although some went to Berlin, and Spandau Ballet even acquired their name from a piece of graffiti on a west Berlin wall.

In the early part of the 1980s, the Conservatives had successfully sold the notion that we are what we buy – and a number of style magazines, such as *i-D* and the *Face*, sprang up to reinforce the idea. (The *Face* was launched around the same time as the

Wire and critics chuckled that only one of them could possibly survive – they were right.) There was a magazine devoted entirely to the new, hedonistic way of life – *New Sounds, New Styles* – but, fatally trapped between a concern for fashion *and* music, it did not survive long. There were shops for heroes, clothes for heroes, clubs for heroes, but in truth there were very few actual heroes, just wannabe celebrities. The striving for celebrity and the music survived, everything else got washed away.

Advocates of this more flamboyant approach complained that independent music had become dark and doom-laden, the wonder of post punk, with its blue-sky, supposedly limitless future, mired in anxiety. For young males coming to maturity around the time of punk or shortly after – having grown up in an age when supersonic flight, adventure magazines for boys and the space race held fascination – the idea of future *was* irresistible, but troubling. Better to live for the hedonistic moment.

There was another way, one that said that the logical end-point of the DIY revolution didn't have to be a capitulation to the demands of the market, with bands packaging their singles in covers with images of imitation perfume bottles, as was the case with Scritti Politti. By 1982 the anarcho punk movement was beginning a gradual slide towards the margins, but it was, not withstanding, a good year for some of those involved. The Crass anti-war flexi disc, 'Sheep Farming In The Falklands' had gone through a first pressing of 40,000 by the time the conflict ended in June. The one-sided release had no song title, band name or matrix number stamped on it. At first, the band denied making the record, but later admitted that they 'had played the song on our recent tour… [We] assume that someone must have taped it and now issued it in bootleg form'. The song drew parallels between warfare and certain sexual acts but predictly what most gained the ire of the establishment was the use of a collage of taped speeches from the Houses of Parliament. Rough Trade had distributed the record by discreetly slipping it into the sleeves of other releases before sending them out to the shops.

What appealed to many was that Crass presented a way of life and philosophy – and didn't focus on themselves. 'They said we were trash/ Well the name is Crass not Clash/ They can stuff their punk credentials/ 'Cos it's them that takes the cash' run the lyrics to their song 'White Punks On Hope'. The band partly operated to help disseminate information, often about pacifism and anarchy. As a result of their stance on the Falklands War, by the end of 1982 it was difficult to find promoters who would book them. When the Jam played their testimonial shows in mid-December, Crass locked themselves into the Rainbow venue, intending to put on a free show in protest at the way they had been treated. Police cut through the chains and evicted Crass but sympathetic squatters went in and temporarily occupied the hall before the police evicted them as well.

Crass operated as more than just an information bureau. Their live shows – where the entry price was often subsidised by some or other political movement – were also meeting points, where the band and their disciples could exchange views and break bread together. Followers were put to work – handing out the literature and paraphernalia, selling badges and making food for the communal masses.

One of those who followed the band around was Ian Astbury who spent a reasonably large part of 1980 'homeless and drifting' and going to a number of Crass concerts where he helped out. He admired their music, in particular, the 'Reality of Asylum' single and the *Feeding of The 5000* album which 'were really different than the punk rock we were listening to, which was the Pistols, the Clash and the Banshees. Crass was certainly more extreme sonically…'

Astbury's nomadic existence had run its course by the start of 1983, and the romanticism of punk had also worn thin for him. He'd earlier told the *NME* in a cover story written by Paul

Morley: 'I was in the army for a while, and then I came out, and I was a punk, and I thought, right, fucking anarchy, this is it for the rest of my life. This has got to last forever. And then I just sat there and thought… what the fuck was that all about?' Instead, as chief lyricist and frontman of Southern Death Cult, Astbury looked more imaginatively for inspiration, finding it in part in the experiences he'd had as a child living in Canada mixing with the indigenous population. He adopted a look based on their apparel and wrote about their general suppression in Southern Death Cult's first single, 'Moya', which simultaneously also lamented the Americanisation of Canada by 'the kids of the Coca-Cola nation/ …too doped up to realise/ that time is running out'.

Southern Death Cult was one of a number of bands that emerged towards the autumn of 1982 and looked out on an indie landscape they found to be bleak and unpromising. Southern Death Cult was no different from Tony Fletcher in worrying about where independent music was heading. Concerns were voiced in an *NME* interview in late summer: 'This is as much '72 as '82 – the scene is stagnant,' the band told David Dorrell. 'This fresh young pop music is an illusion. Something new is coming – and we could be it, or at least part of it.'

With their striking looks and an attitude to match, Southern Death Cult quickly came to spearhead a movement of bands whose members all loosely fitted Tony Fletcher's bill of coming along after punk or being in the suburbs when it happened, those who were fidgety and anxious and now ready to be part of whatever the next big thing was going to be. They were more than happy to respond to the increasing music press calls for more passion, as had been the previously mentioned case when journalist Don Watson reviewed a March Violets gig and came away 'baying for anything with a hint of guts'.

The new bands and journalists like Tony Fletcher weren't alone in lamenting the current apathy and lack of direction. Weller had wasted no time mourning his old band and was back by February 1983, sporting a new flat top, white socks, shades and a Jean-Paul Belmondo mac. His new group was called the Style Council, consisting at present of just him and former Dexys organist Mick Talbot, the 'best young soul/ jazz organist in the country'. Weller, too, had picked up on the whither-rock debate. Talbot was in because he shared 'a hatred of the rock myth and rock culture,' Weller claimed. 'It is boring to go on about "how dull music is at the moment and what I plan to change it" and all the crappy promises the fraud squad groups make… I think the time is right for a new way of presenting music without the usual bullshit.'

These were exactly the sentiments that the positive punks had held when they set out six months earlier. The new music quickly took off, sharing with old-school punk a close bonding between band and audience. Venues had tended to get bigger after punk, to accommodate the audience numbers, and that created an inevitable distance between the band and audience. Positive punk re-established the bond. The concerts for some (largely males) were a release, an opportunity to let off steam in a physical manner that just occasionally ended up in a bout of fisticuffs but more usually than not was an occasion of joyous abandon. Following a band around from venue to venue, as Astbury had done with Crass, with a gang of like-minded souls was almost more rewarding than watching the actual bands perform.

Another band that could excel in the live arena was Sex Gang Children, a group who combined music, theatrics and the occult. At the start of their shows, a skeleton-costumed Grim Reaper figure called Bingo sprayed rings of fire across the stage as a prelude to the band's arrival. Bingo had been a fan who one day decided to take the process of interaction a stage further and so got up on to the stage and began his routine, perhaps getting his lead from the band's logo, which was itself a skeletal representation of Death 'with a scythe, cutting down the old regime', as Andi Sex Gang explained at the time. Like many before (and after), the band had found their name thumbing through the works of William S Burroughs.

Southern Death Cult and Sex Gang Children were part of gothic rock's long tail. Some argue that the genre began in 1979 with the release of the nine-minute epic 'Bela Lugosi's Dead' by Bauhaus, and both in the music of Bahaus (which was anti the Spartan sound of punk) and in the group's imagery the ground-work for what was to follow was laid. Bauhaus realised early on how important visuals were to the sound they were creating and sent out demo videos (not cassettes) when trying to get a deal. They weren't alone in trailblazing, some arguing that Joy Division (particularly in the darker sound of *Closer*) were the true originators, and a number of punk bands including Siouxsie & The Banshees and the Cure played their part.

One band who, like Bauhaus, immediately took their image seriously was UK Decay. They, along with Theatre of Hate, could lay claim to have most inspired many of the bands who rose up at the end of 1982. UK Decay was fiery and discordant, proclaiming the songs of the warrior ('A blaze in their eyes/ death is their glory') on the album *For Madmen Only*. The band blended grand imagery with matching poetry and were one of the first adherents of the all-over black look. But their image and their music were paradoxical, they said: out of their darkness came light, optimism, and positivity. With its fright and melodrama, UK Decay's work mirrors of course the 'pleasing terror' concept introduced by Horace Walpole in his 1764 novel, *The Castle of Otranto*, the first Gothic work of literature.

Some other bands fell into the fold by accident, caught in the moment between the demise of post punk and the rise of the new bands. Danse Society is a case in point. They were more of a pro-gressive rock band than a gothic band, one that would have been far more commercially successful had bad luck not plagued them in the shape of collapsing record companies. 1983's self-released mini-album, *Seduction*, remains one of the era's best releases capturing all the urgency of the new music without succumbing to the usual lyrical and visual clichés. Lyndon Scarf's synth work and Paul Nash's measured guitars create a strong platform for singer Steve Rawlings quite prepossessing vocals and front-of-stage antics. 'We're not and never were a cult band,' Steve Rawlings protested in 1983, before adding: 'Tribal segregation is far too insular too survive.'

Rawlings complaints refer to the fact that the new music was quickly taken up and sanctioned as the *real* sound of the future, or at least the sound of the future according to critics who felt that they now had the ammunition to go to town on all of the ills of the recent past. 'GIVE ME PASSION (WAKE UP BRITAIN)' screamed a Mick Mercer article in *Melody Maker* on 26 February 1983, firing some long overdue mainstream music press shots across the bows of complacency in pop. Written in the form of an open letter to the readers, Mercer approached the problem from what might be called a punkist's viewpoint. 'The '77 generation has grown old and hideously complacent' he berated, adding: 'Punk itself has never been worse. Hard to imagine that it actually can get any worse…' Like Tony Fletcher's 'Statement' in *Jamming!*, Mercer's editorial urged direct action: 'STIR YOURSELF!' In its passion and bravery, the article didn't bother wasting time questioning the moribund processes that produced the complacent pop (which might, incidentally, have included the music press itself) but fingered instead the bands seen as responsible. It wasn't just obvious targets that came in for it, either – such as those he listed, including Echo & The Bunnymen, Scritti Politti, Ultravox, Tears For Fears, and the Thompson Twins – but also those that produced the kind of music that Mercer usually wrote about, such as the Cure and Siouxsie & The Banshees. And he reserved special ire for those second-generation punk bands that had stuck to the ship as it slowly went down, such as the Exploited, Blitz, and the Anti-Nowhere League.

In 1983 readers had two options, as he saw it. 'Continuing what you are already doing (we call it the sleeping sickness) or taking the brisker alliance to your hearts.' The 'brisker alliance' amounted to bands 'inspired by Birthday Party, early Ants, Decay and Bauhaus' and, unsurprisingly, included Danse Society, the Sex Gang Children and Southern Death Cult. There were, however, a number of less familiar names that reader's were advised to look out for who were following in the wake of the above, including Blood & Roses, Bondage, Look Mummy Clowns, the Committee, Dead Man's Shadow and Hagar The Womb.

The week before Mercer's impassioned plea hit the newsstands the *NME* had run a slightly less breathless piece and more or less arrived at the same destination. Richard North's article was given front cover status and trailed with the headline 'POSITIVE PUNK'. It's a curious piece of journalism and on inspection there is less at its centre than there is at the centre of Mercer's rant. But it moved everything on by stressing – by *over*stressing – what it recognised to be the *positive* nature of those musicians and bands involved.

The scene is set when North imagines a fan of the new positive music scene preparing for a night out. He's off to see Blood & Roses at the Moonlight Club in Hampstead. Recently, he's discovered a whole clutch of bands – '*his* bands' – that includes Brigandage, Southern Death Cult, Rubella Ballet, Danse Society and Specimen. 'They're the only ones that mean anything to him any more,' the ones that make him feel 'alive, positive'. He's 'bright and optimistic about the future' and doesn't care that he's on the dole because that gives him time to do things, like play in the band that those above inspired him to form.

It isn't *quite* a washing powder ad and the rest of the article does carry through the positive motif in a less underscored way. Rather than blame 1977 for the current ills North recognises similarities between then and 1983 and sees that the 'same buzz that burned our streets, hearts and minds… is happening again'. Clearly fearful of the backlash (which, of course, came to pass), he cautiously advances the view that there is a collective movement 'that we can now call the new positive punk'.

Positive Punk took seriously the business of having fun. As the 'heavy drumbeat rolls and the harsh chords crash and sometimes even tingle, it's then that the boys and girls come out to play. Playpower!' North's article informed. *Playpower* (later renamed *Play Power*) was the title of *Oz* editor Richard Neville's rambling book on the 1960s underground and the politics of play. Play wasn't the only thing that an old hippie like Neville had in common with the new positive punks. The interests of the 1960s counter culture had travelled through the 1970s and made it relatively unscathed into the early part of the 1980s, via the medium of the anarcho punks whose influence on the positive punks was clear. Shared interests included mysticism, a dabbling into the occult, and a general belief in karma. North refers to the 'inner warmth and virtual energy that human beings regard as the most favourable state to live in. The new positive punk … tapped into this current'.

Michael Moorcock expanded on the connections in a television documentary about positive punk that was aired on the TV programme *South of Watford* at the time. Initially positing the notion that the whole thing might be taken as just another revival, *a la* the psychedelic revival, Moorcock ultimately drew a distinction between punk 1976 style and the 1983 version, comparing the progressive punks instead to those counter culturists of the 1960s. 'In their non-violent antagonism towards Establishment politics and their determination to change themselves before changing the world, positive punks remind me of 1960s hippies, though more realistic and less mystically drug-based,' he commented. 'The music and energy of 1976 is combined with 1967's idealism. It's a fresh angle of attack on the awfulness of 1980s Britain. Style, music, tactics, the modern punk idiom isn't a media fad – it is, in my opinion, nothing less than a moral attitude.'

Listening to the contributors in Moorcock's documentary, it is quite hard to detect *any* antagonism, non-violent or otherwise. 'Anger is an emotion done to death,' comments Jez James from Blood & Roses, whilst another contributor advises: 'Don't moan about unemployment, don't moan about politics, you can't change it.' Personal politics was what was important. Such a politically neutered stance inevitably switched the focus towards the more peripheral aspects of the scene, such as the fashion, which ultimately doomed it.

In fact, after Richard North's *NME* article in February, music press interest in certain quarters began to wane. A piece in the same paper on the Batcave, the movement's premier venue, and on the band Specimen, that had been published the week before read like a parody. Specimen occupied a Soho flat, but it might as well have been the stage set from the *Rocky Horror Show* to which it paid homage. Fake human and animal skulls hung from the walls, a severed doll's head was suspended from the ceiling. There was a blood splattered mannequin in one corner and on the walls were daubed the words 'blasphemy, lechery and blood', borrowed from the diary of the English Romantic painter Robert Haydon who was describing the supernatural motivations of fellow painter, Henry Fuseli.

It was all very appealing to some of the major record labels, not least London Records, who rushed out a compilation album entitled *Young Limbs And Numb Hymns* that cobbled together a ragbag of seemingly unconnected artists (Specimen and Blood & Roses were joined somewhat mystifyingly by Test Department and Jimmy Pursey amongst others) and packaged everything in the most cartoonish way possible. The sleeve notes were hostage to fortune: 'Look past the slow black rain of a chill night in Soho...

Come walk with me between Heaven and Hell. Here there is a club lost in its own feverish limbo, where sin becomes salvation and only the dark angels tread. For here is a BATCAVE... It will endure.'

But it didn't, of course, and the whole thing was over almost as soon as it had begun, descending into a caricature that limps on to this day. Some fans began to embrace the new indie that moved into the original gap that gothic rock had sought to fill. As to the positive punk bands, they, according to Richard North at the time, had been 'fireworks'. Alas, like all fireworks they burned brightly and then fizzled out. Some bands turned themselves into the conventional rock stars that they had always longed to be, while others, it turned out, had been straight-ahead punks, just devilishly caught out of time. And then there were the dandies, the romantics, the *positively* theatrical – it is the image of them that has come to define the world of progressive punk, a world where everybody is scared but happy and Bela Lugosi dies each day after dark, again and again and again.

CHAPTER 6

'FRET NO MORE, POP CHILDREN'

POSITIVITY ABOUNDED AS THE HOT summer of 1983 drew closer. 'The new optimism for '83 continues…' a *Sounds* article on Tony Fletcher's band Apocalypse reported, and Fletcher agreed. 'I hate most pop crap,' he told journalist Karen Swayne, 'but what carries me through is the knowledge that something better will come out of it – people are starting to look now.' Even Mick Mercer was in a jolly mood, of sorts, describing 1983 as the 'best year we've ever had for real music' in an interview with Action Pact for *Melody Maker*. They – Action Pact – were 'one of the best pop-punk outfits that have ever lived', he enthused, whilst reserving some irritation for the lack of coverage his paper gave to similar bands.

Since the closing of the Communication Club, Alan McGee had gone quiet on the promoting front, switching his attentions instead to a fanzine he planned to launch called *Communication Blur*. The first issue appeared in February with a run of 500 and came with a free flexi disc featuring tracks by the Laughing Apple and the Pastels. Printed using different coloured inks, courtesy of the printing firm in Glasgow where Bobby Gillespie worked, it sold out almost immediately.

The fanzine highlighted McGee's blossoming relationship with Dan Treacy. The Television Personalities were the first band featured within the fanzine's covers. McGee had soaked up and shared some of the fanaticism Dan Treacy had for the pop culture of a number of beat and garage bands of the 1960s, and the very first thing the reader saw when opening the fanzine was a roughly pasted down article about garage band the Creation, lifted from an old music paper. McGee used the space above to set out his vision for the future. What was important was keeping the 'soul' and 'feeling' of the past alive while creating something new. 'Only two periods have meant anything to me in recent years,' he wrote. '1965-67, 1977-78. Let's create our own culture, starting now and draw on the ideals of people as once sussed as [Paul] Weller and [Mark] Perry.'

Part of creating the new culture involved demolishing the old and the fanzine took pot shots at various bands it considered redundant. A hand-scrawled article about Andrew Innes' band Formica Tops berated 'the new short-haired hippies' like 'Echo, Bauhaus and Sex Gang' and the bile level was cranked up significantly in a column written by the Legend! called the *Sound Of Music*. The title of the column was deliberately chosen, its content anything but an optimistic, Mary Poppins-style view of the current state of the independent music scene, which it saw as lamentable.

A number of obvious targets were roundly thrashed – the music press, Cherry Red Records (with whom McGee had recently signed his publishing deal) and punk, and the column echoed McGee's editorial in calling for change: 'Let's get something new, leave punk to the people (like Flux, Conflict, Poison Girls, etc) who are taking and shaping it into something positive and challenging, and subvert Joe Normal (yes, that's you) all over again. We've got nothing to lose. Aim for the sky and you might get a look in.' Some final tips included the advice to kill all promoters, replace middle-aged record executives in business suits with young record executives in 'hard times' clothes, can all 'shit bands' off stage, and overthrow the Government and the police and replace them with a state made out of Lego. Readers were finally urged to 'shop early for bargains'.

According to Jerry Thackray , *Communication Blur* was part of a calculated plan of assault. 'The general idea,' he says, 'always was that Alan would start a club in London and with the money he made from the club he'd then start a record label. The fanzine? Well, the first purpose of that was to help him create his own myth.' In fact, McGee had almost finished the first issue when Thackray was asked to contribute and Thackray was far from confident that he was the right person. He had failed his English O Level and been forced to drop out of a psychology course at college because, he says, he couldn't write essays: 'Nobody had shown me *how* to write essays'. The solution to the problem was easy. McGee told him to 'just write a column slagging everything off'. Nobody would be overly distracted by style when the tenor of the text was so explosive.

McGee and Thackray were best friends, *the* most passionate advocates of music, and they whiled away time in the front room of McGee's new home in Tottenham putting the world to rights, two totemic artefacts gazing down upon them from either side of the fireplace that sported McGee's red Rickenbacker guitar and his regency jacket. 'Jerry would often come around our house and get his tea,' McGee says. 'He jumped in on the fanzine and became a big part of it; he was a good guy genuinely into music. He was totally agit-prop and very quickly went from being an ex-public schoolboy to being a fully paid up member of the Socialist Workers Party, or so it seemed. I thought he was a genius.'

In this scenario, McGee might be seen as the working class hero, Thackray the middle class interloper, college educated, well spoken. Thackray had gone to 'a minor public school', but had been accepted on a scholarship and came from a relatively poor family himself. Give or take an accent, they weren't entirely dissimilar. 'I remember going around once and helping muck in with the washing up,' says Thackray, 'which shocked Yvonne, Alan's wife at the time. I think that where she came from the blokes didn't do that. Some of Alan's friend considered me a novelty and took the piss out of me, usually because of my accent, and Alan regularly had to step in and defend me.'

Communication Blur quickly made its mark on the tiny fanzine scene, and, spurred on by the impetus, McGee once more turned his attention to gig promoting. That summer, Patrik Fitzgerald put on a series of shows at the upstairs room of a tiny pub in Conway Street, a stones-throw away from the Telecom Tower that at the time was the most notable feature of the London skyline. McGee was one of those who turned up to support. Ostensibly, the upstairs room of the Adams Arms was given over to a folk club called Dingles, and the floor space, while Georgian in proportion, might best be described as 'cosy'. It was in a great location, if a little on the small side.

'Alan found out about the place through Patrik,' recalls Geoff Stoddart. 'Then one day, Alan called me up and said that Patrik's car had broken down and could I help move the PA in for the show Patrik was playing at the Adams Arms that night. I had access to a car through my job at the post office. He said to me that he was thinking of putting shows on himself at the venue. When I got there, the first thing that struck me was just how relatively tiny the room was. I asked Alan if he was serious about putting amplified bands on in such a small space. But in a way, its size became its beauty because although it never became a hip happening place there was always an atmosphere of sorts.'

McGee booked out the venue and on 4 June, under the aegis of the fanzine, put on a show billed as '*Communication Blur* Presents Here Comes the Summer'. Once again, the call went out to friends new and old. The Television Personalities headlined, with Miles Landsmann (from Miles Over Matter), 12 Cubic Feet and the Legend! supporting. The night was a success, with many more people turning up than McGee expected, given his experience with the Communication Club. The central London location helped, and if there was any of that longed-for optimism in the air, it somehow felt easier to embrace in the warmth of a balmy night that was the start of an unusually hot summer.

'Here Comes the Summer' proved to McGee that so long as expectations were kept in check, running a club was well within his capabilities. The lack of space turned into an advantage, because no matter who was performing, the venue always looked reasonably full. McGee wasn't overly confident that he wouldn't fall flat on his face again – 'I honestly thought the club might last just a few weeks,' he says today – but when the Nightingales played the opening night on 6 August, the place was full. McGee had decided to christen the new club the Living Room, simply because with its doilies on the table and twee table lamps the place reminded him of somebody's idea of a front room.

Entry into the club was £2 and the format rarely varied as the weeks went by – one vaguely 'name' band played, followed by a couple of unknown groups, with the Legend! always appearing somewhere on the bill. Dave Evans, who'd looked after the sound at the Communication Club, took care once again, using a vocal PA, a couple of speakers and a four-channel amp. The bands performed in front of one of the room's two fireplaces and the lighting system was basic, a bicycle wheel with coloured strips of acetate attached to its spokes which was manually spun as white light was shone onto it, although McGee later purchased some liquid slides from an ex-Pink Floyd roadie. 'I took care of the lights as I had been working on all that kind of stuff at college,' recalls Joe Foster who later became house producer at Creation. 'We also had a sheet of metal with holes in it that when you shone light through it from a projector created a kind of strobe effect.'

The intimacy of the Living Room was immediately striking, if, on occasions, a touch overwhelming. In one of the earliest write ups of the club, Mat Snow, reviewing a Three Johns gig for the *NME* in September, noted the quaintness of the band playing in front of the fireplace, the amps on rickety chairs, the low wattage house lighting (two bare light bulbs that night) and the fact that the band was almost audience and audience almost band since there was 'no distance at all between them and us'.

The facilities were basic, as Adam Sanderson of the Jasmine Minks recalls: 'The room was extremely hot in summer and freezing cold in winter. It smelled and the PA system was crap. You weren't allowed to open the windows due to noise restrictions, so basically you cooked. The floor would end up slick with sweat and the place usually stank by the end of the night, not just body sweat but also beer and cigarettes. Your clothes would stink, even your guitar strap would have that "Living Room smell". It was, however, absolutely brilliant. For me, the best time of my young life.'

The week following the Nightingales performance at the Living Room, the Television Personalities played, along with the Jasmine Minks, the Committee and Belinda Blanchard. The Jasmine Minks appeared again the following week, this time on a bill with Patrik Fitzgerald, Ed Ball & the Rain Parade, and the Legend & His Horns. A Whaam night was staged in October, when the Television Personalities returned, along with 1000 Mexicans, the Page Boys and Khartomb. And between then and the end of the year there appeared (and in many cases, reappeared) the Three Johns, Doctor & The Medics, Nikki Sudden, Flowers in the Dustbin, the Revolving Paint Dream, Del Amitri, the Nightingales, the Membranes, Fixed Grin and Death In June.

Not long after Mat Snow's review appeared (and had the effect of attracting even more people to the club) the Pastels played the Living Room. David Keegan of the Shop Assistants helped out on drums that night. Stephen Pastel had first come across Alan McGee when he'd gone to a free Newspeak concert and had later met him in London when the Pastels had played a show there. 'I could see Alan was passionate and to an extent angry about things,' he says, 'maybe not politically, but more of being outside of things he wanted to be a part of. He had strong conviction, which was really good: we were, on occasion, a bit too self-deprecating. We were probably an odd combination. I always think that Alan felt that as a group we under-estimated him and there was a bit of truth in that.'

But Stephen Pastel could see immediately the significance of the club: 'I liked the energy around it and thought it felt small but somehow important. Alan and his friends made it what it was. There was a mixture of ex-Jam fans, people with more of a DIY/ punk/ fanzine perspective and probably a few refugees from the Groovy Cellar scene drifting across with the Television Personalities. And then there were younger people going to those kinds of shows for the first time. The idea of a recognisable scene was still some way off, but there was something good going on and an appreciation of quite a lot of different things. I thought it was great that ATV, the Nightingales and Patrik Fitzgerald all played – it stopped it from being something that was isolated from its predecessors and gave it more of a sense of inclusion.'

Adam Sanderson remembers it as 'a place where introverts were allowed to be extroverts. I felt at home. We used to jokingly compare it to Warhol's Factory, but there was a wee bit of pride in there, too, in that it was something new, something home-grown and hype free, that was attracting a young, genuinely creative crowd. It was a world away from the hip art school/ industrial events that were going on at the time, the Test Department metal bashing. If I recall, correctly, Alan's dad was a panel beater, so he had probably had an overload on that sound anyway.'

As had been the case at the Communication Club, the supports reinforced the camaraderie amongst the central core, Dick Green reappearing with his Richard No Soup For Me, and the Legend! appearing in numerous guises, such as the Legend! & His Ego, and the Legend! & His Fan Club. The support most likely to raise a cheer was the Legend! & His Swinging Soul Sisters, an acapella outfit consisting of the Legend!, his brother Michael, and graphic artist David Smith that performed 'hits' of the moment, such as Elvis Costello's 'Shipbuilding', one of a number of songs they regularly murdered.

'I started the Legend & His Swinging Soul Sisters because me and a bloke at work used to sing along to the radio – Tony Blackburn, Steve Wright in the afternoon, that kind of thing,' remembers Thackray, who worked at the time at a printing firm.

'Then one day I saw this advert in the back of the *NME* looking for "new and interesting" acts to play at what turned out to be a nightclub run by Richard Strange. I called up and he asked me what kind of act we were, and I replied, New Wave Acapella. I explained that we were vocals only, that we wore suits and did a dance routine and that the only songs we covered were punk rock ones. We played, and I had tears of laughter streaming down my face all through the set.'

The Living Room had barely been going a couple of months before the queues to get in snaked back down from the upstairs room to the bar below. On one occasion an impromptu acoustic night took place in the even smaller downstairs bar after a power cut had plunged the whole area into darkness. The choice was to send everybody home or rig up some candles and find some acoustic guitars. 'The Television Personalities were due to play,' recalls Paul Groovy, 'but after we moved downstairs it was decided that anyone who wanted to could take a turn. Nikki Sudden, who was there, did a couple of numbers, and so did Jowe Head. The Legend! and Alan McGee did something together and Jed Dmochowsky played, as did the Jasmine Minks.' Adam Sanderson remembers 'taking a taxi up to Somers Town to pick up a Guild acoustic guitar before returning to the pub. The guitar was passed around and anyone who wanted to play could use it. Jim and I played as a duo, but Jim only had an electric guitar so I rather drowned him out.'

The immediate success of the 'Here Comes the Summer' event and the opening few nights of The Living Room reanimated an idea that Alan McGee had had since the end of 1982 when he had been openly talking about starting a record label. He'd already had the experience of releasing the Laughing Apple singles and knew a bit about how the process worked. But the failure of the Communication Club had put almost everything on hold. Now that the Living Room was proceeding full-steam ahead and the first issue of *Communication Blur* had been a runaway success, his optimism was back. A second issue of *Communication Blur* was published in August and fittingly came with another breathless editorial, this time urging readers to 'Seize that <u>young</u> determination' and 'show the fakers you aren't fooling'. 'The afterbirth of punk, ie a defeated generation – wash them away… Start groups, clubs, fanzines, labels….'

Issue two carried on where the first had left off. Once again, the *Sound Of Music* column pulled no punches, rounding on Cherry Red and the music press, as it had before. There was a cartoon strip – 'The Legend! at Cherry Red' – that featured a drawing of A&R man Mike Alway being machine-gunned while a young folk singer wearing a fisherman's cap (similar to the kind worn by Ben Watt at the time) sobbed tears. 'TAKE THAT REACTIONARY HIPPY WIMP!' ran the text. At one point, the fanzine asked the question, 'Is the lack of good music journalism around due to the lack of good music?'

If that was the case, then *Communication Blur* might be able to rectify the problem. Page three announced the arrival of a new record label – Creation Artifact: 'THE LABEL TOTALLLY COMMITTED TO THE DESTRUCTION OF MEDIOC-RITY'. A few pages further on a small hand-drawn advert also appeared, promoting '"73 In '83', the label's first release which was a record by the Legend!. In fact, copies of the three-track single had gone out to the music papers at the end of July, accompanied by a press release that carried through the editorial tone of *Communication Blur*. 'Fed up with the lack of vital pop noise?' the press release asked. 'Fret no more, pop children, here comes the Legend! '"73 In '83" is a short, sharp shock destined for the destruction of mediocrity… A blast of hope against the current pop dross.'

McGee and Thackray had been discussing making a record for some time, initially one that they would record together. 'We sort of had a band just before that point,' says Thackray, 'but it was never going anywhere since we both wanted to be the lead singer. I don't think we even got as far as a name, though if there was one it would have been Revolving Paint Dream, the name Andrew Innes later took for his band. Alan had an idea of how we might sound, which was basically like the Jam. Personally, I've never seen the point of being in a covers band and that includes being in a band that *sounds* like someone else's. I remember we did a couple of rehearsals, which I believe involved Simon Down and Ken Popple, and we even got up on stage once, when the Television Personalities played the Coal Hole in the Strand in spring 1983.'

On the night in question, Thomas Zimmerman, a German back-packer and later promoter, got press-ganged by McGee and the Legend! into playing tambourine for them. Zimmerman went on to become a promoter, helping set up a number of early Creation tours and tours for the Television Personalities. On the night, the electricity was continually cutting in and out. 'It was a very odd,' remembers Alan McGee. 'The electrics were tripping and the sound was fading in and out and Dan Treacy, who may have taken something beforehand, seemed to think that the weird effects were being created by us. He thought it was amazing.'

McGee and Thackray stopped pretending that they could be in a band together, but carried through the idea of working in tandem when it came to recording the first Creation single, which, when they went into the studio, was to be a split release. 'We went into IPS,' remembers Thackray, 'a studio very deliberately chosen because it was where the Television Personalities had previously recorded. In two hours we managed to record eleven Legend! songs. We spent the next two hours mixing them. Alan was so enthusiastic that he scrapped the idea of a split single and decided that the first Creation release should be a Legend! single.'

''73 In '83' is a mere 70 seconds long but an impressive art ter-rorist statement nonetheless given the circumstances of the time.

''73 In ''83
''73 in ''83
''73 in ''83
I'm looking at them and you're looking at me

it begins, establishing the notion reinforced through the *Sound of Music* column that you really should be looking at him, or looking at McGee, or looking at Creation, or looking at what's going on at the Living Room, or looking anywhere but to the mainstream music business, most of all the press, for any leads.

And why? Because it seemed suddenly as if there was little that was different between 1973 and 1983.

'The song was originally written in 1982, and the title comes from something I read in the music press,' says Thackray. 'I'd heard music from before 1976/7 but hadn't really liked it. The music press was constantly reinforcing the idea that 1976 was some sort of Year Zero, which we all went along with while recognising that it was nonsense. The *NME* had started heavily writing about bands that hung out at the WAG club and people like Duran Duran, who were in the charts. That was the moment when I lost faith in writers like Paul Morley and Ian Penman because regardless of how good their writing was they seemed to have lost track of the fact that the music always comes first. So ''73 In '83' was my response to what was happening at the time and to what was being written about in certain parts of the music press, all of which meant nothing to me.'

With its constant, repetitive vocal hammering, ''73 In '83' sounds like a proto rap record. The only accompaniment to Thackray's vocal is a drum track provided by McGee. The other two numbers are less startling (or puzzling) and are more conventionally delivered, with bass and keyboard and even backing vocals when required. 'You (Chuka, Chuka) Were Glamorous' is Thackray at his more playful, while 'Melt The Guns' is a song co-written with McGee about the Falklands War.

Amongst those contributing to the record was Patrik Fitzgerald, one of Thackray's idols and a man whose music had been the main inspiration for Thackray getting up on stage in the first place. In a nice touch, McGee had arranged for Fitzgerald to come along and play some organ. But Fitzgerald appeared somewhat fazed by Thackray: 'After we'd recorded part of 'You Were (Chuka Chuka) Glamorous' I went and sat on the studio sofa next to where Patrik was sitting. He made a great play of getting up and moving a few spaces away from me, saying, "Whoo, You're scary...."'

''73 In ''83' was, at it turned out, very much an acquired taste and one not much to many people's liking. The mainstream music press largely ignored it. *Melody Maker did* review it (in eighteen words) arriving at a verdict that was somewhat gnomic: '"'73 in '83, all the bands are dead now". Yes. This unprepossessing record may be good for you.' *Jamming!*, the publication that had inspired McGee and whose 'Statement' probably gave Thackray the inspiration for the main song, derided it, mocking one of the tracks on its B-side, 'Melt The Guns' which, as well as being an anti-war song, alluded to some Mods beating up a punk outside the Rough Trade shop. Tony Fletcher himself was the reviewer and complained overall about the record's 'wilful amateurism', damning the whole project as 'worthless'. John Peel gave the white label copy he was sent two or three plays, favourably comparing it on air to another quirky, underground record – 'There Goes Concorde Again' by ...And The Native Hipsters – but didn't play the record at all when he received his finished copy.

There is no doubt that the record fell on deaf ears, or that most people misread and have continued to misread its significance. Alan McGee has himself later called it 'a really dreadful record, almost ever aspect of it rubbish'. The best thing about the record is just how odd and unusual and paradoxically fitting its release was given the music of the time. Stephen Pastel wrote to Paul Groovy at the time of the record's release, saying, 'I like the Legend! single and I don't care who knows it'. His appreciation of the record hasn't diminished over the years: 'One of the things I most liked about "'73 In '83", he says, 'was that it was unexpected in the context of what was going on. It fitted into the DIY punk heritage (one of the main things feeding into the Living Room and Creation) unlike some of the other styles that the label became associated with. Of the first Creation singles, it was the one that made the biggest impression on me, although I liked most of the records in some way.'

Just how impacting the negative critical reaction to "'73 In '83' was on Alan McGee and the start of Creation needs to be seen in the context of the high esteem within which McGee and Thackray held themselves. The hubristic tone of *Communication Blur* left McGee unprepared for the ravages of the critics. 'We were genuinely delusional,' admits McGee. 'When everybody slagged the record off it made me reel and knocked me back, but it also taught me that to succeed I needed to up my game.'

Many purchased the Legend! single but most of the pressing went unsold, later melted down and recycled, or possibly damaged in a flood that may or may not have been the subject of an insurance claim. But in spite of the record's fate, nobody could doubt its integrity or that of its maker: 'The one thing I have always been proud of is that the sound of the record was genuinely me,' says Thackray. 'I wasn't trying to be someone else. What you got was always me.'

But as Christmas drew nearer, McGee shrugged off the disappointment of "'73 In '83' and focussed wholly on the Living Room. He was in no hurry to issue a follow up record and the demands of the club would allow no more time to compose fanzines, but he kept his eye in writing wise by contributing the occasional piece to other fanzines, including the one he wrote for *Groovy Black Shades* praising to the skies the Smiths, a band that he claimed made him feel young again (he was 22 at the time). For McGee, the success of the Smiths was like a dream, Morrissey's comments to *Melody Maker* at the time declaring that he was 'ready to be accepted by everybody' and wanted to be heard and seen 'by as many people as possible' music to his ears.

Alan McGee also wanted to be seen and heard by as many people as possible, or at least wanted that for his bands. Following the failure of the Communication Club and the dismal response to the first Creation single, he had come back strong. What was obvious, also, was that his own personal drive outstripped that of most of those he was involved with. Recycling old bands and even older ideas was noble but clearly not going to lead him to the place he wanted to be.

It was then perhaps inevitable that when on 22 December he threw a private Christmas party at the Living Room to thank those who had supported the club he drew less on the revivalist culture that had influenced the club's earlier period and focussed instead on the future, booking the Legend!, the Revolving Paint Dream, Biff Bang Pow! and the Jasmine Minks to play. Collectively, they would be responsible for the first four singles on the Creation label, which was to be reactivated, reanimated and re-launched at the start of 1984.

CHAPTER 7

MISFITS

IN HIS COMPREHENSIVE STUDY *Death To Trad Rock*, published in 2009, John Robb outlines the qualities that a particular kind of indie band in the middle of the 1980s shared. 'The bands,' said Robb, 'produced loud, noisy, discordant music with a stripped down punk energy. Most of them had a dirty bass sound, shrapnel guitars and surreal lyrics.' The songs themselves were often 'anti-rock songs', with 'short, sharp shocks of wild noise'. There were no guitar solos or any other rock 'n' cliché. Instead, there was the noise of Telecaster guitars overloaded with treble, a plangent bass sound, and, more often than not, the strains of a vocalist struggling to keep the pace, since Death To Trad Rock songs tended to speed up as they reached their climax.

His description nails the music nicely, but, as Robb pointed out, Death To Trad Rock wasn't just about music: it was about *attitude* as well – an attitude inspired by punk, and, in particular, by the Clash, whose incendiary early performances captured all of the contrarian force of rock 'n' roll in its kinetic glory. Those that carried the spirit on were also motivators – more discordant artists, such as the Pop Group, Gang of Four, Joy Division, Wire, the Fire Engines, the Stranglers, the Birthday Party and, perhaps most fittingly of all, the Fall. The bands that drew inspiration from them – the Death To Trad Rockers – picked up on this contrarian attitude and ran with it. The music they produced was 'music for fanatics made by fanatics', and, in a period where creeping conformity was becoming the norm, they were misfits.

Robb's idea of putting rock to the sword, which he'd first touted in the spring of 1984, complemented the earlier calls to arms Mick Mercer and others had made. Mercer's target had been complacency within the indie sector, whereas Robb's, in typical fashion, was broader – a sideswipe at the state of rock generally. It wasn't the indie 'stars' who had conformed that bothered Robb, although, true, they *were* a problem, but the behemoths and giants like Kiss, Duran Duran, Phil Collins, and Bon Jovi, artists whose anodyne music polluted the airwaves and was laughingly sold to the kids in the name of the same sort of subversion as that of the Clash.

Robb pinned the colours to the mast with 'Spike Milligan's Tape Recorder', a splenetic, Dada-esque offering that cleared out a few eardrums nicely when it first appeared at the start of summer 1984. Pre-empting the aural assault of noise bands such as Sonic Youth and Big Black, the record was a step-change not just for the Membranes, but also for indie music. It made Single of the Week in *Sounds*, who described the band as 'seriously disturbed and completely at odds with musical trends'. The assault was all but physical, and the record 'the stormiest punk single since "Anarchy In The UK"', one where 'every riff you've loved to deaf, damaged beyond repair [is] squeezed between a title which bears no relation to the words,' according to reviewer Jack Barron. Or, put another way, it was a Death To Trad Rock song. The words *were* fittingly surreal: dog-eating vicars brought to book by the local rag, radioactive seaweed, casual family violence, cassette tape culture. 'By the light of the pumpkin moon/ On a storm-tossed night of the 12th June', begins one stanza, but sea shanty it isn't.

The experience of growing up working class in the 'tatty seaside town' of Blackpool runs through the work of the Membranes like lettering through a stick of rock. Blackpool is often said to have been the first working class seaside resort, but by the time the Membranes formed in 1977 it was in severe decline. In the 1950s and 1960s it was an entertainment mecca – international stars would jet into the UK and play just two locations, London, and Blackpool. George Formby, one of the biggest music stars pre-rock 'n' roll, lived in a suburban house on the outskirts: John Lennon, taking the annual family holiday from nearby Liverpool, would head there to gaze over the garden wall in awe. It was no accident that the Beatles played Blackpool a whopping fourteen times at the start of the 1960s. But by the 1970s, Blackpool was in decline. The stars had all gone away. And when punk came along, it was, according to Robb, a dead town, 'just a place to get pissed and go to discos'. And since most people reaching a certain age just upped and left, there were no older bands to act as mentors, so forming a band at that time really was a case of DIY.

'I was sixteen going on seventeen when I decided to put a group together,' recalls Robb. 'I had absolutely no idea how to go about doing it. I knew that you needed other people and so in time I roped in a couple of mates, first off Mark Tilton. Neither of us had a clue about playing a musical instrument. We bought a second-hand guitar and a bass from Woolworths with three strings and somehow we managed to get that to work through a record player. Then we put 'Peaches' by the Stranglers onto the record player and attempted to play along to it. Right from the start we did things back to front, the opposite way from how bands conventionally learn.

'The hardest thing was finding a drummer. A Big City band would have been able to take out an ad, but there weren't any drummers in Blackpool and I realised that the only way to find one was to turn one of your mates into one. We were at the bus station one day when we overheard a kid saying that he'd been given £30 for his birthday. He was thirteen. We made him buy a drum kit with the money. That didn't last and eventually Coofy Sid came in on drums and the original drummer moved on to keyboards.'

The Membranes played their first gig in 1978 at a place called Kirkham Palms, supporting a local band called Cyclon B. Cyclon B's guitarist spent the afternoon teaching them how to tune a guitar. 'Wow,' says Robb. 'We were excited – we were being initiated into the dark arts. Prior to that we'd just lined up all the machine heads in a row and assumed that that was how you tuned a guitar. That gig was also the first time that we'd plugged into a proper amp. Again, we didn't know what to do so we put everything into one amp – bass, guitar, the lot – and it came back at us sounding *loud*, really loud – loud and out of tune.' Other shows followed, reflecting the small town nature of where they were – gigs in church halls and occasional clubs where Coofy Sid had to be smuggled in because of his age. They played a talent show in Cleveleys and came last: a six-year-old girl reading a poem won.

At the start of the 1980s, the limitations of operating out of Blackpool were all too real. The nearest large city was Manchester, which was fifty miles away. The music papers didn't send stringers to the town, so coverage in the press was virtually non-existent. And the bigger bands rarely visited, either. Between the start of 1981 and the start of 1983, the only 'famous' band to come to Blackpool had been the Fall, according to issue 16 of *Rox*, the fanzine Robb set up to run in conjunction with his band. Yet by 1983, largely thanks to the industry of Robb and a few others, a scene of sorts was in place. Bands like Section 25, with their doom-laden, bass-heavy sound that predated Joy Division, had a record released on Factory, and other local bands such as Zanti Misfits, in2xs, the Fits, Tunnelvision, and the Urbane Guerillas had also released records. A 'Blackpool Rox' EP that Robb had helped release back in August 1980 had tracks not just by the Membranes and Section 25, but also local acts Syntax and the Ken Turner Set. Other artists, as forgotten now as fish and chip paper blowing along the promenade, had released cassettes, including Hermanns Effey (featuring an early Greg Keeffe from Big Flame), Index 11, Pom Pom 3 and Door 66, a Bunnymen-esque band fronted by the actor David Thewliss.

Blackpool bands were, largely, treated as a novelty, something to be quickly consumed and forgotten. The first real contact that the Membranes had had with the outside music world was when John Peel played the 'Blackpool Rox' EP and people began writing to them, purchasing the record mail order. It wasn't exactly an operation to match Rough Trade, but it created a small platform and helped take the band's message beyond Lancashire. The band's *Rox* fanzine also helped. Robb had the same philosophy as Alan McGee, an attack-on-all-fronts approach. The fanzine promoted the local scene aggressively and disseminated the philosophy of and news about the Membranes. Early on, the plan, according *Rox 14*, was to 'continue blundering away at our sound…make a single every three months, each one a three-track cracker … break into the Alternative Charts on our own merits, gig around the country revitalising the stale scene'. Part of revitalising the stale scene involved setting up a club, the Vinyl Drip Club, named after the label they'd invented to release the EP, which ran for about six months between the end of 1982 and the middle of 1983. For the paying guests there was the excitement of getting to see 'out of town bands' like the Nightingales and Crispy Ambulance, but the club was short-lived thanks to a visit by one of the local gangs co-running the town who decided to rob the door. 'Big, burly Teddy Boy-types,' recalls Robb, 'like characters out of a film. The police arrived, and that was the end of that.'

The Membranes 'Muscles' EP was originally self-released on Vinyl Drip in 1981 and then re-released by Rondolet in 1982, the year they started to make broader forays beyond the limits of Lancashire. A debut at the Moonlight Club in London, which would have been their first appearance in the capital, fell through because Coofy Sid's employers threatened him with the sack if he went AWOL. Unfortunately, the rest of the band didn't find out about this until they were actually in London. The young Coofy's well-being was also of concern to his parents who banned him from playing beyond the county line, causing drummer John McWilliams to be ready on standby for those not-to-faraway gigs. Blackpool, 'the town with the bands and the town without the audience and venues to show them off' (as *Rox* had it), forced the band outwards, and ultimately helped them develop their style. Manchester and Liverpool were the obvious immediate destinations.

'It took a while but we found a friend with a car. Boy did he become a friend. We'd go and watch the bands in Liverpool, Manchester. Manchester was more cosmopolitan, safer, a bit more welcoming. In Liverpool you had to watch they didn't catch your accent, because that could land you in trouble. We began playing venues in those cities, as well – often strange, inappropriate places, clubs that were underground in dingy cellars. On one occasion we were playing at a place that served food and after a while the relentless music obviously got to the chef. He came out of the kitchen and started attacking us with a meat cleaver.'

It's undeniable that the Membranes at the time would have been taken a little more seriously if they hadn't been a Blackpool band. 'I kind of think that we might possibly have been given a bit more respect by the writers on the music papers if, say, we'd been living in a squat at the foot of the Berlin Wall,' Robb jokes today. There was plenty of fun to be had at the band's expense – the subs had a field day thinking up witty headlines that incorporated the words 'tower', or Blackpool' and 'rock' placed next to each other. A 1988 song ('Tatty Seaside Town') spelt out the predicament: the inevitability of the 'autumn lights' (the yearly illuminations for which the place is famous), the dull presence of the 'seaside mafia' and the struggle to not be the object of the 'sheer thrill of violence on an August night' that others are actively seeking.

There was a mini album released in 1983 (*The Crack House*) and another EP ('The Pin Stripe Hype'), both of which hinted at the even more abrasive direction the band was heading in. 1983 was the year they had slimmed down to a trio (Robb on bass, Coofy Sid on 'off-kilter drums' and Mark Tilton on 'nervous-breakdown, treble guitar – played with lashings of psychotic slide blues licks'), the perfect rock and roll combination. Robb had built himself a monster bass, as well, carved out of soft wood purchased from Crossley's wood yard in Blackpool. It was homage to the bass Captain Sensible played on the first Damned album, and with its violin shape a nod to McCartney's iconic Hoffner. It made a racket that was 'huge and evil', according to Robb.

The band had a look to match as well. Again it was a case of a few key influences here and there and a lot of DIY: 'We'd seen an advert for David Lynch's film *Eraserhead*,' recalls Robb. 'Just looking at the picture made us think it was going to be an amazing film. It was a bit like those punk bands in 1976 – you didn't need to hear them, just looking at the record covers told you all about how brilliant they were going to be. The problem we had was that the nearest cinema showing the film was in Lancaster, about 30 miles away. Mark Tilton and I eventually got to a screening and we were the only people in the auditorium. We didn't really immediately get the black humour of the film, but we immediately loved the soundtrack and thought that the Henry Spencer character, played by Jack Nance, was the coolest mother in the world. The big black coat, the shoes, the amazing quiff and haircut. We borrowed the whole look and did our own version of it – we've still got that look, really.'

The powerhouse trio, the refined look and the hammer-headed sound, now all that was needed was a philosophy.

'Tils and I worked away in his back room, sitting amongst piles of vinyl, drinking countless cups of tea, and created our own musical template,' Robb explains in *Death To Trad Rock*. 'We hated what we saw as "Trad Rock" and decided to revolt against it. We decided to oppose it and get off on the adrenalin of that confrontation. We would have no 12-bars – they were too male, too pub rock. We would have no real chords – just discords, they were more exciting and more unsettling. If a song sounded like something else, we would scrap it instantly. The songs had to come from jams and everyone would be playing lead. Everything was about energy, adrenalin and free thought.'

'Spike Milligan's Tape Recorder', the full-on, prodigious first offering of the new sound was recorded at Cargo Studios, Rochdale in early summer 1984. John Brierley, a man who had previously worked with the Fall, Durutti Column and Joy Division, engineered. He was, according to Robb, 'the only engineer in the UK who let you record everything at full blast'. When the record was released in August, Jack Barron at *Sounds* wasn't the only way to rave about it. Mick Mercer in *Melody Maker* reviewed the single thus: 'And The Membranes? Well they've a loud guitar with which to rip the arms off a classic as flies hatch in their hair'. The single ended up being voted 6th favourite in John Peel's Festive 50 and for *Zigzag* magazine it wasn't just 'the single of the week, [but] the best rock record of the year'.

One person who had been present at the recording session had been Alan McGee. McGee had almost certainly been tipped-off to the joys of the Membranes by the Legend!, who was an early admirer and had been present at one of the bands first London shows, in a club in Kensington in 1982. That same year, McGee had wanted the Membranes to play the Communication Club.

'When Alan became interested in us we'd all but given up on London,' remembers Robb. 'We didn't seem to fit in. The odd thing for us about London was that when you went to see a band there you'd hardly meet anyone actually from London. It would be full of people from the satellite areas around the capital. I'm exaggerating, of course, but making a true point. So when I got to know Alan and learned about what he was up to, I was fascinated. We quickly became big friends. His was a pretty similar personality to mine really – he was enthusiastic, into DIY, knew exactly what he wanted to do and wasn't prepared to be budged aside by anybody. People tend to focus on the psychedelic aspect of the early Creation bands, Alan's taste was actually very broad

– he was a big supporter of bands like Five Go Down To The Sea, the Three Johns and the Nightingales, for example. We were probably the most extreme it got, and it shouldn't have worked, but when we played the Living Room it was a big success. And that was partly down to the fact that Alan's enthusiasm fired up an audience.'

In 1981, just as John Robb's band began making first, tentative forays beyond native Lancashire, in neighbouring Yorkshire, the Three Johns emerged, laying down a blueprint for a similar kind of anti-pop to that of the Membranes. A shared love of all-out sonic assault and a penchant for Dada when lyric writing united the bands, and for each, the tipping off point had been punk. Both could produce music that was dronish and dissonant, peppered with the odd psychedelic squeal, but whereas the Membranes generally favoured a bastardised blues approach, the Three Johns 3 often riffed on a form of perverted glam, reflecting, amongst other things, their love of bands such as the Stooges, the New York Dolls and Marc Bolan's T Rex.

The band's frames of reference were educated and wide-ranging – so much so that the critics usually found it hard to say just what kind of band the Three Johns was. It had been the case since virtually the moment the band formed that its genius should be misrepresented. The day before 1981's Royal Wedding had been spent drinking cider in Hyde Park, Leeds, where a plan was hatched to form a band and play the park's anti-celebratory 'Funk The Wedding' gig scheduled for the following day. But the organisers turned the band away, claiming that a band that had been in existence for less than twenty-four hours was 'not a real band'. In the words of singer John Hyatt, writing in 2009, they 'carried on being "not a real band" for the next ten years'.

Early comparisons predictably compared the Three Johns to the Birthday Party and the Fall, as well as the Cramps, the

Stooges, the Seeds, the New York Dolls, Captain Beefheart and 'Marc Bolan gone mental'. Discussing what he saw as their 'disciplined anarchy', Lynden Barber in the *Melody Maker* at the start of 1984 coaxed out of them what *they* saw as some of their influences, which threw a few more names into the mix, including contemporaries the Redskins, '60s Beat bands the Pretty Things and the Searchers, before arriving – tongue in cheek – at the unhelpful conclusion that their sound was a cross between Captain Beefheart's *Safe As Milk*, the Clash's *Combat Rock* and Michael Jackson's *Thriller*. They told *Grim Humour* fanzine that the following were also important to them: 'Scraping Foetus Off the Wheel, Country & Western, Honky Tonk, Hank Williams, Eek A Mouse, the Nightingales, and the first Clash album'. No wonder the critics were confused.

The key phrase in all of the above is 'disciplined anarchy'. For some they were a good time band – a monster rock and roll engine where Hugo the drum machine and John Brennan's chugging bass underpinned the wildcat guitar of Jon Langford and the pure-pop vocals of John Hyatt. In this version there was a fourth John – John Barleycorn, whose liquid presence fuelled many a raucous night. For others, they were a sternly political band – Socialism with a smile and a touch of barbed inter-song banter, an attempt to comment on the times without ramming dialectics down the lubricated throats of their audience. This notion of Apollo and Dionisyus sitting down together, quite possibly with Karl *and* Groucho Marx confused some who never knew quite how to take them. But then from the start, the Three Johns had determined to be different, as they had told the *NME* in 1983: 'We dreamt of something humorous, something interesting, something that was *not* on the wall.'

1981 was the year of the inner city riots as well as the royal wedding and a hot summer saw the streets of a number of big cities set ablaze to the eerily appropriate soundtrack of the Specials' 'Ghost Town', which was riding high in the charts at the time. One of the riots took place in the Chapeltown and Hare-hills area of Leeds, where £2 Million worth of damage was done when disaffected black and white youths looted and set fire to the area. But Leeds was burning for another reason. At the start of the 1980s it had emerged as arguably the pre-eminent city for happening music in the UK. Bands like the Mekons, Gang of Four, Soft Cell and Delta Five had set the bar high, and would be followed by, amongst others, Chumbawumba, Sisters of Mercy, March Violets, and, a little while later, by Age of Chance and the Wedding Present. This was the combustive/ creative backdrop to the Three Johns who, the day after the royal wedding, wrote their first half a dozen or so songs in Jon Langford's flat.

'At the time we started,' recalls John Hyatt, 'there were so many bands it was ridiculous. We used to drink in the Royal Oak pub in Headingley and on a Sunday lunchtime just walking the short distance down to the pub we'd pass about 20 bands rehearsing in their various flats and houses. I shared a flat with Jon King and Andy Gill from Gang of Four and also in the house was Tom from the Mekons. Next door to us was the band the Cassandra Complex.'

Hyatt and Langford had met whilst students on the Fine Art course at Leeds University, a course also taken by various members of Gang of Four. Their time coincided with the tenure of TJ Clarke, the formidable Head of Department whose rigorous Marxist-oriented approach led to the appointment of Terry Atkinson, the conceptual artist, Griselda Pollock, the Feminist/ Marxist art historian and theorist, and Fred Orton, the social art historian/ theorist. Of the 23 enrolled onto the course Hyatt began in 1978, only 9 managed to finish it. 'It was difficult and very, very theory laden,' remembers Hyatt. 'The course was supposed to be 50% theory and 50% practise, but it got to the point where a lot of people just stopped making art, and for them the course became all theory and no practise.'

In keeping with the period, Tim Clarke's course taught its students that it wasn't just the making of art that had to be questioned, but also the politics of the making of it. As Hyatt told John Robb in *Death To Trad Rock*, 'Everything you did was questioned, so much so that it sublimated into the music.' This was clearly the case with Gang of Four whose art-grad Marxist approach had already turned textbook theory into four-line verses and in 1979 given us one of the more accomplished post-punk debut albums, *Entertainment*. For some the exercise was dry and academic, but such criticisms were leavened somewhat by the band's formidable live act.

If the music of Gang of Four was a sort of intellectual Marxism in action (albeit one that relied on the major record label EMI for dissemination), then it's possible to see the Three Johns as more a reflection of the long tradition of the less dogmatic British Left. The idea was to operate in contrast to the 'theory overload' approach and simultaneously encourage those that came to their gigs to have a good time, adopting Thomas More's strategy of telling the most serious statements with a smile and the most flippant with a straight face, according to Hyatt. At one memorable gig, the stage collapsed and the band carried on playing. When the mood took them, they were known to play their sets backwards, just for the hell of it, or programme the drum machine to play non-stop for 50 minutes, turning a performance into a marathon workout for anyone who had naively taken to the dance floor at the start of what they believed to be a traditional set of songs. It was not unusual for a gig to end with a mass invasion of the audience playing air solos on unplugged guitars. Po-faced the band most certainly was not.

In the beginning, the Three Johns consisted of Hyatt and Langford and John Diamond, who played drums, just as Langford had. The Boss drum machine joined the band because neither of the two drummers actually wanted to drum. In early rehearsals, the band used a synthesizer or drummed on cassette boxes and found objects. Everybody sang a bit until eventually it settled down and Hyatt took on the responsibility fulltime, meaning that he couldn't play bass, as had been the original intention, since he found it difficult playing the bass and singing at the same time.

John (Philip) Brennan wasn't at the university studying but worked on the grounds of the student halls of residence. He'd been intending to travel from his native Belfast to Tibet, but got stuck in Leeds. 'He was always on the scene,' recalls Hyatt. 'He was in the audience at our second gig, at the end of 1981, where we did a Christmas concept show based on the story of Charles Dickens' *A Christmas Carol*. We'd bought some suits from Oxfam and painted them with white emulsion, scrawling onto the back of them appropriate messages, such as 'MARLEY IS DEAD'. We'd prepared a whole bunch of songs, all based on the novel. One, I recall, was called 'Phantoms in The Street' and was a sort of pseudo Adam & The Ants/ Goth song. We wore the suits over our normal clothes and once we started playing it began to get hotter and hotter on stage. The paint was all cracking off my suit and so I started to take it off, handing my bass over to this person in the audience who turned out to be Brenny while I struggled with my trousers. Brenny put the bass on and he just started playing, miles better than I ever could. From that moment on, he was in the band. That's how loose the set-up was.'

The first Three Johns single came out summer 1982. 'English White Boy Engineer' was a song of Langford's, written originally for the Mekons. It's one and only outing prior to the Three Johns recording it was a Peel Session, where it more or less stole the show. The song, based on a poem by the ranting poet Little Brother, railed against the evils of apartheid as imagined through the eyes of white English apologists and made Single of the Week in *NME*, where X Moore (aka Chris Deane of the Redskins) praised its 'cashew nut bass, tremolo scratch guitar and SIN-drums'. It was a beautiful piece of work.

Fittingly, Jon Langford sang on the A-side and John Hyatt played guitar, roles that were reversed on the B-side, 'Secret Agent', a track where the lyrics were written by Hyatt, employing a technique that would serve him well throughout the life of the Three Johns. 'We used to rehearse in a room that was full of books,' Hyatt explains. 'Often, I'd pick up a book and start singing lines from it. "Secret Agent" was from Conrad, of course. I never bothered changing the words at all, just read them out verbatim. I used to write lyrics in a little notebook that I carried around and I'd pepper the lyrics in the notebook with the material from the novels.' Other works of literature plundered early on included Raymond Chandler's *Killer In The Rain* ('Lucy In The Rain') and *Farewell My Lovely* (Pink-Headed Bug'), and Lynne Reid Banks' *The L-Shaped Room* ('Windowlene').

Shortly after 'English White Boy Engineer' came out, the Three Johns picked up their first major press article, when Don Watson interviewed the band for the *NME* in October 1982. 'Self-images, alcohol and T Rex are fundamental to the Three Johns,' Watson reasonably observed. Politics then raised its head before being gently swatted back into its box in a memorable quote: 'We all have socialist convictions and obviously that comes through sometimes because it is part of us, but we are not a socialist band – we're a group of socialists who are in a band. It's a fine distinction but an important one.'

The 'self-images' referred to a painting of owl masks that was the backdrop for the *NME* article and created by the Three Johns, 'ART AND LAW AND MARX'. Just as socialism informed their everyday action, so the fine art pedigree of Hyatt and Langford carried through to the physical production of the records them-selves, in some cases acting as a subtle or not so subtle cypher, as in the case of 1984's *Atom Drum Bop* album with its *ROCK 'N' ROLL VERSUS THAATCHIISM* daub and images of fighter jets, missiles and the hangman's gallows.

'With the exception of *Atom Drum Bop*, which incorporated artwork by Terry Atkinson, we always did our own covers,' recalls Hyatt. 'But bear in mind that we'd been trained as fine art students and not as graphic designers, so, for instance, when we came to do the cover for "English White Boy Engineer", everything was hand drawn, because we didn't know what Letraset was.'

The owl-mask motif followed through onto the paper centre label on the first single. The record company itself, CNT, borrowed its name from and honoured the Confederacion Nacional del Trabajo (National Federation of Labour), an anarcho-syndicalist group founded in 1910 to expand the role of anarchism in Spain. CNT singles (which included releases by the Mekons, Sisters of Mercy, Newtown Neurotics and the Redskins) sometimes carried the CNT slogan *Hijos Del Pueblo A Las Barricados*, or, Sons Of The People To The Barricades.

There were two further Three Johns releases on CNT – the utterly charming and wonderfully surreal 'Pink Headed Bug', with its borrowed lines from Chandler ('I was a pink-headed bug crawling up the Civic Hall') and crisp, insistent, post-Buzzcocks guitar riff overladen with a pure-pop vocal, and the equally as unusual 'Men Like Monkeys', a 5-track 12". Opening with the immortal lines

Come with us now back to a land before time began
When rock 'n' roll was just a sound bubbling underground, *maan*

the title track was another slice of classic rock 'n' roll, concerning itself with evolution, or civilisation, or, in the words of the band, about 'the gap between knowledge/ science/ technology and ideology/ belief', none of which does justice to a song more accurately (and viscerally) described in the singles column of the *NME* as a 'chewing and spewing, and sprawling and clawing' thing.

Having once jokily described themselves as 'the social workers of rock', in 1983, the Three Johns did put their skills to the benefit of the community, teaching a rock 'n' roll course to the out of work at a local institute. 'They were men and women from a range of experience and ages,' recalls Hyatt. 'Some couldn't play at all and others felt like they were already proficient musicians. The major difficulty was reconciling the experienced to supporting the inexperienced. There was a sort of skills "class system" which I had to break down.' Later, Hyatt taught a similar course to students at Leeds Polytechnic, helping bands like CUD and Ritzun Ratzun Rotzer to emerge.

1983 also saw the band switch labels, as they moved from CNT to Abstract Records, a label formed in 1980 by Edward Christie that had found success with a number of punk compilation albums (*Punk & Disorderly*, *The Beerdrop Explodes*, etc) and a wider-fringes assortment of punk artists such as UK Subs and the Gymslips. The formidable Janette Garthwaite joined the label at the start of 1983, responsible for A&R and handling press. In quick succession, 1919 – 'a heavy melodic intense dance band with no frills and no intentions', as they described themselves – were signed up, along with Bradford's New Model Army, performance poet Joolz and the Three Johns. In time, Five Go Down To The Sea and the Blue Aeroplanes would also become Abstract artists.

The band's first Abstract release came in October with 'A.W.O.L', a fully-sprung work of genius that put paid to any lingering criticism that the Three Johns were a great rant-and-roll band but didn't really have any tunes. Echoes of the Cramps and the primal scream of rockabilly, of the Stooges, the Rolling Stones, Gene Vincent and 'Jerry Lee Lewis with a drum machine' (to quote from *Noise Annoys* Fanzine) all surface in a work that is recognisably the Three Johns own. To promote the record's release, the band played Alan McGee's Living Room club, where the *NME*'s Mat Snow, picking up on all of the above and more heard in the band's sound 'the same frenzied, Dionysiac whoop of devilment that Ray Lowry heard in the primal dawn when Elvis first sang "That's Alright (Mama)".' One more Abstract release followed, drawing together the previous CNT releases on to one 12" ('Some History'), which gave the band its second Indie Top Twenty hit just as the year ended.

1984 would be good to The Three Johns – cover stories in the music press, a further string of well-received singles and a well-realised debut album, *Atom Drum Bop*. *Atom Drum Bop* was, according to *Melody Maker*, 'a steaming, incautious bable that goes thump in the night' and a record that sounded like '*Safe As Milk* put through a meat mincer'. Lynden Barber wasn't quite as enthusiastic as previously, finding the record a curious halfway mix between what the band was and what it aspired to. 'We always aimed for a live sound but never quite achieved it on record,' says John Hyatt. 'By the timed we got to *Atom Drum Bop* we really knew we never would be able to recreate that live sound so the production of our records evolved, as can be heard on the following album, 1986's *World By Storm*, which is a lot more produced.'

Atom Drum Bop, in a number of ways, took the pulse of the moment, as Mat Snow noted in the *NME*: 'Is it me or do I *really* hear shades of Hank Williams, Roxy's "Ladytron", a '67-style warning to beware of the Notts constabulary, indeed a whole series of poetically encoded messages suggesting that things in the wacky world of advanced capitalism are *not quite right*?' ROCK 'N' ROLL VERSUS THAATCHIISM read thaa slogan on the back cover of the album, mimicking the kind of slogan approach that the Conservative Party was starting to adopt. 'It wasn't just Thatcher you were fighting at the time,' recalls Hyatt, 'but the advertising agency Saatchi & Saatchi who worked for them. That was our attempt at our own slogan.'

The band put its shoulder to the wheel during the miners' strike and shortly after it ended in spring 1985 they released what some consider to be their finest single, 'Death Of A European', this time turning their attention to politics of a transatlantic kind. The song assessed American imperialism through the eyes of a subject who ultimately finds it wanting.

> He rides the lightning
> His snoring drowns the thunder
> Finds his dreams are frightening
> He won't go under
> He's alive...

The record, 'a ballet of East-West politics', made Single of the Week in *NME* and was, said Danny Kelly, 'a huge runaway cement train of a record... absurdly ambitious and devastatingly realised.' 'An ex-GI reviewed the record in the Village Voice,' remembers Hyatt, 'and he had basically left the forces because of that record. Little things like that really pleased me at the time. The song featured some of our best lyrics, but then you never really know if anyone is taking note of the lyrics. The review was like a small victory at the time, although of course the big victories are really just small victories on top of one another...'

The single looked set to get mainstream radio airplay and would almost certainly have taken the band to a new level in terms of sales, but it was not to be. 'Janice Long was due to play the record,' remembers Hyatt, and she said that before she did she just had to pause for an urgent news flash. The news flash turned out to be about the Heysal Stadium disaster which had just taken place. She didn't play "Death Of A European", she played Bruce Springsteen's "Dancing In The Dark" instead....'

The Three Johns continued until 1988, commited to providing a good time and unafraid to use politics to get a message across.

'Eighties feminism had taught us that everything, even the personal, is political, and yes, the songs were purposefully political,'

Hyatt wrote later in a contributory chapter to *Digging The Seam: Popular Cultures of the 1984/85 Miners' Strike*, ed Simon Popple and Ian W. Macdonald, '… but at a gig it is not the words that matter but the attitude, the style, the energy and the optimism. I saw concerts as a way to bring people together to talk in the intervals and support each other with good humour. I saw myself as involved in Folk Music at this time, not Rock Music. Simple structures, sing-along choruses, a riotous happy performance, and sweat and alcohol brought joy and a moment's transport beyond the worries of the grimmest of industrial disputes.'

Transporting people beyond the worries of grim circumstance was something the Nightingales were also adept at. They were, in so many ways, the ultimate outsider band and even John Robb, no stranger to the crown, concedes that they were the limit, 'the misfits' misfits', as he dubbed them. Putting them on at the Vinyl Drip Club in the early 1980s, Robb sat and watched as the band played a game of cards between the sound-check and the gig. They didn't play the game and they weren't bothered with image. To Robb, they were the kind of band that 'looked like they'd been in the bookies all afternoon… Their records smelt of pubs and big record collections. They were funny, scornful, smart and real.'

By the end of 1983, the Nightingales, the Membranes and the Three Johns, were indie's holy triumvirate, each pushing forward the genre at a difficult time – each a lone wolf example of 'genius at work in dark corners of rock music', as David Quantick observed in the *NME*, adding: 'Can there be a child alive today who does not recite that trio of names like a litany before going to sleep?' Of the three, the Nightingales went back the furthest and cast the longest shadow.

Perhaps more than most, Lloyd is a product of the environment he grew up in, the small town of Cannock just to the north west of Birmingham. Commentators like to describe him as a Saloon Bar humourist, a Tap Room wit – a common man's Morrissey, some claim. In truth, his beef is beyond that and runs deeper than pandering to the would-be intellects of the Sixth Form. The claim, once made, that his real subject is the decline of post-Industrial society, is fanciful but closer to the mark. Musing in a macro or micro way upon his place in the world has always been a favoured pastime. For snap evidence of his razor-sharp self-awareness one need look no further than the titles he chose for the two best-of collections of his work – *The Prefects are… Amateur Wankers* and *Pissed and Potless* (the Nightingales).

Lloyd's is a tail of toil, a Sisyphus-like struggle to continually push a boulder up a hill that continues to this day. His musical education began first at home, listening to the Elvis Presley records that belonged to his mum and her partner, before progressing on to the racks of Wolverhampton public library where, in his mid-teens in the mid-1970s, he was introduced to the delights of Captain Beefheart, Can, Faust, Amon Duul and various prog rock artists. It wasn't too long before the lure of wanting to be in a band started to exert its pull.

The problem was that Cannock was 'a Greaser town', as Lloyd later described it, and the lads he hooked up with in a group were intent on following in the footsteps of local band made good Black Sabbath. The saving grace was that they couldn't play their instruments very well, and to Lloyd therefore sounded less like Ozzy and more like the Stooges. They rehearsed in a garden shed, where Lloyd jumped around shouting out adlibbed phrases, stuff that he thought was 'quite good at the time' but later came to realise was 'pretty shite'. A contrarian from birth, when the boys decided to go out on the road, and wanted to christen themselves Witchhazel, in protest Lloyd quit on the spot.

Then came 1976. The shifting of music's tectonic plates reverberated all the way up to the greasers in Cannock. Lloyd read in the *NME* about the 'primitive music' that was starting to emerge, convincing himself, like so many others, that it was going to be brilliant before having even heard a single note. He began going to punk gigs and saw the Sex Pistols first gig in Birmingham at Bogarts before travelling down to London to see the Ramones play their first UK gig at Dingwalls. He had his photograph taken in Camden and it ended up being used in an article about the Ramones that appeared in an issue of Legs MacNeil's *Punk* fanzine. The caption beneath his picture read: 'The Ramones with Robert Lloyd – Europe's number one Ramones fan'. He followed the Sex Pistols around and soon arrived at the logical conclusion that he needed to be in this kind of band himself.

The band that eventually came into being featured Joe Crow on guitar and Paul Apperley on drums, with Andy Lloyd on bass. At one point, comedian Frank Skinner and soon-to-be Swell Mapper Nikki Sudden were in line to play bass, Skinner actually joining briefly, to the great amusement of the rest of the band. With Lloyd at the helm, there was no chance that the Prefects (as the band came to be known) would do anything by halves and one of their first acts was to write a song in praise of the second city, called 'Birmingham Is A Shithole'. Ever the provocateur, Lloyd liked to pretend that the band was going to be called Gestapo, a name given the seal of approval by Johnny Thunders. The Clash suggested Blackshirts instead (on account of it being more *English*), while Johnny Rotten thought they should call themselves Nasty Party. How the name the Prefects was settled on cannot now be recalled.

What happened next was that the call came through to play some dates on the White Riot Tour with the Clash, the Slits and Subway Sect. It was an eye-opener and a defining moment that shaped Lloyd's whole philosophical outlook. 'No-one was interested in us,' he later told John Robb. 'The Clash were already a pop band by then. When we had played the Rainbow I realised that punk was not what I thought it was. It was just serving up the same old rubbish. To me the Clash were just "stars". There was a VIP room at the Rainbow. We weren't allowed in, but Siouxsie Sioux and Billy Idol waltzed in and they weren't even playing! In Chelmsford, the mayor came to visit and the Clash had their photo taken with him for the local paper.'

Lloyd recognised, as did many others (later to include Robb), that there was a credibility gap between what punk was meant to represent and what it actually was. And although his band may have been 'naïve' and 'bog-standard oiks', they picked up quick enough that, for them, reacting against the punk rock orthodoxy was the first stop on the route to being creatively free, even if the journey was likely to be a short one, as turned out to be the case. The irony of the lyrics to their one and only single, 'Going Through The Motions', was lost on most of the punk rock audiences who provided its inspiration – 'I'm going through the motions/ I do it all for you/ Performance by performance/ Doing what you want me to'.

Playing at The Rainbow, the Prefects set had been seen by John Peel and his producer John Walters. Peel and Walters had been particularly impressed by the band's rendition of a song called 'VD', a thirteen-second ode to the horrors of the sexually transmitted disease. The Prefects were invited to record a Peel session. The session was duly recorded and broadcast and, as a result, Lloyd received a telegram from Geoff Travis and Mayo Thompson at Rough Trade: 'Reverse the charges and ring us immediately' it read.

Whether it was to do with his well-documented disenchantment with punk, or the fact that the Prefects were inevitably going to run out of steam, by the time Lloyd made his way to the Rough Trade offices, the Prefects were all but over. 'What was agreed in the end,' recalls Lloyd, 'is that Rough Trade would put out a single by the Prefects, but also put out the first record by the Nightingales, the band that the Prefects were changing into.' Travis also suggested, in keeping with the ethos of Rough Trade, that the record be released jointly, by Rough Trade and a label that would belong to Lloyd. Lloyd chose to call his label Vindaloo.

The inscription on the dead wax of the Prefects one and only single pronounced it an 'Horrendous Doppelganger Parody' and noted that 'Perfection Is A Fault', something that could well serve as a motto/ epitaph for Lloyd. In the Nightingales, Lloyd passed off the wilfully amateur approach and turned instead to his local mecca Birmingham for inspiration, becoming a shrewd observer of the city's mores.

At the start of the 1980s, Birmingham was, in truth, something of a wasteland. When the Nightingales did their first interview for *Melody Maker*, the reporter was aghast at where the assignment had taken him, seeing not tower blocks but 'ugly grey slabs called concrete', not ring roads and underpasses but 'enormous canals of tarmac' and 'evil, orange-lit tunnels'. This then was the canvas that Lloyd had to work with, the basic raw material, as he set out with his new band and began 'narrating the absurd trivialities of city life'.

One problem that blighted the progress of the Nightingales was that they seemed to be constantly switching record labels. The handshake agreement with Rough Trade resulted in just one single – the chopping and magnificent 'Idiot Strength', a riddled tale of the unwritten rules that get 're-unwritten' – before the band were looking for another label. Guitarist Joe Crow and bassist Eamonn Duffy left and were replaced by Nic Beales and Steve Hawkins.

Mike Alway went to see the Nightingales play local venue the Fighting Cocks and came away impressed, eventually offering the band a 'proper' deal with Cherry Red. With the move, the Nightingales quickly found their feet, turning in a clutch of singles in 1982 and a debut album that for many remains their best work to date.

The first release was the wittily-titled 'Use Your Loaf', which drew upon Lloyd's short-lived time spent working in a bakery – it turns out he only did it for the dough. This was quickly followed by 'Paraffin Brain, a far more frenetic song coupled with 'Elvis – The Last Ten Days', a vivid reimagining of the final days of the King of Rock 'n' Roll told through 'recently unreleased diary entries'. 'Day Four: I can see the humour in being a law unto myself' runs one line, as much about Lloyd as it is about Elvis.

The Cherry Red deal led to the band playing the London circuit more frequently, including the date at the Venue in Victoria when the band shared the bill with the Television Personalities and Alan McGee was present. It was after this show that McGee, via Rough Trade, contacted the Nightingales to get them to headline the show he put on at the Africa Centre. From that date on, Lloyd remained friends with McGee, often sleeping on the floor of McGee's living room when the band was in town and watching from close distance as McGee went through the motions of realising his Creation dream.

Summer saw the release of The Nightingales '12" EP', four urgent, rambunctious numbers lifted from a Peel session which duelled on the band's twin-guitar sound whilst simultaneously leaving space for Lloyd's wryness and wit to take full effect. As usual, biting the hand that fed was too tempting for Lloyd, who delivered up one of his best lyrics ever in 'My Brilliant Career':

> I've always hated teachers' pets
> I don't think dogs should be made to smoke cigarettes
> I don't want to hear 'The Ballad of Mott the Hoople'
> Half-wit tunes to amuse the lesser people

By now Lloyd was still barely into his 20s, yet commanded the formidable respect of the veteran. For both John Robb and Alan McGee he was a hero, and even John Peel rang him up when the

Nightingales appeared on the front cover of *Sounds*, saying it was like seeing his son on the cover. An hour later, John Robb rang to say it was like seeing his *Dad* on the cover.

The two releases that saw out 1982 are quintessential. The clattering but controlled racket of 'Urban Osprey', with the trademark counterpointing guitar, hammering drums, colliding riffs and an almost tinnitus-inducing squall as it nears its end, is the Nightingales at the very top of their game, a precursor to the kind of music John Robb's Membranes would look to make when they went into the studio to record 'Spike Milligan's Tape Recorder'. 'Cakehole', the B-side is every bit the equal of 'Urban Osprey' and an uncompromising slab of non-pop. If the city as raptor was the metaphor on the A-side, then 'Cakehole' returns to the otiose, reflective and somewhat downbeat territory of its composer, the song's narrator recognising that it is '…merely inevitable/ That I've reached the final stop/ The bus of life ran out of fuel.'

Just as was the case with the Three Johns, the combination of uncompromising sounds delivered with a deft (and sometimes daft) humour created problems for the critics. The Fall were, quite rightly one yardstick by which all this kind of awkward music was measured, and the Nightingales were routinely referred to as 'Birmingham's answer to the Fall'. But, as with the music of the Three Johns and the Membranes, the comparison told only one part of the story, with the turf each band was treading significantly their own, largely reflecting the very different environments each sprang from. If Blackpool does run through the early work of the Membranes like lettering through a stick of seaside rock, then so too the thinly-distilled black humour of the Midlands, laced with a dash of *weltschmerz*, courses through the veins of the Nightingales. There is a touch of the David Lynch about Lloyd, as well, with his ability to take the commonplace and twist and weave it into something three-parts wry and one-part sinister, something not lost on the 'social surrealist' bands like Bog-shed that followed on after.

1982 ended up being a good year for the Nightingales, and its crowning glory was *Pigs On Purpose*, one of *the* albums of the year and a challenging and impressive piece of work from a band of self-appointed underdogs. The classic, early-80s pop feel of Richard Strange's production is, of course, only knocked slightly off kilter for the unsuspecting listener by the absurd and wry nature of the tales recounted. The crossword-puzzle lyrics fire off at all sorts of tangents – championing social justice, detailing the travails of alcoholic dereliction, calling for cheaper bus fares at one point, to name but just a few subjects dealt with.

'My obsession is with people, the kind of methods they use to stumble through life with,' Lloyd told Dave McCullough for the *Sounds* cover story around the time of the album's release. For McCullough, *Pigs On Purpose* was *the* album of the year, a sort of fidgety homage to the people in all their peculiarity that never the less still struck a chord for those who had come through punk. He compared it favourably to Buzzcocks ('Spiral Scratch to the nth degree'), as well as finding in its hidden recesses shades of Stanley Unwin, James Joyce, Rousseau and Chekhov, all of which Lloyd allowed to go above, or possibly below, him.

At the end of 1982, Lloyd's band again teamed up with McGee to play the Communication Club. The influence the band had on those indie groups that followed had been spelt out in Dave McCullough's *Sounds* piece, where The Nightingales were astutely singled out as a band representing 'a midpoint through the mess of rock currently'.

1983 brought a move to the Ink record label set up by Dave Kitson at Red Flame. The resultant album *Hysterics* and the single, 'Crafty Fag', were both the usual artful creations, hinting not least in the single at the urban folk/ C&W direction that the band was starting to take and which would culminate in 1986's *In The Good Old Country Way*. Prior to the Ink releases, guitarist Nick Beales left to start up Pigbros and was replaced by Peter Byrchmore.

Following the Nightingales appearance at the Living Room, Alan McGee invited Lloyd to join the Creation label, but Lloyd declined – one of the 'many misjudgements made over the years' he now says. Instead, Lloyd rekindled the Vindaloo label and went on to enjoy a moment of success unlike any that could previously have been imagined as Ted Chippington and We've Got A Fuzzbox gate crashed the mainstream charts during the middle of 1986. Then, as now, the Nightingales remain, Lloyd 'stumbling through life' and trying to make sense of it for us – a welcome thorn in the side, awkward and uncompromising but ultimately inspiring.

CHAPTER 8

'THE NEXT PROJECTED SOUND OF 1984'

'MOST PEOPLE SPENT 1983 WAITING for 1984 to happen,' Pete Shelley told the *NME*, wittily contributing one of the more memorable lines to its end of year issue. He was, of course, obliquely referring to George Orwell's novel *1984*, and the ominous spell the book cast since first being published in 1949. For some, the dystopian masterpiece wasn't just a work of fiction, but also a guide to the kind of authoritarian state that would click in to place once the magical date arrived. In fact, the old year turned into the new without incident. By the spring, however, a living hell most couldn't possibly have predicted had broken out as the miners went on strike and whole communities were suddenly thrust into 'civil war without guns'.

Alan McGee observed all of this, but at the start of 1984 had other concerns, having made the decision to launch the Creation Records label properly on the back of the success of the Living Room club. He'd put the disappointment of ''73 In 83' behind him, was inundated with new bands seeking him out for a spot on the bill at his club and was now feeling confident enough, and possibly even experienced enough, to make a proper go of things. Like Pete Shelley, he *too* was getting a mention in the *NME*, albeit tucked away in the more modest record news section which announced in December that five Creation Artifact records would be appearing in January 1984: 'The Flowers Are In The Sky' (sic) by Revolving Paint Dream, 'The Orchard' by Primal Scream, '50 Years of Fun' by Biff Bang Pow!, 'Blue Bus' by the Pastels and 'Think!' by the Jasmine Minks. 'Aspiring acts' were invited to send tapes to the label via Rough Trade. A previous ad had sought 'pop groups with fantastic songs and a hatred for the current pop scene'.

That it was possible to properly launch the label – and with a group of singles released more or less simultaneously – was thanks largely to the money generated by the Living Room, which was more popular than ever in January 1984. It was entering a new phase, as well. The Living Room of the autumn had largely relied on old friends, contacts that McGee had essentially had since the start of 1982 or even earlier. Some of these mates who played in bands had appeared and reappeared at the club in a very short space of time. New and outsider blood was required, and found. On 7 January, the June Brides, an up and coming group from South London, appeared on the bill for the very first time, along with the X Men, and the Surfadelics, setting the tone for future nights at the club that would look beyond the inner circle for bands.

The bill for that first Saturday night in 1984 reflected the broader church of indie and McGee's willingness to give anything worthwhile a go. The X Men played garage punk, '60s beat, psychedelia and old school rock 'n' roll, and the Surfadelics were one of a clutch of new UK bands that, somewhat improbably, made surf music. The June Brides were recognisably post-punk, playing music that took a lead from some of the early Postcard bands like the Go-Betweens but was sufficiently different through the introduction of viola and trumpet. Early critics struggled to define their sound, comparing the band to the Cocteau Twins, the B52s and the Cramps.

By the start of 1984, the Living Room and Alan McGee were becoming of interest to the mainstream music press: the number of journalists turning up at the club had steadily increased all through the autumn and into the spring. So too had the number of customers. On the 4 February 1984 a short article about the club appeared in the *NME*, written by Bruce Dessau. Towards the end of 1983, Dessau had 'wandered into the Adams Arms by accident', looking for some entertainment having been out of the country for a few months. Inspired by what he witnessed (ATV were playing), he wrote an impromptu review of the night and took it into the *NME*'s offices, naively expecting that the review would appear in the following week's paper. The *NME* didn't use the review but invited Dessau's to write something about the club itself, which he duly did.

Noting that the 'informal club' had been running for six months and possessed 'neither the fashionable pretensions of the Batcave nor a stage', the Living Room was, according to Dessau, 'just the tip of a subcultural iceberg'. Dessau had taken McGee to a local pub and then sat back as McGee did what he was best at – namely, enthusiastically reeling of a list of exciting things that he was confident would come to pass. McGee elaborated further on his hopes in an interview a few months later with *Slow Dazzle* fanzine, explaining that Creation was 'more than just a record label... in about two year's time we'll own rehearsal studios, (recording) studios, clothes shops, bookshops...'

Dessau's article was carried in the *NME*'s somewhat quaint 'Clubs' section (with a logo that was an Ace of Clubs playing card) where emerging venues like Bradford's 1-in-12 club and Ziggys, the Plymouth club co-set up by Jeff Barrett, were also written about. It was a section that attracted interest from gig-going readers and Dessau's article had the effect of introducing McGee and his club to a far wider audience than the converted few. The article reiterated the forthcoming Creation releases. As it turned out, the proposed Primal Scream single (recorded with a female lead vocal) was deemed unworthy for release, the master tapes allegedly burned by the band. At the same time, the Pastels declined to release 'Blue Bus', preferring instead 'Something's Going On'. In the end, just the four singles were released.

McGee's restless ambitions – for himself, the club and the artists on the label – constantly demanded further outlet and one opportunity that presented itself just at the moment that the label got going was irresistible. Paul Weller was actively seeking song-writing talent to help drive the artists he had signed to his record label, Respond. The frisson the Living Room was creating, and McGee's avowed love of 1965-7 and 1977-8 – 'the only two periods that have meant anything to me in recent years' – was surely enough to catch Weller's attention if it could be steered in the right direction.

'Alan wasn't one to miss an opportunity and sent off the Revolving Paint Dream and the Biff Bang Pow! records to Weller,' recalls Geoff Stoddart. 'Both Alan and Andrew had always been big fans of the Jam and they used to even write to Paul Weller but would never admit to having done so. Alan would occasionally say to me, "Don't tell Andrew, but I've been writing to him". I seem to remember that Weller was less keen on the Revolving Paint Dream single, which he thought was just *too* psychedelic sounding, but he quite liked '50 Years Of Fun' and was interested in Alan as a songwriter. Alan was very excited for a while, thinking he was going to be writing songs for Paul Weller, but then he heard Tracie, the artist Paul Weller had in mind for Alan's songs, and went quite cold on the idea.'

Weller had 'discovered' Tracie through an advert he'd placed in *Smash Hits* looking for young, female vocalists and, according to Bruce Dessau, did, in fact, consider '50 Years Of Fun' as a song for her, 'but wanted to change the subject matter from the banality of working in a factory to standard boy/ girl love song lyrics'. Given that the song's subject matter catalogues the miseries of working for British Rail, where the only thing to look forward to is a gold watch at the end of it, the mind positively boggles at the notion of the seventeen-year-old from Derby – who at that age could scarcely have worked a day in her life – getting to grips with the song.

Its downbeat subject aside, the first Biff Bang Pow! single is sparkling and uplifting – the sound of punchy pop with just the right amount of jangle and an assured but not overstated vocal from McGee. It is summery and confident, hinting at both the optimism surrounding the Creation camp at the time and the pop sensibility that would serve McGee well in the future. In contrast,

Revolving Paint Dream is self-consciously *outré*, the very name of the band conjuring up the liquid light and smoke fug of the psychedelic sixties it so obviously draws upon. 'Flowers In The Rain' takes a jumble of psychedelic influence and piles it into the pop-sike tumble dryer, but the outcome is as ephemeral as a dandelion floret, beautiful but insubstantial. The B-side, written by McGee, was a different matter, a song that really did catch a mood, conjuring up lazy afternoons lying by the riverbank looking up at the marmalade skies.

> I never asked you for your dream
> Sometimes feelings go beyond words
> And now I cling to tender moments
> And I don't feel real at all
> In the afternoon

Christine Wanless' dreamy, Nico-esque vocal recounts. 'In The Afternoon' has had a hold on the Creation faithful ever since its release, many recognising in it the state of grace that has come to symbolise what Revolving Paint Dream was supposedly all about. The name of the band had been in circulation well before the band itself (Innes and girlfriend Wanless, assisted by Ken Popple) came into existence – it was almost as if it represented some sort of idealised state, a nirvana for early Creation to seek to achieve.

'Andrew rehearsed the whole thing when it came to recording the single,' remembers Joe Foster. 'He had a tape recorder that didn't quite work properly and he wanted to make use of it to create some totally weird sounds. So we sat down and figured out how to do it, using it as an effects box and putting all the instruments and vocals through it to create these odd-sounding songs…'

Revolving Paint Dream became a shape-shifting entity, a thing forever suggested but never properly fulfilled. Members flitted in and out, and Innes reworked material, including a later, trippy version of 'Flowers In the Sky'. A follow up single to 'Flowers In The Sky', planned for September ('Sunny Days'/ 'Wheels On My Scooter'), was never formally released, but did later appear on the 1985 Rouska cassette compilation, *A Tribute To Tricky Ricky*. The same tracks were then re-recorded and released in early 1986 as JC Brouchard feat Biff Bang Pow!, 'Wheels On My Scooter' now called 'Someone Stole My Wheels', illustrating, as had been the case from its start, that Revolving Paint Dream was amorphous.

There was, however, nothing amorphous about the Jasmine Minks, who sprang from the traps with a confidence and assuredness that was striking. The band had arrived in London in 1980 – at which point they comprised of Adam Sanderson on vocals and guitar, Jim Shepherd on guitar and vocal, and Tom Reid on drums – with no plans and even less money. They squatted in various locations (including occupying a building belonging to the Queen Mother), before ending up in a squat in Stockwell, a stone's throw from the squat McGee and Innes and Popple at one time shared. The band took their name from the Scottish slang term used to denote a gentleman of the road or tramp ('a mink') and hailed from Aberdeen, a city that ever since the discovery of North Sea oil had been nicknamed the 'Energy Capital of Britain'. Some of that energy must have rubbed off on them. Pete Astor, wearing his journalist hat, reviewed them at the Living Room in early February, just before the band's first record release on Valentines Day, and noticed their 'tangible reality' (in contrast to the main act In Easterhouse, who he thought were like 'the wallpaper holding up the wall'). He likened them to 'the Byrds crossed with Fire Engines' and praised their 'edginess and nervous energy'.

The Jasmine Minks had started out at the time of punk, and were originally called Bondage before switching to the more appropriate name of Absit Omen when post punk arrived. Whilst squatting in

Camden, they had run into people involved in the Polytantric Circle, the group that helped organise the yearly solstice celebrations at Stonehenge. The group was helping to convert an old Ladbroke Grove cinema into a music venue and in exchange for work done – which involved everything from mixing cement to sewing curtains – the Jasmine Minks were allowed to practise at the venue (booted out occasionally when more established bands like Motorhead and Siouxsie & The Banshees wanted to rehearse there).

'The Polytrantric Circle connection led to our first London gig,' recalls Adam Sanderson, 'which was the "Smoky Bears Free Herb Picnic" in Hyde Park in 1981. We weren't the Jasmine Minks by that point and used the name Passengers. We played first on the bill, supporting, among others, Nik Turner's Inner City Unit. At some point, the gig was invaded by the police, including the SPG, and the truncheons came out very quickly. I escaped by jumping into an MG Midget being driven very erratically by the 1960s underground poet Kristof Jastrzebski-Glinka who pushed a lump of hash the size of a tangerine into my hand and said, "If the pigs catch us, swallow this".'

Two years later, McGee's beady eye fell across the name of the band in the 'Playback' column of *Melody Maker* that reviewed demo tapes sent in by unknown bands. That week's reviewer, Ian Pye, had written a favourable review of the Aberdeen band, lazily referencing the Velvet Underground, Postcard Records, and also the Laughing Apple. No wonder McGee was intrigued. McGee contacted them and they sent him a tape and invited him along to watch them rehearse at Alaska studios underneath the arches of Waterloo Station.

Pete Astor's review had mentioned the Byrds, but New York's Television was the comparison that most sprang to mind. The Jasmine Minks' repertoire at that time consisted of fairly lengthy numbers that echoed the sophisticated, clean and improvisational guitar work of the New York punks. McGee was less impressed with the longer numbers, some of which went on for six minutes or more, preferring instead the few shorter songs the band had written. He picked out 'Think!' as a potential single, something he saw as fitting perfectly into his notion of the three-minute pop classic. Laying the groundwork for the release, he then raved about the band in the second issue of *Communication Blur*, describing them as 'a pop gun buzz' and summing up for the uninitiated reader how they sounded, which was, he said, 'like a cross between Television and Orange Juice'.

McGee gave the Jasmine Minks £50 (a sum they considered a small fortune at the time) to go off and properly record the single. At Alaska, he introduced them to Joe Foster, who was to produce, and also to Dave Musker, whose brilliant keyboard work enhanced the song (as it did so many early Creation releases). 'Alan supplied a small brown plastic electronic organ that he swore was the same one that had previously been used on Orange Juice's "Blue Boy",' recalls Sanderson. 'Prior to recording, I had been listening to Buzzcocks "Spiral Scratch" EP and repeated the two-note refrain from "Boredom" at the end of "Think!". Later, Edwyn Collins of Orange Juice was to reference "Boredom" and repeat the same two-note refrain on the single "Rip It Up". It's a small world.'

'Think!' moves along with all of the pill-popping speed and edginess of a classic Mod song – a well-crafted melody, intersected by chopping guitars, is overlain with a vocal that rises in intensity until the jolting finale, when the title is barked out almost as an imprecation. Two years or so earlier, the same kind of sound was, at least in the case of the Jam, making it all the way into the national charts. On that basis, it seemed to be a logical choice.

In the work of the Jasmine Minks, McGee detected, or thought he could detect, that rare combination – the potential for both pop credibility *and* commercial success. The Jam at the start of 1984 still represented the most obvious example of how that rare elixir manifested itself. Like the Jam, the Jasmine Minks were gritty, partly due to a background spent growing up on council estates in the blue-collar environment of Aberdeen, which had another nickname, 'the Grey City'. McGee, the would-be taxi driver from Glasgow, understood where they were coming from and dubbed them 'my working class heroes'.

'Think!' did exactly what it said on the tin. Its cover – red and black typography on thin white stock – was as dramatically exclamatory as the single's final imploring holler, visually mirroring the positivity of the label and reflecting the boldness of its design approach. As with the bright simplicity of the cover for ''73 In '83', the oil-wheel splash of the artwork for '50 Years Of Fun', or the multiple-frame imagery of the Pastels single, 'Something's Going On', which playfully conjured up associations with the screen-pulled artwork of early-1960s' Andy Warhol, it was tactile and inviting.

'GET READY COS HERE I COME', read the copy on the back cover of Biff Bang Pow!'s '50 Years Of Fun', words lifted from a lyric by the Temptations. This was doubtless intended at the time as a bit of fun. But it doubled up nicely as a statement of intent on the part of McGee, one straight out the Andrew Loog Oldham school of personal promotion. Be in no doubt that McGee was on his way, it said, or that Creation would be 'THE NEXT PROJECTED SOUND OF 1984'.

On 10 February 1984, the Living Room opened for business, as usual. Only two acts were lined up to play that Friday night – the first, Rebel Yell was a punk/ rockabilly act whose one and only recorded track, 'The Angel In My Arms', would find its way a on to a compilation album, *What A Nice Way To Turn Seventeen, Volume 3*. The headline band was the Television Personalities, who were making their fifth appearance at the club. The Television Personalities were one of the Living Room's main draws and the club filled up quickly, the queue to enter stretching back down to the public bar. The surge in numbers had been due partly to Bruce Dessau's *NME* article, which had appeared the week before.

The band performed most of their set before arriving at 'Three Wishes', which Dan Treacy introduced with the sarcastic words: 'This is our last number one single.' The band was barely a couple of minutes into the song, however, before they were forced to stop, and an announcement made from the stage informing the crowd that a police raid had taken place and that the club was being closed down due to the contravening of fire regulations. 'I can't see any fire,' announced one wag over the PA, and Paul Groovy, who was there on the night, doesn't recall seeing any police either. 'They may have been there,' he says. 'But it is a good story, no matter, and it is somehow fitting that the Television Personalities should have been the last band to play the Living Room, having been the inspiration for the whole scene, anyway.'

The Living Room was down, but not out, and in March, McGee was back promoting it, briefly at the Union Tavern in Kings Cross (where the Television Personalities appeared), then at the Oxford Arms in Camden, before settling down to a residency at the Roebuck pub in Tottenham Court Road. Sporadic gigs were put on elsewhere, as well, such as at the Three Johns pub in Islington (which set up the tantalising prospect of the band the Three Johns playing in a pub sharing their name – sadly, it never happened.) But in truth, once the Living Room departed the Adams Arms, the magic disappeared: the intimacy and the atmosphere could never be recreated in quite the same way.

It had indeed been fitting that the Television Personalities should have been the last band to play the Living Room at the Adams Arms. After all, Treacy's creatively playful approach involving performances that incorporated action painting, film

projections and poetry mixed in with live music had been an inspiration for many bands that followed. One such was the Pastels.
In May 1983 they staged a 'SPONTANEOUS HAPPENING
of sorts', at the Venue in Edinburgh, handing out 'Lucky Bags'
to those members of the audience that had arrived early. The
flyer for the event promised 'loads of great noises from today's
pop stars', and listed the Pastels and Jill and Rose (Strawberry
Switchblade) as appearing. It also promised – 'well, maybe' – the
Television Personalities, April Showers, Jowe Head, Scattered
Cushions 'and anything you can do!', before adding: 'IT'S ART,
IT'S FUN, IT'S A JELLY TOT!'

The non-Scottish contingent failed to show, but Paul Groovy
made the long journey from Portsmouth and handed out copies
of his fanzine *Groovy Black Shades*, while on stage the Pastels played
as somebody daubed the words 'BYHOCKNEY' on a hanging
backdrop. This was the first time that the band and Paul Groovy
had met and Stephen Pastel promised to mention Paul and his
fanzine to Alan McGee who he was sure would like it. McGee had
been a fan the Pastels ever since hearing one of the tracks from
'Songs For Children' played on the Brian Ford show on Radio
Clyde. On the rare occasions that the Pastels played London,
McGee would stand down the front near the stage shouting out
comments like 'Pop genius!' as the band performed. Even before
releasing anything on the label, McGee had released a version of
their song 'I Wonder Why' on the flexi disc that came free with
the first issue of *Communication Blur*.

The Pastels were a tenuous link between the new music that
was coming along (of which they were part) and the music that
had influenced the new music. Guitarist Brian Taylor was still
sharing the flat with Alan Horne of Postcard Records (the 'Postcard flat') when Stephen Pastel began working with him. Stephen
Pastel had an idea for the Pastels while still at school but it wasn't
realised until 1981. 'The band really began when I started to jam

with Brian and we were coming up with our first songs,' remembers Stephen Pastel. 'I was more or less starting from scratch but Brian had a sort of punk-plus proficiency. Even at the beginning, he was quite together as a musician and could bring a sort of structure to what we were trying to do.'

In spite of the Postcard connection, Brian Taylor and Stephen Pastel were keen to create something of their own and not merely imitate the music going on around them. In any event, Brian Taylor – by repute, 'the first punk in Glasgow' and a former member of the near-legendary punk band Oscar Wilde (who used to play a song called 'Wow Wow Wow Wow Dustbin') – had seen it all before and had a healthy suspicion of trends. Stephen Pastel by contrast was completely inexperienced: 'I was kind of gauche, but I still knew that we had to make our own way and that it was going to be possible.'

In 1982, the Pastels released their first single, 'Songs For Children' and also an experimental cassette, 'Entertaining Edward'. A fan of the Television Personalities, Stephen Pastel had written to Dan Treacy and sent him a demo of some songs. Treacy offered to release the material as a single on Whaam! 'That was unbelievably exciting,' recalls Stephen Pastel. 'I remember rehearsing the songs for hours with Robert Hodgens from the Bluebells on bass. But when it came to recording the tracks, Robert wasn't around. Our first studio experience was good, I think, but I didn't have anything to gauge it by.'

In August, coinciding with the release of the single, the Pastels did an interview with the *NME*, Stephen Pastel telling Kirsty McNeil that the Television Personalities and Swell Maps were 'the way punk should have gone' and saying that he wanted the Pastels to 'sound like a '60s group with an element of bubblegum in it'. McNeil applauded the freshness of the Pastels single at the same time as lamenting what had to date, she felt, been a pretty miserable year for pop: '…there's not much happening: what's that stale old smell – Yazoo, *Fame*, 'Freebird', *The Wall*, Visage, Cliff, Madness, Steve Miller, Blondie, Haysi Fantayzee (Jeremiah Pratt should be drowned in hot fat)… Dexys?'

The reviews the Pastels single picked up were generally very good, Mick Sinclair in *Sounds* noting that the self-consciously anti-macho approach of the band did nothing to prevent them from being 'a real gem of a garage band'. 'Heavens Above', one of the single's two tracks, was 'pure joy of amateurish pop perfection, crossing fibres of Jonathan Richman, the Turtles, Buzzcocks and Vic Godard into two minutes and tens seconds of fresh, frail, sing-along naivety'.

Two months after the release of the single, the cassette was released on the Pastels own Action Tapes! label. *Entertaining Edward: An Introduction of Sorts…* gathered together early demos and snippets of live performance (including from the band's first gig in May 1981), and featured the Pastels covering 'Part-Time Punks', the Television Personalities song. The release was intended as an experiment and there was a plan to release more Action Tapes! – it was 'a brand new concept in AURAL EXCITEMENT' – but promised releases by the Television Personalities, Jowe Head and the Paintings never materialised.

'My friend John, who was in the Cheap Gods, was into the cassette scene and it seemed interesting and accessible,' recalls Stephen Pastel. 'We would make a total racket together – he had a synth and I had a guitar and fuzz pedal. With the Pastels it was always more song-based but I thought that we should compile something and see if there was any kind of audience for it. Cassette culture was exciting, a sort of grey area and out of control. There wasn't any kind of rules at all – it accommodated the mass produced and the one-off, compilations (mix tapes), bootlegs and beautifully realised official releases like Marine Girls.'

In the summer of 1983, the Pastels had some more songs that they hoped would make a follow up single. This time they sent a copy of the tape to both Dan Treacy and to Geoff Travis at Rough Trade. An inevitable problem of recording for Whaam! was the fact that Dan Treacy at any given moment always had a lot on his plate: as well as releasing records by others, there was, of course, his own prodigious output to take care of. 'I think Dan had really interesting taste and created a strong visual identity for Whaam! While still in his early 20s Dan was magical, charming, funny. It was frustrating at times because he could be hard to get hold of but with hindsight I think he really achieved a lot. It would have been a perfect scenario if the Whaam! label had been run in conjunction with Rough Trade because that would have given him at least a bit of structure.'

Geoff Travis was very keen on putting out the next record by the Pastels and in October 'I Wonder Why' was released. By this time Martin Hayward had joined on bass and Bernice Simpson was now on drums. The band wanted Mayo Thompson to produce, but he was busy and so engineer Steve Parker stepped in to help out. 'I think the drums were recorded in Glasgow and run through the desk drum by drum,' says Stephen. 'It wasn't subtle and it gave the single a slightly dislocated un-group sound. It really wasn't a brilliant experience. I think we were more basic than Geoff was hoping for and we felt a bit patronised by him and the engineer. It took quite a long time for the single to come out – I know that there was a lack of support from some people at Rough Trade who maybe felt that they'd progressed beyond our kind of amateurism. I have to say there was support too – from Scott Piering and especially Richard Boon. Long after the single had sold out I heard that Richard loved bringing up the idea of a repress at the monthly meetings.'

The *ur*-pop nature of the Pastels created detractors as well as supporters, all the more so in a period where even at an indie level increasing production slickness was considered to be the best way forward by some. The spontaneous happening of sorts at the

Venue, for instance, was reviewed by a couple of music papers that simply missed the point. 'Nursery tunes for the under-fives,' declared the *NME* while *Sounds* compared the band to children 'giggling through guitars and cardigans' as they played their 'puerile, boyish pop songs'. The Pastels deliberately cultivated the childlike. 'A big part of that,' says Stephen, 'was as a reaction to what we considered the po-faced faux-sophistication of rival groups. It was really childish, but it was important to be seen to be really childish.'

There was a possibility that Rough Trade would release an album, but in the end it all came to nothing. The band parted ways with the label, more or less at the same time that Dan Treacy's Television Personalities did. In December, Stephen Pastel wrote to Paul Groovy wondering how both could have been dropped from the label just at the time when, according to Julian Cope's celebrated article about psychedelia in the *NME*, 'the psychedelic dream-like revival' appeared to be back on. In truth, it was no great blow since, as Stephen Pastel told Paul Groovy, the Pastels would be going into the studio just before Christmas to record a single for Creation, something that would hopefully showcase the band's evolved sound which was 'much, much noisier/ more punk live now', with 'ten-minute guitar feedback solos'.

'We felt slightly disillusioned by how the Rough Trade single had come out, like we'd lost control of what we were without finding anything new,' says Stephen. 'We made some demos with Davie Henderson (the Orange Juice engineer, not the Fire Engine) on a 4-track in Glasgow and they were a lot more encouraging, closer in sound to our tastes, and more original too. At this point, Alan McGee was trying to persuade us to cut a single for him and by then we didn't have any other options. "Something's Going On" felt like maybe we were on our way and there wasn't a massive gap between that and some of the next songs, such as "Million Tears" and "Baby Honey", so maybe we were becoming more focussed and finding a more defined Pastels sound. We felt that we were improving and that we'd become more of a group, with Martin and Bernice joining. Maybe we sometimes came across as a bit arrogant, other times not confident at all. It was new for us, we didn't really know exactly where we fitted in and I think it was more that our audience knew where we fitted in for them.'

McGee was very taken with the Pastels, and in particular with Stephen Pastel who appealed to him through both Stephen Pastel's obvious love and knowledge of great music and his obsession, shared by McGee, with Dan Treacy and the Television Personalities. And in fact, 'Something's Going On' was a major step forward, a closing up of a gap between the band's more deliberately childlike aesthetic and the noisier element of a sound that lurked beneath. Edwin Pouncey made it Single of the Week in *Sounds* saying that the band shimmied like the new Velvets and looked like the new Love. The Jasmine Minks' single also made Single of the Week in the same paper and together they were the two most well received of the four Creation singles issued. Even if collectively the releases didn't quite live up to the boast of being 'the next projected sound of 1984', it was a solid start and massive improvement on the reaction the summer before to the label's inaugural single.

The next batch of Creation releases followed in the early summer, beginning with a single by the X Men, 'Do The Ghost'. The record was a departure for Creation, a million miles away from the punk rock psychedelia it appeared to be building its reputation on. The X Men were unusual within their trash/rockabilly band milieu in that they were more influenced by the 1960s than the 1950s and took much of their inspiration from the garage punk of the later period. A typical X Men gig would involve covers of classic '60s sounds, such as Paul Revere & The Raiders 'Stepping Stone' and the Who's 'My Generation', along with a number of self-penned originals, usually about ghosts or girls. 'Do The Ghost' was a frenetic, Cramps-esque mock-dance thrash that borrowed from the famous garage band classic by the Novas, 'The Crusher', yet retained a contemporary freshness.

Signing the X Men may well have been speculative on McGee's part – the market for the right kind of rockabilly/ garage single was very solid – but he had to fight to secure a deal with the band, having seen them play at the Klub Foot in Hammersmith where, in typical fashion, he immediately offered to make a single with them. 'There were several A&R men sniffing around and Alan pushed his way to the front, very determined to sign us to his new label and suggesting lunch at a pub near Liverpool Street Station,' the band's Miles Aldridge later recalled. 'Alan turned up in his British Rail uniform, complete with a lantern which he placed on the table next to his pint, and we signed and recorded "Do The Ghost" and "Talk" at Alaska Studios the following week.' McGee's faith in the band proved justified, and the single had to be quickly repressed. It remained the best-selling Creation single for most of 1984.

Normal service was resumed with 'There Must Be A Better Life', the second Biff Bang Pow! single, which was also a summer release. With its swirling organ part (another Dave Musker classic), blocked/ rushed beat and uplifting vocal its sound was even sunnier and more vibrant than '50 Years Of Fun', with lyrics dealing with one of youth's eternal verities rather than the mundaneness of working in a factory. Reviewing the single for *Sounds*, the ever-observant Jack Barron was carried away by its 'out of phase Rickenbackers and Mr Softee organ lines. Like licking peppermint ice cream tainted with microdots. "Life" makes you think about the future as today dissolves into Carnaby Street and '68.' Creation, he noted, was 'a company to keep a dilated pupil on.'

'Biff Bang Pow! Really only came together when I had learnt how to write songs,' says McGee. 'In the Laughing Apple Andrew generally wrote the songs – it was his band. But I gradually worked out how to write a song and formed Biff Bang Pow! at the point when I thought I had a batch of material that was good enough. I'd also started to find my voice and could even sing in tune. Joe Foster really sorted it all out, because he wasn't just a capable producer but also a brilliant musician. In time, Joe got busy and Biff Bang Pow! became more me and Dick at the helm…'

There was a second single, as well, released by the Jasmine Minks, the band that McGee believed possessed, above all others, the most potential for commercial success. McGee's marketing skills had gone into overdrive about the band even before they'd released their first single – he'd not just written about them enthusiastically in *Communication Blur* but also got them to come up with a promotional booklet, with pictures, random text and snippets of lyrics.

'The booklet was just to introduce ourselves,' says Adam Sanderson. 'We gave it a pink cover to be un-macho, anti-cockrock and also because we played pink guitars at the time. I handwrote most of it because Letraset was expensive and laborious. It featured the Gladdog, our symbol at the time, a large blue drunken dog that we painted onto a backdrop and used at our early gigs.'

For the release of 'Where The Traffic Goes', McGee came up with another marketing wheeze, arranging a busking tour across London in July. A press release went out detailing the various stop off points ('Carnaby Street, 11.00am… Camden Lock 1.00pm… Covent Garden 5.00pm' etc…). The band played a set at the Rough Trade shop in west London, miming to their single like a post-punk version of the Monkees.

The publicity paid off and not long after the Jasmine Minks single was released they were awarded a full-page interview in *Sounds*, the most substantial press either they or the label had so far received. Noting the record's 'devilishly intersecting melodies, shimmering tambourines and head-on collision between fast-lane guitars and Jim's freewheeling vocals', Jane Simon placed the band firmly in the camp of classic pop. Pop impresario (and manager of Wham!) Simon Napier-Bell had apparently sought them out (but found their music 'too intellectual'). 'The Simon Napier-Bell thing was very odd,' recalls Sanderson. 'He turned up at the Living Room in a huge car, a Rolls Royce or possibly a Bentley that was gold coloured and had cream leather interiors. None of us could drive at that time, never mind owned a car. We knew he had worked with Burt Bacharach and managed the Yardbirds, so we gave him our kudos, but, to cut a long story short, Jasmine Minks were not what he was looking for.'

Alas, sales-wise, 'Where The Traffic Goes' followed the same trajectory of most of the previous Creation releases which all struggled to break the thousand mark. McGee soon realised that the only way to make the label work commercially was by releasing albums. None of the acts, however, had anywhere near enough material for a full album. The Jasmine Minks would be the first band on the label to make an album, but in the summer of 1984 even they were not quite ready.

The solution to the problem that presented itself was, at least on paper, ingenious. The Living Room had been closed down in February (although it limped on in name elsewhere until an *official* final night when the Mekons played the Roebuck pub in Tottenham Court Road in September). What better way to commemorate it than by releasing a compilation album of live material by bands that had played there?

Given the quality of the available recorded material, some of which was captured using handheld tape recorders, *Alive In The Living Room* was never going to be up there in the pantheon of great live albums. None of the raw material passed through the soothing conduit of a recording studio before making it onto vinyl. But nonetheless it serves as an important document of sorts, capturing a flavour of the nights at the Adams Arms, as much through the background ambience and between-song banter as through the raw music itself. It also illustrates the diversity of bands that appeared there – with tracks from more established bands such as ATV, the Three Johns and the Nightingales presented alongside newer bands such as the June Brides, the Jasmine Minks and the Loft.

Alan McGee's sleeve notes reprise the tone of *Communication Blur* but as epitaph do go some way to truthfully setting out the significance of the club: 'From that first sweaty night with the Nightingales until the police raid at the Television Personalities gig in February, the Living Room stood for something, most importantly something different to each individual. To this lost soul, the Living Room meant a place I could go… Nothing to do with Trends, Fashions, Haircuts or Clothes… Nothing to do with any Cult or Fashion… If you are the type of person that needs deep meanings then ponder this one… The Living Room meant more in its WC1 residency than Bono Vox, Ian McCulloch, Jim Kerr, Kirk Brandon, Ian Page or Jimmy Pursey ever will…'

The first Creation album confused the reviewers, rather as the first Creation single had. Many couldn't fathom out how on earth anyone had thought the quality of the recordings good enough to professionally release. For the few who had attended the club, its amateurishness was just about forgivable. Most, however, agreed with the journalist from *Sounds* who – referring to the police raid which could be heard on the Television Personalities track on side two and alluding to the record's overall production quality – wrote, 'For once, I'm on the side of the law.'

CHAPTER 9

'ATTITUDE HOSTILE'

REMEMBER

SWITCH ON AT SIX

Using major electric appliances — irons, heaters, stoves, toasters, electric kettles, etc. — forces the electricity board to employ more coal fired power stations, and thereby eats up stocks.

If you want to help the strike, switch on at *6 p.m. each day* so that a peak usage time is created, forcing those stations to come into operation now.

If possible try to keep the appliances on till 6.30 p.m., but the important point to remember is the switch on each day at six. Pass this message to six sympathetic friends.

BY SPRING 1984 ANARCHO PUNK had all but splintered off from the main indie caucus and the music papers weren't automatically running news stories ever time one of the bands involved either got in a mess with the authorities or did something controversial or worthy. The long journey, and not just for anarchist punk, was beginning to the point of today where music is appropriately self-contained in easily marketable and mutually exclusive genres. More flare-ups would follow, but two events in 1984 in particular marked the last great occasions when the anarchist voice wasn't marginalised – the Stop The City protests and the miners' strike.

The miners' strike began nationally on 12 March 1984 and lasted almost a year to the day. At first, many overlooked its significance, assuming it would be the usual short-lived conflict in keeping with strike patterns of the time. It took a while to recognise that what was taking place was something different, a drawn-out, full-scale ideological battle between two iron wills, one a Marxist revolutionary, the other, a raging high priestess of the free market economy. Jerry Dammers' contemporary quip in the *NME* that in 1984 there was 'Shit music in the charts and a miners' strike. It must be 1974' was light-heartedly taken in the vein it was intended.

Dammers' dry comment unintentionally echoed the state-of-the-nation concerns about indie that had been raised by Fletcher, Mercer, North and others but the joke hits its mark mainly in caricaturing the blasé attitude to what was perceived to be a commonplace. It wasn't truly until the summer that bands began gigging in earnest for the miners. Even Billy Bragg, whose passion, intelligence and finely attuned sense of politics had already been brought to bear in support of the GLC, only did his first miners benefit gig in September. From then on, typically, he threw his considerable and energetic support fully into the cause in a unique way: all the equipment Bragg needed to perform fitted into a legendary bashed-up Volvo estate and, as he later noted, 'what I could do that others couldn't do was go and play outside London cheaply and effectively'.

Six months or so prior to the start of the strike, one of the last great counter cultural demonstrations had taken place when on 29 September 1983, there was an attempt to Stop The City. There was no organised route or prepared plan and the day, as well as signalling disapproval of the activities of those in 'the Square Mile', was intended to be peaceful and fun, a 'Carnival Against War, Oppression and Destruction'. It was timed to coincide with the day the City's quarterly stock market results were announced. People were invited to descend on the city and then make their feelings known however they saw fit.

Central to the planning of the day's events was London Greenpeace, an anarchist environmentalist collective unaligned to the more recognised nationwide Greenpeace organisation. The national Greenpeace organisation made it clear early on that it wanted nothing to do with the demonstration. Those involved and active in London Greenpeace included Dave Morris, one of the two people sued in the 'McLibel case' (the other was Helen Steel) for publishing a pamphlet critical of McDonalds. But others were also instrumental. In July 1983 an advert had appeared in an anarchist newspaper announcing a proposed event, and in the first week of September a further advert invited people to a meeting at the Conway Hall in Holborn to form an organising committee to help plan the day.

One of those who saw the adverts and was drawn to the meeting was 'Ron', a former student at the London School of Economics who by his early 20s was a veteran of numerous protests. (Ron's voice, under its true identity, features in this book elsewhere, as a member of one of the prominent independent bands included.) 'There were,' Ron recalls, 'around 30-35 people who showed up for the meeting, and an organising committee was formed. The committee was a small group and those on it took on different roles and responsibilities. There were then further planning meetings held at the Peace Centre in Roseberry Avenue, Islington. The general aim was to disrupt the city and thus get publicity for the wrongs that we saw as going on there. At the time, it wasn't just financial institutions who operated from the city – arms dealers did as well, along with fur and diamond traders, and those with interests that relied on repression to function.'

Planning for the day had been above board and open and, as has been noted, as early as summer warning of the event had been served. In 16 July issue of the anarchist paper *Freedom* the nonviolent aims of the organisers had also been underlined: 'The action is intended to be peaceful, not involving violence to people or other animals.' In the event, the day drew from broad channels of dissent, involving CND supporters, libertarians, anarchists, anti-vivisectionists, various feminist groups, anarcho punks, as well as many involved in squatting and claimant movements.

As part of the preparation, on Sunday, 11 September, Ron went to watch the Damned play at the Hammersmith Palais, taking along a batch of the 5000 Stop The City leaflets that had been printed up and handing them out at the gig. The band helpfully made an announcement on stage endorsing and supporting the proposed event. The next week was spent handing out leaflets at other gigs and contacting people to try to get them to similarly participate. At a Poison Girls gig on 19 September, Ron handed out more leaflets, though was ticked off by the venue's bouncer who informed him that he 'approved of war'.

At this time, a reccy was made of the square mile of the City, to ascertain which buildings might be entered on the day itself. Part of the aim was to talk to workers, to get them to understand the reasons for the action and hopefully gain their sympathy. Ron had also taken on the responsibility for organising a 'slow bike ride' on the day that would do a circuit around the Stock Exchange, the

Royal Exchange and the Bank of England. Given the narrowness of the streets in the area, a small number of cyclists would be able to cause a significant amount of congestion. He would also use the bike to move between areas giving people support as and when needed and generally help boost morale.

The plan had been to set up a help point in Finsbury Circus, the largest open space within the City's boundaries, but, in an act that wouldn't have been out of place in medieval times, this was forbidden and the organisers were forced to offer such support as might be needed 'outside the city walls' in Islington. Ron and those involved 'arranged legal back-up and printed up guide notes which we handed out that told people what they should do if they got into trouble with the authorities.'

On one of the leaflets prepared in advance invited people to join the slow cycle ride (in the end, about 30 or 40 did so) and had Ron's contact phone number printed on it. He was surprised to receive a call from a senior-ranking officer in the City Police force. Could Ron give assurances that the demonstration would be a peaceful one? He could not: by very definition anarchy existed without controlling interests. The officer then suggested joining Ron for a meeting, adding, bizarrely, that if it helped he could bring along his teenage daughter.

On the day, the instructions to those attending were simple – turn up any time between 6am and 6pm and run your day as you see fit. According to Ron's diary estimate, around 800 did so, including many from Europe, the Italian anarchist core being particularly welcomed on account of the rare import records they brought to sell to help fund their trip. People arrived and spontaneously made their protest. It was a 'joyous and jubilant occasion, with many specially dressed up for the day', and, of course, a scenario almost impossible to police. The city force had absolutely no idea how to deal with such an unstructured and largely peaceful event, or where to direct their limited resources.

The principal objective, as has been stated, was to disrupt business, and that is what happened. By lunchtime, the police had been more or less outmanoeuvred and were angry as a result. Individual incidents, away from the swarming mass, created further havoc: a women's group that had travelled up from the south-west staged a 'die-in' at the Nat West Tower. An anti-apartheid demonstration took place at the headquarters of Barclay's Bank. A number of buildings were entered and objects thrown out of them. But the violence, such as it was, was largely carried out by the frustrated police who vented their anger on those present. Ron's diary for the day records some 203 arrests, based on his own access to a semi-official source of information.

The story made the lunch time edition of the *Evening Standard*, which dramatically splashed the story across its front page, complete with action photograph of a 'besieged' policeman, arms around a protester's throat, dragging the protester across the Royal Exchange. The story was then dropped in later editions, where it was patronisingly dismissed as 'Peace, punks and a little city anarchy'. The organisers of the day heard later that the editor of the paper had been at lunch when the decision to run the initial story was taken. When he found out about it he was furious and wanted the story pulled to avoid making the event seem more important.

Indeed, the establishment press was curiously silent on the day's actions, to such an extent that 20 or so of those involved paid Fleet Street a visit a day or two after. 'We wanted to find out why the papers had failed to cover the story,' says Ron. 'We were shadowed by about 60 police, so we split up and effectively lost most of them. When we arrived at the office of *The Times*, they refused to talk to us, although the *Guardian* and the *Financial Times* did eventually run stories.'

In the end, the day showed the police to be unprepared and even incapable of dealing with such a spontaneous protest. The effect of the day was, according to the newspapers, to write some considerable millions off the profits during 29 September. It also had the effect of causing great resentment towards the police by many who had suffered the police force's over zealous response. These two factors ultimately meant that the next Stop The City event would be a far angrier affair.

The event on 29 March 1984 is the one that most mythologises the whole sequence of STC happenings. The first day had been more in the tradition of peaceful protests going back to the LSD rallies in Hyde Park in the mid-to-late 1960s and the CND marches of the decade before. They too had been a 'carnival' of sorts, pro-pacifist, typified perhaps by Martin Sharp's psychedelic poster for the 1967 Cannabis rally that drew together a 'Gathering Of The Heads'. But as one protester had it, 'It's banks what fund war, not parks' and March 1984 was very different.

For one thing, Stop The City, whether by accident or design, got more organised. Some anarchist bands such as the Poison Girls and Crass and their thousands of followers had largely kept away the first time around: when Ron had approached Vi Subversa, she had given the blessing of the Poison Girls but, according to his diary, was 'not sure how it would affect people in terms of future actions' and was reluctant to be involved. All this changed by March 1984, partly due to the police's response, and the anarchists came out in force. Mick Duffield and Andy Palmer from the Crass camp even shot footage and made a film of the day.

According to those present, the miners' strike also played its part, many venting their frustrations on how the miners were being brutally treated, and the strike regarded in the media, by turning up to protest in the city. When the second day became more violent than the first, it was undoubtedly partly due to a growing belief that only through physical response could the actions of the Establishment be properly met.

Such a direct response played totally into the hands of the militant group Class War that had itself kept away from the events of 29 September. Class War – which had started out life as a paper – was not, however, of the pacifistic nature of the bands such as Crass but willingly interventionist – getting stuck in was the movement's raison d'etre. Founder Ian Bone in his striking autobiography, *Bash The Rich: True Life Confessions of An Anarchist in the UK*, explains that the pacifist approach, epitomised by Crass with their tens of thousands of followers, had, in his opinion, had its day, torn asunder by the events of the inner city riots of 1981. 'How could you tell the rioters of July 1981 to be pacifists? People were fighting back but Crass were still telling them to turn the other cheek.'

Yet Bone observed that not all of those supporting Crass followed the script. At a Crass gig in Burghfield (site of a nuclear weapons plant), the Crass punks were 'stroppy, upfront, rattling the fence, looking [as if] they'd have liked to break through and have a rumble with the dog handlers'. Although Crass had done more to spread the idea of anarchy than even Kropotkin, according to the second issue of *Class War*, by 'Putting the stress on pacifism, they refuse the truth that in the cities, opposition means confrontation and violence if it were to get anywhere'.

The first issue of the big, 'tabloid brash' paper had been published on 29 April 1983. In setting up *Class War*, the simple aim, according to Bone, was to put '(1) Class and (2) Violence back at the top of the anarchist agenda'. Looking like a 'punkoid fanzine mutated into a newspaper', it used a similar skull logo as the Welsh band Soldiers Dolls and part of its masthead borrowed the anarcho-punk circled 'A' (in a nice touch, though, dripping with blood) in a deliberate attempt to attract 'those anarchists who only purchased any commodities with 'A's on'. The target of its venom would be 'rich bastards', CND and the Labour Party.

In time, the tabloid press dubbed Ian Bone 'the most dangerous man in Britain', with 'a face like Himmler… and a heart overflowing with hate'. *Class War* was the complete antithesis of the seemingly pipe-and-slippers approach of old-school anarchist papers such as *Freedom* and *Black Flag*. One of its many provocative slogans (playing off CND) demanded – Angry Brigade-style – 'BOMBS NOT JOBS' and a popular column was called 'Hospitalised Copper' (recounting particularly successful rucks with the boys in blue in prose that, according to Bone, 'managed to marry that difficult trick of combining violence with humour and alliteration' – as in 'PC ARTHUR ARSEHOLE ATTACKED WITH A 'ARF BRICK'). During its heyday, its circulation rose to nearly 15,000 and actions between those peak years of 1983 and 1985 include attacks on CND and various political events and against Biorex (at the time, suppliers of animals to laboratories for testing) in support of the British Union for the Abolition of Vivivsection, as well as straightforward marches on the parishes of the rich. The Rose Ball at the Dorchester – often regarded as the 'first social event of the season' for those who attend – was targeted, as was a similar Hunt Ball, and in May 1985 a 'Bash The Rich' march on Kensington was organised, complete with invitation cards promising 'Attitude Hostile'. The calling-card tactic mimicked that of football hooligans and indeed the intent was to act 'like a football-away crew'. Ironically, an event Class War had no part in – the Broadwater Farm riot in Tottenham where PC Keith Blakelock was savagely murdered – signalled its decline, the public suddenly having less stomach for such an overtly confrontational approach.

On 29 March 1984, however, Class War had barely begun its rise. Witnessing the first Stop The City day Bone thought he detected 'the dying embers of pacifism, non-violent and direct action and the peace camps'. Writing in issue five of *Class War* he had bemoaned the 'complete paralysis which makes resistance to the police impossible even when they are heavily outnumbered. The paralysis also attacks the brain resulting in its victims patting police horses, chatting to the filth and voluntarily getting themselves arrested in the absurd delusion that this constitutes "direct action" of some kind.'

And so it was that the second day of protest, whilst continuing the pacifist objectives of the first, became more confrontational. Meanwhile, Ron continued to be involved, once again organising a slow cycle ride, and also helping set up a number of fundraisers. The anarchist network included a number of punk squats that acted as information posts. Amongst them were the Burn It Down Ballroom in Finchley, the Bingo Hall in Kilburn, Dickie Dirts in Camberwell, and the Ambulance Station in the Old Kent Road. Ron helped organise a fund-raising gig at the Ambulance Station, putting on a bill that included musicians from Chile, El Salvador, Guatemala and Ireland in a show of global solidarity.

There were many personal acts of generous support as well. '8 March. Anonymous donation of £100', records Ron's diary. An earlier entry delivers the good news that Attila The Stock-broker, the ranting poet who had once been a stockbroker's clerk and was a veteran of the first Stop The City, was prepared to help the cause and write a pamphlet about the Stock Exchange. Once again also, the police had Ron's best intentions at heart, telephoning him and enquiring if anything could be done to help their end. This time, Ron detected a tone less jovial: the police sounded, he thought, 'really worried'.

In fact, on the day, the City police were, once again, caught unguarded. They weren't ready for the numbers and throughout the morning had to draft in reinforcements from the Met and from forces outside London. Even Ian Bone's world-weary cyn-icism was caught unprepared. Arriving mid-morning he steeled himself for the apathetic worst. But then 'A huge forest of black flags legs it out of an alleyway in front of us hotly pursued by cops in a pall of orange smoke'. It is possible the smoke bomb had been thrown by one of the many smoke-bomb wielding protest-ers dressed up as nuns.

One of the best accounts of the day was published a short time later in *Freedom*. It detailed hour-by-hour how the day had unfolded. First Aid, creche and assembly points were set up at 7.00am, at which point the police diverted all lorries from the city. Shortly afterwards, Ron and his slow cyclists set off. London Peace Action managed to occupy the balcony of an arms trading company and set up a banner and balloons.

By 10.00am protests had been made at the Eletricity Board's Headquarters and around 500 were massed at the Royal Exchange, where eventually the police brought in horses to 'kettle' the crowd in. Disruption was caused at Leadenhall meat market and British, American and Russian flags were burned at Bank. There was a die-in at St Pauls and many military statues were 'decorated'. Smoke flares were let off and much graffiti was created.

Banks were targeted in a big way. The windows at Barclays, where yet again an anti-apartheid protest took place, were smashed and banks were generally subject to the anger of the crowd. Large numbers of people wasted bank time by opening and closing accounts. In Fleet Street, there was a raid on chemists Boots where tampons were thrown into the street at protest against their 'luxury item' VAT classification. And in the afternoon, according to the *Freedom* report, around 200 people made a human barricade across London Bridge before being moved on by the police.

Cyling around, Ron saw plenty of what went on as well, as he recalls. 'A meat lorry tried to come through and had its tyres slashed, a number of expensive cars were damaged and at one point a lorry carrying bricks had its load tipped out onto the street. Groups of people would suddenly run off, small numbers in different directions and the police had no idea which section to pursue. There was confrontation but it was still jolly, with lots of street theatre and people dressing up while all this was going on around them.'

The film made by Duffield and Palmer tells a similar story, capturing some of the more visual manifestations of the protest. In one scene a banner proclaiming 'IN THIS BUILDING PEOPLE ARE DISCUSSING HOW TO MAKE MONEY FROM SUFFERING AND DEATH' is draped from a balcony; in another a paper mache trident is carried shoulder high through the streets. A second banner takes the form of a mock-prayer:

'CREATOR OF WEALTH AND PROPERTY
TEACH US TO LOVE OUR CHAINS
GRANT US, WE PRAY, THAT WE MAY SERVE
AND BLESS US WITH CAPITAL GAINS'

Another active participant that day was Simon Crab who was part of the experimental music group Bourbonese Qualk and also a veteran squatter. Crab had moved into and co-ran the Ambulance Station in the Old Kent Road after the original French anarchists involved were driven out by some of the British Movement-supporting locals. The Ambulance Station provided sustenance and shelter for those taking part and as well as putting on benefit gigs such as the one Ron was involved in and also provided a space for people to meet and plan.

'People set off early in the morning and had a variety of tactics to put into place. We interfered with some of the traffic light boxes so that they didn't work properly and the traffic all got congested,' remembers Crab. 'Through contacts we found somebody in the City who sympathised. Beneath the streets of the City is a miniature railway used for transporting documents between various important buildings. He was able to sabotage the railway so that on that day it didn't work. Cars were disabled, sometimes set fire to, or just left abandoned on bridges to block the traffic. We also organised a bust-fund: some of those involved ended up stuck in a police cell with no recourse to help of any kind.'

By 6pm, the focus of Stop The City shifted towards Whitehall and the Ministry of Defence in a show of solidarity for the protestors at Greenham Common who the same day had stopped a convoy of cruise missiles travelling on the motorway. People gathered in an attempt to blockade Whitehall. And then it was over. A Thames TV News report claimed 360 arrests, but the casualty rate was almost certainly higher and the figure took no account of those subjected to what one recipient called 'police hospitality'. 'The police didn't *police* the second Stop The City, they attacked it,' says Ron today. Nearer 400 were arrested by his account, but many more had been penned for hours in small spaces in the city and then herded into police vans before later being released.

The Times did finally report Stop The City, gloomily claiming that 29 March had wiped around £11 Million off the financial balances of those targeted. Ron's diary for the same day, however, paints a much more positive picture, and one epitomising the independent spirit of those involved: 'The action today took a new line in demos – not a sit-down, not a march, not a position, but a resonating protest by an unfixed body which showed it was capable of striking where it wanted to, saying what it wanted to and doing what it wanted to.'

Many indie bands had openly supported or become involved in Stop The City: as well as the Damned, and more obvious sympathisers such as Crass and Poison Girls, many individuals had also joined the carnivals. But with the exception of *Sounds*, a newspaper that instinctively seemed predisposed to this sort of action carried out by the sort of bands involved, the events were more or less ignored, the papers preferring the kind of protest that came with a bit of gloss, such as the antics of Frankie Goes To Hollywood whose anti-nuclear song 'Two Tribes' was released a month or so later and topped the charts in May.

Then, towards the end of spring and on into summer, the mood of conflict spread. The NUJ went on strike and for nine weeks the *NME* and *Melody Maker* weren't published, forcing journalists to walk it in lieu of their usual talking it. Not content with just taking on the miners, the Government also had the GLC in its sights also and as ever youth, as one headline had it, continued to be 'shopped at bargain prices'. In a year officially designated by the GLC as 'Anti-Racism Year' (1983 had been 'Peace Year'), the GLC's Leader Ken Livingstone ruffled Establishment feathers by threatening to ban from appearing at venues owned by the GLC those who had played concerts and/ or supported the regime in South Africa. Artists on the black list included Rod Stewart, Elton John, Cliff Richard and Frank Sinatra. Meanwhile, before the summer was over, deaths on the Youth Training Scheme (or predecessor) had risen to the shameful figure of 26. Even *The Times* labelled YTS conscription by another name, suggesting the Government cynically used the scheme as 'an anti-riot device, keeping 16-year-olds off the unemployment records and off the streets'.

But the fate of the GLC and the plight of youth were battles for later and paled in comparison to those being fought by the miners. The well-documented skirmish most emblematic of the whole strike took place at the coking works at Orgreave between the end of May and the third week of June when up to 10,000 miners attempted on a number of occasions to stop lorries entering or leaving the works with coke. The miners and police (8,000 in total were drafted in) clashed. The legendary photographs of the mayhem at Orgreave by John Sturrock, Don McPhee and others are surreal – cavalry police cantering across an English country field to engage in a pitched battle with those they were ordinarily charged to defend – and to this day sum up the madness of the whole dispute.

Suddenly everyone was behind the miners and everyone was doing gigs in support of them, or so it seemed. As early as May benefit shows had started taking place – New Order, for instance, played a 'Music For Miners' concert on 14th at the Royal Festival Hall. Post-Orgreave, the number of benefits shows dramatically increased. The GLC had been hosting shows in aid of its own defence against threatened demise, but began also organising benefits for the miners, announcing 'Five Nights For The Miners', also at the Royal Festival Hall. It was hoped that £50,000 might be raised, and 'official' buskers (usually the scourge of official-dom) were allowed each night to play outside the venue: money from the buckets would be added into the fund. Musicians who signed up to appear included Bert Jansch, Paul Weller and Mick Talbot, Wham!, Van Morrison, and Misty In Roots. A number of comedians, including Alexei Sayle, Nigel Planer and Rik Mayall, also appeared. Ken Livingstone had made a plea for support, and according to event organiser Ken Hulme had received 'an amazing response' even although there had been 'apathy from people one would have expected to give support'.

The very real sympathy felt for the miners was summed up in one of the first and prominent articles about the strike in the music press when Tony Parsons reviewed a Channel Four News debate between Arthur Scargill and the Head of the Nation Coal Board, Iain McGregor. Tossing around the pros and cons of the tactics of the miners, Parsons very reasonably arrived at the conclusion that 'while having a lump of coal put through your double glazing [was] certainly unpleasant', it was small beer 'compared to telling a man – twenty thousand men – that his job, his community, his family and his future have all been left out for the dustmen'.

Politics was difficult ground for the music business, and always had been. According to Susan Williams – in a slightly fence-sit-ting review of the likely success of the Redskins to combine music and politics – revolutionary activists and liberal hacks were gen-erally agreed on one point: 'music and hard politics are mutually exclusive'. No band had ever talked 'so fine and glorious a revolution as the Clash' yet never had any group 'failed to deliver quite so dramatically' he argued. Writing in *Time Out* a short while later, Julie Burchill took a similar view, arguing that music and politics combined didn't involve more people in the political process and that 'to connect a political doctrine to a plethora of trendy paraphernalia is to portray it in the same superficial light as that paraphernalia'.

This may be one reason why those seen by some as trenchantly 'political', such as the Three Johns, often took a practical rather than ideological approach, preferring to support the miners and their families as opposed to spouting any political rhetoric. 'We turned ourselves 100% towards supporting the miners, without necessarily supporting Scargill,' remembers John Hyatt. 'We supported the ordinary working people around us who were suffering a hard time. For a period, we gave up promoting the band as such and travelled all over the place, from Scotland to Italy, in support of the miners and their families. Three nights a week or more we were going up and down the motorway. That itself created a problem – three blokes in a transit van, must be pickets. On so many occasions we weren't let off the motorway, but forced on by police at the exit slip roads. In fact, they often blocked all the exits to the trouble spots off at night. You'd be driving, endlessly, up a motorway.'

The Three Johns were honoured by the Italian Communist Party and 'by the old men of the anarchist CNT'. Hyatt recalls a particularly memorable Sunday afternoon miners benefit gig (with Billy Bragg) at the Community Centre at Gorseinon in Swansea, South Wales: 'We were always Bacchanal, but perhaps on stage it was more like a Brueghal painting, more a festival of misrule. In Gorseinon, Langford played on a mock crucifix we found (there were Easter props from a play backstage) and when Billy Bragg was singing "Between The Wars", eyes closed deep in concentration, we dragged on an artificial tree and placed it right in front of him. We weren't expecting it, but after the show there was a presentation and we all were made honorary members of the NUM.' In an essay published in *Digging The Seam: Popular Cultures of the 1984/5 Miners' Strike*, ed Simon Popple and Ian W. MacDonald, Hyatt elaborated on the nature of the Three Johns involvement saying, 'We were activists but we were never tame or controlled. Though we accepted honours with a drunken grace, we never joined anything, and our allegiances had to be re-forged on a daily basis. My allegiance was to the families of miners, not the NUM.'

As Christmas 1984 approached, it became apparent that the miners were unlikely to hold out much longer – their funds had been sequestrated and the law had been suddenly changed to make it almost impossible for striking miners to get any kind of benefit save that doled out by the union. In November, Test Department announced an entire tour in support of the miners. The band worked with the Deptford and Lewisham Miners Support Group, and planned to share the stage with colliery choirs and brass bands in venues as far afield as Snowden, Kellingley, Thurnstone, South Wales and Scotland. The same month, Recommended Records announced 'The Last Nightingale', a collaboration of Robert Wyatt, the poet Adrian Mitchell, and three members of the political rock band Henry Cow. Label boss (and Henry Cow member) Chris Cutler had already paid the estimated profit from sales of the 2,500 copies of the album into the strike fund because 'The miners are in dire need of the money… and need the money now'.

As the so-called festive season got under way, the Clash played a two-night Christmas party for Arthur Scargill and Bronski Beat appeared at the Electric Ballroom in Camden on a bill they called 'The Enemy Within – Pits And Perverts'. The Bronski Beat show was organised by a body called the London Lesbians And Gay Men Support The Miners and profits went to the South Wales pit communities. One of the more unusual benefit gigs took place in Cardiff's Star Tandoori restaurant, where Bomb & Dagger played in between the poppadoms, onion bhajis and main courses.

The increasingly dire predicament of the miners was apparent for all to see, but their cause came in for bizarre criticism from some of the more blinkered observers who saw it as a parochial sideshow in comparison to the campaign for Ethiopia that Bob Geldof had launched. The Band Aid single, 'Do They Know It's Christmas?' inevitably went straight to number one and raised millions, but itself came in for criticism, first by those who questioned the motives of some of those involved, the rich rock stars easing their conscience, and then by those who simply lamented the single itself, such as Morrissey. David Quantick in the *NME* made the serious point, when reviewing a benefit gig in Hammersmith by the Redskins and the Three Johns, that some seemed to be confused, mistakenly believing that 'because there is a famine in Ethiopia, the miners strike is vastly more immoral than it might have been'.

The miners lasted barely ten weeks into 1985 before the strike folded. As the new year began, the serious business of raising money now focused on providing funds for the knock-on effect once the strike ended. The collecting tins were still rattled, and the supporting projects rattled on as well. Rough Trade had released a single by the Enemy Within called 'Strike!' towards the end of 1984. A generic Rough Trade advert described it as 'a disco mix that threatens the fabric of society' and implored people to 'SWITCH ON AT SIX' (sudden surges in power demand used up supplies stockpiled by the Government and therefore weakened their position, or so it was thought.) The record, produced by Adrian Sherwood and inspired by the Malcolm X single, 'No Sell-Out', reached 153 in the national charts, but the financial contribution flowed through after the strike had finished. The money, some £1400, went to Women Against Pit Closures, a group still active post the conflict.

Ron from Stop The City continued doing his bit. 'Kent and Northumberland miners had a room at Lewisham Town Hall they used and I went and got a couple of collecting boxes, various sticker such as "Coal Not Dole", and some papers promoting the cause. Twice a week I went and stood at Hither Green railway station and collected. There was only one way out until you hit a T-junction and then there was a choice of two exits – left and right. By standing at the T-junction everyone had to pass me. Each Thursday, like clockwork, a man came and dropped a folded, crisp £5 note into the box. Lots of people contributed, but eventually British Rail banned me from standing inside the station, which had an effect on the amount I was able to collect, given the fact that there were two exits.' Ron's band also played benefits for the miners and he witnessed the hardship the miners were suffering when he was on tour: 'At the service stations on the motorways miners gathered by the coffee stalls asking if we could spare the sugar given out at the till with the drink.'

There were further gestures of solidarity at the bitter end – Frankie Goes To Hollywood lending muscle to a 'Don't Desert Them Now' campaign in February (which utilised the ubiquitous 'Frankie Says…' slogan on a 'Frankie Says Support The Miners' badge and was aimed at keeping involved those whose interest might wain). Many involved in the Stop The City campaigns, or at least associated, continued to gig in support, including Flux of Pink Indians, Poison Girls, Attila The Stockbroker and Newtown Neurotics. There were gigs early in 1985 by, amongst others, Big Flame, the Nightingales, the June Brides, the Higsons, Yeah Yeah Noh, the Mekons and Buba & The Shop Assistants.

In the second week of March, just as the strike collapsed, Test Department and the South Wales Striking Miners Choir released *Shoulder To Shoulder*, a benefit album whose black grooves mark a full-stop to the dispute. The record is every bit as surreal as the strike itself – containing what critic Mat Snow aptly summed up as 'a sound halfway between Cozy Powell's "Dance With The Devil" and Ghengis Khan's galloping Mongol hordes'. It is part metal machine music and part rendition of songs from the Valleys, songs that would have brought a tear to Harry Secombe's eye, classics such as 'Stout-Hearted Man', 'Comrades In Arms' and 'Myfanwy'. It is a fitting if somewhat bizarre tribute to an equally as bizarre moment in history.

The collapse of the Miners Strike and the brutalising reality of what had happened was a jolt to the system. And although it was one that far from proved that rock and politics were insoluble, it highlighted the difficulties of hitching a message to a rock and roll beat. The romanticism of certain movements (such as New Pop) and the escapism of others (like Goth) showed that music was simply not robust enough to deal with such a rupture. At the same time, the kind of sloganeering that, for instance, the Redskins engaged in – Kick Over The Statues!, Reds Strike The Blues! Etc – was off-putting for some and ran itself into a cul-de-sac: almost as soon as the card-carrying SWP band signed a major record deal, the end for them was in sight.

Ian Bone would have shed few tears over their plight and had little time for the 'oligarchic leadership and corduroy-trousered poly lecturer megaphone robots of the SWP' but even Class War faltered. An ambitious plan to try to orchestrate inner city riots at the time of the strike (thus diluting the Government's ability to police the dispute) came to nothing. The clock was ticking for them, as well. But perhaps the most obviously visible decline was that of anarcho-punk, which lost traction after 1984, no doubt stymied when Crass called it a day. The actions of all would also be further undermined by the predictably firm hand taken by the Government in future when faced with similar revolts, which were either hammered into submission or dragged through the courts, usually with the same effect. Just occasionally, the Government would overstep the mark, as with the anti-Poll Tax protests in 1990, but largely the course to fewer civil liberties was unswerving.

On 28 March 1985, the June Brides, Five Go Down To The Sea and the Legend! played a benefit gig for the miners at the Old White Horse in Brixton. Coming from a long line of miners on his father's side, Phil Wilson of the June Brides had seen the effects of a life spent down a pit at first hand. It was both no life to lead and for most the only life to lead. The strike put an end to that.

'An awful lot of people had the wind knocked out of them: every working-class person knew then that they and their jobs weren't safe,' he recalls. 'As for music, you can't help but notice how an awful lot of "rock" music lost a political edge after the strike. Maybe we all gave up believing that rock 'n' roll could change the world?!'

CHAPTER 10

DESTROYING CAPITALISM

IN MARCH 1984, JUST AS the miners' strike began, the June Brides went in to Alaska Studios in Waterloo to record their first single. The journey from formation to the releasing of a debut single had been swift, the band only playing its first show on 6 August 1983, at the Spotted Cow in Hither Green (as part of the pub's Grand Charity Pram Race). At the band's second gig at the George & Dragon pub in Lewisham – another free gig, where this time the band performed on top of the pub's pool table – Frank Sweeney appeared, and offered his services on viola, an offer received gladly by Simon Beesley and Phil Wilson, who were both big admirers of John Cale. That had been in October. By the end of January 1984, the band had played a first gig at the Living Room and was hoping for the call to be invited to record for Creation.

Sweeney's viola added a distinctive sound, and, although rarely used as drone, one not without reference to a past the audience could easily pick up on. But in an indie environment where the dominant species was increasingly becoming a young man with a fast guitar, both in the UK and in America, the June Brides were distinctive in another way. The songs were muscular enough yet in their fragility the antithesis of the more macho rock posturing that still lingered in the mid-1980s (and would get worse by the time the 1990s rolled around). The songs were intended, as Phil Wilson later noted, as 'small joys', music that was punk rock but sought to speak to people rather than shout at them. Even the choosing of the name of the band was an act of equanimity, according to Wilson: 'We liked the idea that the band name was neutral and that you wouldn't know the type of music we played from the name. We liked the idea of it being a bit odd, as well – we were brides without there being any women in the band. That appealed to us given how much we all hated sexism.'

As was the case with so many indie bands in the early 1980s, punk had been the great motivator and its DNA runs to the core of the June Brides. There was no punk by 1984, but the spirit lived on. In the case of the June Brides, it ran a reverse course back through the spikey pop of Orange Juice and other Postcard bands like the Go-Betweens, on through the 'quiet' post-punks such as Young Marble Giants and Marine Girls, and back to the shout-y music of the quintessential punk acts. In the case of Phil Wilson, the sub-strata then drilled down through Bowie and Be-Bop Deluxe and all the way to Queen, Wings and 10CC, his starting point for the moment when Year Zero arrived.

'I learnt how to play guitar, very badly and formed a stupid punk band with a mate in Norfolk. We were called the Smoking Beagles. We only ever played a couple of tiny shows – one in a pub and one at a local talent competition where we lost to an 11-year-old girl playing Bonnie Tyler's "Lost In France" on an acoustic guitar. Then, in 1980, I moved to London to go to the London School of Economics and was briefly in a hard core punk band called the Slugs, later renamed Obsession. We once supported Infa Riot at a pub in Islington with a solid skinhead/ Oi! Audience. We played an anti-Fascist song called "Hitler Is Alive And Living In England" which the crowd greeted with *sieg heil* salutes. Not a pleasant evening…'

The punk diaspora left clusters of inspired innovators producing all manner of interesting sounds, including those drawn to electronic music. For some, such as Mute's Daniel Miller, electronic music and punk were 'totally linked', an idea he'd attempted to express through his alter ego, the Normal and the single 'TVOD'. Shortly after the release of the 'TVOD' single in 1978, which launched the Mute record label by default (since he printed his address on the back of the record's sleeve), other pioneers emerged – Thomas Leer, Cabaret Voltaire, Robert Rental, Throbbing Gristle, the Human League, Tuxedomoon and the Residents amongst them. Aside from its visceral draw – 'Nag, Nag, Nag', for instance, by Cabaret Voltaire remains one *the* great pop singles – the music had an intellectual appeal, sometimes drawing the more fascinating strategies of the art world into the pop music arena. The appeal wasn't lost on Phil Wilson.

Wilson went off in 1981 and did a course in electronic music, busily 'cutting up tape loops of found sound and banging bits of metal for percussion tracks'. But it didn't feel right. 'Making weird noise tapes quickly felt unoriginal to me – it had been done so much better by others, and it offered little in the way of joy. So I picked up the guitar again and started writing pop songs.'

That same year, pepped up with a new pop resolve, Wilson was having a drink with friend and fellow LSE student Simon Beesley when they noticed some posters for a first round of a student talent contest. Beer being the great motivator, they quickly came up with the idea of having a go, and decided to 'do the punk rock thing, have one rehearsal and do the talent contest as a complete piss take'. They played a short set which made up for what it lacked in musical aptitude by offering plenty of running around and falling over and were surprised to make it through to the final heat, where they came second to a jazz rock outfit.

As a result of the competition, one of the judges invited International Rescue, as Wilson and Beesley's pop-up band became known, to appear at the Venue in Victoria as support to the Higsons. According to *Artificial Life* fanzine, recollecting events a year or so later, the night was not an unqualified success, the cover version of Neil Diamond's 'I'm A Believer' a particularly low point in International Rescue's set. Still, the band soldiered on, playing a few more gigs and recording a demo tape before disintegrating, Wilson no longer seeing the point in being 'permanently in a band that was little more than a joke'.

A short time passed and then, at the start of 1983, Wilson and Beesley decided to give it another go, putting together another band, 'a proper one this time'. Thus it was that the June Brides came in to being, Wilson and Beesley on vocals and guitars and Frank Sweeney on viola, along with friends Ade Carter on bass and Chris Nineham on drums. Then, as 1984 got under way, they acquired a further member. The band rehearsed in Wilson and Beesley's house, which was also home to Jon Hunter. One day, whilst they were rehearsing, they could hear Hunter, who was in another room, playing along on trumpet to one of their songs. So he was in. Like Sweeney's viola, Hunter's trumpet worked against the grain, adding an element that usually expressed itself in a muted fashion, unlike the more usual stabbing brass effect that commonly connected the trumpet and pop.

At the end of 1982, another important connection had been made. Phil Wilson had been one of the very few to trek to the Communication Club in the winter of 1982, on a mission to see one of his favourite bands, the Television Personalities. Inevitably, he bumped into Alan McGee who was selling copies of his Laughing Apple singles at the same time as promoting the night. The gig was poorly attended – 'I was amazed at how few people turned up. I thought the Television Personalities were rock stars!' recalls Wilson – but it gave Wilson opportunity to get to know McGee at bit. He bought a Laughing Apple single, departed and, a short while later, plucked up courage and sent to McGee 'a (terrible quality) June Brides demo in the hope of getting a gig for the band'.

During 1982 and 1983 McGee had been starting to realise his dream, and, as has been seen, had surrounded himself with like-minded people, fellow-visionaries usually falling somewhere between friend and acolyte. One such friend was Simon Down. Down was no John Entwistle, but fancied himself a bit on the bass, although, by his own admission, on the one occasion when his playing had made it all the way on to vinyl, on the B side of ''73 In '83', there was 'a clear mistake at the beginning of the song' that nobody troubled to correct. Prior to Ade Carter joining the June Brides, Down had failed an audition to be the bass player, but kept in touch and remained a fan and supporter of the band.

'It was Alan who suggested that I try out for the bass with the June Brides,' remembers Down. 'The audition didn't go anywhere, but it planted the seed of an idea in my mind, I guess. I could see that the June Brides had something different from the usual run of the mill indie bands and they reminded me a bit of Orange Juice, which was no bad thing. Alan didn't seem to have any interest in signing them, which to me seemed crazy. I very quickly came to believe that I could put their record out, that I could do something similar to Alan and start a record label.'

Down came to the June Brides with a proposition – he would scramble together £500 and use the money to release a June Brides single. At this point the band were desperate to release a single but still keen to see whether or not McGee would make a counter-offer. He didn't, in spite of the fact that the band was one of the most popular draws at the nights he was putting on at his club. Indeed, between 7 January, when they first appeared at the club, and the start of July when their single eventually came out, the June Brides appeared *nine* times at the Living Room (in its various locations), almost certainly appearing on more occasions than any other band booked to play there during that period.

Today, McGee barely recalls the matter, musing that 'quite possibly I was just being perverse' in not signing them. It may also be that, despite being hardened anarchists and clearly capable drinkers, the June Brides just didn't fit into the clique that formed around the Living Room. This was a culture, according to McGee, that, 'whilst not exactly Sex, Drugs & Rock 'n' Roll, involved a fair bit of debauchery and non-PC behaviour'. At an age when such minute distinctions matter, the June Brides were also, crucially, just that slight bit older, and having been through the LSE, from a frankly more intellectual background.

In order to release the single Down needed to have a record label and christened what he he came up with Pink. 'I actually knew how I wanted the logo to look even before I had a name for the label,' Down recalls. 'There was a magazine called *Girl* and I so liked the logo that I thought we would try a similar approach, so I spent some time coming up with a four-letter word, eventually arriving at Pink. Perhaps inevitably, the design approach for Pink's first release completely mimicked that of Creation, complete with wrap around paper sleeve slipped between a soft plastic cover. A little bit of agitation in the Creation camp may have been what later led Down to adopt a different visual approach in future, taking a lead this time from Postcard Records whose singles tended to come housed in a generic card cover. In the case of Pink, the design was a tastefully generic white cover overlaid with a pink triangle across the centre, a design apparently suggested to Down by McGee and Foster.

At the recording session for 'In The Rain'/ 'Sunday To Saturday', Joe Foster produced, knowing his way around the studio marginally better than the June Brides. In hindsight, the gloominess of the Alaska studios, nestled between the semi-derelict arches of Waterloo Station, fitted in with the more lugubrious aspects of Wilson's psyche. The spirit of Marc Bolan is said to haunt the building, but there very little about the place that could be described as 'glam'. Indicative of the level of technical sophistication of the time, the whole session was wrapped up in four hours at a cost of under £20. The record, when it finally appeared, came with the distinction of having no formal B-side, but rather an A-side and AA-side, both songs written by Wilson. The reviews, the few that came, didn't entirely fizz with excitement, but Bill Black in *Sounds*, likened the band's 'scrape 'n' strum' to that of the Go Betweens and considered 'Sunday To Saturday' (the side of the single he reviewed) 'a fine song'.

Dispensing with the need for a B-side represented for the June Brides punk rock idealism in action – everything served up with equal merit. The band soaked up the excitement of actually having their own record out – 'I'd been collecting records and been a music nerd for so long, and now the dream had come true,' recalls Wilson – before getting on with the business of attempting to promote it: 'We did the clichéd thing of standing outside Broadcasting House to catch John Peel on the way in and try to persuade him to play the record. It worked!'

If the archetypal sound of mid-1980s' indie is the sound of sunny guitars being played by those who have yet to perfectly master their instruments, then the June Brides fit the bill perfectly. Through the back half of 1984 the band were on a learning curve, and an enormous part of their appeal lay in the fact that the journey they were taking could be shared by those watching. A *Melody Maker* review of the period begins 'The six-piece June Brides played appallingly…' before going on to ecstatically praise the 'grit, wit, guts' of an 'honest and vital band', one making 'bright spanking pop' and 'marvellous music' (in spite of having a lead vocalist who looked like 'a subversive Nick Heyward').

There's music and there's the response that music provokes, and according to writer Dave Eggars, a lifelong fan of the June Brides, sometimes 'we're hopelessly conflicted and confused about what we want from the musicians we love'. Never were these words truer than in the case of the June Brides, precisely because there is a similar kind of confusion and conflict going on within the actual songs themselves. The critic Michael White has noted 'a duality inherent to many of Wilson's best songs: sprightly melodies and galloping rhythms shrouding lyrics that detail a somewhat defeated worldview'.

'In The Rain' is a song full of optimism, but opens with the bleak question, 'Is this the real world/ Is this all I can hope for?' Meanwhile, 'Sunday To Saturday', with its rolling cadences an arguably more progressive song, is almost naggingly cautious: 'We'll learn how to walk then to tumble/ To swagger is worse than to stumble'. Ultimately, though, confusion abounds, and 'Veils of bright beauty hide visions obscene/ And tired old excuses for current abuses/ Mean no-one will say what they mean'.

On 3 July, the June Brides returned to Alaska Studios to record a second single, 'Every Conversation'. On this occasion, the band took care of the production themselves, in association with Iain O'Higgins, the studio's recording engineer. And this time around there *was* a B-side, 'Disneyland', a song written and sung by Simon Beesley that narrowly missed out on being the lead track by a whisker after a vote was held. Four hours was spent mixing 'Disneyland' and barely an hour spent mixing 'Every Conversation', the first indication to the band that they weren't perhaps being recorded quite as sophisticatedly as they could or might need to be. But the outcome, nonetheless, was popular amongst the band's small coterie of fans and, aided by some fine trumpet work by Jon Hunter, remains the song most people commonly associate with the band.

Reviewing the single in the *NME*, Penny Reel compared the sound of the June Brides to that of the Kinks, an observation also made by Janice Long who called the band in for a session not long after the single's release. 'I'm not a particularly good singer,' Wilson claimed at the time, 'but I represent what I've done, as does Ray Davies.' In *Jamming!*, Jonh Wilde made the record Single of the Month, describing it as a cross between Lou Reed and the Marvelettes, adding, 'For all the impotent theorising on pop recently, the June Brides supply a superlative reply…'

No further new June Brides songs were released until the autumn of 1985, an arguably fatal delay that in truth says more about the precarious finances of indie record labels at the time than it does about any lack of commitment on the part of the band. As a stopgap, the first two singles were collected together on a 12" and reissued in spring 1985. In the interim the band toured extensively, in the process turning itself into a first class live act and building up the makings of a small legend. They also spent time considering the nature of being independent, telling Bruce Dessau in the January issue of *Jamming!* that the indie scene was just as moribund as the pop charts and that the only real difference between the two was the scale of operation – 'EMI are simply more successful capitalists' was Wilson's pessimistic view. Music journalists were little better, he opined: 'Only one thing can be worse than making trivial pop music, and that's making a living by writing about it!' But it wasn't all doom and gloom and ultimately it was optimism that motivated the band, and there were always unexpected moments of joy, such as when the band opened Kevin Pearce's *Hungry Beat* fanzine and saw a picture of the Buzzcocks superimposed on an article about them.

In May, the band went again to Alaska to begin work on their debut album, *There Are Eight Million* Stories… Once more it was a parsimonious affair, with five of the eight tracks recorded on one day, and everything wrapped up quickly. Ex-Undertone John O'Neill produced, but the session was beset with problems and plagued by a number of power cuts. The noise of the trains rumbling overhead sometimes bled into the recording and the quieter sections had to constantly be redone. The mood wasn't helped by the fact that while the session was taking place news broke of the Bradford City FC fire disaster, where 53 people lost their lives. At this time the 'live' track 'Enemies', a cover of the Radiator's From Space song, was also recorded, its inclusion on the album ultimately omitted from the track listing on the cover since there was no money available to pay for clearance. 'I'm still proud of the album,' recalls Wilson today, 'but I do wish it had sounded just a bit more powerful; we were a punk band at heart, and that didn't seem (to me) to quite come out on the record.'

As well as reworked versions of the first two singles (added for reasons of budgetary constraint), the album contains some of the June Brides very best songs, including the primordial rock 'n' roll twang of 'The Instrumental', the unexpected (given its title) and uplifting 'Sick, Tired and Drunk' – a classic punk song if ever there was one, and 'I Fall', a favourite from the days of the Living Room, described by the Legend! in his prolix *NME* review of the album as 'a tumultuous, impetuous expression of joy: fragile, soaring, forever bewitching. The guitars rush headlong through a tumbling waterfall of viola and vocals… *"I fall and you drag me down/ No-one is listening so let's shout out loud to prove that we're alive"*.'

An interesting footnote to the album concerns the title. At a certain point the record was going to be called *Destroying Capitalism With The June Brides*, a fitting choice in keeping with the volatile times in which it was produced. But, as Phil Wilson now recalls, it was not to be: 'We all were and are pretty left wing, but none of us really believed in the idea that pop music should be overtly political. We were much more interested in the idea of persuasion/ gentle subversion than browbeating people with slogans. So, the idea of "Destroying Capitalism" by releasing product for people to buy was a joke, obviously. We decided against the idea because we thought there was a huge chance that the joke might be misunderstood.'

There Are Eight Million Stories… topped the indie album charts and stayed in the charts for almost a year. It marked a moment when the June Brides star was at its highpoint, and following the inevitable split with Pink the band were courted by a number of independent and mainstream labels, including Stiff, Parlophone and the newly-founded Go! Discs, a company riding high on the success of Billy Bragg. In the end they did a deal with In Tape, the Manchester independent label that was home to Yeah Yeah Noh, Marc Riley & The Creepers, the Janitors and Terry & Gerry. The two records the band released on In Tape were the most wholly realised records the band had made to date. More money had been made available for recording, and on 'No Place Called Home' and 'This Town' it shows. The band was invited to Ireland to tour as support with the Smiths.

'In Tape were independent and offered us freedom and artistic control,' Wilson remembers. 'Very importantly, they were also hugely ambitious and felt they could get us into the charts on *our* terms. I think that we could and should have troubled Top Of The Pops. We had the pop songs. But we never made it, at least partly because the labels we were involved with did not have the money and/ or connections to get us there...'

For Simon Down, there was a further problem: 'There was a feeling that the June Brides might crossover and become mainstream pop stars, but, with hindsight, I don't think that was ever going to happen. I don't think that Phil ever really *wanted* to be a pop star, and ultimately I believe a corporate A&R man would have sniffed that out.' In spite of recognising his obvious brilliance, Down argues also that Wilson 'was too wrapped up in the Do It Yourself mentality of punk to really sustain success in the mainstream'.

At the start of 1986, in their own act of perverseness, the June Brides declined to appear on *C86*, fearing that they might end up typecast. (Alas, in the end, everyone got typecast.) Down is right about Wilson never feeling comfortable about the prospect of being a pop star – in such a democratic set-up as the June Brides he wasn't even happy assuming the mantle of group leader, preferring to see himself more as 'the local trades union rep than team leader'. The prospect of being another cog in the wheel just didn't appeal. 'Being another product on the asset list of an international entertainment conglomerate was diametrically opposed to everything we believed, and still believe, in,' Wilson says today. 'We wanted to reach a lot of people, of course, but wanted to retain our independence and dignity in doing so.'

When The June Brides had first started playing the scene, they wore bespoke punk shirts and their sound was pure punk, closer to the music of Subway Sect than that of the Postcard bands or Buzzcocks, the band they were most often compared to. In 1983 they had played the Anarchy Centre in Islington and the Ambulance Station, punk venues a million miles from the more stylised confines of indie. They shared a bill with the Mob, Pus and the Apostles. Their live set regularly included punk covers – not just 'Enemies' but other songs they admired as well, such as the Ramones' 'Suzy Is A Headbanger' and the Cortinas' 'Television Families'. They started as a punk band and they ended as a punk band.

The death of the band, like its birth, fittingly took place in a bar. On 1 July 1986, the band convened in the Skinners Arms, a pub on the Camberwell New Road, a stones-throw from the flat where bassist Ade Carter lived, shared a couple of rounds and decided to call it a day. Before leaving the pub, they got down to the business of composing an appropriate press release, which read, quite simply, 'The June Brides have decided to part company and become legend'. They remained in the pub for the rest of the evening drinking, before finally catching the bus home, all except Ade, who alone had the briefest of staggers back to his flat.

No headstone marked the band's passing, but had there been a need for one then Jonathan Romney's live review in the *NME* from January 1985 could have provided a fitting epitaph: 'Flawed, yes; convincing, yes; bound for glory? As if that mattered...'

When Simon Down had reached an agreement with the June Brides to begin releasing their records, Alan McGee, in typically generous fashion, offered advice and practical help, linking Down with Rough Trade, Creation's distributor, in a meaningful way that enabled Pink to land a manufacturing and distribution deal with the company. McGee, aside from being shrewd, had been fortunate in that the money generated by the Living Room had enabled him to release a raft of singles over a short period, giving immediate ballast to his fledgling label, but Pink started up without any significant capital or turnover.

Out of financial necessity, then, Pink moved at a slightly slower pace. Down was every bit as observant as McGee, and the period spent glancing over McGee's right shoulder had not been a waste. For a brief period Down had managed the Jasmine Minks and towards the end of 1983 had set up a club in conjunction with them at the Pindar of Wakefield in Kings Cross. It ran for a ridiculously short period, roughly the same length of time as the Communication Club had lasted, and like McGee's club was broad in taste, putting on a cross-section of weird and wonderful bands, including the Times, the Sting-Rays, the Jasmine Minks and McGee's own band, Biff Bang Pow!.

Having to proceed slowly meant that there was an inevitable delay between 'In The Rain' and the next two Pink releases that arrived in the summer. Prudence dictated that one of these should be by the June Brides ('Every Conversation') and, in fact, the other was connected to the band as well since the Ringing, whose single 'Caprice' was the third Pink release, included the June Brides' viola player Frank Sweeney. 'Caprice' was, at least according to *Melody Maker*, a vital record, 'an unsettling little splinter of pop', but with a sound that fell somewhere between the raucousness of the Boothill Foot-Tappers and the cheerful inanity of the Farmer's Boys, and with violin and viola a heavy feature, the band was something of an acquired taste.

The label was on safer ground with the release of the next Pink single, That Petrol Emotion's 'Keen', which came out in the spring of 1985. The hiatus in releases had, predictably, been caused by a lack of funds, although Pink was not alone in being cash-strapped, and had Creation not being going through a similarly lean time they would have almost certainly released That Petrol Emotion's single since McGee had invited the O'Neill brothers to London to record for Creation. But it never happened. Instead, Pink scraped together the funds, cash injections coming from Down's brother 'Funky' Ed Down and from Paul Sutton who would later take on the running of the label and steer it into its next phase as September Records.

Down had met That Petrol Emotion through his friend Dick Green who was no co-running Creation. The story goes that Green had met a man at college called Mickey Rooney who was a friend of the former Undertone, John O'Neill. Mickey, Dick, Simon and others used to go out for drinks occasionally and in one instance Mickey brought along John O'Neill. 'It was Christmas, 1984,' recalls Down. 'Mickey and John turned up and with them came John's brother Damian and the guitarist Raymond Gorman. They'd already got That Petrol Emotion going, but at this point were struggling to find a vocalist. Paul Sutton was present as well. We all got on well enough and thought no more of it, but a little while later we ran into them again at a Farmer's Boys concert at UCL. Out of the blue, John asked Paul if Pink would have any interest in putting out a That Petrol Emotion single. It was a hugely significant moment for us and one that happened fortuitously in that Creation appeared to be temporarily short of funds at the time otherwise the band would have signed with them.'

The Undertones was a tough act to follow, and with their new band the O'Neill brothers studiously avoided their past. That Petrol Emotion – the very name says it all – was a more explosive, and more visceral entity than had been the Undertones. The name was lifted fully formed from a song by Bam Bam & The Calling and chosen as a deliberately political gesture so that the band 'could present Irish issues more explicitly'. Musically, the plan, as John O'Neill told this author in the *NME* in late spring

1985, was to go 'back to basics' because 'somewhere along its way music has gone horribly wrong'. That Petrol Emotion presented 'the opportunity to start at the beginning again'.

'Keen' was a frenetic thrash that severed any association with the music of the Undertones through sheer force and delivered politically on its B-side, the acerbic and aggressive, 'A Great Depression On A Slum Night'. This really set the tone for the band, avoiding, as Raymond pointed out in the *NME* interview, 'the barbed wire and bomb cliches' of a previous Northern Irish 'political' band, Stiff Little Fingers. The approach, although louder than bombs, was direct but not preachy.

In the eyes of Creation, Pink had committed an unforgivable sin in releasing That Petrol Emotion's record. It would take decades for Down's relationship with his old friend Dick Green to get back on keel and he has barely spoken to Alan McGee since the single's release. As it turned out, the relationship with That Petrol Emotion was but fleeting, the band recording their next single 'V2' for their own Noiseannoys label before signing with Demon where they unveiled their debut album, the wonderful-ly-titled *Manic Pop Thrill*. When the album came out in April 1986 it climbed to the top of the independent charts and even entered the mainstream charts, climbing to number 84.

Pink's next signing was something of a disaster, the first nail in the coffin for the short-lived label. In 1984 there had been an appetite for bands borrowing traditional sounds and fusing them with a kind of punk energy. The usually patchwork effect blended country and western, sometimes bluegrass, punk, rockabilly or any single one of these influences, presenting it with a contempo-rary slant. By the start of 1985, the most significant band enjoy-ing success with this music was the Pogues, whose acres of press near matched that of the Smiths. Some groups took recreation to the furthest extremes, even dressing the part, as was the case with the Boothill Foot Tappers, the Blueberry Hillbillies, and the

Shillelagh Sisters. There were other bands, more on the outskirts but still comparable, such as Helen & The Horns and King Kurt. It was a love of this music that steered Simon Down towards the label's next signing, Jamie Wednesday.

'We got a little bit into all that cross-over stuff,' remembers Down. 'Nights spent down the Mean Fiddler. Jamie Wednesday didn't exactly fall into that camp but they were indicative of the polar extremes of indie at the time, which ranged from the standard guitar band across to rockabilly and back again to the trad-punk side. As far as we could see, Jamie Wednesday was not like anybody else. The band was different and very impressive live.'

The word that sprang to mind, at least for the critics, was 'eclectic'. David Quantick thought so when he interviewed the band in January 1986 and commented that 'pop will eat itself' (a phrase which gave another band its name, no less). He could hear snatches of Elvis Presley and 'nearly all of "Keep The Home Fires Burning"' bubbling under the multi-faceted surface of their 'Vote For Love' single. The single starts out acoustically, ends up brassily, and can't in truth decide what kind of record it wants to be. It's almost, but then not quite, the Housemartins, or rather, the Housemartins as they might have sounded if Peter Sellers or Spike Milligan had been in the band. That might have been one reason why John Walters refused to have the single played on the John Peel Show. Sales of the single, even by Pink's standards, were spectacularly low. The band withered (in spite of *Melody Maker* hailing 'Vote For Love' Single of the Week), died, and then parts of the band exacted its revenge, returning reincarnated as the much more appropriate Carter The Unstoppable Sex Machine.

By 1986, Down began questioning whether he still had the motivation to run a label and whether he was interested any longer in independent music. In spite of sales in excess of 25,000 copies for *There Are Eight Million Stories…* there was very little money around and even less enthusiasm. Respite briefly came in the form of a clever bit of licensing Pink did when it contacted EMI and secured the rights to issue a Wire compilation that drew together eight of the seminal punk band's most widely cherished tracks at a time when the group's albums were all out of print. *Wire Plays Pop* sold an impressive 15,000 copies, but was too late to stop the rot. The future held two very important Pink signings in the shape of McCarthy and the Wolfhounds and the criminally underrated single 'Tugboat Line' by Rumblefish. But it was all too late.

'At some point in 1986 I started to feel that it was becoming too much like hard work,' remembers Down who had always kept up a day job while running Pink. 'I'd stopped working as a meat packer and started working for London Underground, but was still having to do an enormous amount of label work as well. There was precious little money around, and what there was always got paid to the label late. At one point I thought that one of the majors might have licensed the label, as happened with Creation when Alan McGee went off and started Elevation. But none of them seemed interested.

'Paul stepped up and began taking responsibility for more of the work. By then, he already had a better relationship with some of the acts, such as the Wolfhounds and McCarthy. We were convinced that with the Rumblefish single we had found a great pop song – it even got reviewed in the *Sun*! – but the record came and went just like the others. I ended up taking out a £12,000 extension on my mortgage to fund Pink. Then one day I found myself at a conference organised by *Music Week* and realised how vast the industry was and how very far from its centre Pink was. I no longer had the emotional energy for the label, or for indie, and knew then that it was time to quit.'

In February 1969 the acclaimed BBC Play For Today series broadcast *The Big Flame*, a docu-drama written by the socialist playwright Jim Allen and produced by left-wing director and polemicist Ken Loach. A classic example of the sort of gritty and hyper realistic drama that was in vogue at the time, *The Big Flame* told the story of a group of workers in Liverpool who occupy their docks in protest and stage a 'work-in'. In a prescient plotline that anticipated the social shifts leading up to the Thatcher era of a decade or so later, the conflict is only resolved once the Government brings in the army and police to forcibly restore order.

The play caused a significant stir – Mary Whitehouse of the National Viewers Association wrote to the Prime Minister demanding that BBC's charter be reviewed in light of its transmission – and it became the inspiration, or spark, for a political movement that sprang up in Liverpool in 1970 and borrowed the film's name. Big Flame was, by its own account, 'a revolutionary socialist feminist organisation with a working class orientation'. The group produced a paper – which it dubbed 'Merseyside's rank and file paper' – also called *Big Flame*, and, although largely and deliberately self-analysing, participated in a number of industrial struggles before disbanding in 1984, the year that a band in Manchester, who had also taken the name Big Flame, released its first single.

Continuing in the spirit of Jim Allen's play and the movement set up by the Liverpool feminists, Big Flame the group came together in December, 1982. Drummer Dil Green had been in a band called the Dog Musicians, along with vocalist and bass player Alan Brown, and when they folded they decided to form a new band. Green was an architecture student at Manchester University and on his application form had listed 'punk rock' as an interest. By coincidence, Greg Keeffe had also listed 'punk rock' as an interest and as a consequence the university had placed the two in the same halls of residence flat. When forming his new band, Green invited Keeffe to play guitar, even although Keeffe had never previously played the instrument. Although he later relented, initially Brown (says Keeffe) absolutely refused to sanction this: Keeffe was 'just too shit to be in a band with'. Right from the start, there was something internally unstable, something intrinsically volatile about Big Flame.

At the time the band formed, the three members were living in one of the worst manifestations of inner city, run-down Thatcherite Britain. Hulme was a sink, the haunt of the unstable, the addicted, and the violent. Perhaps inevitably, it had a healthy smattering of musicians, since it was also full of places to squat and rehearse untroubled by the day-to-day goings on of 'normal life'. According to Keeffe, 'the huge monolithic curved modernistic blocks' of the Crescent contained about 300 flats, but only a handful of them were occupied. Green and Keeffe were in one, and not too far away, Brown was in another. Like Green and Keeffe, Brown had also been a student at Manchester University but had dropped out after his first year, uncomfortable with what he later described as the 'nicey-middle-classness' of it all. Brown had experienced the brutalising effect of Hulme longer than Green or Keeffe and on one occasion had suffered a broken nose following a random altercation in the street.

The brutal and itinerant nature of life in Hulme fed into the music of Big Flame and from the start the band knew that the sounds they would produce would be more radical than what were considered the prevailing trends. Green and Keeffe worked briefly collecting glasses at the nearby Hacienda Club, but didn't need to go there to see that post punk was seriously running out of steam. They abhorred the rise of Goth, as well, music according to Keeffe that 'seemed so reactionary after the race through punk and new wave that had happened previously'. In a period when journalists as diverse as Mick Mercer, Richard North, Adrian Thrills and Tony Fletcher were all lamenting the morass that independent music was drifting towards, they watched as 'the music scene sort of collapsed in front of our eyes'. 1983 was dead time, and Keeffe spent a large part of it mastering his new instrument. Time was also spent in the pub, arguing about what kind of band Big Flame ought to be.

'We had some touchstones,' recalls Keeffe, 'such as the Fire Engines, early Gang of Four and the Pop Group. We had all been Clash fans and loved their live performances, so we wanted to do something innovative and anti-rock that would somehow reference the energy of the Clash, but also draw in the funk of the Pop Group and A Certain Ratio in a sort of non-decadent art project.'

It was Green's decision to name themselves after the movement in Liverpool, on the grounds that they shared some ideals, such as the re-appropriation of the means of production for the common good, although, as Keeffe points out, 'instead of factory equipment in a post-industrial, bankrupt society, it was cheap guitars and drums in Manchester' that they appropriated. They were interested in theories of chaos, too, at a time when it was starting to be studied in a proper scientific way – James Gleick's best-selling and ground-breaking work, *Chaos: Making A New Science* was just a year or so from publication and ideas about the subject fizzed through the ether in the music of bands like SPK, Test Department, Einsturzende Neubauten and Hulme neighbours, Tools You Can Trust. They also approved of the kind of direct action that Big Flame the political group had engaged in, marching on factories in support of the worker.

As part of the pub discussions, Green and Keeffe also enthused about the nature of that mythical entity, the 'perfect band'. To achieve such a state of nirvana would require rigorous discipline and place demands on the band that would at all times have to be met. As they later stated: 'They wouldn't sell out. They would be accessible but stretch the envelope musically; they would inspire the next generation; they would only do singles; they would be authentic in that they would use no effects on their instruments.

The songs would be anti-decadent, which meant short and with a message; and they would have a short life so that they wouldn't prevent younger bands from having their turn in the spotlight. They would be amazing live...'

The band would also be non-hierarchical. In the case of Big Flame, the equal structure was even carried through to the rendering of the name, which was sometimes presented as bIG fLAME, because, as Keeffe says, 'why should the first letters get all the limelight?'. A similar kind of methodically democratic approach went into the writing of the songs. Although initially, a few numbers from the Dog Musicians were borrowed and reworked into Big Flame songs, when it came to creating new material the following process applied: a jam would be recorded on to tape. The playback would then inspire Keeffe 'to create some crazy guitar riff, which I would do through some sort of interpretive meditation, a bit like a process Jackson Pollock might have used when creating a painting like "One: Number 31". Alan would then work his magic and create a bass line that made sense of all the madness. Dil would then work out the beats and then deliberately un-structure the drumming, so that the guitar became the beats and the drums the frills. I would then invent a title for the song and that would inspire Alan or Dil to write some lyrics. Finally, Alan would create a melody to float over it all. Alan was a musical genius and without him we would have never got anywhere.'

Early in 1984, Big Flame went into a cheap recording studio in central Manchester and recorded three tracks for a debut single they released on their own Laughing Gun records in March. The £500 needed to finance the release was borrowed from Brown's mum. When the record was pressed up, they sat and folded the paper sleeves they'd had printed at the local printing co-op. 'We touted it around shops, gave some to Rough Trade, and posted out 200 or so to the music biz, including John Peel,' says Keeffe.

'Sink', 'Illness' and 'Sometimes' all bore the fiery and abrasive hallmark of the classic Big Flame song – the short, sharp sonic assault that is all the more shocking for being virtually over by the time its impact properly registers. Played, as it needed to be, at the appropriate volume, the noise on the single was almost as deafening as the critical silence that greeted the record. The few that did review the record invariably struggled to fathom the band out, tripped up by what Big Flame referred to as the HDL, or the Hip Difficult Listening factor. *Melody Maker* called the 'tangled net of rasped guitar, discord and hyper-energy pills' something of 'a winsome scrape', while Manchester's fanzine, *Debris*, erudite as ever, praised the lyrics to 'Sometimes' (a song about Sylvia Plath) and likened the overall sound to a cross between the Fire Engines and the Gang of Four.

One person who did immediately *get* Big Flame was John Peel. In July he invited the band in to record their first Peel session and in October booked them on to an ICA Rock Week he was curating. The band appeared on the same ill-fated night that SPK inflamed the audience by playing just two songs, the shortness of the set prompted by the ICA's insistence that all fire regulations be met. At the time, Peel described Big Flame as the best live band he had seen in nearly 40 years.

The seal of approval from Peel, and the money the band received from the numerous repeat airings of the session enabled the band to broaden its horizons, performing beyond the Manchester area for the first time. They played the Lamplighter Club in Rochdale, and also the Hebden Bridge Trades Club where they performed before an audience of six people and a dog. Cath Carroll interviewed them for the *NME* and they gave the first intimations that Big Flame had an agreed upon 'Sell By' date: 'We'd like to have five or six singles at the end of it all saying, "these are extracts from someone's life" – like postcards.'

One other person who, along with Peel, had unscrambled the code was Dave Parsons. Parsons had set up the curiously-named

Ron Johnson Records as a vehicle for promoting the music of his own band Splat! and had released 'The Splat! EP' in 1983. He heard 'Sink' played on the John Peel show, acquired a copy of the record and wrote to the band, offering to release a single. Big Flame immediately wrote back to take up his offer.

At the start of 1985, Big Flame found themselves in Cargo Studios in Rochdale, recording, as the Membranes and others had, with the legendary engineer John Brierley, who had effectively come out of retirement to produce the band. He did an amazing production job, as Brown told John Robb in *Death To Trad Rock*. 'He was deaf, so he turned everything up to the maximum until the needles snapped on the desk. It was a wall of sound.'

'Rigour' was released in March, another three-track EP, featuring 'Debra', 'Sargasso' and 'Man Of Few Syllables', all classics within the Big Flame canon. It was a significant step up from 'Sink', so good that the *NME* accidentally reviewed it twice, first noting its 'angry, controlled violence' and later deeming it 'the week's best guitar record'. The lyrics to 'Debra' were printed on the back cover, part ode to romance, part social statement that offered the advice that 'AN APPLE A DAY KEEPS THE DOLE AWAY'. The record's packaging moved things up a notch, as well. The AK 47 with the words 'HA HA HA HA HA' spewing out of the end of its barrel (the Laughing Gun logo) was still present, as was a variant of the Kangaroo, both images present on the first single, but the typographical front cover, with its vivid red and blue was utterly arresting.

'At the time we really liked Pop Art and Op Art, so we took that as a starting point, along with Italian futurist and Russian constructivist stuff,' Keeffe told the Blastitude blog, many years later. 'In typical Big Flame style it never really came out right, so we got the blue and red Kangaroos. As Jean Cocteau said, "Genius is the inability to conform"…'

The release of 'Rigour' more or less coincided with the release of Big Flame's 'Statement of Intent', a document/ manifesto penned by Alan that codified the band's position in relation to an industry that it largely despised. It listed a number of OBJEC-TIVES and outlined an EXECUTION OF OBJECTIVES as well as defining Big Flame. Big Flame was 'a tense and quirky "three-piece pop group" born out of a common dismay/ disgust/ distrust at the way creativity and individuality in pop music has once again been stifled'. 1977 had proved to be a false new dawn and the profiteers in the record industry were once more back in control. Big Flame would 'provide a positive and constructive alternative... through the application of honesty, integrity and dynamic enthusiasm'.

They would only make singles. because 'all the best and most innovative bands were singles bands – Buzzcocks, Orange Juice, Josef K, and numerous early punk bands'. Seven-inch singles were and always had been 'the ultimate in pop spontaneity'. And when they played live, their set would be limited to around nine songs and last no longer than about 25 minutes. There could be no encores, since encores only arose in post-congratulatory circumstances when the band wouldn't be able to commit 100%.

The Statement went on to list the band's influences and define their sound. Influences included, but weren't restricted to, the music of the Pop Group, the Higsons, the Sound of Young Scotland, Jacques Brel, Gil Scott Heron, Erto Morero and the Meters. The Big Flame sound combined 'syncopation, rhythm, a sense of the absurd and a sense of humour' manifested in 'Well-disciplined funk/ pop drums and bass, with overriding jazz-rhythmic guitar attack' and 'a hint of the old P. Haig nasals to finish it off'.

In *Death To Trad Rock*, Alan outlines the equipment for delivering rock's *coup d'état* – 'a small, cheap 50-watt guitar combo, with bass tone full down, treble and mid full up, and a Marshall bass 100 watt through a homemade extendable bass cab with 15" speakers borrowed from a Leslie cab some years earlier. Drums were stripped back to a minimal kick/ snare/ tom/ hi-hat and cymbal combination'. Oh yes, and everything would be played at 78 RPM. The band's message would be clear and the lyrics personal. The band itself was a political statement: 'We couldn't be anything else, or less.'

The whole thing was exhausting and almost certainly contributed to the demise of the band. To play as fast as they did, and as intently was physically and mentally draining. Agreed operating practice was strict, according to Keeffe: 'Dil wasn't allowed to drink before going on, Alan was allowed one pint to loosen him up and me, two! Most of the gigs were incredible. The audience would try and dance at the front, but the beats would get cut up and they'd fail to keep up. People would come backstage and ask about anything, from politics via French philosophy to guitar string thicknesses…'

The final part of the Statement dealt with target of the band's attack, deftly summing up the state of pop as many found it to be. Things of concern included 'the return to Rockism'; the apathy of those 'caught in a time warp circa '77'; the reappearance of the 'pop star', with all its attendant 'hype/ corruption/ dupery/ rip-offs'; and the rise of video as a cynical and expensive marketing ploy. Finally, the band committed itself to quitting once its purpose had been served, on the grounds that 'Hopefully by then there'll be better bands who will have the same idea and be willing to promote it.'

The third single, 'Tough', came out in the autumn of 1985 – three more shrapnel blasts in the form of 'All The Irish Must Go To Heaven' (a phrase Keeffe had overhead somebody use in a pub), 'Where's Our Carol?', and '¡Cuba!'. In inimitable fashion, Steven Wells, heaping praise upon the single, thought the band 'truly revolutionary – sticking, as they do, sticky fingers through the dry and flakey skin of le pop modern'. Big Flame was a much needed 'monkey boot in the back of the head' of independent music.

As had previously been the case, the lyrics to the songs were printed as part of the package. So often the words to a song were delivered in every bit as dislocated and staccato fashion as the music, emerging in a series disjointed slogans or half-delivered snippets of seemingly personal reminiscence. The delivery and content was always as emphatic as the music: in 'All The Irish Must Go To Heaven' the narrator 'pissed upon the blarney stone... and spat... hate in the snow'. '¡Cuba!' urged "Turn Your HATRED Into ENERGY!' and 'Collect Your Bile, Use It Like ACID!'.

There were two more Peel session in 1985, where, amongst other surprises, the band applied their deconstructing skills in a mind-blowing way to a couple of cover versions – Lee Hazlewood's 'These Boots Are Made For Walking' and The June Brides' 'Every Conversation'. They toured almost incessantly, including shows in Europe, and set up gig swaps with like-minded fellow indie groups. Brown create Ugly Noise Undercurrents to help promote the cultural exchanges, funding it through the Enterprise Allowance Scheme that offered £40 per week support. They started the Wilde Club, hiring out a Jamaican dominoes den called the Man Alive to put on gigs and a disco that was initially DJ'd by Dave Haslam. 'The first thing we did,' recalls Keeffe, 'was get two hand stamps made up, one with 'THE WILDE CLUB' on it, and the other with 'GET YOUR GODDAM HAIRCUT!' on it. If you turned up looking cool, you got the first. If you looked like a Goth, you got the second. We saw it as educational...'

The approach to contemporary indie bands was equally as Stalinist, with fellow journeymen judged harshly. 'We travelled light,' says Keeffe. 'We had very few allies in the business. We set out to be in opposition to all the decadence that was prevailing, so we had to hate all the bands. And we really did hate them, even the ones on Ron Johnson. However, over time, we started to develop friendships with kindred spirits such as the June Brides and the Mackenzies.' The June Brides ran a club similar to the Wilde Club, organised gig swaps with Big Flame and Brown, writing as Helvicta Halbfett, contributed to Jon Hunter's peripatetic fanzine, *Bandits One To Five*.

The penultimate Big Flame single came out in April 1986, the result of another trip to Cargo: once again, John Brierley handled production. By title alone, 'Why Popstars Can't Dance' proved to be one of the more intriguing releases of that spring, and even although its thionic aural assault did little to enlighten the listener as to why pop stars *couldn't* dance, it was appropriately provocative, the record's dead wax on one side bearing the message: 'THIS GUITAR KILLS LIBERALS'. It trod familiar territory, thought Richard Boon in the *Catalogue*, but reassuringly was 'still rigour matched with vigour'. Steven Wells writing in the *NME* agreed, continuing to heap praise on the 'absoscorching wonderful, in like, a really *awesome* way' band. Both reviewers were singing from the same song sheet as Big Flame's producer. 'Perhaps only once in a producer's life does he meet musical greatness,' he had breathlessly commented at the start of the year. 'It happened to me when I was asked to produce Big Flame.'

A final single, 'Cubist Pop Manifesto' followed, and fragments of the first three singles found their way onto an export 10", 'Two Kan Guru' – dead wax message, 'TOO YOUNG TO KNOW, TOO STUPID TO CARE. A six-track 12", also titled 'Cubist Pop Manifesto', was released in Germany. 'Two Kan Guru' came with a sleeve note penned by The Boy With The Pen Up His Arse (Keeffe) and claimed that Green and Brown had once been members of Wham!'s backing back, a boast that some gullible observers fell for.

If the 10" and 12" formats ran against the grain of the State-ment of Intent, then perhaps it was just another subversive twist in the story, although by the time of the release of 'Two Kan Guru', the planned-out ending was already in sight. One of the highlights of 'Cubist Pop Manifesto' was the track 'Baffled Island', a collapsed structure that musically travels from the sublime to the ridiculous and is underpinned by some unusually scraping and unholy guitar work from Keeffe. It was sometimes referred to as '3 Men On Baffled Island' (as one of the Peel Sessions faithfully registers it) and that may well be a more fitting title.

For some, the music of Big Flame was baffling, and the idea of the three of them castaway (as they were) on their own Treasure Island, with all of the intimations of madness it conjures up, is too delicious to avoid. In a band comprised of three, there is nowhere to hide – all the arguments are lopsided. Intra-band tension in Big Flame was part and parcel of their genius. 'There were *many* arguments,' recalls Keeffe. Usually, he says, it would be him and Green siding together against Brown. 'We never knew when to shut up,' recalls Keeffe. 'I think Alan despaired of us. There were many tensions, possibly arising from the differences in our backgrounds – Alan was much more conventional in his opinions, developed from his working class Yorkshire mining background, whereas Dil grew up in a Hippie commune and I had Manchester/ Irish Catholic roots. Alan's dad was an ex-Army Northern Irish Protestant, my dad an Irish Republican supporting singer. Alan was from Yorkshire and I was from Lancashire. Dil held it all together, really, by liking us both and using negotiating skills picked up in the commune.'

Big Flame played for the last time at The Boardwalk in Manchester on 11 October 1986. The flyer for the event billed them as 'MAn ñchesteR's FAVOURITE JAZZ fuck ttrio EXPLOSIONE!'. The Laughing Gun image spitted out the word GOODBYE and offered 'A cheerful 2 fingers to the doubters', before adding, 'For short sighted intellectual puny types this advertises "bIG fLAME say goodbye"'. The night was a success and such were the feelings that the band, for once, broke its own rules and played an encore, but that was it. It is doubtful that there was a shred of energy left to give.

Dil Green went back to university to finish his architecture studies, and Alan Brown quickly emerged with a new band, the Great Leap Forwards. Greg Keeffe returned to his 'shit flat' and just stared at the wall. 'When it was over, even though we planned the end, I became terminally depressed,' he says. 'I had nothing left. I had given everything and it took me two years to get over it. Things had moved so fast and there had been no safety net – we had careered through this reality with no reference points. Now I see Big Flame more as performance art, and not a band in the true sense. It had a life of its own and became existential. Big Flame was '80s anti-matter: something that balanced the excesses of a band like Wham! and the triteness of an event like Live Aid.

'I'm still proud of it, warts and all, and wouldn't change anything. That's why we will never reform: the performance is over; burning is irreversible. It can't be recreated and there is no sheet music to play along to.'

The Crescents in Hulme – 'the worst housing stock in Europe', according to the experts – began to be demolished in 1991, just 19 years after the 'streets in the sky' had first gone up. The passing marked the end of a free if dangerous playground in which Manchester bands of the mid-1980s had run amok, including Big Flame, A Certain Ratio, Frantic Elevators, and Inca Babies. Later residents included Ruthless Rap Assassins and various members of the Stone Roses. Many others passed through the area on the way to the Hacienda or the Grants Arms pub.

One Hulme band whose trace has vanished almost as thoroughly as the rubble from the Crescents is Tools You Can Trust. For an all too short a time the band was a significant feature of the indie landscape, creating a sound that largely dispensed with guitars and utilised the metal of fire extinguishers, beer barrels, old bed frames and the obligatory pneumatic drill. Sonically positioned somewhere within that territory mapped out by PIL, A Certain Ratio and Suicide, with a touch of the Normal thrown in, the band's 'metal pop twang' was more rhythmic than the sounds associated with like-minded metallurgists such as Einsturzende Neubauten, SPK and Test Department. Tools You Can Trust often covered Duane Eddy songs in their live set, a move that eternally endeared them to John Peel who booked them for a session having heard their self-produced first single, 'Working & Shopping'. Strongly politicised lyrics were often half-whispered, creating a seductive yet unsettling listening experience at times.

At the heart of the band were Ben Steadman and Rob Ward, handling bass and tapes and vocals and drums. They were aided by a large cast of others, who added in, where necessary, extra guitar, trumpet and the sound of various bits of industrial equipment. But the band primarily described itself as 'twang', and, as they told *City Life* in 1985 followed 'a tradition of twang, from Duane Eddy, Link Wray, the Shadows', adding, 'It's really where the guitar shines'. The lyrics were crafted cut-up style, a la William S Burroughs, and focused on the socialist beliefs of Steadman and Ward, some of which they unashamedly admitted had been inherited from their parents. The important thing was having the courage to speak out, since most people were afraid 'of being obvious, saying what they believe in', as Steadman told the *NME* at the time of the release of their second single, 'Show Your Teeth'/ 'Messy Body Thrust': 'All those people in the Hulme Crescents who wear no socks... they've got the right ideas but either seem embarrassed or guilty about their backgrounds.' 'Show Your Teeth' had one of the best lyrics ever:

A haircut doesn't matter
Clause Four matters

one that referred to the under-threat clause in the Labour Party's constitution that guaranteed to 'secure for the workers, by hand or by brain, the full fruits of their industry'.

As was the case with Big Flame in full flow, Tools You Can Trust at their best, both live and on record, could be formidable. With its unexpected elements of twang, their music was as eerie in places as a David Lynch movie, and like a Lynch movie, the inclusion of the velvet rock and roll element didn't comfort but rather added a disturbing twist. The titles of their songs echo loudly the political nature of their approach – 'Show Your Teeth', 'Cut A New Seam', 'The Work Ahead Of Us', 'A Knock For The Young'. But in addressing such subjects as the dignity of labour, the working class and the vulnerability of the unions, the songs weren't intended as slogans but instead splinters of resistance in a body where the music and message were all of a part.

There were two further singles, the excellent 'Cut A New Seam' in 1984, and less essential 'Say It Low' in 1986, by which point the band's moment was over. The first three (and best) singles were collected together on a 12", *Sharpen The Tools*. There were two albums – 1985's *Yet More Proof*, featuring tracks culled from a live performance at the Venue, Manchester on May Day 1985, and 1986's studio album, *Again Again Again*. Everything was released on the band's own Hulme-based record label Red Energy Dynamo. Three Peel sessions, recorded in 1983 and 1984, were later released on cassette (label unspecified). A compilation video, *The Tools For Better Labour*, was released in 1987.

And that was it. The band disappeared without trace, at odds with a culture become increasingly flash and proud of it. When they had started out, one commentator had described Steadman and Ward as looking like 'sub-heroes from *The Ragged-Trousered*

Philanthropist'. By the time the band had finished, philanthropy was out and self-interest was the name of the game. Perhaps that is why today the work of Tools You Can Trust is lost in a time capsule, almost entirely overlooked by chroniclers of the music of its age.

CHAPTER 11
STAPLE DIETS – A NOTE ON FANZINES

LONG BEFORE APPEARING IN THE music press, many bands had already been written about in fanzines. Music fanzines were bulletins from the front, first dispatches in a so-called 'war on pop' that served to remind us that the individual view, unvarnished and occasionally erratic, was a valid one. The breadth and variety of mid-80s fanzines was almost as bewildering as the names chosen to anoint them, which included *Trout Fishing In Leytonstone, Adventure In Bereznik, To Hell With Poverty, Bandits One To Five*, and *Attack On Bzag*. In some instances, the editorial approach was abrasive – machine gun graphics dipped in editorial vitriol; in others, the style was more measured, with designed layouts and conventionally represented text, reflecting a design aesthetic that could be traced back to the 1950s and literary magazines such as Martin Bax's *Ambit* where images and words were, for the first time, given equal weight. These fanzines included *Debris, Monitor*, and *Hungry Beat*. Reflecting the generally obsessive nature of the fan magazine, at the extreme best, the fanzine editor was part maverick and part madman, possessively producing work that was jealously guarded yet instantly loveable. At its best, the fanzine always felt as if it had been written by everyone and was for everyone.

By summer 1984 the music fanzine had been through many phases, the celebrated era of the punk fanzine just one in a long line that stretched back to the 1960s and publications such as Paul Williams' *Crawdaddy!* and Greg Shaw's *Mojo Navigator* in the USA, and to Pete Frame's *Zigzag*, Brian Hogg's *Bam Balam* and Andy Child's *Fat Angel*, to name but a few, in the UK. But the punk explosion in 1976/77 came to overshadow everything else, so much so that many people still regard fanzine Year Zero as summer 1976 when Mark Perry launched *Sniffin' Glue*, a samizdat production quickly joined in the racks by Tony D's *Ripped & Torn*, Sandy Robertson's *White Stuff*, Adrian Thrills' *48 Thrills*, and Jon Savage's *London's Outrage* (which was, coincidentally, the first fanzine to print the Rough Trade shop address as a point of contact thus connecting with the alternative distribution network that served the whole genre).

But just as punk fizzled out quickly, co-opted into the mainstream, so too the early punk fanzines were replaced by a second wave, publications that were more visually aggressive, such as Mick Mercer's *Panache*, *Grinding Halt*, *Allied Propaganda* and *Vague*. The second wave also included fanzines with an explicit political focus, anarcho-punk titles such as *International Anthem* (a fanzine created by Crass), *Cobalt Hate*, *Mucilage*, and *Temporary Hoarding*, which grew out of the Rock Against Racism movement. These, in turn, were replaced by a third wave, early forerunners of which included *Artificial Life*, *Rox*, *Groovy Black Shades*, *Juniper Beri Beri* and *Communication Blur*. By 1984 the third wave included, amongst many others, *Monitor*, *Hungry Beat*, *Adventure In Bereznik* and the *Legend!*, all of which were published for the first time that year.

Fanzines epitomised the DIY, independent ethic more than anything else – introducing graphics of resistance and creating a new language to articulate the passions felt for the music and politics they described. This wasn't the dust-dry voice of the orthodoxy, but a sprightly hymn to obsession, unrestricted by laws of design or grammar. This is nowhere more apparent than in the words of seventeen-year-old James Brown, interviewed by the *NME* in 1985 about his fanzine *Attack On Bzag* and its use of chaotic visuals: 'There is a lot of effort that goes in to making *Bzag* messy. [The designer] Neville Brody once said that he wanted people to look at the pages of the *Face* three times before they understood it. I want people to look at Bzag ten times and *still* not understand it.'

Brown's contrarian approach chimed with the element of subversion that had come to be expected by fanzine readers ever since punk, when what was once a 'fan mag' pure and simple became something else, often a gesture of self-expression manifesting itself through disdain for the establishment. As was the case with the underground press of the 1960s in Britain, it was never, of course, *the* Establishment that was under attack but (in this case) rather a music business establishment, which had come to be seen as encompassing the mainstream music press as well. Just occasionally, the subversive approach itself was subverted. In amongst the spleen and bile of early 1977, Jon Savage produced a second and final issue of *London's Outrage* that was simply a photographic record of him having walked around west London to record the decay, some of which had gone unchecked since the end of the Second World War. It certainly stood apart. And writer and artist Edwin Pouncey (aka Savage Pencil) dreamed up a plan to produce a Ramones fanzine called *Pinhead*. Like *London's Outrage, Pinhead* would contain 'no dialogue and no narrative, just images and collages… I wanted it to confuse people. I wanted it to be about an inch thick so you'd need nuts and bolts to put it together.'

A decade or so later, that same joyous and wayward spirit found its way into the letters addressed to Dave Haslam, editor of the Manchester-based fanzine *Debris*. *Debris*, like every other fanzine worth its salt, generated an enthusiastic dialogue, usually in the form of odes of appreciation or rants of displeasure addressed to the editor. 'However, buried among those letters,' says Haslam, 'there was always one or two from some kind soul or other saying that they liked *Debris* and how grand it was to read a fanzine that wasn't full of the usual shit (just the "unusual" shit)'.

(just the 'unusual' shit) – this is what people came to expect and want from fanzines, and the parenthesis is important, since fanzine creators tended to exist in worlds that were sometimes self-imposingly withdrawn, and often saw themselves as outside and downtrodden in some way, even within their own creed. Certainly in the mid-1980s, the mainstream music press, whose intermittent roundup columns remained one of the few serious providers of mass publicity for the fanzines, regularly criticised,

even mocked, their content, in the process usually lamenting the passing of the 'golden age' of *Sniffin' Glue, et al.* The same was also true in reverse. Writing about the same subject, the two cultures were often diametrically opposed. For instance, Sean O'Hagan begins a fanzine round-up in the *NME* on 26 January 1985 in not atypical style: 'There is, in case you are lucky enough not to have noticed, an outcrop of fanzines/ commix, most of which seem intent on combining the worst aspects of both (ahem) genres.'

O'Hagan was certainly right about their being an outcrop, a steady rise in the numbers during 1984 that was at least partly attributable to the new music that was coming through on labels such as Creation Records, Pink, In Tape, and others. Other notable fanzines to appear that year included *Rouska* (whose editor later set up a rudimentary fanzine distribution network), the *Underground*, *Bombs Away Batman*, *Noise Annoys*, and *To Hell With Poverty*. And a number of fanzines that had first been published during 1983, such as *Attack On Bzag*, *Debris* and *Slow Dazzle*, were starting to get seriously into their stride at that point.

The *NME*'s January fanzine round-up had included a review of the first issue of *Monitor*, a fanzine-cum-'pop journal' which had been published out of Oxford towards the end of 1984 with writing from Paul Oldfield, Simon Reynolds, Hilary Little, Chris Scott and David Stubbs. To begin with, *Monitor* carried no interviews and had no reviews (a policy willingly reversed once it received the irresistible offer of 'free' review singles by a PR), but the first issue did carry a lengthy critique of the whole punk fanzine genre at the time. In *Fanzines: The Lost Moment*, Simon Reynolds praised fanzines simply for *being*, suggesting that 'What is significant about fanzines is not what they say so much as what they are, or even *that* they are.' The writing of fanzines was indeed a route to self-expression, but, noticed Reynolds, much of the individuality present in early (punk) fanzines had subsequently become lost, submerged in a tranche of predictable writing that was as conservative as that which the fanzine editors set out to oppose. The work set itself up as 'a seething harvest of quality, vitality and resistance' fighting against the '"apathy", "mediocrity", and "conservatism"' elsewhere, but was it any more?

The argument mirrors similar criticisms made against independent music at the time and shortly before, following on from Mick Mercer's diatribes of a year earlier, Tony Fletcher's 'Statement' of 1982, the comments that had increasingly been raised generally in the music press (particularly in 1982 by critics such as Adrian Thrills) and Richard North's progressive quest for a 'positive' antidote. In fact, valid though the criticisms in *Fanzines: The Lost Moment* are, fanzines by 1984 were once again going through a period of change, reflecting a different approach and culture to those that had gone before, which had been more defined by punk attitudes.

Part of the change also reflected the promotion of lifestyle as way of living, Margaret Thatcher's free market drive hammering home the message that we are, or were about to become, what we buy. As proved to be the case, pop music was the perfect vehicle for realising this, as the proliferation of glossy lifestyle magazines that sprang up in the early 1980s, such as the *Face* showed. Fanzines weren't immune from the effects of all this and, in many cases, became lifestyle extensions for those that compiled them. Even in the usual instance where ego didn't run rampant, there was a shift from the former process of purely commenting on things to placing oneself at the centre and seeing oneself as a part of the process.

Hungry Beat, one of the very best fanzines of the period, appeared in September 1984, 1000 copies printed up using the facilities at the Jackson Lane Community Centre in London's Archway. 'RIDING THE CREST OF A NEW WAVE…' its strapline read, and the new bands featured included the Jasmine Minks, the June Brides, the Loft and the Jesus & Mary Chain. But there was space as well for older music, and the Fire Engines, Vic Godard and the Lovin' Spoonful also featured. Like *Monitor*,

Hungry Beat carried no interviews, just well articulated passions of editor Kevin Pearce, one reason why the *NME* singled it out for special praise, calling it 'a shamelessly enthusiastic fanzine …that could only have been compiled by a fanatic'. It quickly sold out, in the process setting something of a benchmark.

'The motivation for doing it, and for everything since, was to share musical passions,' says Kevin Pearce today. 'That is, this is what I love and I want to tell you about it in a way that hopefully complements the music and becomes part of the art itself. There was an awful lot about the music scene that I didn't like in 1984, and very few groups I liked. Of course, part of that is down to taste. But I could see a pattern where a lot of openness and style of the early 1980s was being rejected in favour of a much narrower musical focus, with the complete disaster of bands who had got major label deals and what I perceived as a very unpleasant underground scene whose musical values I did not share. But as the summer of 1984 progressed with records and live shows from Jasmine Minks, June Brides, the Loft, the Jesus & Mary Chain, allied to enduring favourites like Hurrah!, Felt and Go-Betweens, I was having fun again. All these bands were a little rough and wonderfully inventive in a subtle way. They were also desperately unloved, which added to the sense of being in a battle to get my message across.'

Simon Murphy, whose *Adventure in Bereznik* pre-dated *Hungry Beat* by just a few weeks, also found motivation in a music scene that looked as if it was about to become reignited: 'I really thought during the summer of 1984 that music had reached its lowest point for a very long time – I hadn't been listening to new music for a few years, with the exception of a few bands I kept up with like the Television Personalities. Then a chance meeting with Joe Foster in the Rough Trade shop, where he was playing an advance copy of *The Painted Word* to the people that worked there, led to my discovering the Living Room. This was at the end of 1983.'

Around about the same time that the first issues of *Hungry Beat* and *Adventure In Bereznik* were being printed, the Manchester fanzine *Debris* was reaching its fifth issue and was also being featured in the *NME*. Unlike *Hungry Beat*, *Debris did* contain interviews, and articles on anything that caught the roaming eye of its editor, Dave Haslam. In one issue, Coil featured alongside an interview with the American short-story writer Raymond Carver, in another, a Durutti Column interview sat next to an op-ed piece about the state of the NHS in Manchester. There were articles on the cheldrens animated adventure series *Thunderbirds*, fish and chip shops, the local newsagent and barber, Mass Observation and every so often the most brilliant lists would be compiled. A 'Top 5 Queues' gave not just the worst Manchester queues but the time of them – 'Hacienda (Saturdays 10.30 – 12.00PM)', 'Gregg's Bakery, Rusholme (9.00AM)', etc.

Debris was printed up at the Manchester Free Press – traditionally printers of much radical material – and the initial print run was in the low hundreds but quickly rose into the thousands. Production costs were defrayed by selling advertising (a traditionally taboo area in the world of fanzines), picked up wherever possible.

'The local veggie café (On The Eight Day) advertised,' recalls Haslam, 'as did the hairdressers who were housed in the Hacienda basement called Swing. Swing had a very odd idea about what kind of advert they wanted, and thought that a big picture of Charlie Manson with a strapline 'Hair By Swing' would work. I advised them against that. So then they gave me a picture of William Shatner with a swastika drawn on his forehead. Not really an improvement, but I needed the £40 or whatever it was I was getting paid for the full-page ad.'

Placing music within a broader cultural context enabled Haslam to engage with 'real life stuff' and shine a beacon on the 'huge parts of our lives that were under-documented'. Mindful also of a pedigree running back to the counter culture and Manchester underground papers such as *Mole Express*, *Debris* was also important in disseminating information at a time when information was often supressed or distorted or false as filtered through official channels.

'I was living in the 1980s but interested in the 1930s. There were similarities: economic depression particularly in the North of England and also the threat of war – nobody has quite analysed how nuclear threat invade our culture at the time. I was interested in the way the Mass Observation project of the 1930s tried to pin down (and thus assign value to) "ordinary" lives. And I remember feeling that there was still this information vacuum – the mid-1980s was more like the mid-1960s when information outside of the most obvious stuff couldn't be accessed, unlike today when there is information overload. For instance, we were being told lies about the economy, about Reagan arming the Contras, about the policing of the miners' strike. Really, I think I should have got stuck into that more. Some of this lack of information was just basic stuff about history and ideas and good music and good films and good books. I just wanted to put a few things in the public domain, even if only in a small way.'

Debris came into being after Haslam had left Manchester University and moved to the notorious Hulme estate but had no idea what he might do next. 'I had no real plan for my life apart from a desire to write and a big interest in music, but not just music,' he recalls. 'I've always been a bit confused by the world and want to work out what's going on. Writing things down, then as now, seemed like a step in the right direction.'

Montitor emerged in similar fashion, after the authors had graduated and were scratching around for something interesting to do next. 'As undergraduates, we had done a magazine called *Margin*, which had started out as a fanzine and then become a wall sheet which we stuck up everywhere for free,' says Reynolds. 'That petered out in a final blast that was a series of manifestos.' *Monitor*, unlike *Margin*, which was a more polemical 'poverty of student life'-type publication, was not Oxford-tied, but rather broader in scope – 'music, fashion, ideas'. Stylishly designed (without being *too* stylish), it was printed up in the offices of Daily Information, a company that provided services for students completing PhDs. Reynolds lived in the building and occasionally sneaked down in the middle of the night to take advantage of the facilities free of charge.

With their relatively clean design lines, *Monitor*, *Debris*, *Hungry Beat* and *Adventure In Bereznik* were antithetical of the great mass of fanzines that deliberately adopted the messier, splatter-gun graphics approach. Ever since punk, an anti-style ethos demanded that for a fanzine to be authentic, it needed to be unpolluted by the hand of the designer. The long-running fanzine, *Vague* (considered by many to be *the* best fanzine of the period), and whose design epitomised the visually chaotic approach, once received a letter complaining that it was too well-produced to be 'real fanzine' after an issue came out that was perfectly bound. Of course, the anti-design fanzines were every bit as time consuming (if not more so) to produce as their more designed counterparts.

'There was undoubtedly common ground between those producing that kind of fanzine and what I was attempting at *Hungry Beat*,' says Pearce, 'but I hated that contrived scruffiness and bad-handwriting approach. It did reflect the music those fanzines often covered, but I found it terribly conservative.' Like Pearce, Simon Reynolds was sympathetic to the overall cause but also slightly 'DIY sceptic' when it came to the more freeform design. Simon Murphy was more sympathetic: 'I liked the design in some of the messier fanzines. I liked the way, for instance, that in John Robb's *Rox* every single millimetre of the page seemed to have a stupid drawing, a funny picture or a picked up clipping. I tried to do some things like that in *Adventure In Bereznik* but in a more structured way.'

One of the earliest fanzines to fervently espouse the value of the visually chaotic was indeed John Robb's *Rox* (formerly *Blackpool Rox*) that had been started in 1978, developed out of an A4 single sheet publication called *Broadsnide* that Robb and friends had put together and disseminated whilst still at school. Robb formed the Membranes along with Mark Tilton and began the fanzine after Tilton's father, a printer, showed them the way around a photocopier. Fanzines like *Rox* – full of 'fierce articles and egotistical rants' – are the precursor to the modern day blog, according to Robb. *Rox* drew further inspiration 'from the 1970s books of Spike Milligan, which were often a jumble of text and cut and paste visual nonsense. It was a small imaginative leap to see the process in punk terms – ripping up the culture and putting it back together again', something Robb attempted with his band.

Rox was part of a group that took to calling itself 'the clique versus the bleak' and publications involved included Jerry Thackray's fanzine, the *Legend!*. Thackray had previously written for Alan McGee's *Communication Blur*, famously contributing its crotchety *Sound Of Music* column, but had set up on his own after disagreements about the direction a planned but never published third issue of *Communication Blur* should go in. McGee, through connections with Rough Trade's Geoff Travis, felt he would be able to secure a flexi disc by the Smiths to give away with the issue, but Thackray was uncomfortable with such a move.

Part of the 'clique' was James Brown, in 1985 a precocious seventeen-year-old whose *Attack On Bzag* was described in one music paper round-up as 'perhaps the ultimate fanzine?' This, of course depends upon definition, but certainly with its *uber* scruffy approach and blitzkrieg editorial ranting, it fulfilled part of the criteria in one sense.

'Selling the fanzine was our destiny, our means to exist,' Brown told the *Independent* in 2005. 'I hand printed them on a Roneo Gestetner machine, which had correction fluids that could keep you going long after the printing had finished.' Badly printed and collated by hand – 'we had the paper cuts and ink under the nails to prove it' – it was, claimed Brown, 'the closest I ever came to hard work.'

Brown's fanzine placed him firmly at the centre of things. Interviewed as part of an NME cover story *("'ZINE-AGE KICKS'*, NME 12/10/85), Brown was only half-joking when he said, 'I could say I'm jumping up and down on the corpse of rock 'n' roll.' And presumably the *NME*, a great supporter of *Attack On Bzag*, was only half-joking back when it in turn called him 'thoroughly obnoxious and rude'.

Such faux swagger went with what Dave Haslam calls 'the punchy and combative, ker-pow approach' of the clique writers, people whose text seems to have been punched out on the keyboard rather than typed. The freneticism is summed up quite brilliantly in that same *NME* cover story where Jerry Thackray outlines the reasons for creating a fanzine, which are: 'Boredom, anger, yearning, excitement, hope, egotism. To sell 'em, to corrupt other less fortunate mortals to your brilliant taste, to care, create, caress, carp, to find your own alternatives, to communicate, to wander freely off at multi-tangents, stumble blissfully over historical mistakes and express yourselves.' In the same feature, Thackray goes on to review the best ten of the current crop of fanzines. Top of the list – 'the best, the boss and the brightest' – was issue 4 of the *Legend!*.

Thackray's description does a good, perhaps even exhaustive job of nailing the appeal of the fanzine for creator and user alike. But not every fanzine voice could be as startling or amusing or car-crash engaging as *Rox*, *Attack On Bzag* or the *Legend!*. Indeed, as Reynolds pointed out, the conforming mass did little above duplicating what amounted to more or less the same interview with more or less the same few bands (Three Johns, Redskins, Billy Bragg, etc).

The very best, though, were a notch above, and often enlivened their fare with material addressing the various issues of the day. The five published issues (the clue is in the title) of the excellent *Bandits One To Five*, a fanzine edited by Jon Hunter of the June Brides, always included some sort of investigative story, pointing the finger at the exploitative or those in the moral wrong, such as Uranium company RZT, or fruit canners Del Monte, both of whom had at the time appalling ethical reputations. Another probing publication was *To Hell With Poverty*, where the blight of Thatcher and the presence of Trident were just two thorns the reader was constantly reminded of.

The mid-1980s marked the unstoppable rise of *Viz*, Chris Donald's parody comic that had, interestingly enough, been modelled along the lines of a punk fanzine and similarly relied on alternative distribution. Some fanzines tapped into the spirit of *Viz*, humour being an essential ingredient and the bond that most easily locked creator and reader together. Since most fanzines didn't really critique, they were never detached in a way that the mainstream music press was. The amateurishness was just a further part of the appeal.

One of the funniest fanzines was *Alphabet Soup*, another publication that ran to just five issues, each issue lettered rather than numbered. Edited by Miki Bereyni and Emma Anderson, who together later formed the band Lush, its humour was deliberately aimed low and all the more engaging for that. Issue A had been sold at 5p but by the time Issue C appeared the price had gone up to 10p, a still respectable charge as was indicated on the cover: 'It's Obscene, It's Badly Written & It's Shit – But It's Only 10p'. In amongst the almost relentless self-deprecating humour, the borderline pornography and the merciless mocking of Goths, though, were articles that could be both informative and educational, guides to drugs in issue *C*, for instance, and a note about deaths in police custody in issue *D*.

Trout Fishing In Leytonstone was another fanzine with a sharp sense of the absurd. Along with *Adventure In Bereznik*, it can lay claim to being one of the most brilliantly realised publications, one where the design is perfectly in sync with the content, using different coloured inks for different pages, on occasion, and striking an editorial tone that was very influential on a number of fanzines that followed. An early issue, quite typical of the publication's run, had a cooking page, a pin-up of footballer Bobby Charlton and a double page fashion spread with a cut-out doll of Alex Taylor from the Shop Assistants with clothes to cut out and dress her up in. The look here, and elsewhere in other similar fanzines, reminds the reader of 1970s teenage magazines such as *Jackie* or *Shoot*.

Although they tended to be the ones getting the lion's share of coverage in music papers, fanzines about independent guitar bands weren't the only DIY publications out there. There were reggae fanzines (*Small Axe*, *Chains Around My Feet*), soul fanzines (*Sweet Soul Music*, *Blackbeat*), fanzines devoted to psychedelia (*Kicks*, *Outasite*, *99th Floor*), and a whole raft of publications dedicated to Mod. Mod Nights were still being put on at London's 100 Club and other venues, attracting mainly those who were first turned on by the Mod revival of 1979. Reading matter included *The New Stylist*, *In The Crowd*, *Shadows & Reflections*, and *Empty Hours* (motto: 'We Were Born Originals, Don't Let Us Die Copies'). *Shadows & Reflections* covered a whole range of music, including Power Pop, Soul, New Wave and Neo Psychedelia, the latter also covered in Paul Groovy's *Groovy Black Shades*, which had started out life covering the mod/ new psychedelic scene and graduated towards the music being played in Alan McGee's Living Room where Paul Groovy effectively became house photographer.

Groovy Black Shades had originally been a gazette, a fanzine that reproduced snippets from music press articles, news items and singles reviews and covered bands involved in the neo psychedelic and neo mod movement (Miles Over Matter, Mood Six), before gradually beginning to cover bands that came out of the Whaam! records stable (the Times, the Direct Hits, the Pastels). At a time when most independent releases printed a contact address on the record sleeve, editor Paul Groovy wrote to people like Dan Treacy and Stephen Pastel and eventually Alan McGee, whose fanzine he had been guided to by Stephen Pastel. For a long time, communication was by letter and it was some time before he actually got to meet these people. Eventually, though, *Groovy Black Shades* began covering bands coming through the Living Room scene.

There were contributions in *Groovy Black Shades* from Alan McGee ('The Creation Cowboy'), Jerry Thackray, Jowe Head and others. Thackray, Stephen Pastel and Bobby Gillespie contributed to *Communication Blur*, and Gillespie, writing as Pete Whiplash wrote sometimes for *Hungry Beat* (on one occasion, penning an article about the Jesus & Mary Chain, the band he was in at the time.) John Robb, Jerry Thackray and James Brown regularly wrote for each other's fanzines. As has been noted, the 'Manchester Correspondent' for *Bandits One To Five*, Helvicta Halbfett, was in fact Alan Brown of Big Flame.

If such a thing as a scene really did exist, then these connections helped underpin it. They underpinned it, but also underlined the fact that rivalry between fanzines was no different than the rivalry that existed between the mainstream music papers (who never overlooked an opportunity to knock each other when it arose). Two of the three principal ingredients of the fanzine were paper and staples – but the most important one was ego.

'I wrote about fanzines in an issue of *Melody Maker* and used a Hip Hop analogy,' says Reynolds. 'Just like Hip Hop, fanzines involved massive egos, pouring out all these words and opinions in a "World According To..." way. There was an adolescent, brittle narcissism to it – all very cocky, yet also insecure and easily offended/ wounded. It was certainly a case of delusions of grandeur spilling into paranoia...'

The view from beyond the trenches, that the troops were rallying around together to fight the common enemy, was far from the case, internecine rivalry greater than the joint hatred of the music press that looked down upon them most of the time.

'There is a tendency to lump everything together,' Kevin Pearce wrote in a recent blog on the twenty-fifth anniversary of the first publication of *Hungry Beat*. 'So naturally there is a view that the fanzine world was one big happy family, that the underground music scene in the mid-1980s was a big happy family, and so on. No chance. There were more schisms and factions than you could shake a stick at.'

Like all families, however, what bound the fanzine fraternity together was greater than what set it apart, and just by the very act of *being* they existed in necessary opposition to the mainstream music press. The press became targets of rants – and with no corporate line to toe, no advertisers (largely) to pander to, and no cruel hand of the sub-editor at play, the rants could be skewering, and devastatingly funny, as was the case with Thackray's contributions to *Communication Blur*, (quoted earlier). But there was a symbiosis between the established music business and the fanzine world – many fanzine writers had one eye on future and the prospect of landing a 'proper job' on the music papers, and the press in turn was all too aware of the scouting value of the fanzines.

Forthright views, though, pay no heed. The prime characteristic of Alan McGee's *Communication Blur* was its tone, breathlessly enthusing at the same time as damning, going off pell-mell at a number of tangents and delivering its message in a series of one-word slogans ('Create!', 'Communicate!', etc) buried under a mound of exclamation marks. One critic wittily compared it to 'a slightly broken Dalek', but this misses the point. It wasn't the prose style that was important but the power of the message. *Communication Blur* was very influential and certainly influenced others, including *Adventure In Bereznik* and *Hungry Beat*: 'I didn't necessarily like the bands Alan wrote about in *Communication Blur*, but I loved his attitude and the way that he challenged ideas,' says Pearce, whose first point of contact in the fanzine world was McGee.

In Scotland, a similar message was being relayed in *Juniper Beri Beri*, a fanzine compiled by Annabel Wright (Aggi) with help from Jill Bryson from Strawberry Switchblade, Jill's boyfriend Pete McArthur and Stephen Pastel. The first issue, published in 1983, had been written towards the end of 1982 and was an attempt, according to Stephen Pastel, 'to try to make something beautiful and unique within the limitations of affordable printing techniques... and to document our world and to give space to the music we liked, including the Pastels.' It was beautifully conceived, and idiosyncratic in the best possible way, running cut-out Batman mobiles and plant guides in amongst the music stuff. But it was also refreshingly spikey. Issue one set the tone, complaining that 'a hedonist on a diet of pop music is very likely to starve to death' given the dearth of good music, before launching into a 'Postcard Records Obituary' that pulled no punches.

By autumn 1984, Alan McGee and Stephen Pastel were key participants in a network of like-minded agitators that the fanzine world had helped draw together. The criticism of a stagnant independent music scene, voiced here by Kevin Pearce and Simon Murphy, was becoming endemic and not just the view of fanzine writers. Following an NUJ dispute with IPC, the *NME* had been absent for most of the summer but returned in a sprightly, no-nonsense fashion, declaring 'War On Pop' on the cover of its 8 September 1984 issue, where it vowed to 'slam the flim flam'.

Central to the issue was a two-page Ian Penman essay (*Into Battle*) that delivered a diagnosis on, and possible cure for, 'the state of pop'. Published against the backdrop of the inexorable rise of Frankie Goes To Hollywood ('Two Tribes', with its Gorbachev/ Reagan video had been *the* big hit of the summer),

Penman's dense text (which lengthily quoted from the work of Post-Modernist icon Jean Baudrillard) suggested that pop must be rescued from the banal, but offered up just two curious examples of how that was already being done; the first was in the work of post-Disco rock band Was Not Was, the second, through the output of Frankie's record label, ZTT (where Penman's friend Paul Morley was Director of Publicity).

The article alienated some who found the idea of replacing one shiny pop presence with another abhorrent. They felt also that it smacked of what it was – log-rolling of the first order. Many could perceive little difference in the scheme of things between the corporate antics of a major record label and the supposedly playful intervention of ZTT. Further, set against the deep gloom of the miners' strike, the sentiments seemed hollow and remote. And so the net effect was that it made a number of those setting out on the indie road more steeled in their resolve, underlining for them the fact that if this was what the war on pop was meant to lead to, well it was hardly a war worth fighting in the first place. Looking back, Kevin Pearce isn't alone in thinking that both the Frankie effect and the (later) Band Aid corporate rock engagement of the time were 'triggers for an underground reaction with a burst of activity in groups, labels, fanzines and club nights'.

Certainly, 1985 turned into an acme year – with many indie bands forming or putting out records for the first time that year, including the Wedding Present, Age of Chance, the Primitives, Miaow and Primal Scream. New clubs opened, venues such as Television Personality Dan Treacy's Room At The Top in a pub in north London, Bay 63 (formerly Acklam Hall, under the arches off Portobello Road), and Splash One in Glasgow. There were new fanzines, as well, like *Pure Popcorn*, which in its first wonderful and witty (and, it claimed, 'real corny') issue at the start of 1985 dispensed with machine created typography, to the extent that almost the whole thing was hand-written, and *Are You Scared To Get Happy?*, a publication taking its name from a slogan on an Hurrah! single and its inspiration from Kevin Pearce's *Hungry Beat*.

Are You Scared To Get Happy? in time morphed into the Sarah record label, sharing a similar kind of Stalinist approach to indie detail that began to be reflected in the editorial of some of the fanzines, where narcissism dictated that a fanzine creator shouldn't just comment upon but must place themselves right at the centre of the pop process. By summer 1985, the mood swing was reflected in the sudden fashion for leather trousers, bowl haircuts and a heavily stylised indie look that came in for criticism and was later defended by Pete Astor as reflecting 'a certain time-lessness'. Mythical pop perfection became the quest. Just a few years earlier such self-absorption would have been frowned upon.

In the end, the life expectancy of the average mid-1980s fanzine tended to be short. Most creators worked day jobs, trawl-ing gumshoe-style around live venues at night to pick up sales, or pleading with the local hip record store or Rough Trade dis-tribution to take some, before returning a month or so later in the hope that the income generated would fund the next edition. Some writers went on to join the rock press; others started labels; some just got on with their own thing.

Taken as a whole, the fanzines were a collective wonder – by turns inspiring, infuriating, inventive, infectious, even. And although in truth very few merited the accolade handed out to *Hungry Beat* by one reader, who said that reading the fanzine made him want to go out and buy records he *already* owned, in some small way they all deserved it.

CHAPTER 12

'COMING SOON: MUSIC FOR THE TIME BEING'

THE PRESS RELEASE FOR THE ICA Rock Week of October 1984, at which Big Flame would perform, had signalled its curator's intent by declaring 'JOHN PEEL IS PUTTING THE FUN BACK INTO BEING PRETENTIOUS'. The line-up included Helen & The Horns, the Nightingales and Marc Riley, but the slogan used to promote it borrowed from the lyrics to a song by Leicester's Yeah Yeah Noh, a relatively unknown band who also appeared on the bill. 'Bias Binding' was a blue-collar lament, an urban folk song that was also a witty and self-referential tale about life struggling at the bottom of the greasy pole of pop. It packed an enormous amount into its running time of one minute forty-three seconds, sending up video albums and scratch-and-sniff singles and advocating the bringing back of the birch for those caught home taping. And it ironically presented Yeah Yeah Noh as on a par with pretentious glossy chart acts like Duran Duran and Spandau Ballet in the line that so impressed Peel – 'Going to put the fun back into being pretentious/ Yeah Yeah Noh so full of ourselves…'

Peel had enthused about the song all through the summer, deeming it the stand out track on a Leicester compilation album he had been sent called *Let's Cut A Rug*. *Let's Cut A Rug*, which also notably featured the 'godfathers of grebo', the Bomb Party (a band once signed to Whaam!) and experimental band Deep Freeze Mice, had been put together by the local fanzine *Printhead*, which was co-run by John Grayland, the guitarist with Yeah Yeah Noh. Grayland also helped run a local venue, the Psykick Dancehall, and his house in Leire Street was a stopping off point for many independent acts passing through or playing in the city.

Grayland had played in a number of 'improvisational punk bands' around the Kidderminster area, and later in the Metal Doughnut Band before winding up at Leicester Polytechnic at the start of the 1980s. He blew his entire first term's academic grant on a four-track tape recorder and consequently ended up working part-time in a pub in Oadby for food money, which is where he met Derek Hammond who also worked there. 'I told him I had a band that would be playing at the Polytechnic,' recalls Grayland. 'He told me that he wrote song lyrics. I don't think either of us quite believed the other until Derek came to the gig and I invited him up on stage to read his lyrics to an improvised backing noise.'

The seven-piece band that Grayland referred to went by the unlikely name of Peter Bounds & Dave Springer, and on the night in question Hammond duly appeared on stage and read a couple of offerings, one of which was entitled 'If You Ever Go Down To Kidderminster' and contained the immortal lines, 'If you ever go down to Kidderminster, don't be frightened/ People there have rockeries…' The other members of the band, as Hammond recalls, 'included a bassist that only knew how to play the James Bond theme tune and a girl flute player whose entire repertoire began and ended with Young Marble Giants' "Final Day".'

In spite of the inauspicious beginning, Grayland and Hammond agreed to continue working together, John Grayland's relatively orthodox musical education offset by Derek Hammond's more unusual experiences. In 1972, at the age of ten, Hammond had been given a portable cassette player for Christmas. While his parents were safely down the pub, he would draw the curtains tight before hooking up 'a 20-foot earphone extension on ear-splitting volume. With the coffee table pushed out of the way, I killed all the lights except the sickly blue glow of the TV, and plonked away at my practice putter, strumming it wildly like a single fat string on a very thin guitar. The coffee table, by this time, was a sound monitor for resting my foot on at the front of the stage. If you squinted quite hard, the settee was a bank of adoring fans, busily hurling their pants my way.' As he told John Robb, Hammond dubbed the imaginary group the Mick Lander Band.

Experiencing the disorienting and nihilistic rupture that was punk, and aided by the John Peel show which he avidly listened to, he gradually plotted a route towards the kind of real music he would like to play, but the experience was by no means straightforward: 'I was ... still into rock 'n' roll and '60s pop and the Steve Gibbons Band and even heavy stuff like Motorhead, Deep Purple, Rainbow,' he further told John Robb in 2009. 'I think I was the only person who turned up to see Whitesnake in 1978 wearing a crimplene suit, psychedelic shirt, golf jumper and parka. Confusing times!'

In the middle of 1983, John Grayland recorded some backing tracks with Deep Freeze Mice's drummer Graham Summer and bassist Alan Jenkins, with a view to Derek Hammond adding lyrics over the top. Before giving the cassette to Hammond, though, he had allegedly written on the cassette's inlay card, 'BACKING BAND FOR MARK E SMITH IMPERSON-ATORS'. Hammond quickly scrawled out the lyrics to a dozen or so songs and Yeah Yeah Noh were sort of on their way. There followed a few practice sessions where they used a drum machine, but it wasn't until the start of 1984 that they felt that they had something worthy of sharing with the wider world of the music business. In January, they recorded a demo – 'SEVEN SONGS' – on a four track tape machine in Leire Street before running off thirty cassette copies and distributing them to the music papers, independent record labels and John Peel. 'The demo sounded like a hamster going around in a broken wheel with play in a day twangy guitar,' Hammond recalled later. 'We sent it out hopefully...' All in all, it represented a challenge for even the most redoubtable A&R man.

The tape met with a stony silence, with only Cherry Red Records bothering to write back, and then to tell them that what they had produced was 'hopeless'. 'We didn't get any other responses at all,' remembers Derek Hammond, 'but then in February, just as the tapes had fallen on deaf ears, Jim Khambatta from In Tape got in touch. He'd been hearing 'Bias Binding' played all the time on the John Peel show and wrote to ask if we had any other ideas for songs. So, we sent him a copy of the tape and that's how we hooked up with In Tape. Jim got back in touch and said he'd be prepared to help finance a single.'

'When we started,' says John Grayland, 'I am not sure we knew what kind of music we would make exactly, but we knew it would have a beat and that it would have tunes and swooshy music. I guess we wanted to make pop music with a twist – something you could whistle but that would also take you by surprise. We started as a punk band, because we had more attitude than ability, more ideas than expertise. Later, by the time we were a proper five-piece band, we had completely different ambitions. Perhaps the model was Joy Division, their start as Warsaw and their transformation into something impossible to categorise. Of course, we never found our Martin Hannett, but that's another story...'

Jim Khambatta's offer caught them slightly unprepared. They could make a demo using a drum machine but for a finished recording they needed a bass player and a proper drum sound. And so, Adrian Crossan, and old school friend of Derek's, was recruited on bass and Graham Summers recalled temporarily on drums before the band went into Barkby Road studios in Leicester and recorded a number of tracks, including 'Bias Binding', 'Cottage Industry' and 'Tommy Opposite', the three tracks that would feature on their debut EP.

'Cottage Industry' was released in July and went on to spend an impressive twenty-six weeks in the independent charts, eventually winding up at number 32 in John Peel's Festive Fifty for the year, no mean feat for a rookie band. The EP's wit and charm immediately set it apart, Derek Hammond's wry and observant lyrics introducing a new voice. Richard Cook in the *NME* praised its 'flatcap wit' lifted from a 'potted library of sarky remarks and straight glass observations on this queer little circus called life'. And whilst many quite rightly noted the influence of the Fall (and the Nightingales), there was something more at work here, Yeah Yeah Noh taking inspiration from everything from Eddie Cochran to Philip K Dick, from surf rock and sci-fi B-movies to Aldous Huxley and the Beats. Although cut from a similar cloth, Derek Hammond was a far less impressionistic lyricist than Mark E Smith and it was clear early on that there was always going to be a tale to be told.

Almost as soon as they'd recorded the EP (in spring) the band had realised that in order to play live they needed a drummer, a problem solved when John Grayland's partner and co-editor at *Printhead*, Sue Dorey, was pressganged into joining in spite of having absolutely no experience behind a drum kit. When the band played its first gig, supporting Deep Freeze Mice at Leicester Polytechnic in April, Dorey's equipment consisted of a borrowed bass drum and a recently acquired snare. She'd been a drummer for three whole days. John Grayland and Derek Hammond did originally ask Graham Summers if he'd like to join, but he declined. 'I'm already in one shit band, I don't need to be in another,' he apparently said.

'The early gigs were pretty shambolic,' John Grayland recalls. 'We thought it was going to be easy and didn't spend enough time practising. We'd talked Sue into playing drums before she'd barely learned the basics. Half the time, Ade was the only one keeping the songs going. But the one thing we had going for us was that Derek was a natural comedian and provocateur right from the start. I think some people turned up for the chat between the songs rather than the music. From the reception for "Bias Binding" and all the first three singles, it was obvious that our appeal was more about the words than the music. Our USP was Derek. The music would just have to fight for attention. But

I wanted us to be known for our music as well, rather than just produce a nice backing noise for Derek.'

Hammond's lyrical dexterity was immediately apparent on the EP's title track, 'Cottage Industry', which rattles along skiffle-style, the music fitting perfectly the narrator's brisk measuring-up of a life on the factory floor. But in amongst the depicted drudgery, there is a post-modern twist, as the narrator gives us a few thoughts on the state of contemporary pop, *a la* 'Bias Binding', outlining his attempts to escape his fate.

> I made a move for chart position
> Asked Paul Weller for a place on his label
> He said, 'Are you a New Soul combo
> Talentless but disco photogenic?'
> I didn't bother telling him a lie …

In the end, of course, the narrator is doomed to his lot – to the 'tower blocks and Mills & Boon, Friday night in the city centre'-existence, to the inanity of the factory drink-a-yard-of-tea competitions, and the company-funded Vicars and Tarts nights. The star jumpers and flares peeping out from beneath the overalls are his private acts of rebellion, a dream relegated to bedroom fantasy where he picks up

> A bongo hairbrush and kazoo
> Shouts into condenser microphone
> Portable mixing unit on the desk

This last act, of course, reflects Hammond's own adolescence, time spent in the front room as part of the Mick Lander Band.

Things progressed quickly. It wasn't until July that they performed for the first time outside Leicester, yet by August the *NME* was calling them one of the two 'most significant insignificant bands in Britain' (the other being She He, according to X Moore). They played Alan McGee's Living Room club and received their first full write up in the *NME* in a set 'combining prole art threat with a spikey psych, [and] peculiarly *English* pessimism'. 'If this is the war on pop,' said Mat Snow, 'Yeah Yeah Noh are trainee Vietcong.'

By October, they were on to their second release, 'Beware The Weakling Lines'. Once again, it was a combination of abrasive, repetitive guitar, a rumbling bass line and twisted social observation delivered deadpan. The subject this time was the archetypal indie kid whose 'wraparound shades hide a pasty weakling face'. A witty list of the tell-tale signs of hipsterdom is delivered, before Derek Hammond wraps things up with a surreal nostalgic lament: 'Whatever happened to manual kebabs/ The feeble chant of a favourite brain/ The lilac hand of Menthol Dan/ From the hollow chest of a patent chain?' The record's running time came in, naturally, at not much over two minutes.

The fans, such as they were, loved it, but the critics, including John Peel, seemed slightly less taken with 'Beware The Weakling Lines', perhaps finding it too similar in tone and approach to the band's first EP. In a 'celebrity' singles review in *Melody Maker*, singer Helen Terry called the band 'a more literate version of Jilted John' or the equivalent of a 'mildly subversive Chas & Dave'. In fact, the real meat of the release was to found in the record's B-side which no reviewer bothered mentioning.

'Starling Pillowcase & Why' properly introduced the distorted state realities that began finding a way into Derek Hammond's lyrics and would became a major feature of 1985's *Cutting The Heavenly Lawn Of Greatness... Last Rites For The God Of Love* album. It also saw the band striving for a richer sound – the 'tunes and swooshy noises' that John Grayland previously refers to. Ennui bleeds into paranoia for the narrator of the song, who is caught in an eternal night, interspersed with flickering dreams of a sunlit morning. As Andrew Male pointed out in *Mojo* in 2012, it was a 'shivering, bare-boards nightmare' of song, made all the more haunting by the 'growling bass and the thin, febrile guitar'. It was a sound unlike anything being heard at the time.

To promote the new EP, the band duly played John Peel's ICA Rock Week, appearing third on the bill on the first night in a strange and somewhat incompatible line-up that included Yip Yip Coyote and Pink Peg Slax. They played a short set – for some, very short. The PA was flawed, Derek Hammond read the lyrics from a sheet of paper – a practise that throughout time has always always irritated critics as seemingly pretentious – and one reviewer, by later confession, remained for only one number in the four-song set before retreating to the bar and later grumpily writing about his experiences in *Melody Maker*.

Whatever fun Peel managed to conjure up at the ICA, it was staged against the wider backdrop of a miners' strike that was steadily growing more and more bleak. All through November, Yeah Yeah Noh played benefits in support of the strikers – at the Old Tiger's Head in Lewisham, where Phil Wilson of the June Brides came to see them, at Birmingham University on a bill with the Three Johns and the Membranes (where a profit was made), and at Liverpool University, where Test Department and a brass band also played, and where the organisers lost a whopping £1000 staging the event due to expenses.

The strike was just one topic that cropped up in an *NME* interview that same month, along with the band's broader politics and also where the group might be positioned in the indie firmament. Set against an interview with the Fall on the facing page, the two articles shared a headline – BEFORE AND AFTER THE FALL – that more or less summed up the paper's (or sub-editor's) take in five words. On the facing page Mark E Smith was scathing about bands that appeared to have taken inspiration from the Fall, calling them his 'bitches', although most of his anger was reserved for Marc Riley whose departure from the Fall a couple of years earlier still rankled.

In both *NME*, and in a *Sounds* interview the following week, the subject of the band's next single, 'Prick Up Your Ears', came up. The song took its title from John Lahr's masterful biography of Joe Orton (another son of Leicester) who was brutally murdered when his gay lover took a hammer to his head. The sensational element of the crime, and the somewhat déclassé nature of Orton's work, had ever since been too much to deal with for the good burghers of the east Midlands city – motto, *Semper Eadam*, or, Always The Same – who forever after brushed Orton's legacy under the carpet and beyond view, preferring the Leicester-born but fictional Adrian Mole as a more wholesome hero. Reflecting the work of Orton, part of Yeah Yeah Noh's purpose John Grayland told *Sounds* was 'aimed at kicking people out of their apathy'. Grayland reiterated that the band made no secret of the fact that they were far from proficient musicians – in other words, true heirs of the DIY spirit – but felt they were capable of enjoying the same kind of 'non-glib' chart success of, say, Buzzcocks or the Undertones, only in the case of Yeah Yeah Noh it 'would be weirder'.

'Prick Up Your Ears', the single the band released at the start of 1985, was certainly 'weirder', and a major progression for the band. Derek Hammond had been trawling through the archives of the Leicester *Mercury* when he'd come across a cache of Orton letters and articles. One Orton quote – 'the humble and meek are thirsting for blood' – aptly sums up the more vengeful aspect of the playwright's work, but it was a quote from his *Diaries* that particularly caught Derek Hammonds eye: 'Cleanse the heart... Give me the ability to rage correctly'. The line reappears in 'Prick Up Your Ears', running as a lyrical motif through music that dispenses with the earlier rickety bass and spindly guitar sound and presents a more droning, proto-psychedelic noise, laying out the direction the band was travelling in. 'I cross-seeded some lines from John Lahr's biography with a few more stolen ideas, like Larkin's "books are a load of crap". It was an arch example of Dadaist cut-up technique! Musically, it would have sounded more Glitter Band/ Krautrock if we'd been able to play it properly back then,' he says.

Once again, 'Prick Up Your Ears' highlighted the articulacy with which Hammond delivered his twisted vignettes, unpicking the surrealism of the suburban. Musically, it showed the band to be moving away from the sarcastic style evident on the early singles and towards a dense, more abstract approach, dreamscape elements becoming less comic and more fuzzily dark. The new effect was satirised in the *Bumper Book of Yeah Yeah Noh*, a mail order, 16-page booklet that was given away free with 'Prick Up Your Ears':

'Somewhere in a cellar someone's eccentric uncle is locked in by an overzealous weekend nurse, who recognises his oddity but not his harmlessness. He tells himself stories in an undulant tone to keep his spirit up and to remind himself who he is. His obsession is deadpan entertainment, the listener is never convinced of the seriousness of all this seriousness, and the happy gap between Uncle's ideas and Uncle's reality amuse.

'Meanwhile, next door's home video provides percussion for dancing clocks and Uncle is twitching slightly in syncopation. From upstairs someone can be heard practising quirky circular lines on a guitar, and a couple of bass things tumble around and about like overweight hamsters playing at rats. The whole effect is so English Domestic, the shots of venom can't be serious…'

The more abstract tone – both lyrically and musically – found its way onto the material Yeah Yeah Noh chose for their second John Peel session, which took place in April 1985. The four tracks recorded, 'Temple of Convenience', 'Crimplene Seed Lifestyle', 'See Through Nature' and 'There's Another Side To Mrs Quill', were ambitious and complex. There were still elements of the rumbling, more rudimentary, bass-heavy sound of old, but the progressed sound incorporated new instruments and introduced reverb, sampling, phasing and distortion.

In July, just prior to the band going in to record the album, Tom Slater joined as second guitarist, adding yet more texture and helping further develop the increasingly sophisticated music the band were trying to create. Now a five-piece, Yeah Yeah Noh went into Street Music Studios in Leicester and over five days between the end of July and the start of August recorded *Cutting The Heavenly Lawn Of Greatness... Last Rites For The God Of Love* and a handful of B-sides. The record was not, alas, recorded in the best of circumstances.

'In many ways the album was a disaster. I'm still proud of the songs and the ideas on it but the production was terrible,' says John Grayland. 'We never had any mentors and we never had any money. Actually, we were probably too headstrong, too wilful and too snotty to have any mentors. Our only friends "in the business" were Deep Freeze Mice who provided the only bit of concrete advice we got. They'd recorded an album at Street Music, so that's where we recorded ours. The studio engineer didn't "get" what we were trying to achieve and we were not really listening to him anyway. Everything was recorded in a great rush.'

According to Hammond, 'It's hard to get any perspective on it, but I think if it were another band's work, I'd see it as a complete but intriguing failure.'

Nonetheless, the first release from the session – 'Another Side To Mrs Quill' – received rave reviews when it was released as a single in September and arguably remains a highpoint of the band's studio output. It was a record that quite literally wore its influence upon its sleeve, Sue Dorey's cover art a mind-altering swirl of purple and green typography that perfectly matched the surreal tale told in the song itself. 'It's a record driven by Ade's bassline,' recalls Hammond. 'Lyrically, as the critic Seething Wells pointed out, it's "Eleanor Rigby". It was a pleasure to change tack and try to aim a little higher than the indie charts, to see what kind of words I'd come up with if we were a pop group.'

Mrs Quill lives in suburbia but is filled with the anything but the everyday dreams of the average housewife. She levitates for a start, quite literally lifting herself out of her boring existence, floating around the room naked yet always making sure that she's back on the ground in time to have the absent Mr Quill's tea ready. There's a goldfish called Regret, and a butterfly that always whistles as Mrs Quill floats by. Both musically and lyrically, the song is awash with the dreamy escapism of psychedelia refracted through the numbing boredom of surface-bright domestic life in a song, Hammond points out, 'about alternative realities'.

Indeed, when Hammond sings

It's not what you give, but what you can take
And in what amounts

is he referring to Mrs Quill's daily grind, or is he hinting instead at Mrs Quill's narcotic intake, in a song that might possibly be read as an updated version of the Rolling Stones' 'Mother's Little Helper'?

'There's nothing quite as strange boredom,' Hammond told Andrew Male in 2012. If the new direction the band had taken *was* psychedelic then it was a psychedelia informed not by drugs but by boredom, which could be equally as transportive and perspective shifting. In Hammond's view, something different was deliberately at work: 'My mission was to reclaim nostalgia from the past. The new songs were playing with the idea of the past as an alternative reality: deliberate visions of a past that didn't really exist.'

It all fitted in with the time. In 1985, psychedelia was having yet another mini-revival, the Creation record label, the Paisley Underground and the last vestiges of the neo-psychedelic second coming of 1981 just three things that attested to the subject's longevity. But Yeah Yeah Noh were different, and produced arguably a more relevant and contemporary form of psychedelia. The much bandied about term 'psychedelic punk rock' – or the bolting of a no-nonsense DIY ethic onto the more drug-induced, metaphysical ideas of the mid-1960s – applied far more genuinely to Yeah Yeah Noh than it did to those who more often than not merely aped the period's sounds.

Cutting The Heavenly Lawn Of Greatness… Last Rites For The God Of Love (a title part borrowed from a line journalist Jack Barron had written about the band) appeared at the start of November and visually and musically carried through the psychedelic motifs of 'Another Side To Mrs Quill'. Once again, Sue Dorey's album cover art was apt, this time depicting a Buddhist God of love being smashed to pieces by Japanese soldiers. The swirly lettering bled through to the inner sleeve, which was a collage of lyrics, photos and statements, such as 'Coming Soon: 'Music For The Time Being'. The album cover spine recycled an old piece of hippy wisdom – 'The sky starts at your feet – think about how brave you are to walk around…'

The album opens with a choice track, 'Temple of Convenience', which steals a riff from 'La Bamba' and tells a tale of a religious cult, before moving on to an enhanced, re-recorded take of 'Prick Up Your Ears'. The shimmering 'Married Miss New Jersey' has the song's narrator ('a guy with impeccable taste') recounting a number of marriages to beauty queens, lifting words from the Fun & Games' 'Grooviest Girl In The World', in a story that could be real, or could be a dream.

In fact, throughout the songs on the album, time shifts and dream and conscious states merge. Characters in the songs are invariably caught in a time/ spatial limbo. On the occasions when the song's mood is more melancholic or romantic the effect is deeply unsettling, as in 'Zoological Gardens', a bittersweet tale of adolescent romance, modelled, Hammond told Andrew Male, on his idea of 'a ''60s, Technicolour, Hollywood film, not a very good one', with 'nostalgia that falls down the cracks'.

With its echo and reverb and drowsily repetitive motifs, the album creates its own world, one where the boundaries are frighteningly blurred and the reassurances impossible to quantify – as queasily disturbing as the Monty Python sketch where the character wakes up in an English country garden in brilliant summer and says to his mother, 'So it was all a dream!', only to be told: 'No dear this is the dream...' In one of the albums very best songs, 'See Through Nature', we are even told as much.

Everything collides in the track, the bass melody smashing into a rotary blade cut-up of samples, guitars, piano and other instrumentation that is being sucked towards the centre to only be spat out again. The song's trippy pattern is reflected in the voice of the narrator, which begins confident but quickly turns insecure. He lives in a 'photo-novel dream' and likes to talk to things and then answer back for them. It's a frighteningly schizophrenic tale that gradually descends into hell, Derek Hammond ending the song with a couple of lines taken from New Jersey garage band the Beach Nuts' 1966 single, 'Iconoclastic Life':

My life's nil, I just take pills
I sit for hours, just watching the flowers...

But it is the last track on the album that is arguably the crowning glory, hinting most fully at the place Yeah Yeah Noh were heading for and would most probably have arrived at had they stayed together. Laden with tremolo, the song's undulant tones are simultaneously soulful and harrowing. The 'Blood Soup' in question refers to the slaughter that was the Vietnam War and the story unfolds in a deliberately epic way. There is an even better, perhaps definitive version recorded for a John Peel session, where the song's organ-heavy vibe disintegrates and distorts as Derek Hammond borrows a few lines from the Shangrilas' 'Train To Kansas City' ('Baby, baby, please believe me/ I would never, *never* do anything to hurt you…') in a surreal juxtaposition before an apocalyptic finale that mimics the setting off of an atomic bomb. The dust metaphorically clears, and an audio clip of an old public information film (about how to survive a nuclear attack) is sampled, its message delivered in the reassuring tones of received English: 'Children, we better clear up this broken glass and debris. All in all, I'd say we've been lucky around here. Nothing to do now but wait for orders from the authorities and *relax…*'

'"Blood Soup" evolved over a very long time, and went through more versions than any other Yeah Yeah Noh track,' says John Grayland. 'We wanted an epic finish for the album. If other songs on the record were like day trips, "Blood Soup" was a harrowing week long journey to somewhere more frightening, somewhere that might leave you shaken and scurrying to get back home at the end of it.'

And yet, for all of its obvious qualities, *Cutting The Heavenly Lawn…* appeared to confuse many. John Peel, for one, seemed not as taken with the new material. Some fans also favoured the earlier, more minimal work. The band had prepared for this when they made the album, scratching into its dead wax the joke comment, I PREFER THE EARLIER STUFF, MYSELF. Interviewed by *Sounds* shortly after its release, they were asked, was Yeah Yeah Noh a band of happy go lucky youngsters, or a bunch of angst-ridden sociologists? 'I'm a fun-loving manic depressive,' came back the response from Derek Hammond. The reviews *were* positive, the ever-supportive Jack Barron praising in particular

Derek Hammond's lyrics that made 'so called astute wordsmiths like Paddy MacAloon seem like navvies with broken pencils', but perhaps they weren't quite *as* positive as might have been expected given the quality of the album delivered.

There was one more single ('Temple Of Convenience') and a final John Peel session before they called it a day. 'The album sold less well than expected,' says John Grayland. 'Radio play didn't materialise, John Peel was not keen and the finished sound was not good enough for other shows. Live, we couldn't make the step up to bigger venues and better fees. With hindsight, it is easy to see Yeah Yeah Noh as a product of the socio-economic conditions of the time. We were all working class kids, but not the type for whom playing in a band was our only alternative to going down the mines or working in a factory. We all had degrees and were part of that generation who got grants to avoid going to work. When the band took off, we signed to the Enterprise Allowance Scheme that allowed us to earn a bit of money while still claiming £40 a week to live on. There was a time limit on the scheme, though, and when the album failed we were looking at financial ruin.

'Sue and I were a couple and we had managed to secure a house from a Housing Co-operative at a very reasonable rent. That small terraced house had provided Yeah Yeah Noh with a base, a rehearsal room, a place to store equipment and our main social space. Without that house, Yeah Yeah Noh wouldn't have lasted more than a year. However, the house also provided my way out. I became the Chair of the National Federation of Housing Co-operatives and got a job in housing soon after the split.

Ironically, by the time of the 'farewell' concert at Leicester University on 26 February 1986 the band was at the very top of its game. The practical decision to quit created no personal animosity and was not motivated by the usual 'creative differences'. Derek Hammond became a writer, Sue Dorey went travelling for a year before becoming a teacher, Adrian Crossan went to work in electronics and design and Tom Salter landed a job in communications with the help of a bunch of Yeah Yeah Noh covers, posters and press releases that he cleverly took credit for.

There was a coda. In May 1986, a compilation of the John Peel sessions was released on the band's own Vuggum label. The record was far more evenly produced than the studio album, reflecting not just the BBC's deep pockets but also the knowhow that was beyond the average indie label. 'Hindsight will judge what you hold here a shit hot cult item as rare and beauteous as the Fugs and Holy Modal Rounders,' ran longtime supporter Mat Snow's prescient sleeve notes, summing up to some extent both band and album, telling it as it was but not, regrettably, as it might and should have been.

Derek Hammond wasn't the only wordsmith out there with a biting wit and a fiercely intelligent style. Bumping about the live circuit, Yeah Yeah Noh often shared the bill with a ragged bunch of compadre bands that included Marc Riley & The Creepers and the Jazz Butcher, both of which had main men blessed with a well-honed worldview. Marc Riley shared the same label as Yeah Yeah Noh (and, in fact, co-owned In Tape), while Pat Fish aka Jazz Butcher had begun weaving his wonderfully idiosyncratic work since 1983 when he'd released the esoteric album, *In A Bath Of Bacon*, and the equally as wonderful single, 'Southern Mark Smith'. Butch, as he was affectionately known, had overheard someone use the phrase and turned it into a song about 'the soft underbelly' of 'the Saturday scene'. The title was, as he later explained, incongruous, since 'a southern Mark Smith is an impossibility'. 'Southern Mark Smith' was just one gem from an artist who, according to Ian Gittins in *Melody Maker*, was, like Derek Hammond, 'using thought and language precisely to remind us how strange is the business of living'.

Pat Fish had started out making tapes at home without any real thought of developing things further. On a whim, he decided to send a tape to his friend Dave Barker who in 1981 had set up Glass Records. Barker's aim in setting up the label was, according to a 1984 profile in the *Catalogue*, 'not to develop a house style of music or graphics, but a standard of quality'. Barker contacted Fish and immediately offered to release the material, which led first to the album that came out in March 1983.

Nothing if not eclectic, the Jazz Butcher revealed himself to have a neat turn of phrase and an idiosyncratic line in song titles, as numbers like 'Southern Mark Smith', 'Big Foot Motel' and, indeed, *In A Bath Of Bacon* showed. He also had an equally natty line in tunes, causing some to draw the conclusion that he was an artist in the mould of Robyn Hitchcock, when Jonathan Richman, John Cale or possibly Kevin Ayers, was nearer the mark. And whereas the average indie kid was just learning to mimic the sound of the Velvet Underground at the start of 1984, it seemed to be genetically pre-built into the DNA of the Jazz Butcher.

'Southern Mark Smith' was followed by 'Marnie', an everyday tale of a girlfriend who wants to keep a lion in her room, and shortly after that, in September, by a cover version of Jonathan Richman's 'Roadrunner'. 'Roadrunner', like R Dean Taylor's 'There's A Ghost In My House' or Norman Greenbaum's 'Spirit In The Sky' is a song hard not to make something of, and that proved to be the case, giving the Jazz Butcher its first indie charting. However, abnormal service was resumed with the release of *A Scandal In Bohemia* that hit the racks in November. Named after a Sherlock Holmes short story – apparently Fish was later asked by a commentator in Germany, 'What *is* this scandal?' – the album included the two singles as well as further outpourings in a similar vein. Earlier in the year, *Sounds*, had raised the possibility that the Jazz Butcher was 'almost genius', a man whose songs were

COMING SOON: MUSIC FOR THE TIME BEING'

'part beautiful, part ruthless… like some pissed-up Bob Dylan, or drug-crazed Piccadilly Circus busker, strumming acoustic guitar attractively, yet in a manner which suggests brain patterns very disturbed…If so, why isn't he famous?' Songs on the album ranged from a wonderful ode to being tied up in 'Just Like Betty Page' (which referenced the American 'Queen of Pin-Ups') to the Fall-esque 'Caroline Wheeler's Birthday Present', a perennial favourite ever-after whenever the Jazz Butcher performed live.

By mid-1984, the Jazz Butcher, which now comprised of original duo the Jazz Butcher (guitar/ vocals) and Max Eider (guitar/ vocals), augmented by David J (bass) and Owen Jones (drums), had very much spread their wings beyond the home turf of Oxford/Northampton and were regularly playing some of the key indie venues, such as the Pindar of Wakefield and Alan McGee's Living Room Club in the Tottenham Court Road. As befitted the Jazz Butcher's maverick approach, the shows were anything but a routine run through of a prearranged set of songs. As the critic Robin Gibson pointed out, in an interview conducted in June 1984, the shows more often than not consisted of 'the Butcher setting the tone with humorous little asides in keeping with the humorous larger asides that are his songs'.

The variety of the material, in terms of content *and* tone, could sometimes bewilder – Jack Barron reviewed 'Marnie' and considered it 'stupid, rather than silly'. Speaking with Robin Gibson, the Jazz Butcher considered such observations anything but insulting, saying that he liked 'the dumbness of pop music. Some of the best pop records have been really dumb: stuff like "Speedy Gonzalez"'. The Jazz Butcher didn't set itself up as having any particular style, instead it was 'like pop music being a big toyshop', with the band 'just running around, poking with this and that'. The band itself was the common element.

Such a broad cultural approach makes for a prolific output and in February, 1985 the band went into the studio to record its third album in as many years. *Sex & Travel* was released in May and featured a clutch of songs more personal to the Jazz Butcher, but nonetheless still refracted through Fish's strangely strange but oddly normal world-view. Once again, the range challenged, one critic pointing out that in some ways it sounded more like a compilation album of different artists than one band's work. But underpinning it there was a prevailing attitude, even if the attitude was peculiar.

One song, 'Red Pets', was inspired by the Jazz Butcher's Tom cat, Sterling (the cat, apparently had a mother called Mo…), while another, 'President Reagan's Birthday Present', imagined a cold war incident, the President lamenting communists in MiGs who pay him a visit in the skies. The chorus, 'Red Russians shot my rocket down' was lifted from a tabloid newspaper headline of the time. Another song also dealt with East/West relations, 'Walk With The Devil', which, the Butcher told *Debris* magazine, was 'about a spy defecting… and a love song, a song of parting, of leaving'. The self-explanatory 'Holiday' returned to the more day-to-day subject matter of old and concerned a prim and proper Englishman on holiday in Prague. It was an example of what the Butcher called his 'Dutch cycling songs', or lighter work.

The work continued to pour out of the Jazz Butcher, finely-crafted pop songs built in classic fashion upon the 'idle notions' that came to him from time to time. Years of not fitting in (or rather, not being always *allowed* to fit in) ended when the band signed with Creation in 1988 and released a string of albums buoyed up by the support of a label boss who loved the band. At last the future looked promising – if a little weird.

Like Pat Fish, Marc Riley was something of a willing outlier. He had begun his career as a roadie for the Fall at the tender age of fifteen, before joining the band on bass in 1978 and then switching to guitar and keyboards, thus adding a major ingredient to the overall sound of Mark E Smith's band during the period he was with it. At the end of 1982, though, a general weariness with where Riley was headed with the band, the effects of the fall-out from a punch-up in a nightclub on the Fall's Australian tour, and Mark E Smith's employment revolving door policy found Riley out on his ear, a man with the sound but with nowhere to make it heard.

Seven year's man-and-boy in the Fall (by the age of 23), Riley's early solo work sounded, not unsurprisingly, a little like that of his former employers. Indeed, 'Favourite Sister', which was released in April 1983, featured then ex–and current alumni of Mark E Smith's band in the form of Steve and Paul Hanley and Craig Scanlon. The single also launched the In Tape label that Riley set up with occasional keyboard player and manager Jim Khambatta, and Khambatta joined him in his new venture, Marc Riley & The Creepers (that also included Eddie Fenn on drums, Paul Keogh on bass and Paul Fletcher on guitar). The new band's first release, the single 'Jumper Clown' appeared in the autumn, a hurtling thrash of a song that contained the immortal lines, 'I don't buy the evil rock press any more/ Please may I look at yours...'

Although Riley's lyrical style wasn't quite as fleeting as that of Mark E Smith (some of whose songs by 1984 were becoming *so* impressionistic as to be lyrical gibberish), he didn't waste words, songs delivering little tales of wily observation in a way that was appealingly barbed and disjointed without being self-indulgent. 'The songs,' he told Gavin Martin in the *NME* in March 1984, 'are usually about groups of people, fanatics of one kind or another.' Like Derek Hammond, he wasn't above making observations about the world the Creepers operated in. In 'Location Bangladesh', for instance, which tongue-in-cheek partly tells the story of a rock band scouting for a video shoot location, he offers up the following: 'We went to Sri Lanka last year/ But we didn't like the beer/ And we didn't chase the women there/ I want to make that very clear'.

The band recorded their first John Peel session (of five) at the end of 1983 and the tracks were released on a 12" in March 1984, 'Creeping At Maida Vale', which included 'Location Bangladesh', 'Blow', a song parodying the white funk brigade's use of brass, and a marvellous rant entitled 'Cure By Choice', which contained the immortal lines, 'I wear mascara, lipstick and rouge/ Baggy trousers, patent leather shoes/ Carmen rollers and a whining voice/ I listen to the Cure by choice'. The single was followed by the release of a compilation album of the early singles (*Cull*), and then in July by the studio album, *Gross Out*. The album was allegedly recorded in eighteen hours at a cost of £85. It was inevitably patchy in places, its endearingly rough-hewn charm salvaged by a couple of stand-out tracks including 'Gross' (a particularly lurid tale of sexual conquest) and 'Railroad', another 'trade' tale, this time one poking fun at the then-fashionable countrybilly fad.

The album made it in to the indie charts, as did *Cull* and the following two singles – summer's 'Polystiffs' and October's 'Shadow Figure', which once again featured tracks recorded for a John Peel session. The band played John Peel's ICA Rock Week, at which point, according to the ever-astute Richard Cook reviewing 'Shadow Figure' in the *NME*, they were 'turning out the best and most playable garage music in Britain'. Certainly 'Shadow Figure' was a leap forward, a piano-heavy stomp all about Freud and bingo (according to Cook) that smoothed away the rough edges, even if, as ever, the lyrics remained wilfully obtuse: 'I'm a tall guy/ Taller than him/ But he's really *bigger*...'.

1985 saw just one album and one single and seemed like a period of summing up of kinds for Riley. In the case of both the single ('Black Dwarf') and the album (*Fancy Meeting God*) there were a number of axes to grind, 'The Bard of Woking' taking a pot-shot at Paul Weller and the album blasting all manner of things – journalists, cocktail bar radicals, laid-back activists and obscure artists. In an interview in August, Riley claimed that two of his main inspirations had been the comedians Lenny Bruce and Bernard Manning (the latter because 'nothing is sacred to him, which is perfect to me').

Marc Riley & The Creepers could have gone on for ever – as far as wit and talent went, the tank looked as if it was never going to run dry. As it transpired, there were just a couple more albums and a couple more singles (the last released on Red Rhino) before Riley hung up his boots, returning to the Manchester flat he shared with his wife, a tarantalu, an Indian python called Sabu and a dog going by the name of Timothy Malcolm Riley.

There would be no more Marc Riley records, but the airwaves wouldn't be lacking his voice for long.

CHAPTER 13

WHO KILLED
BO DIDDLEY?

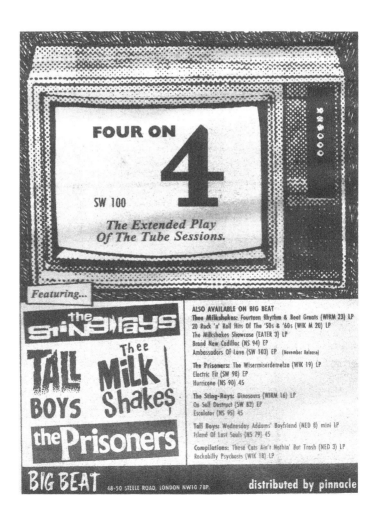

THE RELEASE IN JUNE 1984 of the X Men single 'Do The Ghost' illustrated how close the ties were, in a pre-segregated age, between the different strands of indie. One of the very best venues for live music was the Klub Foot in the basement of the Clarendon Hotel in Hammersmith, a key location for the various types of music that grew out of the neo-rockabilly movement at the end of the 1970s and included psychobilly, garage trash, psychedelic punk and countless variants of the basic sound of old school rockabilly and rock 'n' roll. Alan McGee had signed the X Men on a predictable whim, having witnessed the band playing at the club on a night during the spring of 1984.

McGee had fought his way past a number of other interested parties, and promptly introduced himself, as guitarist Miles Aldridge later recalled: 'There were several A&R men sniffing around and Alan pushed his way to the front, very determined to sign us to his new label and suggesting lunch at a pub near Liverpool Street Station. Alan turned up his British Rail uniform, complete with a lantern which he placed on the table next to his pint, and we signed and recorded 'Do The Ghost' and 'Talk' at Alaska Studios the following week.'

The neo-rockabilly movement had introduced a generation of young fans to the charms of stripped-down, basic rock and roll, but it was brought to them for the most part by imitators riding the wave of a '50s revival, which was happening in music and film and, to a lesser extent through fashion, with retro stores like Flip opening in Covent Garden and selling upcycled American fashion from the decade. It wasn't the music of Johnny Burnette or Charlie Feathers or Sun Records that was exciting most of them initially, but rather the sounds of the Stray Cats, Match-box and others. They were experiencing a similar kind of ersatz '50s culture on television through films like *Grease* and shows like *Happy Days*. When this heavily-concocted reinvention began throwing up contenders for the mainstream charts, it turned off some of those who had been at first impressed but subsequently underwhelmed as gradually they discovered for themselves the more authentic sounds of rockabilly and rock 'n' roll.

It was the outer fringes of this culture that excited, the more frenzied and demented work of exponents such as the Trashmen, the Phantom, Hasil Adkins and the Novas. In 1984, Big Beat issued a landmark compilation album, *Rockabilly Psychosis & The Garage Disease* that brought together work of some of the more obscure and oddball practitioners from the 1950s and 1960s and presented it alongside the work of some contemporary groups. The album included the above bands, as well as the Sonics, the Legendary Stardust Cowboy, the Meteors, the Sting-Rays, the Gun Club and Tav Falco's Panther Burns, leavening out the psychosis with a healthy dose of garage.

The desire for a more dangerous thrill than that offered by the mainstream neo-rockabilly acts gave rise to psychobilly, which took the staple rockabilly format of double-bass, guitar and drums, and presented it with the same kind of urgency and attitude that had marked out punk. The Meteors, a band fronted by the irrepressible P Paul Fenech, got things rolling with their debut album, *In Heaven*, recorded in just a week and released on Lost Soul Records in 1981. *In Heaven* featured largely original songs by Fenech and bassist Nigel Lewis and opened with a 'wrecking crew' of some of the band's fans chanting a song from the film *Eraserhead*, before Nigel Lewis urged the album's listeners to 'Go Mental!'. The same year *In Heaven* came out, the band secured a prestigious session for John Peel and appeared in a short film, *Meteor Madness*, a seventeen-minute, B-movie tale about the Devil's attempts to take over the world through a fiendish keep fit regime that starred a young Keith Allen in the main role.

Where The Meteors led, others followed, bands such as Guana Batz, a four-piece west London band who played 'modern rockabilly' (as they called it) and the band that was for most the mainstream representation of psychobilly, the more cartoonish King Kurt. King Kurt had originally been called Rockin' Kurt & The Sour Krauts and at one point, when scrambling around in search of a singer, had placed an advert that read: 'WANTED: EX-RAMPTON PATIENT. MUST HAVE FULL CONTROL OF MOUTH AND SILLY HAIRCUT. OAPs CONSIDERED'. An ex-patient applied. In time, they released an album called King Kurt's *Big Cock*, flirted with the charts and were effectively the public face of the movement.

In tandem with the rise of rockabilly, another music emerged. With the inclusion of bands like the Sonics and the Trashmen, *Rockabilly Psychosis & The Garage Disease* had also introduced many to the delights of a subterranean music that, since the 1960s, had lain dormant, but was now being rediscovered in the wake of the neo-rockabilly boom. It was through the garage music and trash of the period that the cross over between indie and the post-neo-rockabilly scenes was most apparent, as the signing of the X Men to Creation showed. The visceral music of garage and trash was less self-consciously theatrical, and offered up, in the words of Lester Bangs, 'twenty years of rock 'n' roll history in three chords, played more primitively every time they're recycled'.

Played more primitively is the key. At its best the music was stripped back and buzzing, and even although garage and trash bands usually dispensed with the classic trio format of rockabilly they rarely extended themselves beyond the classic four-piece rock 'n' roll line up of guitars/ vocals, bass and drums. While the music stole and borrowed from some of the same sources as the neo-psychedelic revival, which included Leadbelly and Link Wray, Texan psychedelic punks the Thirteenth Floor Elevators and the castaways gathered together on Lenny Kaye's seminal 1972 compilation, *Nuggets*, it also took from the British beat bands of the Star Club era, with their hard-edged, amphetamine-driven raucous rock 'n' roll.

One jumping off point had been 1982, when a series of 'Night of Trash' concerts had taken place, the last at the 100 Club in October. Three bands came to the fore – the Cannibals, Thee Milkshakes and the Sting-Rays. Of the three, the Cannibals had the most visible pedigree, having released a first single (as Mike Spenser & The Cannibals) in 1977. By 1982 the band had a few notches on their belt, and an album ...*Bone To Pick*, which featured one of the all-time great record covers with its blood-splattered skeleton lying on a filthy mattress clutching an electric guitar. Spenser had formally been in punk band the Count Bishops, a band that at its best sounded like a dirtier version of the Pretty Things. By 1982 he was a mover and a shaker on the nascent trash scene.

Spenser invited the Sting-Rays, a young north London band, to appear on the 'Night of Trash' bills, initially placing them low down on the bill before catching their infectious live performance and moving them up a rung or two. He also invited Thee Milkshakes to appear, a band from Medway that had been knocking around in various guises since the time of punk and was fronted by the hugely talented poet/ painter Wild Billy Childish (nee Stephen Hamper). The shows were a great success, the bands playing to a packed out and enthusiastic audience. Such was the buzz that Channel Four invited a number of bands on to the *Tube* television programme for a 'Trash On The Tube' special, a ten minute feature that stood out in amongst the more anodyne fare the programme usually served up.

In the film, Thee Milkshakes, the Sting-Rays, the Tall Boys (Nigel Lewis's band after leaving the Meteors) and the Prisoners, a band who, like Thee Milkshakes, were from Kent's Medway Towns area, were given the chance to run through one song and then make some comments on the new music. The performances were later released on an EP by Big Beat – 'Four On 4: Trash On The Tube' – complete with suitablty cod-retro sleeve notes by

Meteors' manager, Nick Garrard – 'This dynamic programme is a feast of powerful beat music – a "knockout" for every teenager', etc. On the programme itself, as for comments made by the bands, Thee Milkshakes offered up the wisest kernel of truth in their tongue-in-cheek appraisal of their own sound, saying, 'We play simple, basic music for… simple basic people, for simple basic reasons.'

The programme showed the high esteem in which Thee Milkshakes were held. The band also put in the best performance, stripping their sound back to its beat essence in 'Out Of Control' in a way that didn't even bother competing with the more frenetic Sting-Rays, who also made a strong fist of things with their self-penned 'Come On, Kid'. The Tall Boys and the Prisoners were less engaging, although the latter group's outfits (they were all dressed in *Star Trek* costumes) provided a diversion.

Thee Milkshakes had started out life as TV21 (a band that did cover versions of Gerry Anderson theme tunes like 'Fireball XL5' and 'Stingray'), before morphing into the Pop Rivets in spring 1978. The Pop Rivets were 'all dressed up as mods because we thought that was funny,' Childish told Cynthia Rose in an early interview in the *NME*. The piss-taking carried through to their songs – one was called 'LambrettaVespaScoota', another 'Beatle Boots'. The debut album appeared in 1979 – 'the finest, most honest rock 'n' roll record I've heard this year', said *NME*'s Monty Smith – and a second followed shortly after, the well-titled *Empty Sounds From Anarchy Ranch*, a liquorice allsorts box of contemporary styles with a heavy dose of punk pastiche.

By a strange coincidence, the Pop Rivets found themselves in Germany and began picking up shows at small clubs dotted about, including playing in Hamburg at the Star Club. They were, so legend goes, the first British band to appear there since the days of the Beatles, although by the time of their appearance the club had been renamed and was now called The Salambo

Erotic Sex Theatre. Back in Britain they cut an EP, 'Back From Nowhere', which featured a track called 'Going Nowhere', which Childish later said had been written about the band. They split up shortly after in 1980.

There were a number of line-up changes before The Milkshakes came into being, taking advantage of a compensation pay out guitarist Mick Hamsphire received following a car accident to quickly record and release the album *Talkin' 'Bout – The Milkshakes* on their own Milkshakes record label in 1981. The album ran a whole gamut of influences yet came out tough sounding and original and was, like all the best garage music, as Cynthia Rose pointed out, a forever 'modern noise'.

Straddling the whole rockabilly/ garage phenomenon was the music of the Cramps whose early singles had first reached the UK shores on import at the tail end of punk. Their 'modern noise' influenced a whole range of groups involved in or skirting the rockabilly genre, including the Meteors, the Sting-Rays and Thee Milkshakes (to say nothing of the Gun Club and many others whose music fell outside the genre). The Cramps always resisted the 'revival' tag (and, for good measure loathed labels like 'psychobilly'), Lux Interior rebuffing the idea that the band were in any way a parody, saying that such a view was 'either a misunderstanding or misapprehension of what rockabilly… was all about'.

To begin with the band had two drummers (the first, the appropriately named Pam Bamalam) and *no* bass player, the main thrust of the music coming through the guitars, which drew on vintage rock 'n' roll but also on the surf sound of '50s artists like Dick Dale and the Ventures. They first sought fame and fortune on America's east coast, just as punk was breaking in New York, before being rebuffed, at which point (around 1978) the band drifted across to the west coast where they began building up a following based on their live performances (including one legendary show at the Napa State Mental Hospital where some of the inmates thought the band must be from the Lifer unit). The cover versions they played were always genuine off-the-wall oddities and included Jimmy Seward's 'Rock On The Moon', the Sonics' 'Strychnine', Little Willie John's 'Fever' and the Kasenetz-Katz Singing Orchestral Circus' 'Quick Joey Small'.

The first few Cramps records to reach the UK – the singles 'Human Fly', 'Surfin' Bird', 'Garbageman' and 'Fever', and the albums *Songs The Lord Taught Us* and *Psychedelic Jungle* – were jewel boxes stuffed full of the weird and wonderful. The music took the tough men sounds of the 1950s, from the work of Billy Lee Riley, Onie Wheeler, Alvis Wayne, Ronnie Dawson and Carl Perkins and other artists that even the critics knew little about, fed it through a blender and sprinkled some Glam stardust and the rawness of punk on the top. All served up with the kind of sleaze usually depicted in the B-movies the band were so fond of, including the work of Herschell Gordon Lewis, Russ Meyer and Nick Zedd (whose 1983 comedy horror film *Geek Maggot Bingo* the band were said to be particularly enamoured of).

In 1983, the Sting-Rays paid their own particular homage to the Cramps when they released a three-track single on Ace under the name the Bananamen. Taking time out from recording their debut album, *Dinosaurs*, the band cut 'The Crusher', 'Love Me' and 'Surfin' Bird', partly as an ironic attempt to silence those who continually brought up the name of the Cramps when describing the music of the Sting-Rays. The choosing of the alter ego name the Bananamen alluded to the fact that two of the songs, by the Trashmen and the Novas, had been first released on the obscure Hava Banana label in Minneapolis.

The Sting-Rays had formed in at the end of 1976 but didn't play their debut show until 1981 when the line-up of the band had settled down to Bal Croce on vocals, Alex Palao on drums, Mark Hosking on guitar and Keith MK Cockburn on double bass. They recorded their debut EP, 'The Sting-Rays On Self Destruct' at Pathway studios in one night (bill – £50) and released it on Ted Carroll's Big Beat label in 1983. The EP included a cover version of the Thirteenth Floor Elevators' 'You're Gonna Miss Me' and the record sleeve had a photograph of the band taken beneath a wall resplendent with a giant mural of the cover of the first Thirteenth Floor Elevators' *Psychedelic Sounds Of...* album.

Many bands gravitated towards Big Beat, for reasons put succinctly by Billy Childish when interviewed by *Sounds* at the start of 1985: 'Big Beat is one of the few labels doing this sort of thing. It's time somebody gave them credit. Most labels try to get hits, but Big Beat realise they've got a bunch of losers so they don't bother.'

Big Beat wasn't the first label that Ted Carroll had set up. In 1975, he'd co-launched Chiswick Records and released a run of punk and proto punk singles by bands that included the 101ers, the Count Bishops, Johnny Moped, the Hammersmith Gorillas, and Johnny & The Self Abusers. Carroll had an eye for the curious and nights spent going to garage gigs at Dingwalls put on by Mike Spenser from the Cannibals led to him offering to make a compilation album and the start of the Big Beat label proper. In 1983, he gave Thee Milkshakes, the Cannibals and the Sting-Rays £100 each and told them to go away and record four tracks each, the results bundled together on *These Cats Aint Nothin' But Trash*. The album's back cover was partly mocked up like a movie poster, the tale of trash snappily outlined for the uninitiated buyer in one hundred or so words.

'I TELL YOU IT JUST WON'T GO AWAY…. IT'S BEEN BURIED MORE TIMES THAN BELA LUGOSI AND STILL IT KEEPS RIGHT ON BOUNCING BACK… EVERY TIME THE BLAND START LEADING THE BLAND UP THE CHARTS…. ALONG COMES…

THEY CALLED IT *ROCK 'N' ROLL*, THEY CALLED IT *ROCKABILLY*…

THEY CALLED IT *BEAT*, THEY CALLED IT *PUNK*……

IT'S FOUND IN GARAGES LIVING OFF THE CARBON MONOXIDE FUMES AND EVERY NOW AND THEN IT CRAWLS OUT OF THE PIT AND ONTO A STAGE, THE 100 CLUB, THE HOPE & ANCHOR, BRIXTON'S 'GARAGE' AND EVEN DINGWALLS HAVE ALL HOSTED A NIGHT OF TRASH. NOW FOR THE FIRST TIME THE THREE BANDS AT THE TOP OF THE HEAP, TOGETHER ON ONE RECORD.

The label flourished, bringing in fresh talent like the Vibes and the Guana Batz and reissuing out of print classics, including albums by the Chocolate Watch Band and the Damned. It released the Naz Nomad album, *Give Daddy The Knife, Cindy*, and even briefly signed the Cramps, releasing the classic *A Date With Elvis* in 1986. Another excellent band that the label signed was the all-girl garage outfit the Delmonas, a group that took their name from a Bo Diddley song and had started out as the Milk-Boilers, backing vocalists for Thee Milkshakes.

Thee Milkshakes returned the favour, acting as backing band for the trio. There were two brilliant EPs released in 1984 – 'Comin' Home Baby' (the title track a cover version of Mel Torme's 1962 hit) and 'Hello We Love You', a reworking of the Doors classic. The band also did a mashed-up version of 'Peter Gunn' and 'Locomotion', and elsewhere, as on their full-length album, 1985's *Dangerous Charms*, recorded songs written by Billy Childish and Micky Hampshire. Clearly Thee Milkshakes had a blast providing what the record's back cover called 'a column of noise', their 'blitzkrieg of slashing cymbals sitting on top of a vast, primitive horde of chundering bass and guitars'. The formula was repeated, but alas the Delmonas, who at their best sounded like a revved-up version of the Shrangri-Las, made too few records in all too short a period.

Sadly, there were hardly any female rockabilly bands during the early years – no prominent latter day Wanda Jacksons or Sparkle Moores, although there was a cross over between the garage, trash and rockabilly music and the brief rise of cowpunk that became something of a fad at the start of 1984. The Boothill Foot Tappers, the Bluberry Hillbillies, Yip Yip Coyotee and the Shillelagh Sisters all had prominent female band members and took elements of the rockabilly sound and threw it into the mix of a punk-coated music largely made up of bluegrass, skiffle, gospel and western swing. The boundaries were often blurred. The Shillelagh Sisters, for instance, used an upright double bass and saw themselves as less a country band and more a rockabilly outfit, telling *Sounds* shortly after the band signed to CBS at the start of 1984, 'What we're playing at the moment is traditional rockabilly'.

The rockabilly and cowpunk look wasn't too dissimilar, either, both trawling the 1950s for inspiration, both (in the case of the men) fond of washed out denim and brothel creepers and both sharing a penchant for the flat top when it came to men's hairstyles, or beehives, bobs and Betty Page fringes when it came to the ladies. The classic white T-shirt was popular as ever it had been since the days of Marlon Brando and *The Wild One*.

The styles and looks also reflected the social demographics of the scene. In spite of supposedly working class origins, punk had very quickly become a middle class plaything (as was indie), but genres such as psychobilly were resolutely working class. Many shared the lingering fashion traits of skinhead culture and indeed in 1984 the skinheads had far from gone away, as fanzines like *Hard As Nails* and bands like Burial and the Oppressed showed. But having witnessed the debacle of the racist movement Oi's involvement in politics, many on the rockabilly/ psychobilly scene deliberately adopted an apolitical stance. Many considered themselves to be so much the underclass of Thatcherism that they didn't bother articulating *any* kind of political response, giving themselves over, instead, to joyous abandonment.

What Mike Spenser's Brixton venue the Garage was to trash, the Klub Foot in the basement of the Clarendon Hotel in Hammersmith was to psychobilly. The club had started in the early 1980s (at one point promoting heavy metal nights) before becoming a top spot for many of the neo-rockabilly, psychobilly and garage bands to play. The club's heyday coincided with, and contributed to, the seemingly limitless outpouring of compilation records that appeared to service the music. *Stompin' At The Klub Foot* came out towards the end of 1984 and featured live performances by Restless, the Sting-Rays, Thee Milkshakes and the Guana Batz. It was a cleverly recorded work that captured the fidelity of the individual band's sounds but also highlighted the atmosphere of the club, when on any given night the sweat-soaked atmosphere of the mosh pit would be heaving. 'So, who killed Bo Diddley?' ran the headline of the *NME*'s review of the album upon release, before pointing out that part of the record's charm was its inclusion of 'all the nervous blunders and bad tempered gaffs' of the bands in question. This was 'not only the legitimate expression of arty temperament, but also forgiveable'.

Bands took gigs wherever they could find them, as the X Men's appearances at the Living Room showed. Simon Down, prior to starting the Pink label, had put garage and rockabilly bands on at the short-lived Gladdog Club at the Sir George Robey in Kings Cross, including one night when the Sting-Rays played there. 'The independent scene and that rockabilly scene ran in tandem,' he recalls. 'People were in and out of the various clubs and sharing bills in a way that wasn't quite as mutually exclusive as it might seem. Some of the shows were awesome. There was nothing quite as powerful, for instance, as seeing Thee Milkshakes in full flight...'

Such was the success of *Stompin' At The Klub Foot* that *Volume 2* appeared less than a year later. This time bands were allowed just two tracks and those asked to contribute included Demented Are Go, Frenzy, the Tall Boys, the Rapids and the Pharoes. *Volumes 3 & 4*, a double album, appeared in 1986 and there was even a *Volume 5* and a *Volume 6*. Such was the cache of the venue's name that a number of bands, including Demented Are Go and Guana Batz released whole albums of stand-alone Klub Foot material. In fact, the Klub Foot would probably still be going today but for the fact that the owners of the Clarendon Hotel sold up in 1988 and the building was demolished to make way for a new post office. Regular fans of the venue vented their spleen by helping the process along, smashing up the toilets in quite spectacular fashion just before the whole edifice was pulled down.

By the start of 1985, Thee Milkshakes were up to a staggering tenth album, the commercial considerations of flooding the available market offset by the fact that the cost of production tended to be low: 'We record very simply,' Billy Childish commented at the time. 'Everyone else releases records at set times to sell, but people don't like us anyway, so we *can't* flood our market! Everyone else doesn't do enough work, it's not that we do too much…'

Thee Milkshakes releases included compilation albums, instrumental albums, albums of cover versions, all recorded with a healthy disregard for the finer points of posh fidelity that put even Mark E Smith's anti-image stance to shame. The albums were often recorded in the studio in one 'live' take. When Dave Henderson of *Sounds* asked Billy Childish whether or not Thee Milkshakes would ever like to make a record using hi-tech, even digital equipment, he replied yes, but didn't see the logic in it. 'We've used modern equipment, we know how to get the best out of the technology, though there's not much point with our sound! You *have* to be good to make thousands of pounds' worth of equipment sound like a cassette player. Production is our thing…

In fact, we used to find cassette versions of our stuff were better than the finished versions!'

Thee Milkshakes called it a day in 1985, Billy Childish going on to form Thee Mighty Ceasars and then Thee Headcoats (and, later, other bands). He continued, as he had been doing through the period of Thee Milkshakes with his 'riting' and poetry and painting. In *The Man With The Gallows Eyes: Selected Poetry 1980-2005* (Aquarium) he summed up 25 years of small press publishing experience in a way that could equally stand testament for his musical output, saying, 'By my late 20s I was planning armed robbery as a means of financing my small press ventures and as a way to publish my novel [called] *My Fault*. A sawn off shotgun was promised by a fellow riter but never matirealised and I was saved again. I could see a pattern forming: I have always been saved from success and destruction; Failer is great indeed and is ultimately the only way to succeed.'

The Meteors weren't quite as prolific as Thee Milkshakes in the short term but still managed to work their way through fifteen albums during the course of the 1980s. Band members joined and left bewilderingly fast (sometimes only surviving a matter of a few months), with P Paul Fenech the only constant, as remains the case to the present day. Mike Spenser remains at the helm of the Cannibals, although their most productive period drew to an end as the 1980s wound down. The Sting-Rays more or less imploded after the release of 1987's *Cryptic & Coffee Time*, the follow-up album to their debut, *Dinosaur*.

Ultimately, the fate of the various sub-genres thrown up by the neo-rockabilly explosion of the late 1970s and early 1980s was the same as that dealt out to hard core punk – a gradually sliding into the margins as independent music became more and more compartmentalised. Rockabilly started out as part of a communal well everyone dipped a beak into but ended up pushed out, a tributary sought by only the truly committed. Played by those that were mad, bad and dangerous to know, the music – gone but not forgotten – is an enduring testament to the claim that in rock music the Devil really does have all the best tunes.

CHAPTER 14

'SMASHING UP POP MUSIC'

THE INDIFFERENT REACTION TO *Alive In The Living Room* couldn't dampen the enthusiasm generated at Creation following the release of its first album. A second quickly followed, in September 1984. The compilation *Wild Summer, Wow!* featured a clutch of tracks from earlier Creation singles by the Pastels, Biff Bang Pow, Revolving Paint Dream, the Legend!, the X Men, and the Jasmine Minks. It also featured 'Winter', a previously unreleased song by the Loft, recorded during the session for their debut single, 'Why Does The Rain', which appeared at the same time as *Wild Summer, Wow!*.

The Loft were an impressive addition to the Creation stable and a band that could hardly be tarred with the psychedelic revivalist brush. They had broad tastes, with an appreciation that took in everything from the conceptual art of the avant-garde through to the Beatles and jazz, via New York intellectual punk, reggae, and Kraut rock. They bravely expressed an unfashionable (for the time) admiration in interviews for the work of Paul Simon, Creedence Clearwater Revival, Don Henley, the Band, Randy Newman and Bobby Womack. What journalist Danny Kelly called Pete Astor's 'angular non-voice' and the interlocking melodic and rhythmic guitar in the sound of the band also acknowledged a far more urgent debt to Television.

Guitarist Andy Strickland and bassist Bill Prince met Pete Astor towards the end of 1981 when, along with drummer Andy Knott, they went to watch the Fuck Pigs (later Turkey Bones & The Wild Dogs) at the Pied Bull in Islington. Support on the bill was a group called News of Birds, a guitar band whose main songwriter and vocalist was Pete Astor. Prior to News of Birds, Astor had been in a post-rock group called Damp Jungle, a band that sometimes incorporated a DJ and record deck on stage and whose members occasionally swapped instruments mid set. The band's one projected release (a cassette on the Fuck Off tape label) never happened. Astor formed News of Birds after 'aesthetically tiring of trying to write songs without a tune, of trying to reinvent the wheel when it didn't want to be reinvented'.

Unlike Astor, Strickland and Prince didn't quite yet have a band but were very keen to make one happen and thought that Astor would make the ideal frontman for what they had in mind – he certainly looked the part with his white Burns Duo Sonic guitar and striking looks, and his songs were a literary cut above the above the average. All three exchanged contact details and then six months went by with nothing happening before a cassette of songs by Strickland and Prince dropped through Astor's letterbox for him to listen to. Astor listened, liked the music, but decided that due to final year college commitments he wouldn't join.

Astor had made his decision but had no way of relaying the information since the squat Strickland and Prince lived in didn't have a telephone. He decided, therefore, that the only thing to do was to go along to where Strickland and Prince rehearsed, but not take his guitar. 'I didn't take it because, in essence, I was simply going along to tell them that I couldn't do it,' recalls Astor. 'When I turned up to the squat we chatted and we got on well together. There was a spare guitar lying around and they suggested that I join them on a song. They also told me that they too were in their final year at college and that perhaps we could arrange rehearsals with that in mind. I played along and enjoyed it and so we decided that we would meet every Sunday. It was all very ordered, and since that was a day off, it was more like a recreational arrangement. So that's what we did.'

Astor began bringing songs along to the rehearsals, tossing them onto the pile that already contained a few Strickland riffs and some material worked out by Strickland and Prince. 'Pete had a few songs in his back pocket when he joined and Bill and I had done a few rough recordings, including some weird instrumentals,' says Strickland. 'I remember we also had one dreadful song called "Domestic Politics" which was all about eight students living in the same house. It sounded OK, but the lyrics were not exactly brilliant. Pete was something of a poet, he was a good fit.'

The band rehearsals took place in a house that was squatted in Tuffnel Park and used by a number of bands – 'there was one group who were a metal/ industrial type band and all wore dyed black boiler suits, another was a group of radical feminist punks: going there was a bit like an episode out of *The Young Ones*,' recalls Astor – but the venue gave them inspiration to come up with a name, which they duly did, christening themselves the Living Room. It was a name not without connotations, some people mistakenly assuming it was modelled on an English translation of *lebensraum* (or 'living space'), the Nazi's racist ideology used to justify human-geography expansion.

They played their first gig in November 1982, booking out the London Musicians Collective building around the same time that Alan McGee was hosting the Communication Club there. 'We joined the LMC simply to be able to play a gig there and went about the whole thing properly, arranging for two other bands to play with us and bringing in a load of beer to the unlicensed premises to sell through the old raffle ticket dodge,' remembers Astor. 'The night was a great success for everyone except us –we went on first and were dreadfully out of tune.' Helping the band out was Danny Kelly who acted as an unpaid manager/ roadie and Kelly brought along his friend Richard Cook, the *NME* critic. 'It was a bit daunting, really,' says Strickland. 'Richard Cook saw the show and then was quite cool about it after, encouraging us, but not *too* much…'

It took the Living Room a little while before they came play a second gig but in April 1983 they managed to get a support slot at the Kings Head pub in Crouch End where Julian Cope was meant to be making a secret appearance. Cope failed to turn up but the Living Room went down a storm. They were not, alas, able to immediately capitalise on their success as drummer Andy

Knott quit the band and went off to live in Hong Kong. A chance meeting with Dave Morgan in Dick's Bar in Crouch End saw him eventually take over the role as the academic year drew to a close.

'The "rehearsal" year was over and we had to make a decision about how we would go on,' explains Astor. 'We came up with a plan to give it six months or so and if in that time we hadn't got anywhere we'd chuck it in. There was a definite date we fixed on as a point when we would review the situation. Andy and Bill had done a media course at college and had already got work placements. I was on the dole.'

All three of them went to the first night of Alan McGee's Living Room club in August and immediately decided that it was a venue they wanted to play. 'There was a mention of the place in the *NME* the week before it opened,' says Astor, 'just two lines which, as I recall, referred to it as a Rough Trade club. That was what caught my interest. The other thing is that it was one of the very few venues in London where a band like us could get a gig. If you tried to play other smaller venues like the Rock Garden, not that you'd necessarily want to, you'd hand over a tape but always find yourself turned away. That was the way it was.'

After a discussion with McGee, the Living Room decided to change their name and McGee agreed to put some thought into giving them a gig. The band turned up regularly and on one occasion gave Alan McGee and Dick Green a cassette to listen to. 'We'd recorded a song at Horsney Boys Club called "The Day Lies Like A Lion",' remembers Astor. 'It was very much in the vein of Syd Barrett and quite long. They listened to it and agreed to put us on, although they told me later that they didn't like the song on the cassette very much. I'm certain the fact that we had journalists in the band helped sway Alan's mind.'

The Loft, as the band was now called, played their first gig at the Living Room in December as part of a three day 'London tour', the other dates being two nights at a derelict squat gig called Number 39 in Vauxhall. The Living Room gig was the first of many and on that occasion they supported the Television Personalities and Ut. In spite of their reservations about the demo cassette, both Alan McGee and Dick Green found the Loft to be surprisingly good.

'It took a couple of shows but I came to really like them,' says Alan McGee, 'and in Pete Astor they had a fantastic talent. He was probably the closest thing to a rock star I'd ever met at the time, as much as anything through his self-belief. I knew straight away that I wanted them to record a single for the label.'

The Loft continued to rehearse and work up material, one day coming up with 'Why Does The Rain?', a song based partly on a Little Willie John lyric. With its strong melody and poetic mien ('Why, when the thunderstorm is gone/ does the air, the blue-grey air, ring like bells?') it was a song the band knew to be one of their best and one that immediately went down well at the Living Room. It remains a classic Pete Astor composition, the subdued nature of its subject matter redeemed through the very act of narration. As Astor later told *Sounds*, the song worked a little bit like a blues song: 'If the music is good it becomes an uplifting experience to hear about something miserable.'

Alan McGee agreed, and told Astor that he would finance the release. 'Pete came and told us the good news, nervously excited,' says Strickland. 'Then he immediately panicked and said that he *thought* that that was what McGee had offered. He had to go back and ask him again since he always had a real problem understanding Alan's Glasgow accent.'

McGee sent them in to the studio to make the single with Joe Foster producing. 'We had very little experience of studios,' recalls Strickland, 'and were just ecstatic at the fact that we were being given the chance to make a record. Danny Kelly came along and acted as our ears while we just soaked up the experience. Danny would occasionally stick a head around the studio door and tell us when he thought something didn't quite sound right. As a producer, Joe wasn't at that point much more experienced than we were.' With a total budget of around £100, the recording was a quick affair. 'It was all done in a rush – less than half a day to record and the engineer was a complete snob thinking that we couldn't play and that I couldn't sing,' says Astor. 'After I had done the vocals, I realised one more take was needed to get it right. But there was no more time.'

Recorded in June, there was slight delay in the record's release – McGee called up Astor to say that Bobby Gillespie, who was printing the sleeve, was experiencing difficulty 'acquiring' the necessary paper from the warehouse. The delay was no bad thing. All through the summer of 1984 the NUJ dispute with IPC dragged on and the *NME* didn't appear, one of the key papers where the Loft could expect their single to be reviewed, not least because Danny Kelly was freelancing there, having been introduced to the paper by Richard Cook.

The record was eventually released in September and became an instant favourite of Janice Long who played it regularly on her Radio One Show (and later hailed it her *second* favourite single of the year after Echo & The Bunnymen's lachrymose 'The Killing Moon'). John Peel also played it, and included it in his weekly broadcasts for the World Service. And the band got their review in the *NME*, where Danny Kelly complimented them on their 'stack of fine songs' but complained about the record's 'less than thrilling production'. The record, pressed up in the usual Creation run of 1000, quickly sold out on the back of the radio play: 'I remember thinking that if the single got into the lower reaches of the indie charts I'd be happy. It went straight in at 26 and I thought that I had achieved my dreams,' says Astor. 'Talk about aiming way too low…'

In December, the Loft recorded a session for the Janice Long show, four tracks that were 'Skeleton Staircase', the live favourite

'On A Tuesday', the homesick lament 'The Canal & The Big Red Town' and 'Lonely Street', a superb outsider song in the classic sob vein of 'Heartbreak Hotel'. The session was broadcast in January, not long before the band went back into the studios to record the follow-up single.

The success of the first single, McGee's belief in Astor and his expectation that the Loft would become part of the mainstream, coupled with the general growth of the Creation label during 1984 meant that the Loft were this time sent into a better studio with a producer with a track record when it came to recording 'Up The Hill & Down The Slope'. They travelled up to Woodbine Studios in Leamington Spa and John Rivers was at the controls, a man whose CV included working with Swell Maps, the Specials and Felt. 'We spent two days in a B&B – living the dream! – and John Rivers did a brilliant job,' says Astor. 'He made little changes to the song but everything he did was really useful helping us get the great sound that we got. He even made my really scranky guitar solo, the moment when I fleetingly believed I could play music as good as that of Thelonius Monk, sound good. It was really excellent work.'

With its almost classic construction, 'Up The Hill & Down The Slope' shows just how far Creation had travelled since the label's first release in the summer of 1983. The stripped-down, basic agit prop of ''73 In '83' is a galaxy away from what the Loft track aspires to be. According to Dave Cavanagh in *The Creation Records Story*, 'Up The Hill...' took its 'skipping bass line... from a Derek & The Dominos track, "Why Does Love Got To Be So Sad?"' and 'the snare drum crack that [opened the song] came from the first bars of Bruce Springsteen's "Born In The USA".' Especially good is the sound of Andy Strickland's chiming guitar. Richard Boon in the *Catalogue* praised the 'neo-classical guitar runs... on the rousing title track', noting that the classic sources had been 'used and treated well'.

The four tracks spread across the 12" were all of a rare quality by the standards of indie production. As well as a studio version of 'Lonely Street', there was a stunning take of 'Your Door Shines Like Gold' – the live version had been one of the few highlights of *Alive In The Living Room* – and a cover of Richard Hell's 'Time'. Back in 1981, Astor, who had been fixated by the song, had written to Richard Hell asking for a copy of the lyrics: eighteen months later, he received his reply.

The band could measure the success of the single by the amount of mail they received. They had taken the step of printing an address on of the back of the record sleeve and, as Astor recalls, the letters flooded in: 'Bill heard from a guy at Virgin that after the first Culture Club single flopped they made Boy George come in to the office and personally reply to every letter. We didn't bother – our letters just mounted up in a corner. We did quite a good job of looking cocky and I am amazed at how cocky we could appear to be, but at the same time as being arrogant, we didn't harbour any sense of self-worth or entitlement.'

'Up The Hill & Down The Slope' made Single of the Week in *Sounds* and *Record Mirror* and a month after its release, in May 1985, there were short interviews in both *Sounds* and *NME*. Bill Prince had been contributing to *Sounds*, in some cases lengthy articles, under the name Bill Black, but amazingly almost throughout the life of the Loft very few people realised that Bill Black and Bill Prince were one and the same. Andy Strickland wrote for *Record Mirror*, and eventually, Pete Astor began writing, contributing to the *NME*. 'Bill was working for *Sounds* and one night I went with him to see the band the Passion Puppets, who were terrible,' remembers Astor. 'On the way back, Bill suggested to me that I should start reviewing. I wrote a review of the night and sent it in to the *NME* and thought no more about it. Amazingly, they ran it. So that's how I started writing journalism, although I deliberately stopped once the band got going properly.'

In the interview for *Sounds* the band revealed how Alan McGee had wanted them to make an album, but they spurned his offer as being 'too pompous'. Asked what made them special, the band were lost for words, although Bill Prince tentatively suggested that it might have to do with taste – 'We just filter out so much garbage: the clichés and the easy options'. In the *NME*, Danny Kelly had no problem singling out the band's essence: the 'twin tensions, the first between the rhythm and the guitars, the second between the guitars themselves. Strickland plays chiming, sometimes beautiful figures while Astor's battered Strat (sic) nags and snarls, snags and gnarls.'

One person who had been carefully watching the progress of the Loft was Mike Alway, formerly of Cherry Red and then Blanco Y Negro. 'Mike approached us and took us out to lunch one time,' remembers Strickland. 'He was interested in licensing the Loft for Europe, where Creation, at that point, had no foothold. We certainly had enough songs to make an album, and, looking back, making an album would have seemed to be the logical next move.'

Janice Long continued her support of the band and invited the band to appear on the television programme, the *Oxford Roadshow* in a weekly segment she oversaw called 'Bands To Watch'. During the short interview, Bill Prince had made a casual remark about forming the band with Andy Strickland and 'picking up the others along the way', a comment that immediately sat ill with Astor who had come more and more to creatively represent the band. Hairline cracks within the structure that had probably been there since the formation of the group gradually began to open up.

'Bill's comment was both unintentional and unfortunate,' says Strickland. 'If only at that moment, Pete had yelled out "Cut!" or something and then had it out with Bill, we'd probably have all thought about it and laughed it off. One part of the problem was that nobody, apart from Pete, seemed to hear Bill's remark, another was that there was no-one neutral to help sort it out. Had we had a manager, or roadie, or even driver, I am sure they would have stepped in and knocked our heads together. There might have been a big row but we'd have got over it, instead of what happened, which is that we limped on for a bit and then for 25 years Pete and I never spoke…'

The timing couldn't have been more calamitous. The Colourfield were also appearing on the Oxford Roadshow and Terry Hall witnessed the Loft's performance and asked them to support his band on their upcoming nationwide British tour that began in May. The highlight was intended to be a show at the Hammersmith Palais on 14 June. The Loft played a number of dates with the Colourfield in the provinces before returning to London to do some warm up shows at small venues like the Pindar of Wakefield in preparation for the big night.

Since the appearance on the *Oxford Roadshow* tensions within the band had been visibly strained, but they had carried on, playing a Creation/ Kitchenware festival at the Riverside in May along with Hurrah, the Daintees and Jasmine Minks. That the band had progressed during the past year or so was apparent from the presence of Rob Dickens of WEA Records who turned up to the Riverside night to check the Loft out with a view to possibly signing them to a major deal. In fact, he left early, allegedly finding them 'too punky', although his departure was of less concern to Strickland than the presence in the audience of Robert Forster and Grant McLennan of the Go-Betweens. 'They'd had a conversation with Pete about how much they liked the guitar sound on "Up The Hill" and especially on our version of Richard Hell's "Time",' he remembers. 'As we began playing "Time", I saw Robert Forster making his way further and further towards the stage until he was standing right in front of me. I think he wanted to check out if we were using any foot pedals or stuff like that, which of course we weren't. I got so nervous with him standing right in front of me that I completely cocked up the guitar solo.'

As it turned out, Strickland's lapse was of little consequence since shortly before the Hammersmith Palais show Pete Astor phoned Bill Prince and told him that he was breaking up the band. He intended, he said, to keep the name and carry on working with Dave Morgan. Astor told Prince that he would play the Hammersmith Palais gig if Prince and Strickland wanted him to. 'Bill rang me and was very upset,' remembers Strickland. 'Of course we wanted Pete to play the Hammersmith show – it was meant to be our big moment. In the end, it just turned into this very odd experience. We didn't talk, and I certainly didn't really understand what the problem was. At the Hammersmith Palais, really, I just wanted to punch Pete, but when the moment arose he was standing in front of the guitars – six guitars, we each had a spare – and I could see that if he fell he was going to fall on my guitars, so at the one moment when the chance arose, I held back...'

For Pete Astor, the issue was one of valued worth: 'One of the key problems for me was that when I joined the band, I was joining *as a singer*,' says Astor. 'But the songs had gone from being songs that we all worked on to songs that were being written by me. At first, I had no idea about who "wrote" the songs, it was only later that I began to realise that ownership was mine. So when Bill made his remark on television, it pissed me off and on the television you can see that I look like I am about to be sick.'

The Loft went ahead and played the show at the Hammersmith Palais, but just before playing 'Up The Hill & Down The Slope' (which was always the last song the band played), Andy Strickland announced from the stage that the band were splitting up. During the song, when Astor often extemporized lyrics just before the song reached its finale, he made a number of comments about Strickland and Prince, effectively comparing them to the 'sad, tearful journeymen' contained in the songs lyrics. 'I improvised words that were germane to what was going on in my head. In many ways it was truly horrible,' he says today. 'I then threw my guitar down and quoted a couple of words from Lou Reed's "Street Hassle" – "bad luck" – before storming backstage where I sat thinking that somebody was probably going to hit me and that I wouldn't blame them if they did.'

The rest of the band finished the song and then trooped backstage, at which point both Astor and Morgan had left, taking the tube home. 'Pete was gone by the time we came off, as I recall,' says Strickland. 'We'd had a bit of Dutch Courage to get up and do the gig in the first place and when we came off, I was in a rage. I've never seen Bill so angry, before or since. We thought that we might have it out when we loaded up the van, but the Pete and Dave were nowhere to be seen. Dave Morgan must have taken his drum kit home on the tube.'

A review in the *NME* the following week effectively confirmed the band's fate – 'WARNING: THIS GROUP WILL SELF-DE-STRUCT IN THE NEXT SONG' – and whilst not wholly hampering Astor's plans to carry on with the name probably helped him to decide otherwise.

'When I think back now, I was the main person but I wasn't the *only* person in the Loft,' says Astor. 'Failing to realise that properly was the error and it was compounded by the fact that Alan McGee always saw bands in terms of the main person rather than the whole.' Shortly before the show McGee had been invited on to the Janice Long show to talk about Creation and inevitably made a few comments about Janice Long's favourite Creation band. 'I remember Alan commenting that the Loft was a great band but that Pete Astor was a genius,' adds Strickland. 'He said something to the effect that Pete Astor was the only person on the Creation roster that could write a song like "Mull Of Kintyre".

I think that probably told the story of where Alan was coming from. I am sure his line to Pete would have been, "You're the singer, you're the songwriter, maybe you don't need them…" I think he felt that he had to nail his colours to a mast and he decided to go with the singer.'

'Andy and I were at each other, yet not one word passed between us at the time to sort things out and I completely regret that,' says Astor. 'For Andy, he was adamant that the show at the Hammersmith Palais would be the last gig by the Loft, and I stupidly thought I could keep the name. On reflection, I was wrong to want that. But we didn't talk and we didn't work out our differences. And that was a great pity, because the consequence was that we never got to make the album we should have made.'

In time, Bill Prince formed the Wishing Stones and set aside grievances to do some shows with Pete Astor's new band, the Weather Prophets. Andy Strickland formed the Caretaker Race, but didn't have contact with Astor at all. 'We were tight-lipped and never discussed anything between us when we should have done,' he recalls. 'In the end, I didn't speak to Pete for 25 years. We didn't make the album, but the real tragedy is the 25-year gap in our friendship. Only once in that period did our paths cross, in an off licence in Walthamstow in around 1990. I just growled at him…'

Shortly after The Loft's 'Why Does The Rain?' single was released, there was second and final single for Creation by the Legend! 'Destroys The Blues' was every bit as cantankerous towards the hand that fed it as ''73 In '83' had been, with a David Smith cover design depicting the Legend! taking a handsaw to an electric guitar which he is also frantically biting as the top of his head explodes. The song served up more outpourings of social conscience, but this time was aided by the assistance of a more fully formed backing band. With its slices of feedback and messy, garage-rock blast, the record captures perfectly the indie zeitgeist, but its drifting Stooges-like dirge, with vocals meshed deep into the mix, proved a bridge too far for both the label and audience: in a late summer dominated by the sanitised outrage of Frankie Goes To Hollywood, such severity was out of step, even although anticipating the social surrealist sounds of a number of bands that would break through in the next twelve months such as Bog-shed and the Noseflutes.

As autumn turned into winter, Creation released its third album and also began attracting the first proper profile articles that outlined the label's progress throughout the preceding year and took soundings of where it might be going in the future. *1-2-3-4-5-6-7 All Good Preachers Go To Heaven* by the Jasmine Minks was a mini album running to just eighteen minutes, recorded at a cost of £400. In summer, the band had been given demo time by London Records, and although the relationship never pro-gressed, they did manage to walk away with 'Ghost Of A Young Man' which was one of the very best new tracks that were added together with the second single to make up the album. Although some quibbled over the content – *Sounds*, for instance, wonder-ing aloud if the band knew in which direction they were really heading, such was the melting pot of influences – the record generally picked up good reviews, *Melody Maker* praising the 'edgy rebellion of their music' and suggesting that they offered 'an escape route from our lemming-like march into the jaws of Product Pop'. 'They may not be the Chocolate Watch Band,' thought this author in the *NME*, 'but they may be the chocolate band to watch.'

'The album was a big step up for us,' recalls Adam Sanderson. 'It was also a bit of a departure from previous planning, which had been to release a series of classic seven-inch singles. We had to accept that releasing seven-inch wrapped up in polythene bags with a two-colour wrap hand-folded had failed to revolutionise the world. Due to the usual budget restrictions, the album had a lo-fi element. We never quite captured on vinyl the exuberance of how we were live. Our punk influence was more noticeable at gigs than on record.'

At the start of November, another and more substantial profile of the Creation label appeared in *NME*, once again, written by Bruce Dessau. Not mincing his words, as ever, Alan McGee got straight to the root of the problem with pop, as he saw it: 'The music business at the moment is absolutely sick, and Creation is the medicine.' He vowed to release 24 albums in the forth-coming year and unveiled his new weapon in the war on pop, a band from East Kilbride named the Jesus & Mary Chain. McGee called them 'shock troops... they'll smash down doors which more subtle bands like the Loft and the Jasmine Minks will discreetly sneak under'. In an earlier interview with *Slow Dazzle* fanzine, McGee had likened Creation to a kaleidoscope – 'you turn it one way and you see a pop-art thing, you turn it another and you see a punk thing, turn it another you see quality, turn it another you see shit...' A further article about the label appeared in the *Catalogue*, written by McGee himself. Once again, it took a retro-spective view, and once again McGee was no wallflower: 'I told you twelve months ago that I was going to set the world alight with my brand new shining pop groups... You laughed aloud. I'm still laughing, the joke was on you.'

In the same week the *NME* profile appeared, what many might have seen as one of the Creation label's very best 'pop-art' bands released a new single. The Pastels' 'Million Tears' was the first Creation twelve-inch and picked up where the promise of 'Something's Going On' left off. It saw Stephen Pastel making good on his earlier pledge to toughen up the sound of the band. The Pastels were McGee's favourite band in the autumn of 1984, or at least were *primus inter pares* since McGee was never less than wildly enthusiastic about any of his acts. He wrote to Paul

Groovy describing them as 'sons of the soft side of the Velvet Underground' and called 'Something's Going On' 'by far the best Creation release so far and that IS official.' He continued: 'If there is any justice in Pop, and I personally don't believe there is, then Stephen should be a pop star…'

'Million Tears' kept up the fragile *almost*-Pop of the band's earlier releases, but reflected a new-found confidence, and if, as it sometimes seemed, the Pastels was a deliberately on-going experiment, it showed them inching towards some sort of ideal state. 'I think the main thing was that we'd gained some experience and maybe had more of a sense of what worked for us,' says Stephen. 'Even in different studios, in different situations we were able to get it to come out sounding like the Pastels, so that was a bit of progress. And although we often weren't that great live, more people were coming to our shows and it started to feel that there was a scene developing which was exciting at first and then maybe something that we felt trapped by.'

One song from the single that proved particularly popular, not least when played live, was 'Baby Honey', a seven-minute long, hypnotic, droning yet classically composed ode of love:

There is magic in her fingertips
There is magic in the lips I kiss
There is magic in her beautiful eyes
Justify the tears I've cried

It is not too fanciful to suggest that the track anticipates the indie/dance crossover that would follow a few years later, although its hypnotism owes more to spikiness of the Velvet Underground than to the motoric beats of, say, Kraftwerk.

'When we played live, we felt that sometimes we lacked a little range but we were really happy with "Baby Honey" from the moment we started to play it as a group, and could see its potential,' says Stephen Pastel. 'It wasn't the first time we used feedback but it was probably the best use of feedback we'd made and everyone in the group seemed to know their place in the song. It was a song that Brian seemed to have an image for which we discussed and agreed on. He could dig in properly to notes and we played off him, including Bernice, which was maybe slightly back to front but actually gave us originality. We always played it, it was my favourite song from the time.'

For their first few years of existence, the Pastels were something of an anomaly – concrete pop artists in a Scottish music environment that was increasingly filling up with derivative, faux-sophisticated bands trailing in the wake of Orange Juice but lacking Orange Juice's sparkling originality, wit and talent. Amongst the followers of the Pastels was a two-piece band called the Daisy Chain that featured guitarist/ vocalist Jim Reid and bassist Douglas Hart. The Daisy Chain lived in a concrete new town on the edge of Glasgow called East Kilbride ('Stonehenge with windows,' according to the brilliant description of Douglas Hart) and rehearsed in a disused paint factory where they consumed magic mushrooms and dreamed about creating the perfect band. They made a demo tape but had no joy with local promoters. On one occasion, though, they went to the Candy Club, a venue in the Lorne Hotel, Glasgow, to see the Pastels play in a show promoted by a promoter called Nick Lowe. A little while later, they decided to send Lowe a copy of their demo, the songs hastily duplicated onto a used cassette that featured a Syd Barrett compilation on the other side.

Lowe listened to the tape and decided that he didn't like it, but the Syd Barrett material on the demo's reverse side was good and would appeal, Lowe thought, to his friend Bobby Gillespie. It took him a good six months to get around to sending Gillespie the tape, at which point Jim Reid's brother William had joined the Daisy Chains, bringing with him some of his own songs and instantly doubling the band's repertoire. Gillespie listened to the tape, Barrett side first, and then flipped it to listen to the the Daisy Chain. The Daisy Chain material – which included the songs 'Upside Down', 'Never Understand' and 'Taste The Floor' – cast an immediate spell on him. As he told Zoë Howe in *Barbed Wire Kisses: The Jesus & Mary Chain Story*, 'I played it about six times. I thought it was fucking incredible.'

Gillespie rang the number on the cassette tape's inlay and spoke with Douglas Hart, mentioning to him that he had a friend in London called Alan McGee that ran a club and record label called Creation. The tape duly made its way to McGee in London and he listened and liked what he heard but felt the best way forward was to include the band on a compilation album he was planning to put together called *Are You In Love Or Are You A Car?* He also decided to give the band some proper demo time to see if they could come up with something worthy of being released as a single.

The Daisy Chain recruited a drummer called Murray Dalglish and went into an East Kilbride studio to record a version of 'Upside Down' that they then sent down to McGee. McGee was unconvinced, but given Gillespie's enthusiasm, he decided that there would be no harm in giving the band a gig at the Living Room, which by then had moved to the Roebuck pub in the Tottenham Court Road. The band, who had decided to change their name to the Jesus & Mary Chain, travelled down to London on the coach leaving at midnight on 7 June, fuelling the journey on stolen beer that Douglas Hart had acquired from the pub where he worked part time.

McGee had booked the band onto a bill that included the Loft and the Irish band, Microdisney. As he later explained in his autobiography, he wasn't quite prepared for what he got when the band showed up at 6pm, as arranged. 'They were punk rockers from East Kildbride, six years too late,' he recounted. 'Scruffy clothes, hanging together. The brothers – they looked like a punk version of the Bay City Rollers, they looked like punks by accident. Don't get me wrong, they looked cool, but there was something wrong about it too, a small-town version of a movement that was dead.'

The performance when it came was every bit as shambolic, the band coming to blows during the sound check and Douglas Hart attempting to remove the make-up that Yvonne McGee, Alan's wife, was diligently applying to Murray Dalglish's face. The short set consisted of three covers, Syd Barrett's 'Vegetable Man', Jefferson Airplane's 'Somebody To Love' and Subway Sect's 'Ambition', and the overall sound was a mesh of white noise, partly caused by producer Joe Foster turning everything up on the mixing desk to its maximum volume, as McGee later claimed.

Feedback in rock was hardly a novelty by the summer of 1984 and was frequently an element in the music of many of the bands the Jesus & Mary Chain admired, such as the Stooges, the Gun Club, the Birthday Party and Einsterzende Neubaten. On songs like 'The Friend Catcher', the Birthday Party used feedback as a shock tactic, a surprise weapon used sparingly. There was more feedback in the music of Einststurzende Neubauten (Collapsing New Buildings) who created their art out of material found in the debris of their hometown Berlin and blended the concepts of art and daily toil – or so they said – through the use of pneumatic drills, Black and Decker power tools, lead mallets, crowbars, girders and old radios, together with old-fashioned bass and rhythm guitars. But no groups previously had woven feedback into the basic canvas of their sound quite as emphatically as the Jesus & Mary Chain did.

'Even the sound check was confusing,' remembers Dave Evans. 'The noise was ear-piercing loud, almost hideous, yet at the same time totally thrilling. I was standing there thinking: is this it? Is the noise going to stop? Are they going to do any actual songs? I had no idea what would happen. It really was like nothing you'd ever heard before. And since Jim wasn't a particularly loud singer, the vocal microphone was turned up and that added further to the feedback. But there was more than that, and the way that they had absolutely no interest in pandering to the audience was equally as shocking for some...'

The effect was simply to knock McGee for six and he immediately offered the band a one-off contract to make a record, sending them into Alaska Studios in September to record 'Upside Down' and 'Vegetable Man'. The sessions were booked to commence at midnight, the cheapest possible time to rent the studio. The band went in with producer Joe Foster and engineer Pat Collier and recorded the two tracks. They put the guitar through a rack-mounted digital delay and cranked up the input so that it distorted appropriately. Extra feedback was added during the mixing stage. By the end of the session, when each of those involved took away a rough mix of the recording, everyone seemed happy.

Played through studio speakers, the recordings sounded imposing but when played on an average hi-fi they sounded more like an extreme version of FM radio rock. Consequently, McGee and William Reed returned to the studio the following morning and remixed the two tracks, piling on as much feedback as the recordings would take. Satisfied, McGee then returned home, eager to send the results to Bobby Gillespie to see what he thought. As Zoë Howe recalls in *Barbed Wire Kisses*, 'McGee was so enthusiastic... that he bought a £10 Stagecoach ticket from London to Glasgow and travelled overnight to play it to him in person.' McGee took with him the original mix (by Joe Foster) and the cranked-up version that he and William had created and played both to Gillespie. Gillespie said that he preferred the latter.

In the same month that the Jesus & Mary Chain recorded the single, drummer Murray Dalglish left the band, taking up an apprenticeship with a firm that built buses. When McGee announced that Creation would be doing a package tour of Europe and that the Jesus & Mary Chain would be involved, it was a matter of urgency, therefore, to recruit a new drummer as quickly as possible. In fact, what the band did was ask Bobby Gillespie to stand in on drums: Gillespie had once been a roadie for Altered Images and on more than one occasion had acted as a makeshift drummer when the need arose. His style was, putting it mildly, primitive. He used a snare drum and a floor tom and drummed standing up. He played with the Jesus & Mary Chain for the first time at the Venue in Glasgow on 11 October (with his own band Primal Scream supporting), helping design the tickets which part-copied the original poster for Lindsay Anderson's seminal film *If.* and featured a hand grenade and the words, 'Who's Side Are You On?'

The new line-up of the Jesus & Mary Chain returned to London to play a warm-up gig for the European tour at the Three Johns pub in Islington on 24 October. Prior to the show, McGee had done his usual rounds of the music papers and his distributor Rough Trade, attempting to whip up excitement for the band that he was rapidly coming to see as the future of rock and roll. The set the band played was less frugal than the one at the Roebuck, running to almost 30 minutes, and was all the more imposing for being played in a room that was considerably smaller than even the Living Room had been when the club was held at the Adams Arms. At moments, the performance was cataclysmic, not least in the rendition of 'Vegetable Man' that was always performed at a level of madness that matched the intensity of the song's creator.

The *NME* review of the gig at The Three Johns (by this author) used language in praise that was almost as unrestrained as the show, likening the band's impact to that of Joy Division and comparing the excitement they generated to that created by the Sex Pistols at their height. The only other review to appear was in *Sounds*, calling the band 'a pile of shit' and their performance 'an exercise in gullibility'. Such diametrically opposed views cannot fail to intrigue, as proved to be the case. 'We returned from our little mini-tour in Germany to find that all of our delusions had come true,' says Joe Foster, recalling the moment the band opened up the old music papers and read the reviews just as they got off the boat home.

On 23 November they played their first gig since the tour at the Ambulance Station, the squatted building in the Old Kent Road where Simon Crab and others lived and worked and used as a base for various activities, such as the fund-raising shows for the Stop The City events. Many more people turned up at the show than had been expected and it proved to be a combustive night with a threat of violence hanging heavy in the air.

'I remember setting up the show,' says Joe Foster. 'It was the most amazing venue – a sort of derelict, bizarre squat. The guy that organised it looked like Peter Cook in *Bedazzled* and dressed like him as well. When the show started it was obvious that things were likely to get uncomfortable. I was with Alex Palao from the Sting-Rays and our partners and at one point the job at hand was to get everybody out because there was a real possibility if we stayed that everybody would get beaten to fuck the way things were going.'

The set was short, the sound terrible, and the band fairly well intoxicated. At one point Jim Reid responded to heckling from a member of the audience with a ferocious outburst. 'We don't fucking want to know you… We hate you,' he screamed in a rare pause between songs. 'We fucking despise you. You're a fucking shit. Where were you six months ago you fucking cunt?'

The shocking outbursts and the response of people to the band needs to be set in context. The *whither indie?* arguments of 1982 and 1983 had cooled into frustrated resignation by the end of 1984, many not even expecting things to improve as the mainstream charts began to be increasingly clogged up with slick, nodule-free pop. Frankie Goes To Hollywood was the least of it. The rise of the pop video, satirised by bands such as Yeah Yeah Noh and Big Flame, added to the malaise. Ever since the accompanying video for Duran Duran's 1982 single 'Rio', which had featured the band miming along to their song dressed in Anthony Price suits whilst on a yacht in the Caribbean, high-end pop videos had become ever more grand, coming to represent wanton excess and needy glamour.

Jim Reid's anger was also aimed at those who revelled in the Jesus & Mary Chain's overnight success but missed the six months of hard toil and rejection that had led up to it. The anger reflected the brutal time, generally, with many growing increasingly upset with how the miners' strike was playing out. By Christmas, the miners were desperate – three had died digging for coal on dangerous slag heaps, while a taxi driver had been killed ferrying a miner to work when a slab of concrete was dropped off a motorway bridge and onto his taxi (causing Paul Weller to momentarily withdraw his support for the striking miners). There would be six deaths in total during the dispute, with some 20,000 involved hospitalised, over 900 men sacked and some 200 sent to jail.

Then came Band Aid, which, as has been seen led some to question the motives of a number of those involved. The miners' strike and Band Aid became linked in a way that caused some anger when one of the organising and senior pop stars involved with the Ethiopian Band Aid effort claimed that no similar fund raising ought to be undertaken for the miners since *they had a choice* and didn't need to be on strike. The choice, as John Brennan of the Three Johns later pointed out, amounted to one of 'struggling to maintain their jobs and community or being bashed into the ground by Thatcher'.

While Band Aid epitomised the supposedly caring society, the Jesus & Mary Chain were the antithesis, the we-don't-care society, a nihilistic affront to traditional values and the supposedly good taste of the masses. The journalist Simon Price, writing in 1991, put it neatly in a review of the band's *Peel Sessions* album, where he compared the 'altruistic guilt of the New Pop Bourgeoisie' who were engaging in 'a grotesque orgy of caring' with The Jesus & Mary Chain's don't-give-a-fuck approach, as epitomised by the lyrics to the group's 'The Living End' where Jim Reid sings, 'I'm in love with myself...'

At first, the press didn't know how to handle the band; their uncompromising music – all the more emphatic when all there was to go on was the live performances – seemed to be contradicted when in conversation they expressed their desire to be on to *Top Of The Pops* and be written about in *Smash Hits* (both of which came to pass). Lyrics weren't important (they claimed to come up with them in the toilet). In *Sounds*, Robin Gibson wrote about the experience of seeing the band live and being thrust into 'screamingly dense, bottomless wells of untouched rock 'n' roll energy' but pointed out that 'Upside Down' carried the sound away from the pure noise of the shows, comparing it to Subway Sect's 'Nobody's Scared' and Felt's 'Index'. 'We've got good songs... certain people just won't realise that,' Jim Reid told him. 'You could play our songs on acoustic guitar, they'd still sound good.'

The key point was the songs. There was sweetness in there, and in amongst what Howe describes as their 'cocktail of psychotic noise, Spector rhythms and dark lyrics' there was something genuine and original, something captivating that took them beyond pastiche. Pop music is and always will be an exercise in reinterpretation – as Richard Cook once pointed out in the *NME*, '*all* pop music is revivalist' – but the Jesus & Mary Chain, like other great bands, transcended that. 'They were,' said Howe, 'past, present and future rolled into one'.

Courted by all the major labels, in January they signed with Blanco Y Negro, coaxed to the hybrid label by Geoff Travis whose judgment they respected and whose experience building Rough Trade made them feel that they were still keeping one foot in the independent camp even although they constantly made noises about wanting to leave it. McGee continued to manage them but was entirely realistic about the fact that the fledgling Creation label was incapable of holding on to the band. The group went from helping fold the sleeves of the endless represses of their first single to receiving £1000 each, a small fortune for them at the time. The deal with Blanco was for one single, 'Never Understand', which was released in February and made good on Jim Reid's promise that lurking beneath the white noise there were tunes.

'I met them at the Ambulance Station,' recalls Geoff Travis. 'That was an event, a totally thrilling experience. It seemed to me that what they wanted was money and success, and they *knew* that they were good. "Upside Down" had been enough to convince me that there was something incredible going on. I went up to see them in East Kilbride and chatted to them about what we might be able to do for them. All four sat on the sofa and didn't say a word – like four catatonic robots. But we got on well enough and they agreed to sign to Blanco.'

Although they were never *actually* described as such in the *NME*'s live review of the Ambulance Station gig, the 'new Sex Pistols' tag hung around a bit, papering over the real essence of the Jesus & Mary Chain's dissent which, as Jim pointed out to journalist Chris Roberts in February, went back far further than punk and travelled right back to rock's kinetic roots when Bill Haley was inciting teenagers to tear up cinema seats. According to Chris Bohn, writing in the *NME* in the same month, the phenomena was best viewed in non-lineal terms and was more a part of an on going 'pattern of disintegration', a 'dynamic that keeps the rock rolling'.

Such disruptions as occurred tended to flare up more commonly in London – the city Peter Ackroyd has called the city of 'violent delights'. But at the start of February, an incident occurred at a gig in Brighton after a member of the audience climbed on top of the PA and bottles and glasses began being thrown (both to *and* from the stage). 'We were bottled off,' Jim Reid later told Zoë Howe. Unlike the bacchanal of the Ambulance Station, where violence had always been threatened but never properly materialised, Brighton spelt danger and marked the first example of serious trouble at a Jesus & Mary Chain show.

The band simultaneously lived up to and played down the image created for them. A series of petty indiscretions, some real, some invented, all trivial, found a way into the press (in some cases, even into the tabloid press) as a die of sorts was cast. Alan McGee played his part, feeding stories and then acting like a suitably horrified parent called into school to explain its child's behaviour when they appeared. It was often said of McGee that he was a quick learner and the burlesque of the Jesus & Mary Chain perfectly illustrates that. 'The comparisons with the Sex Pistols had inspired me,' he wrote in his autobiography, 'and now I was really up to being Malcolm McLaren, trying to generate cash from chaos. Douglas Hart had brought me a video … of *The Great Rock 'n' Roll Swindle* and I watched it over and over.' So much so that he often regurgitated lines from the film when talking to the band, using the cod language of the script.

The show at Brighton had been arranged as part of a tour to help promote 'Never Understand'. A further gig was scheduled for North London Polytechnic on 15 March, where the band would be supported by fellow Creation act the Jasmine Minks, and also by Meat Whiplash, a new band who, coincidentally, also came from the Jesus & Mary Chain's hometown of East Kilbride. The show was a typical student, Ents-run affair, and the Polytechnic later admitted that a number of tickets had, in its words, been 'overprinted'. There were too many people inside and a few hundred people outside who were denied access, some of whom had legitimate tickets.

To call the mood inside the hall fighting would be an understatement – for many this was the first opportunity that they had been given to see a band that had been written about in ever more breathless language. 'There was a sense that something historical was about to happen,' writes David Cavanagh in *The Creation Records Story*, 'although people disagreed about what.' For Adam Sanderson, the spectacle was eye opening in a number of ways: 'The Jesus & Mary Chain had money now and new amps. Previously, Creation bands had pooled their gear, amps in particular, as we were always broke. The early Creation acts were mostly Scottish and poor, so to see a brand new Fender Twin amp on stage was the equivalent of a guy with a moped seeing a Bentley car for the first time.'

Sanderson noted that the bar quickly ran out of alcohol and as staff pulled down the bar's shutters and closed, they were the recipients of some angry abuse. He watched Meat Whiplash open the proceedings and the atmosphere in the hall turned even more ugly after singer Paul McDermott picked up an empty wine bottle and viciously slung it back into the crowd from where it had come. Some of the audience climbed on to the stage and began attacking the band. The troublemakers were eventually bundled off stage and Meat Whiplash finished their set.

The Jasmine Minks were the next band on. 'Tom, our drummer, used to have a problem with creeping drums,' says Adam Sanderson. 'He would hit the drums hard and the kit would inch forward during the set. In a small venue like the Living Room he would start the set five feet behind you but be up against your arse fifteen minutes later. We solved this problem at the North London Polytechnic by nailing his kit to the wooden floor. Given how Meat Whiplash had fared, I decided to keep the steel claw hammer I had used for banging in the nails about my person. When we went on, I had the hammer sticking out of my back pocket. If I was just playing and not singing, I'd turn my back to the audience so they'd see the hammer. After a while it almost became choreographed, like a routine by the Shadows, but with a blunt instrument. Maybe it worked. We certainly didn't get any trouble that night.'

The Jasmine Minks departed the stage and then there was a delay. Two announced 'technical faults' clearly added to the volatility of the crowd and was then compounded by the playing of the usual short set. Some of the crowd then got on to the stage, kicked over the PA and began vandalising it, stealing the more portable bits of equipment. The police arrived and a number of scuffles broke out. 'People were laughing and giggling,' remembers Sanderson, 'the middle-class youth of England, swept along on the euphoria of doing something *reaa-lly* wild for the first and probably last time in their lives.'

Fanzine writer Andrew Perry, quoted in *The Creation Records Story*, found it 'all so liberating. You imagined if you went to see the Eurythmics, say, it would be an hour and forty minutes of synchronised, over-staffed bollocks exactly like their records. But here was patently a band that wasn't capable of even playing the most rudimentary of music. Jim Reid had a guitar around his neck that he didn't play at all. It was just hanging there, feeding back. It was total noise and anarchy.'

Many of those involved directly with the band, such as McGee, were oblivious to what was going on – McGee, for instance was with the Reid brothers who, he says, 'would have been too scared to go on stage until they were absolutely hammered'. Joe Foster, however, was in the thick of it, later pulling Jim Reid out of the middle of an angry scrum at the foot of the stage: 'I was doing a PhD and teaching Spanish at the college and later got fired as a result of the night. I was seen as one of the night's prime movers by the authority, someone who had helped destroy the building, even although it was all the work of childish students…'

McGee preferred to see it another way, once again slipping on his Situationist hat when issuing a press statement after the calm of a weekend had passed. 'The Jesus & Mary Chain deny all responsibility for the proceedings on Friday night. Friday night proved that people are crying out for the first division excitement that the Jesus & Mary Chain provide. In an abstract way the audience were not smashing up the hall, they were smashing up pop music…' According to Joe Foster, after the night had ended, they went back to McGee's place and deliberately set about 'creating a press release as out there as a surrealist manifesto. Of course, it was preposterous, but we were going to be ahead of Malcolm McLaren, ahead of Andrew Loog Oldham… Maybe we were.'

The storm in a tea cup that was the North London Polytechnic gig had the potential to create serious problems for the band, not least with timid booking agents, and the group decided to retreat from playing London shows for the immediately foreseeable future, turning their attention to the album that they would be making having agreed new terms with Blanco. In truth, the North London Polytechnic incident was an aberration: the need for shock value was a thing of the past. The aim now was to focus on turning the promise of their songs into the kind of reality that 'Never Understand' had hinted at. There would be just one more release – the stripped-down, Spectoresque 'You Trip Me Up' – before they retreated to John Loder's Southern Studios and began work in earnest on the album.

The giddy ride that was the Jesus & Mary Chain took up a lot resources and in the six month's between the November 1984 release of 'Upside Down' and May 1985, there were only three singles issued by Creation. Unquestionably, the Loft single was the most important but there was a second release as well for the

X Men. 'Spiral Girl' didn't quite hit the heights of the band's debut, 'Do The Ghost', but was every bit as frenetic, 'the toughest, most tuneful trash on the block', according to Gavin Martin in the *NME*. Alas, it would be the last single the band would make for Creation. Slightly less obvious – in fact baffling, for most – was the single Creation released in April. McGee always prided himself on his punk ethos, but Les Zarjaz' 'One Charmyng Nyte'/ 'My Lady Owns A Falle Out Zone' owed less to the age of Jimmy Pursey and more to that of Purcell, whose work it appears to be loosely based upon: the spirit of '77 for sure, 1677. Offering classical music presented in a modern idiom, it might be said to have anticipated the playful humour of the label Mike Alway would shortly launch, él, but any qualities largely passed over the head of its few listeners.

Biff Bang Pow!, on the other hand, was more direct. Alan McGee and Dick Green might have deliberately kept the path clear for the Jesus & Mary Chain but did find the time to come up with an album of their own. In March, the same month as the North London Polytechnic gig, and the month that the Miners' Strike ended, they released *Pass The Paintbrush, Honey*. The album was as much a visual statement as an aural one – McGee's red Rickenbacker bass leans against a couple of vintage amps and a copy of Kevin Pearce's *Hungry Beat* fanzine is strategically worked into the tableau.

The record blended the more obviously pop arty ('There Must Be A Better Life', 'Waterbomb') with the experimental ('The Chocolate Elephant Man'), combining punk and beat-boom psychedelia and revealing, according to one reviewer, 'the hand that drew up the battle lines' to help clear the advance of the Jesus & Mary Chain. Inevitably, the name of the latter crept into many of the reviews, the *NME* pointing out that 'the main danger for the cats at the hub of the Creation operation now is one of being completely overshadowed by their own bastard offspring'.

In the event, the label managed fine. Media interest in the Jesus & Mary Chain died down while they were busy recording their album and Creation Records got back to what it was good at, digging pop art singles out from the black morass.

There would be more bands and more records as 1985 progressed, but no more talk of smashing up pop music.

CHAPTER 15
THE PAISLEY UNDERGROUND

THE PSYCHEDELIC REVIVAL OF 1981 had been an easy target for those critics worn out with the dressing up antics of the New Romantics. They had seen the revival as the same kind of empty clotheshorse, one lacking substance, and the band's involved as little more than grave robbers ransacking the carefully cultivated plot where '60s rock rested. As neophiliacs, critics were disdainful of anything that smacked of revival. At the same time, the need to constantly revive seemed pronounced in Britain at the turn of the 1980s when the nation was perhaps subconsciously starting to question its place in the world pecking order.

But the fascination with psychedelia remained, and in America, which had no similar inferiority complex, sheer geographical scale meant that many and all things were happily subsumed into the melting pot. So when in 1982 a batch of groups emerged on the west coast, all to a greater or lesser degree influenced or inspired by the music of the psychedelic era, there wasn't the same impulse to supress. Once again, the question arose – what was and what was not psychedelic? Sylvie Simmonds, writing in *Sounds* in April 1984, astutely observed that the first wave of psychedelia was less a movement and more an era, and that you couldn't tie it into a style: 'folk rock, garage punk, country, pop and crashing primitivism ran concurrently; the Standells and the Byrds existed side by side'.

Simmons article was headed 'THE PAISLEY UNDERGROUND', borrowing its title from the name that the small group of bands had taken for themselves. 'As with the old psychedelia,' it said, 'there's not one single sound: you've got the country-Byrds of the Long Ryders, the Mamas and McCartney of the Bangles, the fragile folk of Wednesday Week, the fragile Hollies of the Three O'Clock, the Dylan/ Doors of Green On Red, the Syd Barrett of Rain Parade, the Velvet Underground of Dream Syndicate and the Unclaimed's grungy, garage punk.' And although the material the bands played was 'original if somewhat derivative', it was, for the most part, 'increasingly well written and well played'.

As had been the case with the Living Room set up by Alan McGee, who was drawing inspiration from Paisley Underground bands such as the Rain Parade at the time, a small number of people were involved initially and very few bands. For many observers, the core group extended no further than the Three O'Clock (originally called the Salvation Army, a name dropped when the charity threatened to sue), the Dream Syndicate, the Bangs (who quickly became the Bangles) and the Rain Parade. It was a small community and a number of other bands got drawn in simply through association, such as the Long Ryders and Green On Red, while others were later deemed part of the group through sharing the same UK record label, groups such as True West, Thin White Rope and Naked Prey. Very few of the bands involved were overtly psychedelic.

As early as 1980, when most of those involved began descending on LA, a nascent scene of sorts already existed. According to Simmons, 'the Last, a raw, intense garage band' were 'the founding fathers of the whole thing, the only band of its kind in LA until around 1980'. The band formed in 1979 and began covering the more obscure classics of the 1960s, works by the Sonnets, Syndicate of Sound and Chocolate Watch Band. Other, early pioneers included the Unclaimed, a group put together by singer Shelley Ganz the same year that the Last formed. With their black turtlenecks and pageboy hairstyles, the Unclaimed, wrote Simmons, had 'the 60s down to a holistic art that [gave] you flashback chills', playing 'fuzzy, grungy guitar, cheesy Farsifa [in] brash, wild rave-ups'. Early on, the band included Sid Griffin, and their self-titled 1980 EP included a couple of tracks by the man who went on to form the Long Ryders.

By late 1981, most of the Paisley Underground bands were either playing at or frequenting small LA clubs such as the Music

Machine, Dancing Waters and the Cathay de Grande. At a time of hard core punk and the rise of bands like Black Flag, Minutemen and Agent Orange, they stood apart. Inevitably, they began socialising. They were all first and foremost music obsessives, and it was the music that drew them together. By the middle of 1982, many of the bands had started playing together. As bassist/ guitarist Michael Quercio of the Three O'Clock told the *Guardian*'s Michael Hann as part of an excellent oral history in 2013, '… we became really fast friends and by June of '82 we all took a trip to Catalina Island – the Dream Syndicate, the Bangs, some of the guys from the Rain Parade … and just kind of camped out and bonded. There was nothing else like this going on. The new wave scene was over, and even the hardcore scene was on the wane because there was so much violence that the clubs wouldn't let a lot of those bands play.'

All four of the core bands had records out by the middle of 1982, including the Three O'Clock, who were interviewed by *LA Weekly* around the time of the release of their EP 'Baroque Hoedown' and asked if the scene had a name. Michael Quercio flippantly called it 'the Paisley Underground', a name that stuck. Towards the end of the year, the Bangs (now the Bangles) signed a record deal with the major label Columbia and Dream Syndicate released one of the movement's defining albums, *Days Of Wine & Roses*. Partly a response to the music of the times – it was released during the heyday of synth pop – *Days Of Wine & Roses* helped rescue the guitar from seeming oblivion and motored along at a brisk pace. There was a touch of Dylan and a dash of Velvets in the sound, and an overall garage rock feel broken up by the kind of experimental exercises more commonly found in jazz – the band's name is said to reference Tony Conrad's experimental NY ensemble, Theatre of Eternal Music.

The album came out in the UK on Rough Trade and its release was more or less contemporary with that of REM's first album, *Murmur*, helping fire the first shots across the bows of the UK market. And although the Dream Syndicate possibly weren't quite as rapt and compelling as REM, whose music sat easy, for instance, on the ears of those weaned on such Postcard bands as the Go Betweens and Aztec Camera, there was the same kind of musical self-referencing. 'I've always said I don't think there would have been a Dream Syndicate if somebody else had been making music like that,' Steve Wynn told Michael Hann. 'When we made *Days Of Wine & Roses* I was imagining a record that I'd want to buy, which is not a bad way to go about making music.' He later told the website One Nation Underground: 'We felt more like messengers for music that matters than rock stars.'

Things began picking up in 1983, when the Long Ryders signed to PVC Records and released the 5-track mini-album *10-5-60*. The same year the Rain Parade signed with Enigma and released *Emergency Third Rail Power Trip* and the Three O'Clock released *Sixteen Tambourines* on Frontier. The records made their way across the Atlantic on import and began making an impression in the UK. 'When we were starting the Living Room at the Adams Arms, those records by the Rain Parade and the 3 O'Clock were a big inspiration, we played them all the time,' recalls Alan McGee. 'Later, in 1985, the first time I'd ever been in America, I was walking down Melrose Avenue in LA with Jim Reid from the Jesus & Mary Chain and a guy jumped out a doorway at us. He said, "Are you Alan McGee?" I was pretty taken aback. "I'm Danny Benair," he continued, "drummer with the Three O'Clock, I fucking love Creation Records." I was shocked but pleased and I was able to tell him how much I liked *Sixteen Tambourines*. I tried to licence the Rain Parade's first album to Creation, but wasn't successful. There were definite similarities between what we were trying to do at Creation and what was happening with the Paisley Underground.'

Since the scene in LA revolved around relatively small clubs, as the bands grew more popular they inevitably hit a glass ceiling. Even with a few major record labels mooching around, the scene remained very much an underground phenomenon, as early supporter Adam Bomb, DJ at the student radio station KXLU, told the *Old Grey Whistle Test* for a feature broadcast in 1985. Asked how popular the music was in LA, he responded: 'Unfortunately in LA, it is almost ignored.' That this was the case was reiterated by Rain Parade's Matt Piuci, when speaking in 2013 with Michael Hann: 'Rain Parade never did shit in LA. It was England that made us. All I remember is getting issues of *Bucketfull of Brains*, reading them and thinking: "Wow – these guys get it." That mattered.'

The fanzine *Bucketfull of Brains* had been set up by Nigel Cross in 1979 and, along with John Platt's *Comstock Lode* and a handful of other publications, was one of the few music magazines at the start of the 1980s to not toe punk's line that the music of the 1960s, and in particular the ideas of the counter culture of the period, were risible. While *Comstock Lode* favoured the west coast sounds, *Bucketfull of Brains* explored the kind of garage punk that had seeped into the collective consciousness ever since Lenny Kaye's 1972 compilation album, *Nuggets*. By 1984 it was covering outliers like the Barracudas, Thee Milkshakes and the Sting-rays and picking up on the LA scene. An early issue wrote about the Bangles and issue 9 ran a lengthy article entitled 'The US Invasion' and featured a picture on the cover of the Long Ryders.

'LA '83; IT'S NOT NOSTALIGIA, IT'S NOW!' screamed a headline in issue 6 of *Bucketfull Of Brains*, as contributor John Holland flagged up the presence of unknown hopefuls Dream Syndicate, the 3 O'Clock, the Last and the Rain Parade, bringing the names before the UK public for the first time. In the same issue Nigel Cross fairly frothed at the mouth in an article headed 'THE MARCH OF THE LA FLOWER CHILDREN', covering at further length the same bands and tracing one of the new music's sources firmly back to a specific album, Pink Floyd's *The Piper At The Gates Of Dawn*, which did for the nascent Paisley Underground the same job that Iggy & The Stooges had done for punk and Captain Beeheart had done for post punk. 'LA's beginning to burn again!' he concluded. 'Listen to the march of LA flower children in 1983.' Issue 7 of *Bucketfull Of Brains*, in early 1984, featured articles on the Bangles, Plasticland and the Rain Parade. Issue 9 carried a *seven-page* article on the Long Ryders.

The writers at *Bucketfull of Brains* weren't the only people in England taking an interest in the Paisley Underground. That same year, Zippo Records was founded, developed out the Clapham record store that was unquestionably the best rock record shop in London at that time, one filled with all manner of treasures from the latest indie releases to punk artefacts to psychedelic posters. The ceiling of the shop and one wall had a large mural painted on to it that was an exact eye-popping replica of the image on the front of the Thirteenth Floor Elevators' album, *Psychedelic Sounds Of…* Bands queued up to have their photographs taken in front of it. The label Zippo was a logical extension of the activities of the shop and set up in conjunction with Demon Records, the reissue label founded by legendary A&R man Andrew Lauder and former Stiff supremo Jake Riviera in 1980.

'We were one of the few record shops in the country where you could buy the records,' recalls Pete Flanagan, owner of the shop. 'Nigel Cross used to come into the shop and leave us copies of *Bucketfull of Brains* to sell and he started enthusing about the new music coming out of LA, so we started stocking it. Edwin Pouncey, who was writing for *Sounds*, was also singing its praises. I used to go up to the distributor Shigaku Trading in west London and buy all the stuff and then come back to the shop and play it. We played an import copy of the first Rain Parade album in the shop maybe three or four times a day at the time and there would always be someone who would come up and tell us how amazing it was and ask if they could buy a copy. One time I was up buying more stock, I sat down with Seth Justman who ran Shigaku and Andy Childs who worked at Demon and told them about how many we were selling and we just agreed to start up a label to release the stuff in the UK.'

The first Zippo release was the Rain Parade's *Emergency Third Rail Power Trip*, released late spring 1984. One of the defining records of the genre, it was instantly popular and was quickly repressed multiple times. 'We had a reputation for stocking a lot of original psychedelic albums and garage albums from the 1960s and the Rain Parade album literally sounded like it could have been made at that time,' says Flanagan, himself a leading expert on the period's music and culture. 'It was a hugely important record, and one that has stood the test of time, which is the only real test that counts.'

The record picked up the kind of reviews that artists dream of in their sleep. 'The first time I played *Emergency Third Rail Power Trip* I thought I had a visitation from God,' wrote Martin Aston, going on to call the album 'a staggering debut' in *Melody Maker*. He praised the 'delicate, shimmering music' that was tough enough to conjure up images of early Pink Floyd, the Byrds *and* Television, yet at the same time avoided the whole clichéd psychedelic imagery of crushed flowers seen through a velveteen haze. The jingle jangle of sublime melodies on tracks like 'This Can't Be Today' and 'Ihr ½ Ago' intersected with fuzzy, droning and complex arrangements. Writing the first mainstream press review of the album in the UK in *Sounds* in July, Edwin Pouncey had already laid the way for all that followed: 'The thunder gets louder, America's new music revolution is turning into something bigger than those critics, who casually passed the whole concept off as an hallucination that would swiftly disperse, can handle... Quality, care and pride make up the only revival on display here.'

The second Zippo Records release was *Let It Be* by the Replacements. The Replacements were a Minneapolis band whose punky, hardcore sound was quite the opposite of the more nuanced Rain Parade, and took influence from bands like Big Star and the Faces and punk rock luminaries such as the Clash. The third release was *Native Sons* by the Long Ryders. It drew a line between Buffalo Springfield and the Velvet Underground and was described by one imaginative critic as 'psychedelic western' music. The band played mandolins, banjos, steel and pedal steel guitars tuned modally for a drone effect, as well as (occasionally) bugle, auto-harp, and harmonica. The complex mix was a long way from the bands that Sid Griffin had started out in, 'straight ahead punk bands with a rat's nest shag', as he once revealed, that he had quickly tired of.

Quite different music, quite different sounds, yet Zippo seemed to naturally draw them all in together. The power of the record shop had its part to play and the power of vinyl. 'What linked almost all the bands on the label was the fact that they all had impeccable influences – often tracing that line from the Buffalo Springfield to the Velvet Underground,' remembers Flanagan. 'The influences really were superb, and that comes through on the records, I believe. The bands were, first and foremost, huge fans of music with impeccable taste and big, big record collections…'

Zippo was doing a smaller version of what Rough Trade had begun doing in 1978 – releasing music for fanatics made by fanatics. The shop, the music, the fanzines, the *fan*aticism, the bands; everything was part of the same process. The signing of the Long Ryders illustrated the process, Zippo picking up the band following a trail that started with the group being written about glowingly in an obscure fanzine. The label was savvy as well to recognise the culture reference built into the cover of *Native Sons*. As Sid Griffin told Michael Hann: 'The cover of *Native Sons* is the rejected album *Stampede* by the Buffalo Springfield and they immediately got it, being old record collector dogs. It took us forever to find a cabin like the one Springfield used – it was way out in the desert, rusting apart. It was in the middle of nowhere, a real American west town that was dead. And they [Zippo] got such a kick that we knew the Buffalo Springfield *Stampede* cover that they thought: "This is a great record; these guys are obviously savvy – call them up".' (In an era of pop-group-as-packaging-exercise, Griffin had a thing about the power of record covers, commenting once on how Sir Douglas Quintet's *Together After Five* album obviously couldn't fail as a mere glance at the cover testified – 'there's five guys on the cover – three white guys and two Mexicans – and they stand out like a cheeseburger in a medicine cabinet…')

Zippo released one further album in 1984 – *Drifters* by True West, an album that 'fitted squarely into the Paisley Underground bag, but in a different and very refreshing way', according to Flanagan. The band had moved away from their deeply psychedelic beginnings – in 1982, they had self-released a cover version of Pink Floyd's 'Lucifer Sam' (the wittily imagined B-side was the song played backwards and called 'Mas Reficul') – and now played music that remained psychedelic but focussed on the twin guitar thrusts of guitarists Russ Tolman and Richard McGrath. Tolman and singer Gavin Blair had briefly played in a band based in Davis, California, a fertile Paisley Underground town that, in time, threw up others drawn into the genre, such as Thin White Rope and Game Theory.

The popularity of the Paisley Underground peaked in the first half of 1985. By then, Zippo had issued the debut album, *Gas, Food & Lodging*, by early originators Green On Red and the Long Ryders appeared both on the front cover of the *NME* and in the UK for a nine-date, month long tour. The Long Ryders were supported by True West and finished the tour with a gig at the Marquee. 'They were spectacular live,' says Flanagan, 'and played some great shows on the tour. All those bands we signed, and in particular the Long Ryders, ended up really accomplished musicians. In Sid Griffin, the Long Ryders had a terrific front man.' The knock-on effect of the publicity saw the sales of *Native Sons* pushing up towards the 10,000 mark and all the releases on the fledgling Zippo back catalogue benefitted.

The Old Grey Whistle Test ran a mini feature on the Paisley Underground, presenter Richard Skinner travelling to LA (when he might, perhaps, have been better served staying in London) to find out more. The feature began with Skinner noting 'a renaissance that looks like it is going to equal the big explosion of talent in the 1960s' before going on to question whether or not the whole thing amounted to a revivalist fad. 'To a certain degree, yes,' thought Island A&R man Ian Matthews, 'but to a greater degree it's a new wave.'

Back in the UK, Edwin Pouncey picked up on the phenomenon he'd predicted a year earlier in a review of Green On Red's *Gas, Food & Lodging* that appeared in *Sounds* in May 1985. 'All of a sudden, it's happening,' he wrote. 'Seems like every LA outfit that you ever read about in these pages, moons ago, is over here with a TV slot, a night at Dingwalls and an interview with some short-haired reporter in a paisley shirt to their credit. The big labels have marched in too, scraping off the cream to pour down hungry punter's gullets at the next summer of love.'

Island Records, alone, signed six bands (including the Rain Parade and the Long Ryders) as suddenly the genre – or handy marketability of its name – seemed to know no bounds. 'I sat at the Columbia Hotel [in London] and one by one major record labels came in and spoke to me,' Sid Griffin recalled later. 'I didn't go anywhere for five or six hours because we had one every hour on the hour. They'd leave after half hour, 40 minutes, and we'd take a break. It was one of the most brilliant experiences of my life to have people come in and basically tell you you're great.'

The backlash was inevitable, and came soon enough. 'You couldn't get better press than the Long Ryders got,' Griffin later told Hann. 'I've got no complaints – even about the backlash over here [UK], which we were warned about. When we came over for the second tour, the guy at customs at the airport said, "Oh, the Long Ryders – I've been reading about you. You know what will happen now? They've set you up and now they're going to knock you." Which is what happened.'

In the *NME* alone, in little over a month between the end of June and the start of August voices of discontent stirred. Part of the problem was the absolute overload of bands (*Melody Maker* in a single 'State Of The Union' feature on new American guitar bands listed no less than 36), many on major labels, who had all jumped on to a bandwagon that was moving along nicely and picking up plenty of press. In contrast, some of the UK independent bands claimed to struggle in every respect – lack of coverage was just the tip of the iceberg that nine-tenths amounted to lack of funds. What made matters worse was that in terms of musical competence, many of the American bands made their British indie counterparts look inept. But, of course, that wasn't the point.

'HATE ASHBURY' ran one *NME* headline; 'SOD OFF '67 IN '85' ran another. According to Don Watson 'the hundreds of … psychedelic revivalists spreading over the States' amounted to either a 'beautiful flowering vine or a colony of nasty insects, depending on what kind of trip you're on'. In an *NME* interview with Primal Scream in the summer of 1985, Bobby Gillespie, a great supporter of vintage American psychedelic music, argued that British bands were prejudiced against. In an open letter to the paper, staff writer Mat Snow disagreed, arguing that American bands simply had more experience and more things to say that could be written about hence the added coverage.

'Everything has a moment and then fades and the interest in the American bands began to wane,' remembers Pete Flanagan.

'That was evident from the reaction of people in the shop. People began getting fed up of it. There were too many bands drawn into it and not enough talent.' This view is borne out by some of the reviews. As is so often the case, during the transition from independent to major record in many cases something gets lost. The Long Ryders first album for Island Records received two stars (out of five) in *Sounds* when it was released in late 1985, reviewer Roger Holland, a fan of the music, complaining that it sounded like 'Rockpile playing Chuck Berry' and was a disappointing 'return to pub rock drudgery'. The Rain Parade, who, along with the Long Ryders, were one of the two most esteemed Paisley Underground bands, fared no better. They had two albums released on Island in 1985 and, critically, neither was particularly well received. While loyal supporter Nigel Cross stuck with them, complaining in his *Sounds* review of *Beyond The Sunset* that the band were 'no re-tread' and had 'as much right to be deemed old hat as the Smiths', Donald McCrae in the *NME* complained that their swift follow up, *Crashing Dream*, was 'a studied exercise'. The two best 'psychedelic' pop songs of 1985, he claimed, were the Jesus & Mary Chain's 'Just Like Honey' and the Pastels' 'Baby Honey' (which had been released at the end of 1984).

In fact, the decorous 'Just Like Honey', released in September 1985, spoke the language of Paisley perfectly, but during summer a new sound had risen up, one more in tandem with the East Kilbride band's noisier side. Weeks before the release of 'Just Like Honey', Sonic Youth/ Lydia Lunch's 'Death Valley 69' had appeared, its gory video simulating the events of the Manson Murders in 1969 that had informed the writing of the song (which came about, the band later said, after band members had all read Vincent Bugliosi and Curt Gentry's true crime account, *Helter Skelter*, Ed Sander's unnerving tale of the Manson cult, *The Family*, and Roman Polanski's bleak and frank autobiography, *Roman*).

Sonic Youth had been around since the start of the 1980s (unorthodox, emerging out of the No Wave and influenced by musicians like Glenn Branca and writers like Kathy Acker) and had even released a couple of albums before their UK debut on Paul Smith's Blast First label, which began trading in the spring (and was later called by John Peel 'the most important label of the age'). Sonic Youth were 'post-hard core', the softer end of a spectrum that found its limits in the work of bands like fellow New Yorkers, Swans, whose extreme, psychotic music and violent lyrics (inspired by the works of Jean Genet and the Marquis de Sade) reflected the Birthday Party and the European chaos of Einsturzende Neubaten. In contrast, Sonic Youth worked with but usurped the orthodox: 'Our idea is that the instrument is not the guitar, as much as it's the chain,' guitarist Lee Renaldo told *Melody Maker* at the start of 1985. 'It's the guitar, the chord and the amp with the electricity pummelling through. The instrument doesn't end where the guitar meets the wire. It starts where the sound comes out the speaker.'

Late summer, just as Paisley was being put to the sword, the new American guitar bands began descending on the UK in earnest. Husker Du, led by Bob Mould, made their UK debut in September, playing the Camden Palace. The Minneapolis trio had slowed down considerably from the thrash of their 1982 debut live album *Land Speed Record*, but still were LOUD, tearing the house down with a searing ten-minute rendition of their classic 'Reoccurring Dreams'. A Month later the Butthole Surfers appeared at the Ambulance Station (supported somewhat incongruously by Miaow). The band's album, *Another Man's Sac*, was a riffing, metallic mess, a jagged wreck and an altogether different kind of surf music. In time, the shock value of some of the more extreme bands dropped away (along with the charges of bigotism, homophobia, sexism, etc). Blast First scoured the source, going on to release material by US and UK acts, including Big

Black, Dinosaur Jnr, Head of David and AC Temple, music that *did* represent an echo of an LA sound from 1981: it was, however, not the pastoral jangle of Paisley but the abrasive hard core punk of Black Flag, Fear, the Germs, Minor Threat.

Of the four original Paisley Underground groups, the Bangles and the Three O'Clock both continued into the late 1980s, going on to record songs written for them by Prince, who, it is said, became intrigued by the Paisley scene and named his record label, Paisley Park, after it. The Rain Parade split in 1986 (although David Roback had left after the first album, eventually forming Opal with Kendra Smith of the Dream Syndicate and later forming Mazzy Star with Hope Sandoval.) The Long Ryders disbanded in 1987. In time, both the Zippo label and the shop came to an end.

The long, strange trip was over and the paisley-hued music returned to the underground.

CHAPTER 16

ROOM AT THE TOP

THE ROOM AT THE TOP

upstairs at The Enterprise
haverstock hill nw3 opposite
£2·00 £150 CHALK FARM TUBE

WED 11TH at THE ROCK GARDEN, COVENT GARDEN
the MIGHTY LEMON DROPS

SATURDAY 14th T.V. Personalities
"I'VE GOT A FUZZBOX AND I'M GONNA USE IT !?

THURSDAY 19th DEC the Shop Assistants
and NOT HERE - A NEW CROSS!

SATURDAY 21st DEC Jamie Wednesdays
AND GO! SERVICE

SUNDAY 22nd DEC ONE THOUSAND Violins
with theServants

Later :- THE Stingrays + Bad Karma Beckons + The Rockin' Razorbacks

IN THE SECOND ISSUE OF the Television Personalities fan club magazine, published in February 1985, an announcement was made: 'The TV Personalities have helped to set up a new live venue to cater for the many new and exciting bands around. Since the demise of the Living Room there has not really been a focal point for new groups. The new club will be called "THE ROOM AT THE TOP" and is situated at THE ENTERPRISE public house, next door to CHALK FARM TUBE STATION, north London. It's a large room upstairs and already we have booked some of the top independent bands to play.'

The club opened on Saturday 2 March when Yeah Yeah Noh played and were supported by fellow Leicester band the Bomb Party. The week after saw the Television Personalities appear, followed in the weeks after that by Mood Six, the X Men, Obvious Wigs and Terry & Gerry. From the start, the club was popular, and the crowds upstairs often spilled back down to the bar below. The Enterprise was an old pub and the rafters above the ground floor bar regularly shook with the collective weight of the crowd, the pub's landlady on more than one occasion halting a band's performance to tell the audience to stop jumping around.

The Television Personalities newsletter also announced a forthcoming single by the band, 'A Good & Faithful Servant', a title lifted from the works of Joe Orton. The B-side was to be a track called 'The Dreams Of A Factory Girl'. In fact, 'A Good & Faithful Servant' finally appeared on 1989's *Privilege* album, and the B-side was never formally released. The single was important since the plan was that it would launch a new label that Dan Treacy was setting up. 'DREAMWORLD will carry on from where WHAAM! left off,' the Fan Club newsletter revealed. 'Bringing you tomorrow's sounds today. Trouble is we are usually too far ahead! Do people remember we released the first TRACEY THORN record? Or recent TV celebrities DOCTOR and THE MEDICS, not to mention the Pastels and 1,000 Mexicans.'

Dreamworld very much carried on where the Whaam! label had left off. One Thousand Violins (who had previously been the Page Boys and released 'You're My Kind Of Girl' on Whaam! the year before) had a new release, 'Halcyon Days', and that along with a 4-track EP from American band the Impossible Years became the first two new label releases. Forthcoming records were promised by Jane Bond & The Undercover Men, Real Traitors and Go! Service, whose 'It Makes Me Realise' 12" in fact became the third Dreamworld release. Go! Service was Jo Bartlett and Danny Hagen (later of Bluetrain) and one of the label's best new finds. They had supported the Television Personalities on a European tour in autumn 1984.

In the April issue of the *Catalogue*, Dan Treacy further elaborated on his plans for the label, giving some taster information on what was to come. The Impossible Years were 'the Violent Femmes meets the Monkees', One Thousand Violins were 'the Smiths on synths' (which quoted *Sounds*), and Jane Bond & The Undercover Men were 'politics and spy intrigue with a spaghetti western soundtrack'. The *Catalogue* also corrected the Television Personalities release, which it said would now be an LP of unreleased material (1978-84) called *Is This Some Groovy Happening?*

One band not mentioned in the Fan Club newsletter, or in the *Catalogue*, was the Wolverhampton band the Mighty Lemon Drops whose demo tape dropped through Dan Treacy's door around about the time the *Catalogue* appeared in print. The band had tried their luck with a number of independent record labels, including Creation, who received the tape but passed on the band, and Subway Organisation, who did respond positively but took things no further. Dan Treacy received the tape enthusiastically, writing to the band on 22 May saying 'heard tape, absolutely brilliant!!', and inviting them to come to London and play a show supporting the Television Personalities at the Room At The Top on 22 June. In fact, the Mighty Lemon Drops did perform with the Television Personalities, but not until the following month, supporting Dan Treacy's band and 1000 Violins at the Deptford Crypt on 12 July before finally playing the Room at The Top on the following night (the day of the Wembley Live Aid show) where they supported the Membranes.

Events moved at a swift pace for a band that had only formed at the start of the year and not even played a gig until 15 March, when they opened for the Man Upstairs at Peacocks in Birmingham. That gig itself had taken place just a month after the band had first rehearsed together and the band recorded their first five songs a week after the first gig. Those were the songs duplicated onto cassette the band had sent off to Dan Treacy.

'We recorded two sessions,' recalled guitarist Dave Newton in 2014. 'Five songs were recorded at an inexpensive 8-track studio on a farm near Worcester, and [there was] another session at a studio in Rugeley, near Cannock. We combined them and made an eight-song mini-album that we sold at gigs called *Some Of My Best Friends Are Songs*. This was a mission statement. We initially made fifty, which took a little while to sell, although after our first *NME* mini-feature, we sold about another hundred all over the world, which we couldn't believe.'

The band was dedicated and self-sufficient, and had enough pedigree between them to make it work. Bassist Tony Lineham and drummer Keith Rowley had previously been in a power pop/mod band called the Pow and had met Dave Newton at a time when Newton was writing a fanzine called *S.O.S.* and had gone along to write about the band. Tony Lineham modelled his bass playing on the melodic style of Bruce Foxton, and although the Pow never progressed far, the experience of the band was useful in helping Lineham hone his song writing abilities – Newton and Lineham wrote all the songs in the Mighty Lemon Drops.

After editing *S.O.S.*, Dave Newton had been in a number of bands. A band called Active Restraints had featured both Tony

Lineham and vocalist Paul Marsh. The band gigged through 1982 and recorded a single that got played on the John Peel Show. An EP was recorded at Cargo but the group disbanded before it was released. Dave Newton went off to join the Wild Flowers, releasing an album and couple of singles and touring in support of bands like Simple Minds, the Chameleons and the Bluebells.

The gang got back together at the start of 1985 and 'decided to form a band, but this time do it right'. The circuit they played on consisted of the pubs and clubs of Birmingham, which was, apparently, not quite the hippest of scenes at the time. As Dave Newton would recall: 'It was pretty dull locally... There was a kind of psychedelic scene in Birmingham, bands like the Great Outdoors and Surf Drums and clubs like the Loft and Sensetaria, but it was safe and not edgy or exciting.' Many of the local bands, remembers Newton, didn't look or sound as if they ought to be in the same band 'Your typical Wolverhampton band,' Tony Lineham later told *NME*, would have 'a mohican on guitar, a heavy rock bass player, a skinhead drummer, and a New Romantic singer, or at least some mix of those ingredients.' It was a scene the Mighty Lemon Drops was keen to avoid.

The band was not only musically focussed but paid attention to other detail as well. The overall image was important. 'We thought of the "Beatles in Hamburg" look combined with early Velvet Underground playing Wah! Heat's 'Seven Minutes To Midnight' louder and faster, with a strong emphasis on the melody,' was Dave Newton's description of how the band's image and music conjoined. 'That was it, basically, with our own Black Country charity spin.' Tony Lineham has noted how he liked bands that looked like they belonged together, 'bands like the Clash and the Ramones'. The Smiths and the Jesus & Mary Chain might be added to that short list.

The Beatles Hamburg look was honed in 1960 after George Harrison walked into the Meyer-Schuchardt Sport Und Leder store in Hamburg and purchased a leather jacket. It had elasti-cated cuffs and waist, angled pockets and was zip fastening. It was the only jacket he wore professionally when the Beatles played Hamburg, which they did on 281 occasions, including a staggering run of 91 consecutive nights (usually playing 12-hour sets) in 1961.

The Beatles had started out wearing leather jackets with jeans and cowboy boots. Their look then mutated as the jeans were replaced by leather trousers (supplied by Paul Hundertrunk), making them look less hokey and more dirty, or, as John Lennon put it, more 'like four Gene Vincents'.

The Mighty Lemon Drops took this lead but rejected the leather trousers in favour of drill trousers. Nonetheless, when they walked onto the stage at the Room At The Top, they could have been walking straight out of an early Astrid Kirchherr pho-tograph. There wasn't quite the air of menace or threat that the look carried during the proto rock period, or in the case of the Beatles where it somehow seemed to enshrine the seaport grub-biness of Hamburg, with its raw energy and tension, its streets awash with amphetamines and readily-available sex, and its port home to prostitutes, sailors and gangsters. But the Mighty Lemon Drops still managed to cut an impressive figure, and whilst their experience didn't quite run to ninety-one consecutive twelve-hour sets, they were very tight musically.

In other words, the impact that they made was quite dra-matic. The *NME* review (penned by the Legend!) of the show at the Room At The Top, although slightly challenging text-wise, attempted to get across the energy of the band (not least in its use of thirteen exclamation marks in the short, three paragraph review). The Mighty Lemon Drops had squeezed 'every last drop of perspiration from their thirty-minute set', the perfect antidote to the 'Curse of London, apathetic audiences'. The Legend! wondered whether he could hear any traces of the sound of the early Echo & the Bunnymen in their set, and then decided it didn't really matter. After all, any serious indie guitar band in the middle of 1985 that possessed a half good-looking front man with a powerful voice was compared to Echo & the Bunnymen, as was the case, for instance, with Mighty Lemon Drops contemporaries on the scene, the Bodines.

The Mighty Lemon Drops never moved to London, preferring to keep a base in the midlands and to sleep on Dan Treacy's floor in Clapham when the need arose. They were insulated from the London scene and the London scene was insulated from them, at the start. This was another reason why the made such a dramatic impact when they played those first few London shows. In fact, in summer 1985, most of the very best bands playing the London circuit weren't from or based in London. The two other new bands that were most often on the tips of tongues at that time – the Shop Assistants and the Wedding Present – were also from outside the capital, the former were Edinburgh based, the latter from Leeds.

The response to the Might Lemon Drops initial performances, and to the review the Legend! wrote in the *NME*, prompted Dan Treacy to speed up plans for releasing a Mighty Lemon Drops single. Treacy sent them into a tiny north London studio in studio in August to record tracks for a proposed EP that he planned now to rush release.

'One of the most popular, affordable studios was Alaska in Waterloo, but Dan thought it was too expensive,' Dave Newton later recalled. 'He sent us to Electro Rhythm in Hornsey, half the price of Alaska. It was in the living room of an affable Scottish guy [and] filled with '60s/'70s recording gear and the mixing console. We ran through "Like An Angel" in one take and [he] played it back. It sounded huge, incredible… we couldn't believe it was us… Over the years that followed, we would spend months in some of the best recording studios in the world with great producers and engineers, but "Like An Angel" will hold its own to any of these.'

The big sound was created in part by the drum kit that Keith Rowley had borrowed for the occasion. The ride cymbal had a huge crack in it, as did the crash cymbal. The snare was gaffer-taped to the bottom skin of the snare drum and the bass pedal had been repaired at a steel works in Tipton a couple of days before and squeaked a lot. But all the faults just seemed to enhance the overall sound, as Keith Rowley later recalled: 'The cymbals sound huge because the delay caused by the cracks goes on forever. You didn't so much play that kit as fight with it and the whole thing had to be strapped down with yards of tape or it would just walk away.'

Dan Treacy only had enough money to pay for five hours recording but the band managed to squeeze in five tracks at a total cost of £96. As well as 'Like An Angel', the band recorded 'Something Happens', 'Sympathise With Us', 'Now She's Gone' and 'All The Way'. According to Tony Lineham, 'the warm sound of the vintage recording gear, the nervous energy of the performances and the maverick genius of the engineer combined to [create] the only recordings that ever came close to capturing the real sound of the band.'

The Mighty Lemon Drops continued gigging through the autumn, playing with the June Brides the same month that they recorded the single and also appearing at the Ambulance Station for a Dreamworld Records night (along with the Television Personalities and 1000 Violins, and also Paul Groovy & The Pop Art Experience, who Treacy had invited to play). The *NME* interview took place in October, when David Swift interviewed them. The band was holding off playing live until the single was released. They still, however, managed to squeeze in gigs with Bog-shed, That Petrol Emotion, the Bodines, the June Brides for a second time (at the Hammersmith Riverside 'Week of Wonders') and the Servants before November was out.

Just prior to the single being released in December, the Mighty Lemon Drops did a session for Andy Kershaw – they were simultaneously offered a session on the Janice Long show and therefore given the luxury of having to decide which Radio One show they would appear on first. They tossed a coin and it fell in favour of Andy Kershaw, although they recorded a session for Janice Long barely a month later at the start of 1986. The two sessions highlighted songs that would later find their way onto their debut album *Happy Head*, as well as a track that appeared on the B-side of the 7" version of 'Like An Angel' ('Now She's Gone') and a cover (on the Janice Long session) of a Teardrop Explodes song, 'When I Dream'.

'Like An Angel' was released in December, originally available in a 3-track 12" format only (the other two tracks being 'Something Happens' and 'Sympathise With Us'). With its lush textures, spacey sound, layered guitar landscapes and haunting vocal, for many 'Like An Angel' arrived fully and perfectly formed. The *NME* called it 'quite simply brilliant'. Very few indie singles, even by the end of 1985, were able to conjure up such a classic pop feel or deliver work that was so unashamedly garage in content yet mainstream in potential appeal. Whether by chance or design the band never really matched what was achieved in the Hornsey front room of producer Wilson Sharp, as Tony Lineham noted in the sleeve notes to *Uptight: The Early Recordings 1985-86* when he referred to the recordings as 'lightning in a bottle'.

Indeed, such was the headiness of the brew that Dreamworld realised quickly that they had a potential hit on their hands. The 12" version entered the independent charts at the start of January and remained there for an extraordinary 40 weeks (peaking at number 4). However, the label realised that they were unlikely to get serious daytime radio airplay for a 12" single and in early spring announced that they would be releasing a 7" version of the single on 21 April. The release coincided with the band suddenly becoming a magnet for major label A&R men. Even without major label support, the Mighty Lemon Drops was, claimed a Dreamworld press release in March, selling out venues with a capacity of 800. 'It looks like this could be one of the few successful independent records in the 'Proper Charts', wrote Dan Treacy and Emily Brown in the same press release, 'but hopefully for DREAMWORLD and many others outstanding in the independent sector, both groups and labels alike, this could be the starting point for success and acceptance.'

At the start of 1986, *NME* had invited the Mighty Lemon Drops to contribute 'Like An Angel' to *C86*, but the band declined, preferring instead to go into a studio and record some new material for the compilation. In the end, 'Happy Head' ended up on the cassette and all three tracks that were recorded in, according to Dave Newton, 'a cheap Wolverhampton studio' found their way on to the band's debut album, also called *Happy Head*. 'We made a mistake,' Dave Newton later commented. 'Of course we ought to have given the *NME* 'Like An Angel', especially after hearing what some of the other bands contributed, such as Primal Scream and the Bodines.

In their first extensive interview, also in the *NME*, Adrian Thrills distilled the essence of the band's sound, noting the New Merseybeat influence of the Liverpool bands of 1979 and 1980, a period that had produced more classic singles than the time of punk, and suggesting that such influence was what enabled the band to create classic pop and make it sound easy. In the interview, Dave Newton put to rest the criticism that the band sounded just a little bit too much like Echo & The Bunnymen, pointing out that a closer influence was the power of Wah! Heat and the tunes of the Teardrop Explodes.

After 'Like An Angel', there was talk of the band recording a mini-album for Dreamworld, but the lure of a more fully-funded offer proved too great, and in any event, as Dave Newton had told Adrian Thrills, 'We never said, we *don't* want to sign with a major label... We want to be heard by as many people as possible.' In the end, the Mighty Lemon Drops signed a deal in the

UK with Geoff Travis and Blue Guitar (a subsidiary of Chrysalis) and a deal in the United States with Seymour Stein at Sire.

The album that followed *Happy Head* was 1988's *World Without End* and it made it all the way into the mainstream Top 40, or the 'proper charts'. Three of the next four singles after 'Like An Angel' also charted, reaching the lower reaches of the Top 100. Derek Jarman produced a video for 'Out of Hand' in 1987 (he also worked with the Smiths). Almost everything that needed to be in place was put in place for the band to succeed commercially but the break through never fully happened.

The 'lightning in the bottle' that Tony Lineham later spoke about was like a genie: once released, it was never going back in again and the Mighty Lemon Drops finally called it a day in 1992.

Both in the execution of the music and in the presentation of their image the Mighty Lemon Drops paid particular attention to style. When they played the Room At The Top for the second time, on 9 November 1985, they were supported by another band whose attention to detail in every area was equally as fastidious. The Servants had taken their name from Joseph Losey's *The Servant*, a 1963 film about class and sexuality that starred James Fox and Dirk Bogarde (developed out of a sexually risqué novella by Robin Maugham). Screened at the time of the salacious Profumo Affair, in a sedate Britain primed for scandal post-Suez but still largely pre- the explosion of the Beatles phenomenon, the film was guaranteed to find an audience, its plot enhanced by a Harold Pinter script and some clever camera work. Twenty-two years later there was a similar kind of monochromatic sharpness to the work of the band the Servants. 'It occurred to me at the same time,' says David Westlake, 'that the name could seem to have a distant echo of the lyric of the Velvet Underground's "Venus In Furs" – "Come in bells, your servant, don't forsake him". That was a record I liked.'

The Servants was formed by singer-songwriter David Westlake who in 1984 joined forces with his school friend Ed Moran who took up bass. By having a drum machine instead of a drummer, the duo was able to rehearse at David Westlake's parent's house. Ed Moran recruited a friend of his own and John Mohan joined on lead guitar. Work then forced Ed Moran away and David Westlake took out an advert in the *NME* that read: 'Velvets. Smiths. Postcard. Bunnymen. Enthusiasm. Potential…' Guitarist Phil King responded, writing a letter to David Westlake and enclosing a cassette of some recordings he had made with a former band the Beautiful Losers. David Westlake wrote back with a tape of his own, which included the song 'She's Always Hiding'.

'David lived in Hayes, and I lived in St Margarets, which wasn't too far away,' recalls King. 'I used to drive a 1964 two-tone Humber Sceptre and one night I jumped in it and decided to pay David an unannounced visit. His mum let me in and I think David was a little taken aback at my arrival but we got on well, and he suggested that we have a practice with John Mohan. I remember sitting in his bedroom listening for the first time to Love's 'Between Clark & Hilldale', which blew my mind.'

The three rehearsed together, either in David Westlake's bedroom or in John Mohan's house, and, since the band already had two guitarists, Phil King eventually moved on to bass. 'They had a Fender Musicmaster bass and a Peavey bass amp that I used,' says King. 'The rehearsal went well and everything fell together quite quickly. I used to get on a coach bound for Heathrow and change at Hatton Cross for a bus to Hayes. On the way I would quite often listen to *Highway 61 Revisited* or *Blonde On Blonde* and try and pretend that I was on a Greyhound bus travelling through America – not the dull suburbs of London.'

Early recordings were made on a Portastudio using a drum machine, before Eamon Lynam joined on drums. 'Eamon played drums at most of the early Servants shows and on the early recordings' remembers David Westlake. 'Phil nicknamed him Neasden Riots – like the Clash's Tory Crimes. Eamon had been put on police curfew following his alleged involvement in said fracas. Of course, it meant that he was unavailable at the time of day a drummer is most needed. The Trees' drummer John Wills agreed to join us for the single "She's Always Hiding", just a few weeks before we were booked to record it in December 1985.'

By then the band had already begun playing gigs, the first at the Pindar of Wakefield on 1 July 1985 supporting The Television Personalities and Cabaret. Dan Treacy and his girlfriend Emily Brown were impressed with band and were given a demo tape to take away and listen to. 'We made some demos and put our phone numbers on them,' says Phil King. 'Emily rang my number to offer us a gig at the Room At The Top. My dad answered and she asked him if she could speak to one of the Servants, to which he replied that he was sorry but we had no servants in the house. The first gig at the Room At The Top was in November, but we'd actually appeared at the Enterprise pub in September, our third gig, when we'd supported the Jasmine Minks and played to an almost empty room.'

Also present at the first gig at the Pindar of Wakefield had been Simon Murphy from the fanzine *Adventure In Bereznik*. He immediately fell in love with the band's music, briefly mentioning them in issue four of the fanzine in a section called 'BRILL NEW BANDS!' that also included Go! Service, the Bodines and Easter & The Totem. In the next issue of *Adventure in Bereznik*, published towards the end of 1985, Simon Murphy more fulsomely explained the band's appeal: '… some joy, some cynicism, the occasional knowing smile – songs! –melancholic ditties, "evocative of buses, parks and bedrooms, taking in sea and sky between" – your attention, please!' He called the band 'the best unsigned band I've seen in ages – too subtle for Creation?', adding, 'yes, subtlety; combined with straightforward, obtuse pop sense'.

The songs were certainly subtle, and also straightforward, refreshing and uncomplicated. One of the *NME* adverts referenced the Velvet Underground, an influence possibly carried through to a number of song titles that used one word female names ('Stephanie', 'Meredith'), but the work itself was often more reflective of the lyrical and poetic elements found in songs by troubadours such as Nick Drake, Kevin Ayres, Peter Perrett and Syd Barrett. There are songs about absence – 'She's Always Hiding' – and about displacement ('She Whom Once I Dreamt Of'). There is a timeless quality to them, and while they sit comfortably with the work of some of Westlake's revivalist contemporaries, they are unique, crisp and contemporary. Often, at the centre is a conundrum.

> She whom once I dreamt of is invisible
> She whom once I dreamt of is unseen
> She whom once was said to be
> Is now more conceivably
> Said to be
> But, Oh, she could have been

Early admirers of the Sevants included Jeff Barrett, the former record shop owner and club organiser whose infatuation with Creation eventually led to him working at the label as a publicist. Barrett was keen to release a single by the band and along with Bill Prince from the Loft set up Head Records to facilitate it. He wasn't alone in recognising the band's potential – Alan McGee had also heard the band's demos and was keen to put the band out on Creation, as he later told Phil King, but when he telephoned the number on the demo cassette there was no response. 'The first, unreleased Servants recordings were for Statik and the late Adrian Borland (of the Sound) produced the session,' recalls Westlake. 'But the proposed deal was for an indefinite number of albums on onerous terms, so we politely declined. We also talked to Philip Hall at Stiff, a good and kind man, and Mike Alway at él got in touch as well.'

'She's Always Hiding' was recorded in Alvic Studios in west Kensington at the start of 1986. Richard Preston was chosen as producer, having just worked with the Go-Betweens on their *Liberty Belle & The Black Diamond Express* album. The band recorded both sides of the eventual single (which had 'Transparent' as a B side) and also a track called 'Loggerheads', a bittersweet tale of love and resignation ('If I can't satisfy you/ I guess I'll go find someone new…') with a ringing, chiming guitar and tripping organ motif.

Just at the time when the Servants were recording their single, the *NME* was starting to put together a track listing for its forthcoming *C86* cassette. The Servants were approached and asked to contribute 'She's Always Hiding', but David Westlake declined to give them the track, thinking, like many, that to throw away the song on an itinerant tape that would soon be forgotten was a waste. In the end the band submitted 'Transparent', the single's B-side. 'No-one expected that *C86* would be remembered in 1987, let alone now,' he says. 'Had I known it would still be talked about thirty years on, I would have chosen a better song. I always hated "Transparent". It was amongst the first songs I wrote in my teens, while I was still learning how to put a song together.'

Westlake was also aware of the fractured nature of *C86*, and the dilemma of attempting to artificially unify something: 'If the bands on *C86* shared anything, it was a residual punk ideology. I was conscious of there being a scene centred on a number of disparate bands. There are precedents for different people on a scene or in a putative genre having a productive contrariety or antipathy to each other, be it artistically or personally. That went to the heart of *C86*, I think.

'I also sought to distance the band from whatever it was that started to be described as "shambling". I didn't feel the Servants *shambled*. It felt like an insult to be included in that club, if one existed. That and other descriptions which started to be used were only insipid and pejorative – "twee", "fey", "cutie". I remember being surprised after *C86* had been out for a while that bands and labels not connected with the compilation started to appear, happy to embrace and even become the caricature of what for a while *C86* became fashioned into in the press – this jangly omnishambles performed by anoraked virgins with pudding-basin haircuts.'

After the recording session at Alvic, they discovered that not everyone shared their casual approach to *C86*. 'We finished the session,' recalls Phil King, 'and we all piled into a florist van that John used for his work to head back home. Jeff Barrett was with us and had a tape of the track that Primal Scream was contributing to *C86*. He played "Velocity Girl" as we were driving back in the van and we all sat gobsmacked. It just blew our minds.'

The Servants picked up their first substantial write up in the mainstream music press in the first week of January 1986, when Bill Prince interviewed the band for the *NME*. The article compared them to the Velvet Underground, noting 'the giddying suggestion of melodies conjured from the ether' and the 'striving for a sound as perfect as (eek!) silence'. David Westlake claimed to have been listening to the Velvet Underground since the age of 13, regarding them as important 'texturally'. He also said that he believed with a 'confidence bordering on a sense of inevitability' that the band would succeed. 'We've definitely got a classic album under our belts already,' he told Prince. 'Definitely a case of every home should have one, filed away besides *With The Beatles*.'

Accompanying the article was a Jayne Houghton photograph of the band sitting before a pair of Ian Breakwell paintings that hung in the Tate, surreptitiously appropriate in that Breakwell had worked with Ron Geesin and Kevin Coyne on music projects (although he demanded money from the *NME* after the article appeared, claiming the paper had no right to use his images in such a way). The band sits almost coyly, David Westlake studious, Phil King sporting his recently acquired bowl haircut (copied from a picture of the Walker Brothers in a *Lady Penelope* annual that King had shown the hairdresser.)

Bill Prince did a good job of promoting the band prior to the single's release, also writing it up in *City Limits* under the alias Bobby Surf. In that article, he compared David Westlake to the 'rich harvest of '60s artists, incorporating the novel lyricism of Buckley, Barrett and Lover-Lee', before addressing 'She's Always Hiding'. 'The band's debut single,' wrote Bobby, 'turns on its head the criticism that Westlake sometimes wears his art on his buttoned-down sleeve by suggesting (heresy!) that MAYBE his songs are better than the ones he's supposedly ripping off!'

The single was released at the start of May and duly received praise, Andy Strickland (another ex-member of the Loft) calling it 'one of the most delicate and tuneful love songs released this year' and praising its 'ringing, mournful guitar and unaffected vocal'. The record came out at a busy time for the Servants. That same month they played the Hammersmith Palais (on a bill that included the Jesus & Mary Chain, Sonic Youth and Pink Industry) and were interviewed by Sorrel Downer for *Melody Maker*, where David Westlake confessed to being 'obsessively romantic, and not just in my life'. Asked whether or not the 'bedsitter images' conjured up in his songs wallowed in cliché, he responded: 'It's not cliché, it's self-indulgence. I love self indulgence.'

The *NME* ICA Rock Week took place in July, a series of concerts designed to celebrate the release of *C86*. The Servants appeared mid-week, on a bill that included Primal Scream and the Wedding Present. All three acts were on top of their game, Primal Scream choosing 'Velocity Girl' as a finale and the Wedding Present hurtling through a twenty-minute set with gusto. Sorrel Downer, reviewing the night for *Melody Maker*, praised David

Westlake's ability to 'find lazy notes and love words to stretch into something sweet, warm and melancholy' and also the 'beautiful, boyish fragility' of 'The Sun, A Small Star'.

In fact, 'The Sun, A Small Star' became the second single after the Servants went back into the studio with Richard Preston at the controls, to record five more tracks, four appearing on an EP that was posthumously released in October. The title track, with its acoustic backing and crisp drum sound, was poppy, confident and assured, reinforced by three further tracks of quality – the faster and more rambunctious 'Meredith', the naggingly beautiful 'It Takes No Gentleman' with its wonderful guitar structure and deliciously tautological lyric ('If I could spend less time thinking how I could tell you/ Maybe I'd tell you…') and the molten rock and roll-tinged 'Funny Business'.

The 'classic album' that David Westlake had referred to at the start of the year would have appeared shortly after, had there been a correct script to follow, but there wasn't. The band played for the last time, with Felt at Bay 63 on 6 August, the occasion of Lawrence Hayward's infamous acid gig when he became incapable of performing before the assembled masses of record company people there to witness a showcase gig. The Servants single was going to be on Creation, then wasn't on Creation after Jeff Barrett (who had paid for the release) refused to promote the record if appeared on Creation and not Head.

'The line-up I had at the time of *C86* drifted apart the first time the Servants got dropped. In Morrissey's *Autobiography* he uses a mock tragic phrase about Johnny Marr going off to play with Talking Heads: "monogamous I, polygamous, he". But at age 21, I felt the same way about being in a band. I hoped that whoever was in the Servants would want to do only that.'

David Westlake placed another advert in the *NME* (in 1986) and joined forces with Luke Haines for the next incarnation of the band. 'The Servants didn't again receive the attention that

C86 had begun to attract early on, but for me it wasn't the end of my world,' he says. 'My own favourite Servants record is the *Small Time* album, recorded 1991, released 2012.'

In April 1984 Scottish band Buba & The Shop Assistants went into the studio to record their one and only single, 'Something To Do'. At the band's core was songwriter David Keegan, a multi instrumentalist who had put the group together in February 1983. As well as David Keegan, Buba consisted of John Peutherer on bass and Moray Crawford on drums: a female singer (Lucy) had come and gone, as had a second guitarist and a manager. The band was struggling on, encouraged and assisted at times by Stephen Pastel and Annabel (Aggi) Wright. In the fourteen months of their existence, up until the point when they recorded the single, they'd played just once, performing in June 1983 under the name the Crispy Crunchies.

In fact, by the autumn of 1983, the band didn't really have a name. David Keegan wrote to Paul Groovy in October 1983, fishing for a feature in *Groovy Black Shades*, and explaining that he was the only band member that *liked* the name 'Shop Assistants'. He wasn't sure, as well, whether or not the other band members even liked the song that his friend Stephen Pastel had taped and already sent to Paul Groovy, a rough take of 'Something To Do'. But he was determined that the band would go into the studio and self-finance a proper demo. He had other songs, even although he couldn't send them to Paul Groovy right now: 'I'll list some songs – so you can use your imagination!' he wrote. 'They are: "Switzerland", "Shopping Climate", "Nature Lover" (… about life in the Highland village where I come from), "Secret Beach", "Alone" (bit depressing that one, the tune is quite jolly though), [and] "Woe" (…about cars getting stuck in the snow)…'

Having raised the funds to record, David Keegan enlisted the support of Stephen Pastel and Anabel Wright and together with

Moray and John the five of them recorded 'Something To Do' and 'Dreaming Backwards', planning to release the record on the Villa 21 record label in the summer. The label would also release an EP by the Pastels, 'Teatime Tales' that drew together the band's Whaam! release and a live version of the tracks on the Rough Trade single. Acetates of the Shop Assistants recording were ready by June, but there were no sleeves prepared and the record eventually was released in November.

Keegan had been aware that the lack of enthusiasm amongst his fellow original members for both the name of the band and the song ultimately meant that regardless of how the band progressed, the Shop Assistants would end up a separate project. In May, Buba & the Shop Assistants played a second concert, and played three more at the end of July and the start of August, before breaking up. Just before the live shows, Alex Taylor had joined on vocals but didn't at that point play live with the band.

Even aside from the fact that Stephen and Aggi played on 'Something To Do', the aesthetic influence of the Pastels on Buba & The Shop Assistants is noticeable, 'the nearest reference point', as David Keegan admitted at the time. 'Something To Do', with its layer of noise rested upon a beat band intro and sparky vocal from Aggi, lives up to the 'much, much noisier/ more punk' approach Stephen Pastel had written to Paul Groovy about at the end of 1983, and anticipates the Pastels more muscular work that began in earnest with 'Million Tears'. Stephen Pastel was the record's producer. Ahead of its time, 'Something To Do' is very much a pre-cursor of the velvet-sheathed noise epitomised by the Jesus & Mary Chain's 'Just Like Honey' and *Psychocandy*.

After Buba & The Shop Assistants split, David Keegan and Alex Taylor immediately set about recording some new material on a portastudio, with David playing all of the instruments. In October 1984, Sarah Kneale joined on bass and the three began working up songs that David and Alex were writing. In spring

1985, they recruited not one drummer but two, Laura McPhail often playing snare drums (and tambourine) and Ann Donald taking care of the floor toms. When the Shop Assistants played live, the two often drummed standing up, creating a formidable visual effect.

Just after the missing parts of the rhythm section slotted in to place, the Shop Assistants went into Pier House studios in Edinburgh and recorded the four tracks that appeared as 'Shopping Parade'. The EP was the familiar mix of Keegan's buzzsaw guitars and Taylor's harmonic vocal, underpinned by the work of what the Legend! later called 'the deadly, dourish drumbeat duo'. One of the faster songs, 'Switzerland', was reworked from a Buba & The Shop Assistants song. It opens waltz-time and features a Swiss harmonica no less, before launching into a frenzy of guitar. 'All Day Long' is equally frenetic, all pounding drums and swirly guitars, whilst 'It's Up To You' and 'All That Ever Mattered' are slower, more sparse creations that provide contrast. The EP was Single of the Week in *NME*, but fared less well in *Sounds*, the cloth-eared reviewer asking the question – Is this what all the fuss is about? – before comparing the EP to something that might have been made by Bananrama backed by the Exploited and recorded in a 'make-your-own-record-booth'. In an end of year poll, Morrissey declared 'Shopping Parade' his favourite record of 1985.

The EP was released in August on a new label, Subway Organisation, a label based in Bristol and owned by the ambitious Martin Whitehead. Whitehead had promoted gigs and published the fanzine the *Underground* before linking everything together under the name Subway Organisation and starting a cassette label.

'I ran several club nights between 1985 and 1988,' he now recalls. 'The first was the Mission Club on board a converted boat called the Thekla in Bristol Docks which had formerly been an alternative theatre venue and host to mostly folky and acoustic performances. I put on six gigs there – the Loft, Jazz Butcher, Jasmine Minks, the Pastels/ Shop Assistants, and Marc Riley & The Creepers – before we got booted off for being "horrible people". We moved then briefly to running a club called the L Shaped Room at Bristol's infamous Dug Out club before moving at the start of 1986 to the Bunker at the Tropic club, a venue I co-promoted with the Flatmates drummer, Rocker. The Flatmates played their proper first gig there on 21 January, supporting Half Man Half Biscuit.

'At the end of 1984, I'd heard John Peel play a single by Buba & The Shop Assistants and sent off my couple of quid to get the record as it was only available mail order. I enclosed a list of my Subway cassette releases. David Keegan wrote back and said the band was thinking of recording a cassette for release and would I like to be involved. The Shop Assistants were the antithesis of the Goth scene that had dominated the post punk years – exactly the sort of band I wanted for a Subway record label. The idea of the label had been swilling around my mind for at least five or six years. A friend lent me half the money we needed to get the first thousand copies pressed, but we were still on such a tight budget that we drove from Bristol to Southampton docks to collect the pressing ourselves and save £20 on the delivery costs. We went from selling, at best, 200 copies of a cassette title to selling 12,000 Shop Assistants singles.'

To promote the EP, the Shop Assistants played a few shows in London, including one at the Room At The Top with the Pastels. In the band's first bit of mainstream music press publicity, the Legend! reviewed the night and instantly fell in love with their sound, calling it 'a storm at the centre of that whipped-out, laid-back, dog-tired, bland mud pool we currently call pop'. The band played fast and slow, used xylophones and tambourines, and at one point during the slower numbers, Alex Taylor told the audience, 'You can cry to these if you want...'

Like that of the Mighty Lemon Drops, who were playing the same circuit at the same time, the Shop Assistants live experience was something formidable to behold. The aural assault of the guitars was leavened by Alex Taylor's contrapuntal vocals and bewitching stage presence. The whole was all the more effective in a period of relatively dire mainstream pop, as Danny Kelly later pointed out, noting that generally when playing live 'they positively dazzle, and when they do you could bottle the resultant atmosphere and sell it as Faith Restorer'.

Bananarama, not, then. And it wasn't just the sound that distinguished the Shop Assistants, it was the attitude, as well. As Alex Taylor told this author in the summer of 1985, 'I don't want to sound 1976-ish or anything, but there is a lot to get angry about at the moment.' She challenged the notion of what being in a girl group usually was taken to represent – the average view that all girls in groups could do was 'sing and look pretty' – pointing out that all the members of the Shop Assistants were more than competent musicians. And shortly after, she told Robin Gibson in *Sounds* that the portrayal in the media of the 'capable' woman often did a disservice to those other women who weren't coping, singling out Britain's most popular actress at the time for criticism: 'I hate Felicity Kendall. She's so coy and twee and disgusting. I hate women who make you feel that everything's alright, because everything *isn't* alright…'

As had been the case with the Mighty Lemon Drops, before too long the major label caravanserai began to circle. But before they did, the Shop Assistants released a second EP, this time on a label David Keegan had specially created with Stephen Pastel and also Sandy McLean, who had previously worked at Fast. 'Safety Net' was the inaugural release on 53rd & 3rd, the label they had chosen to name after a song on the first Ramones album, and came out at the start of 1986. Like the first single, it travelled at two speeds, the exhilarating thrill of 'Safety Net' offset by

'Somewhere In China', one of the very best slow songs the band ever came up with. The record copied the success of 'Shopping Parade' in also making it to virtually the top of the independent chart (both stalled at number two) where it remained for a very respectable thirty weeks. Both records appeared in John Peel's Festive Fifty for their respective years.

'Prior to 53rd & 3rd, I'd been involved in Villa 21, the label that had released the Buba & The Shop Assistants single,' recalls Sephen Pastel. 'David was very positive about the Shop Assistants coming out independently and I was enthusiastic about trying to run a label with him. Sandy Maclean was the facilitator running the Scottish part of the Cartel, and with a connection to Fast Product, which was still something strong for us. I'm extremely proud of the label, but neither of us was completely focused on it and it suffered as a result. There was no real structure to it, and after David dropped out I often wondered why I was doing it. I became really busy with my post-graduate year at university and it became harder and harder to stay on top of things.'

In the summer, just prior to playing the *C86* ICA Rock Week, the inevitable happened and the Shop Assistants signed to a major label, joining Blue Guitar, the same subsidiary of Chrysalis that had signed the Mighty Lemon Drops. They utilised the talents of producer/ engineer Stephen Street (at the mixing stage), although Mayo Thompson was the band's credited producer. Just one single and one album followed.

In August, the Shop Assistants went into Hart Studios in Edinburgh to record 'I Don't Want To Be Friends With You'. By now drummer Ann Donald had left, but the band's signature wall of sound still remained, Alex Taylor's vocals tracing the usual melodic patterns upon it. Possibly, some of the extra production polish had knocked off a bit of the charm of the rougher edges of previous releases, or possibly, like so many bands written about in this book, the molecular structure was never capable of being stretched beyond a certain point, but the single wasn't quite as well received as previous releases. Having been released on a major label, it further didn't have the comfort zone of the independent charts to fall back on (or in), either.

The same fate befell the album *Will Anything Happen?* that was released towards the end of the year. If the object of major label business is to get records into the mainstream charts then the Shop Assistants album succeeded but represented a pyrrhic victory: it's highest chart placing was the lowliest available, number 100.

The band split in 1987 when Alex Taylor went off to form the Motorcycle Boy with ex-members of Meat Whiplash, but reformed two years later with Sarah Kneale assuming lead vocal duties. Two singles were released on Avalanch Records (run by Sandy McLean) – 'Here It Comes' (1989) and 'Big E Power' (1990) – before the group finally split for good, with David Keegan going off to join the Pastels for a period.

The Shop Assistants only recorded once for Subway Organisation but the release got the label going properly. Martin Whitehead had quite a lot on his plate. He continued promoting as the label started to take off and also carried on writing and publishing his fanzine. At one point he was also freelancing articles for *Record Mirror* before realising that he couldn't (quite) do everything and holding back on his music press journalism. The aim from the start was to present Subway in a way that paid attention to its visual look: 'As promoters, we tried to have better posters and fliers than other gigs. We wanted everything to be more visual, more fun, more anarchic than just "going to see some band".'

Whitehead also set up connections with other promoters, such as Roger Cowell in London and Jeff Barrett who during his pre-Creation days was promoting Wednesday night gigs in Plymouth. 'Jeff might call and say he had a band for Wednesday in Plymouth and they needed a Thursday night gig before playing London or Birmingham on the Friday,' remembers Whitehead.

'It felt like we were all on the same side, and it didn't matter if you or another promoter was doing the show as long as a good band got a gig. When old timers claim, "I fought the indie wars for the likes of you", it's not all hot air and rhetoric. It really did feel like we were part of some bigger underground movement, finding bands "safe" venues to play and chipping away at bland corporate rock, one gig poster or DJ set at a time.'

One of the driving engines for the whole Subway structure had been the fanzine. Whitehead had begun publishing *Underground Romance* in 1981 but after five issues he shortened the name, in 1983, to the *Underground*. He became an integral component of the whole fanzine support system, helping distribute the work of others and in turn passing on his fanzine for others to distribute. 'I started producing a list of fanzines I had for sale and including it with copies of the *Underground* I mailed out,' he says. 'The list expanded to include cassette releases and some seven-inch singles, and then I started my own cassette label. The umbrella name I gave to all of this activity was the Subway Organisation. It was at the height of the Cold War and the name, to me, had elements of U.N.C.L.E or S.M.E.R.S.H about it.'

Subway Organisation releases through 1986 included the Soup Dragons, the Chesterf!elds, the Flatmates and Razor Cuts, all presented with the trademark attention to visual detail. Singles were often issued with an added printed insert. The Subway Organisation 'house look' was largely a creation of Simon Barber of the Chesterf!elds, who designed many of the distinct and bold covers on the early releases. 'He pretty much had free reign over what he wanted to do,' remembers Whitehead, 'but his ideas were very close to the ways I wanted the label to be represented visually and graphically.

Whitehead had come across Barber's own band after seeing them play as support to the June Brides on the Big Twang Mystery Tour in Temple Combe, Dorset in December 1985:

'Great tunes, smart lyrics, real song writing. From the moment I first saw them I thought the Chesterf!elds were a band that could record a great album as well as a bunch of singles. They certainly did that – *Kettle* was one of the albums that defined that sound and that period.'

The Subway Organisation would go on to great things in 1987 and beyond, with releases by the Rosehips, the Clouds, the Groove Farm, Rodney Allen and others before everything came to a shuddering halt as the 1980s itself drew to a close. 'Subway ended because Revolver Distribution stopped providing upfront funding for the label,' says Whitehead. 'By 1988 I was more than £25,000 in debt to Revolver, and whilst they continued to pay pressing and manufacturing costs, they wouldn't advance any money against future sales. That meant I couldn't pay recording costs or designers, and as all sales income was retained by Revolver I couldn't pay bands mechanical royalties, which for indie labels was payable on pressings, not sales. The irony was that if I had a record sell 10,000 copies, the mechanical royalties alone due on it would have made me personally bankrupt before I ever saw the royalties or sales income from it. I had to stop because I would have been made bankrupt and homeless if I'd had another successful release on Subway.'

CHAPTER 17

SOCIAL SURREALISM

THE DJ JOHN PEEL COINED the term 'shambling' and it didn't take long to stick, yet in the eyes of many (not least those bands involved) it was a lazy and inappropriate label. Writing in the *NME* at the start of March 1986, Adrian Thrills referred to Peel's 'rather patronising' term, whilst recognising that it 'pinned the point where the rambling meets the shambolic in an awkward, angular sonic shuttle' in certain cases. The term was not just patronising, considered Thrills: it was woefully inadequate when used to describe any number of bands such as the Shop Assistants, the Pastels and the Soup Dragons (all of whom at one point or other were dubbed 'shambling') yet whose music clearly bore no relation to the flippant descriptor.

Initially, Peel had used the term 'shambling' to describe the music of one of his favourite bands that began breaking through at the end of 1985. Bog-shed were unique and although the band never liked the term 'shambling' to a great extent it adequately defines at least one aspect of their appeal, the spontaneous and all-incorporating nature of the music they made. When recording final takes of songs, singer Phil Hartley would retain any vocal misreadings from previous takes in a way that was both chaotically wilful but also suggestive of the song having a life of its own, Hartley merely the conduit through which it passed. The very name Bog-shed was conjured in a similar Ouija-board fashion, it coming after Phil Hartley mispronounced a lyric and thought the word would make a great name for a band. The songs themselves took the listener into what John Robb called 'a strange world of macabre black humour', delivering up 'a surreal social commentary embedded in superbly catchy, bass-driven garage-punk songs'. It wasn't John Peel that nailed it but the formidable critic Steven Wells, who referred to the music of Bog-shed and other loosely associated groups as 'social surrealism.'

In fact, it didn't get much more socially surreal than Bog-shed. The band lived and rehearsed in the town of Hebden

Bridge in west Yorkshire, rehearsing in a run down cottage that in the mid-1980s still sported an outside lavatory. Hebden Bridge had cobbled streets and had been the location for a mawkish and nostalgic Hovis bread advert in 1970. Although later, the town would become hip and bohemian, in 1985 it was, as Phil Hartley told this author that same year, 'a place of faded things', home to a Trades Club for working men in a place where there were very few men working. PJ Proby was, somewhat bizarrely, recording in the town at the time, creating the only buzz since the Hovis ad. A frequent visitor to the cottage Phil Hartley lived in and where the band rehearsed was a horse that would regularly wander up to the window to see what all the fuss was about.

Bassist Mike Bryson had met singer Phil Hartley whilst both were enrolled on a Fine Arts course at Leeds Polytechnic. At college, Hartley made collages, often perplexing his tutors with his choice of subject matter. On one occasion he handed in a collage of the teeny-bop group the Bay City Rollers made entirely out of tartan. In time, the two moved to Hebden Bridge, Mike Bryson moving primarily because he had found some free space within which he and guitarist Mark McQuaid could live and rehearse the band they shared together. The band was called the Bippies. About a year after the move to Hebden Bridge, Phil Hartley joined the band on drums, switching quickly to vocals, a role his attention-grabbing personality was somewhat more suited to. Tris King joined and replaced Hartley on the vacant drum stool and the nascent Bog-shed were up and running.

'The way it happened,' recalls Mike Bryson, 'is that one day Phil just decided he wanted to be the singer. "I don't want to be the drummer in your band," I recall him saying at the time. "I want to be the singer and I want you to be in MY band".' Phil Hartley promised to get things done, organise gigs and generate publicity, a promise made good upon, at least to begin with when the band began gigging in nearby Halifax and Bradford. Having only been in existence for less than a year by the time they came to release records in 1985, they already had a repertoire of some 100 songs.

The songs were created out of jams, the words of Phil Hartley overlaid on music composed essentially by Mike Bryson and Mark McQuaid. The early sound was a cross between Prog rock and Captain Beefheart, according to Bryson, 'with plenty of twiddly bits going on in between'. The songs were more than musically competent and Phil Hartley's lyrics right from the start veered into the territory of the absurd. There was a song called 'Hardly Manky', and one called 'Another Neck Tie Murder', subject matter conjured up in the fevered imaginings of Hartley. It was work that, according to John Robb, 'saw into the gloomy inner psyche of a rain-swept culture and turned it on its head'.

A slightly warped world view wasn't Phil Hartley's only attribute: he also possessed one of the earliest and best four track tape recorders, which the band used to produce a six-track demo that in spring 1985 they began distributing to independent record companies. Songs on the tape included 'Panties Please' (with the immortal line, 'Bring out your dead') and 'The Amazing Roy North's Penis Band', a song inspired by the TV presenter of the same name. 'Roy North was Basil brush's sidekick,' explained Phil Hartley to this author in the *NME* in August 1985. 'He went on to do a programme called *Get It Together* with a woman called Linda Fletcher. Every week Linda would sing requests of songs that had been in the charts six weeks ago – the worst possible time to cover a song.'

Bog-shed visited Creation in London, meeting up with Alan McGee, but declined to sign with the label, opting, instead, to take up an offer John Robb made to release an EP on his Vinyl Drip label. Robb had fallen in love with the demo, and the tape's accompanying letter, ending with the declaration 'we are not dickheads', enthused him further. He went to watch the band when they played in Manchester, one of the few northern strongholds where their talents up to that point weren't appreciated. On the night in question, Robb and his partner were the only members of the audience, doubling the number of a previous appearance in the city when only one person had turned up to see them. 'Oh yes, we played that night and the only member of the audience was the snooker player Alex Higgins who must have wandered into the venue by mistake,' says Mike Bryson. 'He was a nice bloke and he bought us all a drink.'

In the middle of August 1985, Bog-shed went into the studio and recorded six tracks for a 12" EP christened, somehow appropriately, 'Let Them Eat Bog-shed'. The tracks included 'Fat Lad Exam Failure', a wailing screech of mournful blues that sounded as if it had been sucked through a straw, 'Panties Please', a perennial concert favourite whose title was repeated like a mantra, and 'Hand Me Down Father', with its 'wie ist der purer fuhrer' ('as is the pure guide') lyric. This wasn't the common-all-garden blues of worry and depression but something more refracted. The characters in Phil Hartley's story of the blues may well, like Oskar Matzerath, the narrator of the *Tin Drum*, have prefaced each tale with the disarmingly innocent confession, 'Granted: I am an inmate in a mental institution…'

By the end of the month of August the band had played thirty-three times, twenty-eight of them to desultory audiences and only a couple of the remaining handful at venues in the capital. They played the Lie Detector in London, supporting John Robb's group, and picked up an *NME* review from the Legend! who claimed to have 'never witnessed such a welcome for an "unknown" band'. '*Whisper it softly now…*' he enthused, '*but tonight even the totally incredibly awesome Membranes paled a wee bit in comparison.*' Bog-shed even had the cheek to rip off parts of 'Spike Milligan's Tape Recorder' in their set.

As independent music began its move into highly stylised fashion – the leather trousers and the bowl haircuts were just starting to come in – Bog-shed looked visually anachronistic, like 'four gardeners enjoying a day off', as one wag noted. The anti-style, taken with the absurdity of the songs, threw some off balance. *Sounds*, normally champions of this kind of absurdism, took a misstep when reviewing the band's first album, calling their music 'Northern, bloody-minded pop' and berating them and 'a host of other grimy specimens who have contracted pop to a constricting equation'. The music, claimed the paper, asked us to disregard 'all grace or melody' and subjugated 'real music' to a 'scruffy, shapeless energy… a racket rudimentary and joyless'. In fact, all the music of Bog-shed and bands like them was asking for was the right to exist.

'We're a pretty easy band to put down,' Phil Hartley told *Air Strip One* fanzine at the time, 'because they [the press] don't really know what we are about.' Many of the songs were pastiches of lots of different sounds, he added. Some individual songs, such as 'Panties Please' were amalgams of many previous songs. The band didn't have a particular *style*, thought Mark McQuaid. The members didn't listen to contemporary bands. 'I find the more you make music, the more you hate it,' admitted Mike Bryson. 'I don't even like Bog-shed.'

The EP climbed quickly into the independent charts. Bog-shed recorded a John Peel session in November and took little time in becoming the DJ's current favourite band. 'In many ways they were the archetypal Peel band,' John Robb later noted. 'Their angular neo-Beefheart weirdness that somehow sounded like pop music from another planet, or at least some weird parallel universe in some rain-soaked mill town, fitted in perfectly with the show's eccentric shtick.' Two more sessions followed in quick succession during the first half of 1986.

'We didn't like Peel's use of the term shambling to describe our music,' remembers Mike Bryson. 'If we were shambling, then part of it was due to the fact that we never managed to get a decent recording of anything. Phil, inevitably, had a novel approach to subverting the shambling label we were branded with. "I know," he once said, "let's do an absolutely perfect cover version of a Benny Hill song, that'll prove we're not shambling."' It came to pass, and one of the more perverse delights of Bog-shed's third Peel session, broadcast in July 1986, was the faithful rendition (complete with spoken word intro) of 'Gather In The Mushrooms', a song that had been a hit for the comedian in 1961.

In spite of the good work that Vinyl Drip had done in breaking the band, Bog-shed left the label and released their follow up single, the jaunty (for them) 'Morning Sir' on their own Shelfish label. 'Sadly, the move away from Vinyl Drip was really to do with Phil's need to have control of everything,' says Mike Bryson. 'There was a sort of creeping megalomania and at times he could be irrational and quite unwilling to listen to other people. We *all* had strong characters. I seemed to be the one spending most time trying to keep it together.'

By the time of the release of the album, *Step On It*, in late 1986, the band was starting to unravel. A clutch of new songs was unveiled that, once more, typified the extraordinary range of Phil Hartley's vision, not least in his vocal delivery that could range from his natural falsetto to any kind of mimicking style he favoured at the time – singing in Cockney, trying to match his beloved Doris Day, screeching, yodelling, sneering and sometimes just simply delivery the song in standard fashion. Once again, the mind boggled at the contents of songs with such titles as 'Packed Lunch To School', 'Tried To Hide But Forced To Howl' and 'Tommy Steele Record'. But, of course, decoding the language of a Phil Hartley lyric was a fruitless exercise: the observations were warped, fractured and deliberately obtuse. 'Fat Lad Exam Failure', for some the band's best work, is about the closest Bog-shed came to a song that was constructed in any kind of vaguely conventional way Phil Hartley later claimed.

'It's better not to know the words,' Tris King told *Airstrip One*. 'The fun is making your own meaning up.' People wrote to the band mishearing in a way that only added to Phil Hartley's glee. One person wrote enthusing about 'I Lay Stuck', which, when it appeared on the album turned out to be 'Oily Stack' – it was too late, otherwise Phil Hartley would have gone back and changed the words. 'Imagine what the words would look like on paper,' Mike Bryson told the fanzine. But Phil Hartley would never sanction that: 'If you want to print the words,' Hartley said, 'you might as well print the music as well. Don't even have a record in the album cover and let people find out when they buy it.'

Shortly following the release of the album, Phil Hartley moved back to his native Liverpool and Bog-shed for the last eighteen months operated remotely. The band played live less and less and Phil Hartley seemed to retreat into himself. 'Phil didn't seem to have the same sort of drive that he had before, and I wonder whether he got scared of taking the whole thing on a level,' remembers Mike Bryson. 'We'd climbed pretty high up the indie circuit but Phil seemed to suddenly become set in his ways. It was difficult for the band to operate properly.'

Some of the John Peel sessions were bundled together and released as 'Tried & Tested Public Speaker' and in 1987 there was a second album, *Brutal*, and one last single, 'Excellent Girl!' The band played its final concert at the Town & Country Club in London, supporting That Petrol Emotion before 2,000 people on 19 May 1987. After the split, contact between Phil Hartley and the others was non-existent. Phil Hartley had a brief solo career but then retreated entirely from music. The rest of the band heard from him sporadically, on one occasion after a tax bill arrived that needed sorting, and then nothing.

During their short career the band sold a lot of records by indie standards and it was when the PRS cheques dried up that they learned the saddest next stage in the Bog-shed story.

'Mark rang up PRS to find out why we weren't getting paid and during the conversation, the PRS guy informed him that they'd been told that Phil Hartley had passed away in 2006,' says Mike Bryson. 'I was quite disbelieving, so I went through all the obituary notices in the Liverpool *Echo* and eventually discovered the relevant entry. We were just in shock.' Tragedy struck further in 2008 when Tris King also passed away.

During his lifetime, Phil Hartley resisted reissuing the Bog-shed back catalogue, in spite of the many offers and deep love that still remains for the band to this day. Perhaps it is fitting that something so wonderful and unique should remain untrammelled. It seems to fit, also, Hartley's view that the master take, warts and all, should be the final take.

The genius of Bog-shed has retracted back into itself and left very little trace. But then perhaps that was always going to be the case. When, during the band's heyday, *Melody Maker* asked Mark McQuaid how he wanted people to remember Bog-shed, he came out with the most fitting of responses.

'I'd like people to forget us completely,' he said.

Bog-shed weren't the only artists to have a record issued on John Robb's Vinyl Drip label in 1985. Having quit Creation, the Legend! resurfaced with a whole album of material whose very title – *Some Of Us Still Burn!* – might have been taking a not too subtle a dig at his previous paymasters. Although kindred souls, the Legend! and Bog-shed made music whose only real connection was a shared label. There was a far greater nexus between the music of Phil Hartley's band and the music of the third artist to appear on Vinyl Drip in 1985, Pigbros.

Pigbros had one foot in the social surrealist camp and one foot in the misfits camp of the Membranes, the Three Johns and the Nightingales. Indeed, guitarist Nic Beales formed the band after a stint in the Nightingales, unveiling Pigbros in June 1984 with Jonathon Cooke on bass, Svor Naan on sax/ guitar and Fuzz Townsend on drums. They made a formidable racket, as the website Maggot Caviar neatly pointed out in 2013, likening Nic Beales vocals to those of 'Ian Curtis impersonating a heavy smoking Dalek with binary coded lungs saturated in phlegm' and calling Fuzz Townsend's drumming a 'powerhouse' of funky grooves.

'From 1980 I spent a couple of years in the Nightingales,' says Nic Beales. 'We recorded two albums and seemed to be doing a John Peel session every other week. We had some great times but tensions were pretty high in the band, especially after an aborted tour with the Fall where the group basically split into two – the one half getting together to write uncomplimentary songs about the singer (they were quite good actually and were eventually recorded when we'd kissed and made up – with different words mind!)'

When Nic Beales parted company with the Nightingales, he decided to move away from a sound that took a lead from Captain Beefheart and instead to the kind of sound he'd created on a song he'd written for the Nightingales called 'How To Age'. On 'How To Age' and on other early Pigbros songs such as 'Cheap Life' and 'Hedonist Hat', he'd created a drone effect on his guitar, the basis for the way he wanted Pigbros to sound.

First into Nic Beales new band was Jonathon Cooke, with his rumbling bass sound thrashed through a Watkins Copycat echo machine. The formidable Fuzz Townsend then joined – 'a human drum machine', according to Nic Beales. When the band played Peacocks club in Birmingham, Svor Naan was present and invited to join, introducing not just more guitar but also roaring, echoing sax into the mix.

When Vinyl Drip released 'The Blubberhouses' in late summer 1985, Pigbros hit the ground running. 'This Is The Blubber-houses – The Home Of Corruption – Core Of The Malaise' proclaimed the promotional flyer, but there was more of a groove thing going on rather than anything out and out abrasive. 'Hedonist Hat' remains the standout song on the EP, a sonic workout of muscular proportions where wandering, circling guitars meets the kind of tribal drumbeat not heard since the days of Adam & The Ants. Over everything, Nic Beales delivers an almost laconic vocal. The effect, whilst paying post-punk homage to bands such as Wire and Gang of Four (in its dislocation) is pop-oriented and original, not least in the context of the abstract music of the time.

'We started with a style – droning guitar, echoing bass, metronome drums and Hawkwind noises, singing songs about powerlessness and those we saw as figures of fun,' recalls Nic Beales today. 'Hip hop and dance was massive on the indie scene at the time and we got sucked into that and away from the original template. It also seemed to take us forever to write new material and longer still to release it, which might show in the changes of style even though I've always hated the idea that a band can only have one style and has to rewrite the same song forever.'

While Fuzz Townsend was smashing away on the drum kit, Jonathon Cooke chugging away on bass, and Svor Naan either blasting out on sax or guitar, Nic Beales remained a focal point, often wearing the kind of silver sparkly outfits not seen since the 1970s – looking 'like a silver lamé Elvis on the dole', according to John Robb.

'It's not a great claim to make these days, for obvious reasons, but in the early 70s I was a big Gary Glitter fan and I loved the idea of that glam look – especially having come out of the drabness of the Nightingales. We wanted to be entertainers!' recalls Nic Beales. 'I remember we played a gig in Hammersmith supporting Alternative TV – I think it was our first London gig. Me and Jonny went in search of shiny clothing, eventually discovering a sparkling purple dress that did the trick for bass playing glam wear for that night! Fuzz had a fantastic image of half his head shaved, the rest in long dreadlocks. Well, let's say, it was an interesting band image all in all!'

Nic Beales told the Legend! in an *NME* interview at the start of 1986 that the wearing of the outfits was to 'present a corporate image of the group so people won't forget us easily. It could be taken as a joke, but really it is more symbolic – symbolic of the society we live in, superficially shiny and glittery, but underneath... a mess.'

Indeed, Pigbros set itself up with a political agenda – 'We aim to show the way forward to a better life', they proclaimed at the time, and railed against the kind of political apathy that blindly accepted, for instance, Cruise missiles. And they were fiercely democratic: Nic Beales claimed to have experienced more than enough of autocracy in action during his time in the Nightingales. There was no leader at the helm of Pigbros, deliberately.

The band recorded two well-received Peel sessions between August 1985 and April 1986 before moving to Backs Records for a follow-up single, 'Cheap Life', that once again reprised the band's core sound. Fatally, there was a gap of almost a year between the first and second single. Fuzz Townsend set up the label Cake (along with Peter Byrchmore of the Nightingales) and released Pigbros' only album, *From Now On This Will Be Your Ideal Life*, but not until 1987. A couple of further releases followed (including an EP recorded jointly with the Membranes that included a brilliant cover version of Cameo's 'Word Up') before the band called it a day.

In the minds of the audience, it was difficult to get a grip on just what kind of band Pigbros was. 'One of the big problems was that we could never really settle on a sound or style,' Svor told John Robb in his *Death To Trad Rock* book. 'The fact that I switched back and forth between saxophone and guitar was proof of that.' It was quite possibly then a case of over ambition, but they never quite achieved the 'Rod Stewart level' of commercial success that they told the Legend! they craved. In fact, the band's fate was foretold in the very same *NME* piece. 'Pig Bros, what does that name conjure up in your mind? Surely not yet *another* bloody noisy tongue-in-cheek northern Peel/ Rox/ sub-Fall independent band who'll release a couple of Beefhearty 12"-ers on some hip, totally obscure label and then break up…?'

Pigbros were part of wave of bands that washed up on independent music's wilder shores during the latter part of 1985 and the early part of 1986. Another such was A Witness, a group who could lay some claim to having helped create the whole discordant scene whilst students at Lancaster University at the start of the 1980s. Lancaster was the unusual setting for a small group of abstract musicians who, by the early-to-mid part of that decade, formed something of a vanguard: musicians whose music became increasingly tagged with the shambling or social surrealist label. John Robb had been at the Polytechnic for a short time, meeting Vince Hunt and others from A Witness and also Noel Kilbride who later went on to form AC Temple.

Bassist Vince Hunt and guitarist Rick Aitken knew each other from their hometown of Stockport and began working together in 1980. They wrote a few songs, but very little happened until Hunt went away to do a Modern Studies course at the Polytechnic and met Noel Kilbride, another guitarist. Hunt began writing some further songs, this time with Kilbride. At some point during 1982, Keith Curtis joined on vocals and A Witness was born. The band had no drummer and began rehearsing using a drum machine.

A Witness continued through 1983, *the* college band in the area, and played every kind of venue they could find – working-men's clubs, wine bars, pubs, even an old people's home (where, famously, they received payment in the form of a pushbike). The band came up with a novel solution to transporting their equipment – forming a college society and therefore becoming entitled to use the college minibus. The minibus was used to ferry A Witness all over the country under the aegis of the non-existent society.

That carried on for a while, then, at the end of the college year, Noel Kilbride left to study in France and the band continued as a threesome, a state of affairs that remained until 1986 when Big Flame's Alan Brown joined on drums. The 1984 trio line-up ushered in a new, more urgent sound, partly influenced by the kind of music the band had started listening to (such as the Swans). One of the earliest manifestations of the new sound was 'Kitchen Sink Drama', a song Hunt had written in autumn 1984 while waiting on the platform at New Street train station in Birmingham. The new song had an extraordinary effect on singer Keith Curtis, as Vince Hunt later commented: 'Keith started screaming like he'd been shot as we played it and the new A Witness was born: confrontational, loud, aggressive and passionate, coming off stage with fingers shredded and the drum-machine controls flecked with blood. Much better.'

As 1984 progressed, the band's popularity grew. They played a couple of gigs at venues organised by Alan McGee, and played the first night of events organised by Leigh Goorney at Thames Polytechnic where they appeared on the bill with the Membranes and Heads On Sticks at the start of September. They returned to Thames Poly in November, playing again on the bill with the Membranes and also Bog-shed. At a gig in Nottingham in spring 1985 the band bumped into Dave Parsons who offered to release a record on the Ron Johnson label. The label was very flexible in terms of how the band wanted to proceed. 'We explained that we only wanted to do 12" singles, so as to avoid that 7" syndrome where a record is only judged on its title side,' Vince Hunt said at the start of 1986.

'Loud Hailer Songs' was released in December 1985, the same month that the band did the first (of four) Peel sessions. Reviewers immediately latched on to the dislocated nature of the five songs on the EP, Mr Spencer in *Sounds* deeming it 'pop music perfectly perverted' and calling A Witness a band 'that do[es] not put the listener at ease'. The *NME* praised the 'neurotic buzz' that 'systematically batters you'. The aim to not unwittingly showcase a particular track certainly worked, and although the prominent use of a loud hailer on the track 'Lucky In London' made that many people's favourite, there was something deeply insinuating about the other tracks, and 'Kitchen Sink Drama', with its portentous, throbbing-bass intro and immortal opening lines – 'Someone's been dying in the kitchen/ And its not the first time this has happened…' – gripped equally as hard, as did the eight minute, skittering cut-up epic, 'Drill One', a particular audience favourite when played live. The kaleidoscopic 'Drill One' set to music a novel approach Keith Curtis outlined in an *NME* interview with this author: 'If you take out the white liner sleeve of a record and place it on the cover, each time you move it you get a different picture with a new meaning. That's what approaching songs should be about.'

Holed up in Stafford, the band took their inspiration from wherever they could find it. Like Rob Lloyd in Birmingham, band members discovered the delights of a well-stocked music library, borrowing everything from Throbbing Gristle to John Coltrane, Cecil Taylor, Charlie Mingus and Nurse With Wound. As well as the music of the Swans, Vince Hunt was listening to Philip Glass, Steve Reich, Ice T and baroque composer Tomaso Albinoni. He was picking up inspiration for the lyrics to songs and images for covers by simply keeping his eyes open. The suspension spring on the cover of the 'Loudhailer Songs' EP was found in a scrapyard and kept in the kitchen where it was regularly kicked around for fun. He found lines for the song 'Smelt Like A Pedestrian' from lines in a guide book – 'What time does the garage close?', 'Do you think it is going to rain or snow?', etc.

A Witness contributed a track to *C86* ('Sharpened Sticks') around the time they began recording their debut album in the spring of 1986. Typically, they chose the name for the album –

I Am John's Pancreas – randomly, lifting it from a Readers Digest series about parts of the body and when they set about making it, Vince Hunt was determined to showcase the band's formidable talents. 'I didn't just want to be loud and aggressive – I knew there was more to me than Doc Martens and bloody fingers,' he later said. All manner of weird and wonderful things made their way onto the record, including some furtive recordings of the rhythm of steam engines (snatched at Manchester Air & Space Museum). The sound of the steam engines was added to some looped horns, put through graphic equalizers and an old radio and the hypnotic track '4.49 Stool' emerged out the other side. There were other surprising tracks on the album, as well, such as 'Car Skidding', with its delicate piano and clarinet, and 'Dipping Bird' with its sloweddown and overdubbed bass and snares and symbols.

The album followed 'Loudhailer Songs' into the independent chart – a second EP, 'Red Snake' had fared less well – and the band joined the Ron Johnson Pop Noise Tour of Europe in October, the month the album was released. Following the tour, Big Flame split and bassist Alan Bown joined A Witness on drums. But the cultural winds were blowing differently from how they had been a year earlier in the autumn of 1985 and making progress became harder, not just for A Witness but for all of the bands sheltering under the social surrealist umbrella. A Witness moved to Manchester, surviving largely on the patronage of John Peel who continued to support his 'shambling' bands.

The band released two further 12" singles, including the infectiously catchy 'I Love You, Mr Disposable Razors', and a compilation of Peel Sessions. Alan Brown departed in 1988 to join the Great Leap Forward and Tris King from Bog-shed stepped into the breech. The same year, the Ron Johnson record label collapsed. Then, just as the band was getting itself back on track in 1989, tragedy struck. Whilst on a climbing holiday, Rick Aitken fell and fatally injured himself. The tragedy occurred just before the release of the 'I Love You, Mr Disposable Razors' single. The release was put on hold and a slot on a major tour with the Wedding Present was cancelled out of respect.

Such was the camaraderie, the intensity and the friendship of the original trio that it was impossible for A Witness to continue. It would take twenty-five years for a reformed A Witness to begin playing the songs again, and only then in tribute to their former guitarist. In the period between, where once there had been the most magnificent and maverick sound, there was only silence.

Like Pigbros, the Noseflutes were part of the Birmingham noisenik mafia and another band signed in time to the Ron Johnson label. There must have been something in the local water, or quite possibly it was a reaction to living in a depressed second city yoked to Thatcherism in the mid-1980s, but the Noseflutes, like many bands from the West Midlands took a jocular approach to the business at hand. Prior to settling on their name, they'd tried a few others out for size, including the Blaggards, the Cream Dervishes, Extroverts In A Vacuum, the Viable Sloths, Pantaloni Brothers and Shitstormer.

The band had been around since 1981, but it took them a while to get going on the recording front. Like Bog-shed, they constructed their songs out of jams, and like Bog-shed, in Martin Longley they had a witty and wry singer/ lyricist. The title track to their debut EP 'Girth' typified Martin Longley's somewhat unusual take on things: 'God made heavy demands on me/ Women would never lay hands on me'. Thrashing away behind Martin Longley were Mark Rowson on drums, Chris Horton on bass, John Horton on guitar, Dave Pritchard on guitar, Chris Long on violin and Roger Turner on percussion, although often band members hid behind Beefheartian aliases such as Leg Akimbo, Rene Libido, Kit Bageldish and Motic Necrojam.

The four-track 'Girth' EP was released on Reflex in early autumn 1985, a touch of swamp-blues here and R 'n' B riff there, discordant guitars and violin wandering free-form with Martin Longley's irrepressible vocals floating on top. The EP had been recorded in June at the legendary Birmingham Arts Lab studio where Mark Rowson's brother worked and where the band consequently got some studio time free. In the 1960s, the studio had been part of the old ATV set up and sported stunning acoustics, as can be heard on the EP and on the band's debut album, part of which was also recorded there.

The object right from the start, as Martin Longley told this author in the middle of 1986, was to make art not money. 'It seems ironic,' he said at the time, 'that so many people are forced to make music in their spare time... yet society relies upon them for entertaining. Your parents laugh at you until you make money or the media writes about you – it's as though you've got to justify yourself in a way they can see before you are free to work.'

It was probably just as well that the Noseflutes ambitions lay in the direction of art since that first album was given the slightly challenging title of *Several Young Men Ignite Hardboard Stump*. The album cover featured a shot of New York's twin trade towers rising up into the sky, a pair of cut off, upside down legs of rising between them at the bottom of the cover. But inside it was an extravaganza of angular and quirky yet resolutely melodic music, best summed up by 'Perfect Cockney Hard-On', one of the band's most beloved songs, a scattering, tumbling melange of scratchy guitar and frenetic drumming with the song's title repeated almost ad infinitum over and over, or by 'Dreamboat', a warped romance of a number with the engaging lines, 'Dreamboat/ From table to table/ Before the next ladle/ My little noodle/ We could be good!'.

John Robb once described the Noseflutes as being maverick even by the standards of their maverick contemporaries. Their live performances were as perplexing as they were formidable, as one dazed critic pointed out reviewing a performance where Martin Longley swung 'between the club's ornate lamp-posts, plastic flora and fancy chromium balustrades like Harold Lloyd playing *The Fly* for a night'. Theirs was the art of the impossible, as Martin Longley further explained in the 1986 interview with *NME*. 'Most bands are actually a variation of their favourite [band] and this shows in their writing. But in our case we realised that trying to mix Alice Cooper's 'School's Out' with African rhythms and Doctor Feelgood was totally impossible.'

And so it proved to be. Two further EPs followed the album, both released on Ron Johnson Records and sporting such irresistible titles as 'Legs Full of Alcohol', 'Catcheel Maskhole', 'Hanging A Scarface' and 'Body Hair (Up In The Air)' but the band remained an acquired taste. A second album, *Zib Zob And His Kib Kob* appeared on the band's own Rictus label after Ron Johnson ended and a couple more releases followed before the band quit in 1991.

Their music, as *Melody Maker* at one point concluded, was found at a 'sardonically cultural crossroads, a meeting point for African melodies, tribal rhythms, music hall drama, American art rock and northern intellectual cockiness'. The description summed them up well, but perhaps not quite as well as the 2001 mention of their charms in the Birmingham *Evening Mail*.

They had been, said the paper, a 'wonderfully perverse avant weird outfit'. It was a pithy and fitting obituary

Around the same time that the Noseflutes debut 'Girth' was perplexing the uninitiated, the Shrubs formed, born out of the ashes of a Watford group called the Kevin Staples Band. The history of the Shrubs had a long tail, at least in the case of singer Nick Hobbs who, in 1977, had found himself managing the 'anti-commericial', avant-rock band Henry Cow that boasted Fred Frith and Tim Hodkinson in its ranks. Henry Cow existed beyond the mainstream music business and, as Nick Hobbs later cheerfully recounted, punk largely passed him by, or at least the commercialisation of it did. Nick Hobbs witnessed it all from a distance, then retreated to the more wide-ranging music he had discovered whilst at boarding school in Portsmouth, which included the work of Captain Beefheart.

In the early 1980s, Nick Hobbs moved to Sweden and joined a band called Kraeldjursanstalten – 'proper musicians', he called them later – but returned to London when the band folded and then scoured the wanted ads in the music papers for a new opening. He joined an early version of Stump, but was allegedly sacked for being 'too serious' and shortly after, in May 1985, the Shrubs started up.

From the start, the emphasis was on the spontaneous, the drawing out of the creativity that, according to Hobbs, lurks 'just beneath the surface in all of us'. '[T]here's no point in working to forms or norms,' he told this author at the time. Such an unscripted and automatic approach was inevitably hit and miss but when it worked the results were far more satisfying than taking the more conventional route. It led to some interesting lyrics. 'When I write the lyrics I don't think about what I'm writing and I don't think about why I'm writing,' he claimed. 'The sun sets over the plaza/ The cleaners wave their brooms at the matadors/ Go home! Go home!' run the lyrics to 'As You Hunch Over Your Gin', perhaps proving the point.

The Shrubs took their influences – the Fall, Pere Ubu and Captain Beefheart, according to Nick Hobbs – and twisted them until they either turned into something new or fell apart in the process. The understanding that things could hopelessly misfire was an important aspect of how they worked. 'What elevates a good group,' the singer claimed at the time, 'is the ability to recognise influences but not worry about them. What is more important… is what inspires you.'

The band signed with Ron Johnson after Nick Hobbs sent label boss Dave Parsons a demo of songs that ended up on the six-track EP 'Full Steam Into The Brainstorm'. The songs ranged from the more straightforwardly melodic, such as 'The Dealer', through to the more obtuse, such as 'Carbreaker' and

'Bullfighter', a track that found its way onto *C86*. 'The Shrubs sounded a bit like Beefheart,' recalls Dave Parsons, 'but at its best their sound was less obviously bluesy and more angular. The Shrubs came to the label at the right time since by the middle of 1986 Big Flame had ceased to exist and we were looking for bands to fill the considerable gap that they had left.'

A follow-up EP 'Blackmailer' (co-produced by Tim Hodkinson) came later in the year and followed in the same vein as 'Full Steam', before the band's debut album was released in 1987. *Take Me Aside For A Midnight Harangue* was less splenetic, the trademark twisted folk leavened in places by more melodic interludes. The *Underneath The Volcano*-style madness of narration still peeped through but overall the sounds reflected the record cover, which showed a picture of simple folk revelling by the wayside. The band travelled to Amsterdam to record with Dolf Planteijdt, a producer who had previously worked with label mates the Ex.

Following the collapse of Ron Johnson, the Shrubs recorded a further single and album, linking up with the Hertfordshire label Public Domain for both releases, issued in 1988. The band split in 1989, Nick Hobbs eventually moving on to promote in eastern Europe before later involving himself in performance art.

According to Paul Walker, the drummer in Splat!, Ron Johnson was the last man to be hanged in Nottingham. There is no concrete evidence to suggest that this was the case but in any event Ron lent his name to one of the more unusual independent record labels of the mid-1980s. Certainly, no Ron existed at the label, but Ron nonetheless became the recipient of many letters and tapes from fans and aspiring bands at the time. John Peel did little to disabuse people of the notion that Ron was living flesh and blood, often cheekily making reference to his supposed existence in Long Eaton, a town between Derby and Nottingham where Ron Johnson Records was based.

Splat!'s first EP (and the first Ron Johnson release) had appeared at the tail end of 1983 and although it went largely uncelebrated in the mainstream music press, the band were written about in *Sounds*, trooping off to the pub with Mr Spencer and, according to Dave Parsons, 'talking about James Joyce and coming across as pretentious fools'. The EP ('Yeah The Dum Dum' and 'Bookface' backed with the enigmatically-titled 'Biggles Bloodbath') sold a respectable 1000 copies, a number that neither set the world alight nor reduced the ambitions of the band to ashes.

Dave Parsons had caught the music bug in 1977 when he went with his older sister to see Thin Lizzy play. The support band was the Radiators From Space, his first introduction to punk rock music. Shortly after, Parsons heard the music of the Sex Pistols and fell in love with punk. He was fifteen at the time and ended up spending all his spare pocket money and dinner money for school on punk rock records. *Never Mind The Bollocks* was an early purchase, but at Select-adisc, his local, well-stocked and well-informed record store, he was in time turned on to other delights: product from labels like Fast, Factory, Small Wonder and Rough Trade and an early introduction to the more noise-oriented bands of the time, such as Cabaret Voltaire. Like others before and after, he ended up running a label quite possibly because he started out a *collector* of labels.

In fact, the plan with Splat! was to be signed by somebody else. 'Where we were, up in Nottingham, there was not a lot happening,' remembers Parsons. 'It felt quite isolated. We didn't even bother sending demos to anybody, although we did try to get signed by All Trade, Rough Trade's booking agency. They came and saw a couple of shows but turned us down. I suspect that they thought we sounded too much like the Birthday Party. After that we thought that we might as well put the record out ourselves.'

'Yeah The Dum Dum' did sufficiently well enough for the distributor, Nine Mile, to encourage the band to release a follow-up. This time the band delivered a self-titled, four-track EP, 'Splat!'.

As had been the case with the first single, the influence of the Birthday Party was apparent, not least in the thrashing drums and in the deep and unrestrained vocals. But once again, Splat! found a market and when the single ran its sales course, Nine Mile asked the band what they planned next. Since they didn't have enough material for an album, the distributor suggested that they look around for other bands to sign to the label.

Dave Parsons had set the label up with friend John Allsopp and had got funding through a Manpower Commission Services scheme whereby the Government matched money they put up to help float the business. In order to keep the business running, Dave Parsons had a job in the local biscuit factory, working nights where he would load biscuits onto lorries for overnight delivery to supermarkets. On one particular night, as he told the *NME* in passing in November 1985, he loaded 9,600 boxes of Jaffa Cakes in a single shift alone.

'We had the radio on when we worked,' he says. 'We'd always listen to the John Peel show and one night he played 'Sink', the single that Big Flame released on their own Laughing Gun label in 1984. It really stood out for me and sounded different from everything else that I was hearing at the time. I must have got in touch with them via the address they put on the back of the record's sleeve and they wrote back to me asking if Ron Johnson would be interested in releasing a record by them. At that point they had already recorded 'Rigour' with John Brierly at Cargo Studios. I think they had planned to release the record on Laughing Gun but had run out of money. When the project came to me it was more or less a finished thing. They'd done the artwork, and the record was mastered. I went up to the Crescents in Hulme and met them, and got on very well with them, although there was a degree of tension between them and it was clear that in some ways they didn't always get on with each other.'

'Rigour' became what Dave Parsons considers to be the first 'proper' Ron Johnson release (and also the first to carry the ZRON catalogue number prefix since Ronco records objected to the use of the prefix RON). By rights, the next Ron Johnson release would have been by A Witness who had sent Dave Parsons a demo of the songs that ended up on 'Loudhailer Songs'. But sneaking in between was a third Big Flame EP, 'Tough', featuring the immortal tracks 'All The Irish (Must Go To Heaven)', 'Where's Our Carol?' and '¡Cuba!'.

The label was quickly developing a sound. Dave Parsons had had an early education in punk and post-punk but some of the final touches were added by Splat! (and later Shrubs) bassist Mark Grebbly, who educated his label mate in the finer nuances of the more unusual. 'Mark had a bizarre taste in music that covered quite a few extremes. He introduced me to the music of the Residents, to Matching Mole and Hatfield & The North, and to Etron Fou Leloublan and stuff on Chris Cutler's Recommended label. This all went into the mix and I liked also the notion that a label could have a particular sound. Early on, I remember buying those Earcom samplers and the Factory sampler that were almost aural magazines. All of that surfaced somehow in the Ron Johnson approach.

The label itself began attracting attention – the small feature on Dave Parsons had appeared in the *NME* at the end of 1985 and the *Catalogue* featured the label on the front cover of an issue in spring 1986 along with a free Ron Johnson flexi disc ('Solid Glod' – featuring tracks by Big Flame, Stump, A Witness and the MacKenzies). Many years later, Dil Green from Big Flame would quite possibly put his finger on the essence of both the label and bands signed when he told Dave Parsons that Ron Johnson was 'a confederacy of *Not*s rather than a collective of any sort', defined by what it wasn't and not by what it was. Certainly the label didn't go out of its way to curry favour. 'We were conscious that we were doing something different,' recalls Dave Parsons, 'although if someone said that they liked us we tended to get suspicious...'

By the end of spring 1986, Ron Johnson had hit something of a high point. Five of its acts had appeared on *C86*. Releases by Big Flame ('Why Pop Stars Can't Dance'), A Witness ('Loud-hailer Songs'), Stump ('Mud On A Colon') and the MacKenzies ('New Breed') all made it into the independent charts and all four had Peel sessions broadcast between the end of 1985 and July 1986 (Stump doing two sessions), as did the Shrubs. All of the bands involved picked up major coverage in the mainstream music press, usually in the form of lengthy profiles.

Speaking for all of them (perhaps), the Mackenzies when interviewed by this author worried about how this abstract music was being compartmentalised, not least by tags such as 'shambling'. The four-piece band from Glasgow consciously avoided emulating Postcard or the Velvet Underground, unlike any number of their hometown compatriots, and even condemned the use of the word 'rock' within their creative discussions. As their single 'New Breed' revealed, and their *C86* track, 'Big Jim (There's No Pubs In Heaven)', amplified, they injected a fair amount of funk into their discord. That still, however, left them open to the charge of following in the steps of the great Don Van Vliet, John Peel calling 'New Breed' 'the spirit of Beefheart in the 1980s'. The band claimed that it sometimes took six months to write a single song – which maybe why it left little trace, recording just three singles for Ron Johnson, gradually moving away from what journalist James Brown called a 'hand-grenade attack on Kew Gardens'-sound towards dance. The last release was in 1988, and credited to the MKZ's before the band imploded, the formidable rhythm section of Paul Turnbull and Graham Lironi going on to be part of the Secret Goldfish with ex-Fizzbombs singer Katy McCullars and guitarist John Morose.

The records that saw out the summer of 1986 marked, according to Dave Parsons, the end of the 'first phase' of Ron Johnson and the start of the label's decline. The label became holed below the hull line quite severely after releasing the Ex's double-disc single, '1936 – The Spanish Revolution'. The Ex was a Dutch anarchist band with a long pedigree and one well known to the UK. In 1984, for instance, the band had toured the UK in support of the miners. '1936 – The Spanish Revolution' was a lavish work, presented in a gatefold sleeve with a 150-page booklet. The four songs that comprised the set – 'They Shall Not Pass', 'El Tren Blindado', 'Ay Carmela' and 'People Again' traced the story of the Spanish Civil War, focussing on the activities in Catalonia of the FAI and CNT organisations, who were anarchist, trades-union affiliated, popular and armed. Danny Kelly, writing in the *NME*, called the release 'the best and most adventurous singles package of the year', trumping the usual freebie pin-up posters offered up by mainstream record companies that were 'by comparison, lining for budgie cages'.

'We sold around 15,000 copies of the Ex single, which was very respectable, but unfortunately the distributor didn't realise how much it had cost to make and it retailed at £2.99,' says Dave Parsons. 'That price meant that we were receiving around £1.54 per copy. In fact, they were costing around £2.50 each to make, so we lost roughly a pound on every copy sold.'

In 1986, Dave Parsons was just 24 years old and, by his own admission, not quite as financially astute as he might have been. He ran the label soley out of love for the music it was producing. 'I didn't like the idea of being a bossy head of the label,' he admits, 'and at the same time there was more pressure on me from the distributor to start releasing albums, which were much more expensive to make.'

The first Ron Johnson album was *I Am John's Pancreas* by A Witness, released at the end of 1986. It sold around 4,000 copies and was, impressively, even licensed in Greece. It cost just £500 to record. Later releases proved to be not quite so cost-effective. 'The Shrubs album ended up costing £4000 to record, far more than we could afford and ended up selling less than a thousand copies. By mid 1986, we no longer had Big Flame, either. Their singles regularly sold around 3000 and always sold quickly, reaching comparatively big numbers within a few weeks. But they were also expensive – they often had inserts and Dil, who designed the sleeves, liked to use colour schemes that were costly, or didn't work and ended up having to be redone. The band famously wouldn't make an album or 12" but the distributor wanted something for export. They flatly refused the 12" format so we ended up compromising and did a 10", 'Two Kan Guru', but that ended up costing more to produce than a 12" would have.'

Throughout 1987 and into 1988 new acts joined the label, including Twang, the Great Leap Forward, Jackdaw With Crowbar and the Sewer Zombies, but overall sales dropped off as costs rose and even the love affair the press had with the label began to cool. Just before the business went under, one outstanding debt to a studio hit the £40,000 mark (or nearly double the cost of an average house in the area at the time). The business eventually folded and Dave Parsons was forced to declare himself bankrupt.

'Afterwards, I never heard again from many of the people whose records we put out,' he says. 'Today, people think of Ron Johnson Records as a reasonably big name in independent music at the time, but really it was relatively small in the scheme of things. In retrospect, people see it as being more important than it probably was.'

At the start of 1986, Noel Kilbride of AC Temple had released a cassette compilation called *Skin & Bone*. *Skin & Bone* collected up many of the more discordant and Death To Trad Rock bands, such as A Witness, Big Flame, Marc Riley & The Creepers, the Membranes and Five Go Down To The Sea. Splat! were also on the tape, which was released from Skin & Bone HQ, not far from Ron Johnson's base. An interview with Brix Smith and Craig Scanlon of the Fall, and another with the Very Things, gave the tape a magazine feel.

Noel Kilbride was also involved in putting on gigs – promoting bands such as the Swans, A Witness and We've Got A Fuzzbox And We're Going To Use it. One band he had come across was Stump, a four-piece group based in south London who had been around for a couple of years but only recently settled their line-up. Bassist Kev Hopper had been visiting a friend in Whitstable when he met guitarist Chris Salmon. Hopper had brought with him a fretless bass that he proceeded to play throughout his stay, impressing Salmon with his original style of playing. Hopper was at that time still at Coventry University, completing an art degree but the two hatched a plan to meet up again when Hopper had finished his course and put together a band.

They ended up in south London and set about forming a band, looking out for a drummer and a singer to complete the line up. For a while Nick Hobbs was in the band, but left not long after drummer Rob McKahey joined. McKahey had arrived in London from Cork and had an unusual drumming style, often playing in Irish jig time of 12/8. When it was decided that Nick Hobbs wasn't quite the right fit, McKahey asked around in the community of Irish musicians and bumped into Mick Lynch who was squatting in Brixton at the time. Tall and thin and with a Tin Tin quiff, Lynch was visually striking and instantly charismatic. Following a rehearsal in a basement the band used on the Old Kent Road, the other three quickly decided that they wanted Lynch in.

In 2014, Kev Hopper summed up the band's approach in that period when they were just starting: 'I originally had in mind a band that would play a cross between 'Suction Prints' by Captain Beefheart and 'DMZ' by Brand X – with a little bit of Pere Ubu thrown in. Splintered structures and dissonant harmonics combined with a post-punk flavour a singer might bring – but nothing too po-faced.' Nothing too difficult, then, for a singer/ lyricist to weave his words into... Luckily, Lynch had been weaned on a diet of the metafiction of satirist Flann O'Brien and was able to conjure up the most amazingly absurd lyrics, usually constructed as ballads, adding another incongruous element.

One song, 'Bit Part Actor' carried the lines

Charlie in the factory
And Benji on a tractor
And a woman from Max Factor
And an Irish sub-contractor…

Another, the hugely popular 'Tupperware Stripper' from 1987 ran:

Bulging of biceps for the Tupperware ladies
Grinding of groins for the Clip-Top Brigade
Winding down his yellowing Y-fronts
Madeleine screams
As he pulls at the string…

Stump were then, to say the least, unusual, with a charismatic front man and capable lyricist in the face-contorting Mick Lynch and a fretless bass and guitar sound that turned pitch bending and the use of the whammy bar into an art. Their fiery, off-kilter method of playing appealed to Kilbride who suggested to them that they contact Dave Parsons with a view to Ron Johnson taking them on.

'Mud On A Colon', the band's debut EP, came out in February 1986 and is one of the very best Ron Johnson releases, not least because by the time that the band came to record they had acquired a sound that was unique and wholly different. 'I received a letter and a demo from Kev Hopper,' recalls Dave Parsons. 'At first, I really couldn't relate the sound to anything I'd heard before and it fascinated me. Kev Hopper was worried initially that I might take them for some sort of comedy band, but I loved the 'Mud On A Colon' demo.'

Just after the band signed with Ron Johnson (and were given £500 to make their record), they were asked to record something for *C86*. According to Hopper, they didn't take the invitation all that seriously and managed to spend £50 of the £100 that the paper gave them on beer. The track that the band submitted, 'Buffalo', went on to become their most well-known track with its famous 'Does the fish have chips'-lyric. At the time, Mick Lynch outlined for this author the song's genesis: '[It] is a brilliant song. Big bottom swing! It's... basically about Yanks (as opposed to Americans). I was on the bus one night when I heard from downstairs this Yank asking, "How do I get off the bus?". It just creased me up.'

During the summer, Stump departed Ron Johnson and began work on a mini album, *Quirk Out*, which was released in October on Stuff Records, a label the band set up itself. Stump had been keen to make the transition to a larger label, and had received money from Stiff to make a demo of 'Our Fathers', the opening track on *Quirk Out*. The cheque bounced and Stiff Records went into receivership the following week. The album was eventually recorded in a very short two weeks at Rockfield Studios with Hugh Jones producing and lifting from Stump some excellent performances, as Kev Hopper later recalled. The record did well, climbing to number two in the independent charts by the end of November and not dropping out of the charts for another six months.

By the time of the release of *Quirk Out* – 'one of the pleasures of 1986,' according to *Melody Maker* – Stump's reputation on the tour circuit was formidable: the band's live performances during 1986 were, if anything, even better than their records. Lynch's eye-popping antics were irresistible and the ferocious delivery of songs such as 'Ice The Levant' and 'Tupperware Stripper' was such that the band's performances had, in the words of the *NME*, 'been known to frighten dogs'. Channel Four had made a video of 'Buffalo' that got shown to great acclaim on the *Tube* and the band suddenly found itself the recipient of interest from the major record labels.

The band signed to Ensign, went off to record with Holger Hiller, fell out with Holger Hiller, fell out somewhat with each other and ended up with an album that was eventually finished off by *Quirk Out* producer, Hugh Jones. The single lifted from it – 'Charlton Heston' – entered the mainstream charts for one week before dropping out again. Ensign inexplicably rereleased 'Buffalo' as a single in 1988 to try to revive fortunes but by then the band had effectively disintegrated. Kev Hopper had become more and more drawn to the use of samplers while other in the band favoured a move towards a more basic rock and roll sound.

For all of their quirky genius, Stump ultimately suffered the same fate as the other social surrealists – the inability to outrun the history train. The so-called Second Summer of Love swept all before it as rave culture took a hold. People, as Hopper later conceded, didn't want to go to gigs in small venues, preferring instead to stand in a field getting stoned. In a period of increasingly rampant hedonism, the old music looked anachronistic and academic.

The journey to unlocking creative potential through the juxtaposition of contradictory musical passages was too difficult to comprehend and no match for that of taking a little pill with a smiley face on it.

CHAPTER 18

DISTANT VOICES, DISUSED LANGUAGE

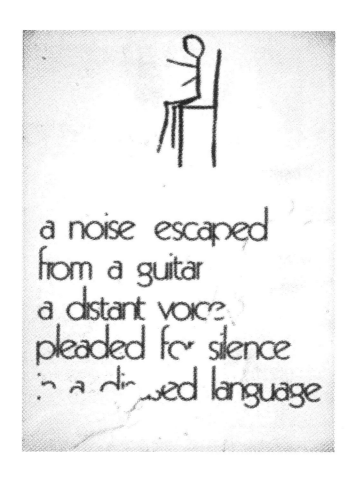

a noise escaped
from a guitar
a distant voice
pleaded for silence
in a disused language

NOT EVERYONE REVELLED IN A culture that deliberately cherished the perverse. Some plied their trade in a more direct way. There were those, like Alan McGee, for whom success represented escape from an otherwise predestined life of drudgery, and others who bemoaned the 'low ceiling' of indie – their destiny, as they constantly iterated, was to escape the 'ghetto' and delivery up their art to the broader audience it so rightfully deserved. Then there were those few for whom the prize was fame alone, even though it could be fickle and cruel and often hiding. In spring 1988, just as he was setting out on a solo career, Morrissey was telling writer Simon Reynolds, 'I always had a religious obsession with fame. I always thought being famous was the only thing worth doing in human life, and anything else was just perfunctory… I wasn't terribly impressed with obscurity.'

Since before the days of Elvis, the first rule of fame had been to create the appropriate self-myth for delivering up to others. This remained the case twenty years later, as many of those emerging through punk but still holding on to the reins knew only too well. Elvis had become so famous that people dispensed with his other names. Mononymity can be an indicator of fame and a well-adopted strategy on the way to it. Two of the biggest stars of 1985 were Prince and Madonna, and most of their fans were unaware of their real names. The identity they had assumed was the *real* person they had become.

At a slightly descended level, (Steven Patrick) Morrissey of the Smiths and Lawrence (Hayward) of Felt carried on their businesses. In so doing, both adopted mononymity as they set about delivering up some of the more accomplished indie music of the 1980s. Both were obsessed with fame, yet in each case fame had been difficult to deal with – either through being elusive, as in the case of Lawrence, or through being a burden, as was the case with Morrissey, who frequently moaned about it. Both Lawrence's group Felt, and the Smiths, the band Morrissey co-founded, left a legacy of beautiful work, but in the case of both artists, their greatest creation remains the myth of themselves.

Felt's first album, released at the time of their second single, barely troubled the record shop display stands when Lawrence was telling the *Master Bag*, in 1982, 'We're trying to build a legend; people are going to look back and say, "they never made a mistake". We want to give people the perfect band... When they do the *Record Mirror* feature on the Lost Underground, we don't want to be there. What I'm working for is *Vogue!*' Four years later Morrissey was more specific, using the voice of the narrator of the Smiths song *Frankly, Mr Shankly* to serve up his view: 'Fame, fame, fatal fame/ It can play hideous tricks on the brain/ But then I'd rather be famous than righteous or holy/ Any day, any day, any day...'

Morrissey and Lawrence were like two sides of the same coin, both working towards an identical centre. The Smiths set about the process of having hit records with quite some vim, letting little get in their way. Felt made ten singles and ten albums in ten years. Neither group could be accused of not trying. But whereas the Smiths ended up the ultimate, mid-1980s indie band that crossed over into the mainstream, Felt had to settle for cultdom and a retirement spent popping up in exactly the kind of 'Lost Group' articles that Lawrence had earlier bemoaned. The cult of Morrissey was established quickly, with the band barely having a record under their belts: in contrast, Felt were largely misunderstood and sometimes mocked, but thirty years on *Felt* are the most obsessed over indie band of the entire period.

Johnny Marr had first heard about Morrissey towards the end of the 1970s, but it wasn't until 1982 that they joined forces to create the Smiths, as guitarist Johnny Marr told this author in 2009. Marr had been in bands since his teens but had struggled to put together something with the right front man with the necessary level of commitment that he was looking for. He was looking, he said, for 'someone who took themself as seriously as I took myself, and was as serious about music and having a decent proper band as I was.' Morrissey, for his part, connected well with Marr whose looks, he later said, reminded him of Tom Bell, the English kitchen sink drama actor and star of such films as *The L-Shaped Room*. They began working together, 'Formulating writing systems and mapping out how best to blend our dual natures…' as Morrissey recalled in *Autobiography*. For the first time in his life, the future was more important to him than the past. In what must have amounted to one of the few unimaginative moments of their working lives together, they decided to call their band the Smiths.

In time, Morrissey and Marr found an excellent rhythm section in the form of bassist Andy Rourke and drummer Mike Joyce and began rehearsing above Crazy Face, a clothing shop owned by Johnny Marr's boss, Joe Moss. The band got into their musical stride quickly, as Morrissey noted in *Autobiography*: 'The Smiths' sound rockets with meteoric progression; bomb-burst drumming, explosive chords, combative bass-lines, and over it all I am as free as a hawk to paint the canvas as I wish.' They rehearsed together – almost religiously, as Johnny Marr later noted, three or four times a week –and quickly put together a set, one where 'nothing ever failed, nothing ever stumbled'.

Early on, the Smiths played shows in Manchester – on one occasion, the Hacienda, and on another supporting Richard Hell – before travelling down to London to sign with Rough Trade. 'Hand In Glove' was released in May 1983, the initial 6,000 copies selling out quickly. That same month, Cath Carroll interviewed them for the *NME*. The band had, Morrissey told the paper's readers, 'a very basic, traditionalist structure, with the four-piece set-up that has been severely underrated in the past couple of years.' He bemoaned the current vogue for synthesizer bands and the trend to smoother everything in effects and gizmos. 'Songwriting just isn't there, that's why we're important,' he said. Johnny Marr predicted a return to the classic song-writing partnership, such as that enjoyed by Goffin and King or Lieber and Stoller.

In *Document & Eyewitness: An Intimate History* of Rough Trade, Johnny Marr told this author that on practically the first day he met Morrissey they 'had a conversation about many things and made a mental wish list'. On that list was that the band should sign to Rough Trade. Morrissey, in his dislocating autobiography, paints (with the benefit of hindsight) a bleak picture of what he found when the deal was done. He discovered that the company that had – through the quality of its release curation and distribution arm – almost single-handedly created the independent sector was in desperate need of overhaul. He describes the company's then collectivist ethos as 'tubercular' and its image as that of an 'hysterical intellectual spinster'. The company was admirably open-armed and political, but ended up producing and distributing records that were not just 'anti-Everything' but also 'anti-listenable'. Into this unreconstructed environment sailed 'Hand In Glove' shattering 'the afternoons of wok rotas, poetry workshops and *Woman's Hour*'.

The Smiths arrived at just the right time, for independent music in general as much as for Rough Trade, which anyway had little of the clichéd 'brown rice' approach Morrissey later complained about. Both post punk and pop music had become alienating, an increasingly synthetic sound tethered to abstract concepts. During live sets, Morrissey would twirl bouquets of flowers before tossing them into the crowd. The two things were connected, he told *Melody Maker*'s Frank Worrell in September 1983: 'The flowers actually have a significance. When we first began there was a horrendous, sterile cloud over the whole music scene in Manchester. Everybody was anti-human and it was so very cold… It had got to the point where people were really afraid to show how they felt… The flowers offered hope.'

Morrissey's lyrics, direct and unadorned, reintroduced realism and an out of vogue expression of emotion that took the listener back to a less complicating pop period: back, for instance, to the cheerful and cheering songs of early period Beatles or the optimism, albeit manufactured, of the hit factories of old. The mini tales Morrissey told were bruising and romantic, and troubled in the fashion of the old kitchen-sink drama films of the late 1950s and early 1960s that he admired so much. The same month Morrissey spoke to Frank Worrell he was a subject of the 'Portrait of the Artist as Consumer' column in *NME* where he outlined a fascination with the much mythologised (and often northern) English culture of some of his favourite films. He admired, amongst others, *Hobson's Choice*, *A Kind of Loving* and *A Taste of Honey*. Beloved writers and 'Symbolists' included Oscar Wilde, Shelagh Delaney, Sandie Shaw, Hilaire Belloc and Viv Nicholson. The work of Sandie Shaw featured on a list of favourite records ('Stop Before You Start') along with that of Cilla Black ('The Right One Is Left') Billy Fury ('Never Quite Get Over You') and a number of American girl groups that both Morrissey and Johnny Marr admired, such as the Tams, the Marvelettes and the Cookies.

It is no exaggeration to say that the mainstream music press fell at the knees of the Smiths as 1983 segued into 1984. The writers positively fawned over them (in one typical interview the writer confessed himself overawed by Morrissey's ability to engage with *any* subject in a way that was 'uncommonly sensible, thoroughly engaging, often touching in its persuasive sincerity'). The Smiths represented the kind of saviour that the more subterranean writers had been calling for every since the end of 1982 but packaged in a way that less hysterical 'senior' writers could enthusiastically promote without being made to look stupid. The tone of the texts of many of the early interviews is oleaginous: in contrast, Morrissey is clear-eyed and forthright, his answers intelligent and succinct. He often has to finish an interviewer's question for them, or answer, like a politician, the non-existent question that they meant to or should have asked.

The formidable status of the band – classically constructed, emotionally mature songs, a literate and witty front man, and the added attraction of fripperies such as the flowers (later props would include National Health spectacles and a hearing aid) – saw them rightfully enter the charts with their second single, 'This Charming Man', a polished song that took away (to the dismay of some) the more rough-hewed charm of the debut single. The plaintive harmonica of 'Hand In Glove' was an unspoken volume of wail, but one rarely repeated as the production values became increasingly polished. No matter, everyone loved 'This Charming Man', Paul Morley in the *NME* accurately defining it as 'rapture, not dialectics' and calling it one of the great singles of the year, on a level with New Order's 'Blue Monday' or, Culture Club's 'Karma Chameleon' (the biggest selling single of the year).

The Smiths went away and made another single – with its rumbling rockabilly bass a better one, if one less well received – before beginning work on a debut album that arrived in February 1984. At the same time, the band began working with Sandie Shaw who they helped record a version of 'Hand In Glove'. Later Morrissey referred to the singer's haughtiness but at the time called the experience of working with her an 'endless thrill… almost like meeting oneself in a former life'. Sandie Shaw returned the compliment (sort of) in the form of song. It is difficult to imagine a anything more lamentable than 'Steven (You Don't Eat Meat)' (a reference to Morrissey's vegetarianism) with its lines, 'Steven/ You dressed me in my glad rags/ You in your Gladioli/ Just like those other lifetimes/ At least that's what you told me…', but the turgid 'Go, Johnny, Go' (another B-side, from 1986, and an ode to Johnny Marr) comes close.

The band had problems recording *The Smiths*, initially working with ex-Teardrop Explodes musician Troy Tate before scrapping the work and re-recording the album with producer John Porter. When it arrived, *The Smiths* was something of a disappointment for some, at least when set against the power and ferocity of the band's live performance where, in the words of Johnny Marr, they delivered 'like devils'. The critics were, predictably, unrestrained in their breathlessness and praise of the band, but in some quarters uneasy about the thin and tinny sound of the 'turgidly disappointing' album. Don Watson, writing in the *NME*, had a further beef. Yes, he recognised the mordant wit, the melancholia and the irony, but criticised a 'philosophy of pop [that] seems all too neatly prepared to appeal'. He took Morrissey to book over his claim to be 'a country mile behind the world', seeing artifice in such wistfulness. Morrissey's view was 'visibly strained through the early '60s films and late '50s novels – a notion of reality three times removed'.

Morrissey's artistic sensibility was openly informed by the literary and the cinematic, but in 1984 – one of the most troubling years of the 1980s, he didn't shy away from the political. 'You have to be interested in politics,' he told journalist Ian Pye. 'There's absolutely no excuses for people who aren't politically aware. I really believe that complacency is bred. It's a recurring theme by a government that says, "Look, do not worry about nuclear weapons – we will look after you".'

On the band's first visit to America, Morrissey was asked about the politics of the UK and commented that the only thing that could save politics would be the assassination of Margaret Thatcher (the then Prime Minister). When the comment appeared in *Rolling Stone* he was swamped with calls from the British media asking what would he do if a fan of the Smiths went out and shot the Prime Minister? He would immediately marry the person, he replied. He returned to the theme on his first solo album, *Viva Hate*, and in an interview at the time was asked by Simon Reynolds if he was happy to see her dead ('Instantly'), the death carried out in a cruel and bloody way ('Yes'). Asked if he would be prepared to carry out the execution, he replied: 'I have got the uniform ready.'

The Smiths put their shoulder to many causes, including supporting CND, the miners and the besieged GLC, and, most explicitly, in championing animal rights through the song and album, *Meat Is Murder*. Morrissey's open politics was just another appealing aspect and differed from the preaching of that of some old school pop practitioners who were more forceful and crude in delivering their messages.

In September, *The Smiths* was temporarily withdrawn from a number of High Street retailers following complaints about the song 'Suffer Little Children', which dealt with the gruesome subject of the Moors murders of Ian Bradey and Myra Hindley. The song was a track on the album and also the B-side to the band's fifth studio single, 'Heaven Knows I'm Miserable Now'. Matters were aggravated by the choice of 'cover star' for the single – each single by the Smiths featured a cover co-designed by Morrissey who ran through an extensive catalogue of cult icons in delivering up photos for use. The single featured a 1961 shot of pools winner Viv Nicholson, but with her blonde mop of hair, the picture of Nicholson might loosely be mistaken for a shot of Myra Hindley. Some of the families of the murdered children complained and Morrissey spent time with one family at the same time Rough Trade issued an apology over what it said was no more than a 'memorial to the children'.

'Heaven Knows I'm Miserable Now' in fact became the band's biggest hit to date, a wonderful, self-referencing fur ball of neuroses by Morrissey that managed to provide a walk-on part for Caligula (who might have blushed at its narrator's plight). The controversy caused potentially more trouble for Rough Trade, who by then had come to heavily rely on the sales of records by the Smiths. The company donated £4000 to the NSPCC and a company memo circulated outlining the implications should the high street ban persist.

Things got back on track in late autumn when Morrissey came up with the idea of releasing a budget-priced compilation album of songs that featured some singles, B-sides, and tracks from the BBC radio sessions the band had done. 'It was,' Johnny Marr later recalled, 'breaking the mould of what a rock band did at the time and it was done in the spirit of those old Marble Arch and Decca compilations like *The World of David Bowie*.' *Hatful of Hollow* came with a mock price sticker announcing that it retailed at '36/11'. The record was, in some ways, far more representative of the sound of the band than the group's debut album, possessing a garage feel in places and reintroducing some songs that merited more than merely B-side status, such 'Handsome Devil'. Some called it patchy and erratic and all the better for being so.

1985 began and the Smiths released 'How Soon Is Now?', a single that for many remains the band's crowning glory. In *Document & Eyewitness: An Intimate History of Rough Trade*, Johnny Marr described the genesis of the song: 'One of my favourite bands at the time was Gun Club and I had this weird piece of lateral thinking – I remembered they'd done a Creedence Clearwater Revival song, "Run Through The Jungle", and in my mind I was doing something similar, in a similar key and with a similar chord change... When it came to [recording] "How Soon Is Now" we put some red light bulbs in at the studio and got the atmosphere right, *maan*, and we created this monster through the night. I'm glad we did. It's obviously a great, great track and it is what I thought the band should be doing at that time. At that point I still felt that how far we could go was limitless...'

The second album proper arrived in February. Its very title – *Meat Is Murder* – shocked some, although the Smiths received none of the kind of censoring from Rough Trade that they received from their US record label who had declined to release a number of Smiths songs for reasons that weren't entirely apparent. The cover featured a still from Emile De Antonio's *In The Year Of The Pig* and the press release a quote from Morrissey: 'Only an army of people could confront the institutions that perpetrate animal slaughter.' A 24-date British tour to promote the album sold out within days.

The band had 'come along way since their muted, at times moribund, debut,' thought Bill Black in *Sounds*. There was a new sophistication to the sound of the band, where 'Morrissey's proselytising endeavours to take the Smiths beyond the cloisters of his own introspection'. In fact, it was an album where Morrissey, for the first time, had begun writing in the third person. Songs like 'Rusholme Ruffians' created a three-dimensional world – in its case, a world of fun fair thugs, stabbings and teenage suicides: furniture in the song had to be moved around in a way that offered less scope for the former introspection. In other instances, songs must surely have related to a past Morrissey always claimed to have forgotten or considered to be of little interest, songs such as the beastly 'The Headmaster's Ritual' (reflecting Morrissey's own real-life 'very deprived' school where 'the only activity of the teachers was whipping the pupils', as he once said). The title track, 'Meat Is Murder' began and ended with farmyard sounds and the noise of an abattoir, in a grisly reinforcing of the album's liberating message.

The album's release marked the end of a whirlwind period for the Smiths – a year and a half during which the media's fascination (in particular with Morrissey) had grown monstrous. The 'greatest pressure' the band faced at the time, Morrissey claimed, came from the press, one reason why in March, Morrissey decided to grant a round table interview (via *Melody Maker*) to a chosen panel of fanzine writers who were disarmingly frank in their questions. 'Do you think that now you are successful you've merely traded in one form of misery for another?' asked Tim Barlow from *Eat Yourself Fitter* ('I don't feel absolutely, entirely miserable,' came the response); picking up on themes of adolescence in the work of the Smiths, Dave Haslam from *Debris* wondered if Morrissey had made a myth out of it. Morrissey replied that adolescence was special, forming a person's views in later life ('we really shouldn't underestimate it'). Morrissey spoke of the violence of modern life, which included not just the threat of nuclear annihilation but also the interconnected violence of the personal ('Barbarism Begins At Home') and of the institutional, as in the case of violence towards, for instance, animals ('Meat Is Murder').

His most striking comments, however, dealt with the position adopted with regard to previous observations about the IRA's bombing of the Brighton Grand Hotel in 1984 during the Conservative Party Conference and current thoughts on Band Aid. Shortly following the IRA bombing, Morrissey had voiced 'sorrow' at the IRA's failure to assassinate Margaret Thatcher. He told Alan Jones, chairing the fanzine meeting, that he had been 'hounded from pillar to post' following his remarks: 'every time I woke up there was some journalist sitting on the end of the bed – but we won't go into that.'

Band Aid had similarly provoked his ire. Asked if he would have joined Band Aid had he been asked he replied: 'I think I would have read the letter at least 18 times and then I would have begun to think about it. If I had listened to the record beforehand, I wouldn't have done it because I think it's tuneless and I think that's really important. I mean it is one thing to want to save lives in Ethiopia, but it's another thing to inflict so much torture on the British public. It's quite easy to sit here and agree and feel very passionate about the cause. Everybody does. But what about the record? Nobody's actually mentioned that foul disgusting thing.'

Shortly following the release of *Meat Is Murder*, the first stirrings of trouble in paradise arose. There had been some concern at Rough Trade that singles were coming too thick and fast, arriving sometimes with as little as a month or two in between, and when the band delivered 'That Joke Isn't Funny Any More', Geoff Travis considered it inferior to the standard that the band had set previously. The band disagreed, and so Travis did the noble thing: having made his point, he then graciously dropped it and continued supporting the band. The single charted considerably lower than some of the band's previous releases, although the band later claimed that that was due to not enough singles being pressed and what Morrissey referred to as 'a monstrous amount of defeatism' on the part of Rough Trade. Critics were starting to tire somewhat even before the release of the single. 'Shakespeare's Sister' preceded it and in the reviews Morrissey took a pasting in some quarters. 'I've found less and less to interest me about the anorexic that fronts this band,' began a *Sounds* review by the normally equable Glyn Brown.

By the middle of 1985, the Smiths were looking to leave Rough Trade and a solicitor's letter to the record company offices contended that an agreement that the band had previously struck with the label was terminated. In July, Rough Trade sought an injunction contesting the claim. Incredibly, the band went into Jacob's Farm studio in Surrey to record *The Queen Is Dead*, the album many consider to be their masterpiece, with their relationship with the label in tatters. An injunction was finally delivered on the band on 20 December, served personally on Morrissey. By then the album had been recorded and now sat locked in limbo.

In the New Year, Johnny Marr could bear the stand-off no more, and one Friday night set off from Manchester in a blizzard with his guitar technician to rescue the tapes of the album from the studio where they languished. They arrived at the studio seven hours later and, amazingly, the door was open and so Marr just proceeded in and began to hunt for the master tapes. At that point, someone who worked at the studio arrived and said that they couldn't hand over the tapes until they had called Rough Trade. Marr lost his nerve and went away empty handed.

The issue was finally resolved eight weeks later and the album and a single ('Bigmouth Strikes Again') could finally be released. The single, released in May, was something of a disappointment, virtually a parody, according to Danny Kelly, writing in the *NME* where he imagined a competition where those taking part would send in a Morrissey lyric for the great man himself to sing. Certainly, as Adrian Thrills pointed out in the same paper a month later, the most recent four singles by the Smiths ('That Joke Isn't Funny Any More', 'Shakespeare's Sister', 'The Boy With The Thorn In His Side' and 'Bigmouth Strikes Again') paled somewhat in comparison with the band's first four singles ('Hand In Glove', 'This Charming Man', 'What Difference Does It Make' and 'Heaven Knows I'm Miserable Now').

The Queen Is Dead, however, more than delivered on its promise. From the first few opening verses of Cicely Courtneidge singing 'Take Me Back To Dear Old Blighty' from the film *The L-Shaped Room* that stormed into the thrilling rush of the title track, through to the closing trivia of 'Some Girls Are Bigger Than Others', it was clear that the Smiths had once more raised their game. 'The Queen Is Dead' was Morrissey in fine paradoxical fettle, the song both a commentary on an England he could have scarcely experienced and on the repressive England he knew all too well. Here, and elsewhere such as in the music hall-inspired song, 'Frankly, Mr Shankly', the spirit of George Formby, the Lancastrian comic actor and ukulele player, was in attendance. 'For me, one of the greatest lyricists is George Formby,' Morrissey had told Biba Kopf six months earlier. 'His more obscure songs are so hilarious, the language... so flat and Lancastrian and always focused on domestic things. Not academically funny, not witty, just morosely humorous...' There was further paradox as well in the way that Morrissey's obsession with a particular kind of English culture found extra resonance through the guitar work of Johnny Marr that journeyed increasingly towards a source of influences (rockabilly, etc) of primitive, American rock and roll.

The Smiths swore that they would never make a video, but in the autumn of 1985 allowed the *auteur* film maker and artist Derek Jarman to make a video that interpreted some of some of their songs, including 'The Queen Is Dead', the popular 'There Is A Light That Never Goes Out', both from the album, and the current single, 'Panic'. Jarman's work was artful and beautifully composed, and scarcely a sop to commercial demands since it was unlikely to be shown on such mass market television programmes as *Saturday Superstore*. In fact, Jarman's work was premiered at the Edinburgh Film Festival, no less, and toured the national cinema circuit as warm-up film for Alex Cox's *Sid and Nancy* biopic.

'Panic', with its insistent hook and 'Hang the DJ' lyric, was the release that Rough Trade bullishly hoped would restore the Smiths fortunes: not since 1984's 'William, It Was Really Nothing' had a single by the Smiths entered the national Top Twenty. Critics chewed over some previous comments of Morrissey, such as his flippant comment that 'reggae is vile' in 1984 and his more recent claim to not know what hip hop was, but such controversy was starting to look passé and the single stalled at number eleven in the charts.

There were four more singles ('Ask', 'Shoplifters Of The World', 'Sheila Take A Bow' and 'Girlfriend In A Coma') before Johnny Marr quit the Smiths in August 1987, partly exhausted, he later claimed, from the effort of trying to keep a band without a manager on the straight and narrow. A decision had been made to sign with EMI, but it was largely academic since the band had disintegrated anyway. The last studio album, *Strangeways Here We Come* – with its lush and sometimes acoustic leanings, it was, for many, the best – was released a month later.

'Looking back, they set the bar so high for the kind of music they made,' says Geoff Travis. 'They were very successful and they had a right to be very successful because if you have that much talent and you are more original and work harder than anybody else then you deserve it. In the end, of course, Morrissey's madness was the thing that capsized everything, and it's difficult to not be tainted by that when looking back, but on the other hand, they were just incredible.'

After the split, Johnny Marr did session work and helped out with the Pretenders and The The before co-forming Electronic with New Order's Bernard Sumner and releasing the highly successful 'Getting Away With It' at the end of 1989. Morrissey recorded his first solo album, *Viva Hate* in 1988, with the help of guitarist Vini Reilly and others. The album was brilliantly real-ised, the songs on the record continuing his obsession with the myths of English suburbia. As for The Smiths – the band that had created (according to the lyrics of 'Rubber Ring') 'songs that made you smile and the songs that made you cry' – they were, in the words of Morrissey, now 'buried in a shoebox in the garden'.

Felt's first single, 'Index', was released in 1979. According to a later article in *Record Collector*, Lawrence recorded the single's two tracks onto a basic tape recorder, using two five-watt practice amps and a £7 microphone from the electrical retailer Tandy. An atonal assault of detuned guitar, 'Index' was completely at odds with the increas-ingly sophisticated sounds of the new wave and consequently fell on deaf ears. The first 100 (of 500) came complete with a verse insert that set out a poetic mien that the music all but obliterates:

a noise escaped
from a guitar
a distant voice
pleaded for silence
in a disused language

According to Lawrence, Rough Trade took a hundred copies of the single and sales-wise that, more or less, was it. When, however, Lawrence had put together a band he decided to send out the remaining records for promotion. A copy arrived at the door of journalist Dave McCullough who listened to it and made the record Single of the Week in *Sounds*. In his review, McCulloch made a reference to the comedy sit-com *Fawlty Towers* and an episode where the hapless waiter Manuel bursts into the hotels's dining room with a Spanish guitar and launches dramatically into a Flamenco song. As McCullough obtusely saw it, Felt's song, like Manual's entry, was the throwing down of a gauntlet of sorts.

Cherry Red's Mike Alway read McCullough's review and was intrigued. He arrived at the very sane conclusion that by comparing the record to an episode of *Fawlty Towers*, McCullough had cleared the field for him, and that all other A&R men would instantly write the record off as a novelty. 'It was great, really,' he later wrote, 'because you could procure that record and hear the madness of that record, and see the potential in it for you, in full knowledge that no other label would touch it with a bargepole.'

Lawrence posted off a tape to Mike Alway of some of the band's more contemporary songs and Alway went to see Felt play live on a couple of occasions while he made up his mind about signing them. The performances were shambolic, but there was enough in the new material, not least in the poetic demeanour and vulnerability of Lawrence's songs and the melodic guitar work of the classical-trained co-writer Maurice Deebank, to show that an original vision was at work.

Where 'Index' favoured noise, 'Something Sends Me To Sleep', the band's next single, issued in the summer of 1981 on Cherry Red, favoured abstract. Less brash than the debut, but more confident and bold, it created through the textured guitars a template for an overall Felt sound that would serve them well into (and arguably beyond) the point when Maurice Deebank finally left the band in 1985. Lawrence's vocals are assured and punchy, each couplet of the fractured lyrics delivered with a mannered aplomb, even if the confidence is gossamer thin and underneath vulnerability lurks. The single was released at the height of popularity of the Postcard Records label, but Felt presented something more dissonant and dark than the music of the Postcard bands who, with their increasing slickness, were heading for the mainstream.

Taken as a whole, the debut album was even better. *Crumbling The Antiseptic Beauty* (another poetic title, which some thought referenced the inner city riots of 1981) was released at the start of 1982. The six tracks were, according to early champion Steve Sutherland, 'mantras that restore respectability to the long-maligned guitar solo'. The overall sound was 'lazy but damaged, dainty but somehow dangerous. Like, say, the Velvet's "Femme Fatale" or early Byrds'. The record was '1982's first – and possibly most – beautiful music'.

Lawrence, in an early airing of one of his obsessions, told *NME*'s Paul de Noyer at the time that he would have preferred the record to have been released on Elektra (home of Tim Buckley, Stooges, etc), one of his favourite record labels, a label whose art director during the 1960s, William S Harvey, he would later immortalise in song. Like some of the Elektra bands of the mid-to-late 1960s, such as Love and the Doors, Lawrence also wanted his band to commercially succeed, 'making the transition from the Velvets to the Monkees', as he saw it. Most of the band's career would be spent figuring out how to make the shift from the avant-garde to the mainstream, invariably without compromising.

Crumbling The Antiseptic Beauty established the classic, early period Felt sound – acoustic guitar laying down the rhythm, Maurice Deebank's ornate, electric guitar work taking care of the lead. The bass is mixed back and the drums are played for simple effect, with no cymbals. 'Lawrence hated cymbals,' drummer Gary Ainge recalled when interviewed for the Felt journal *Foxtrot Echo Lima Tango* (2010). 'He wanted the drums to sound like "Peggy Sue", so the first two albums were just drums with the snare off.' A full kit wouldn't be introduced until the fourth album.

On top of everything rests Lawrence's cool and mannered vocals, delivering up what could be fragments of lost diary entries or forgotten poetry stanzas; scrambled messages from the void – the 'Stories Of Lawrence', as one critic later called the Felt oeuvre, 'a mixture of enigma, arch-poetry and bits of existentialism, the kind that wears a long overcoat draped over its sensitive shoulders'. In places, the lyrics are highly personal (contrary to the more anodyne pop song lyric of the time), serving up volumes of experience in a well-delivered line or two, as on 'Something Sends Me To Sleep', where Lawrence sings, 'I've been asleep for years/ It's just that we preserve…', giving a hint at all that has been stored or bottled up to arrive at this point.

The mini visions in the songs also reflect the music and literary culture that Lawrence became immersed in. Two of his favourite albums were Television's *Marquee Moon* and Patti Smith's *Horses* – both the work of poets – and amongst his favourite authors were the Beats writer Jack Kerouac and also Charles Bukowski, a man dubbed 'the laureate of American lowlife'. Lawrence shared with Bukowski the same sort of fascination with the minutiae of life – in the case of Bukowski, it turned into prose poetry the social and economic nightmare of those downtrodden in LA: Lawrence tended to write about things more immediately in front of him, not least the travails of being in a band. His favourite books have included Kerouac's *On The Road*, Hunter S Thompson's *Fear & Loathing In Las Vegas* and Jim Carroll's *The Basketball Diaries*. He also admired the work of the literary stylist Celine and that of the lesser-known underground novelist John Fante. In 1989 he posed for a photograph holding a copy of Beat critic and novelist Herbert Gold's *The Man Who Was Not With It*, a tale of lost innocence in amongst the conmen, freaks and addicts of 1950s Florida.

The formal music, the cryptic poetry and the mannered delivery – none of it ought to have worked and yet it all worked together brilliantly. Never less so than on the single the band released in autumn 1982, 'My Face Is On Fire'. From its pounding drum opening and acoustic intro it is a tangle of perfect pop and a classic Lawrence vignette. 'Six thirty the rain is falling and the sky is a yellow balloon,' he sings. 'I was waiting for the revolution and the Mexican sundown blue.' Biblical images – references to Naomi and a burning bush – collide with the narrator's sense of his own fate ('Don't let them break you down') at the hands of 'the new generation and the makeshift haulers of time'.

'Penelope Tree', the single that followed in the middle of 1983, was even better, with its bright and glittering sound (Lawrence plays all the guitar on the A-side) begging to be crossed over into the mainstream. It was, according to Lawrence at the time, 'the best record of the year'. A picture of the 1960s model whose name inspired the song adorned the cover but, once again, Lawrence was the subject in a lyric that possibly counterpointed the glamorous (if imagined) silver spoon life of Penelope Tree and that of Lawrence where 'loneliness is like a disease'.

Felt took more imagery from the Swinging Sixties when it came to releasing the second album, *The Splendour Of Fear*: it mangled Alan Aldridge's famous poster for the theatrical release of Andy Warhol's 1966 *Chelsea Girls* film on its cover, replacing the Chelsea Hotel sign with the word Felt and the film info with the title of the band's album. But whereas *Crumbling The Antiseptic Beauty* had, vocals-wise, borrowed partly from the Velvet Underground of 1967, the vocals on *The Splendour of Fear* took a lead from the New York punk of the 1970s, and in particular the work of Tom Verlaine whose vocal rendering of the word 'felt' in Television's song 'Venus' had allegedly inspired Lawrence when looking for a name for his project.

Once again, the album comprised of six tracks (three each side) and had the usual running time of roughly thirty minutes. It opened with the epic, eight-minute instrumental, 'The Optimist & The Poet' (were they both meant to be Lawrence?) where

Lawrence creates cascading 'towers of guitars', running through a number of tumbling notes before arriving back at the point where the song started. Three other tracks were also instrumentals, with lyrics only accompanying 'The World Soft As Lace' and 'The Stagnant Pool', which caused some to see the album as a 'contemplation piece' or 'pacific' diversion from the other business (of the singles) of conquering the mainstream. A double A-side single was released off the album, featuring the cinematic guitar pickings of the instrumental, 'Mexican Bandits', and the chiming, rising and descending chords of 'The World Is As Soft As Lace' where Lawrence declares:

> If I could I would change the world
> But you know my visions they're absurd
> And all my great plans get blurred…

The Splendour of Fear was Lawrence's favourite Felt album and the one he considered to be the band's best, the one with 'a complete atmosphere, a complete mood'. Following its release there were more mainstream music interviews for Lawrence to navigate. He berated the *NME* for reading into the cascading guitar music of Felt a strain of psychedelia, telling Amrik Rai, 'We're definitely not psychedelic, I don't even know what that means'. Albums should be no longer than around thirteen minutes per side, considered Lawrence, short enough to avoid the need for filler. 'We want to make records that know instinctively that they're important, so that it is an event to buy them. We want people to be able to remember the exact day they bought one of our records, the whole day. And when they come and see us, we want them to go home crying.'

Sounds travelled up to Lawrence's hometown to visit him, where Lawrence struggled to fathom out the band's failure to find the kind of fame he sought. (A year later he would tell journalist

Chris Heath that nothing less than 'legendary famous' was what he was seeking – a global, Mickey Mouse-level of fame, rather than the 'underground' fame enjoyed by heroes such as Lou Reed or Johnny Rotten). The band that had set out to make 'weird albums and pop singles' had, claimed Lawrence done everything right, but still success eluded them. 'The only thing I can think of,' he told Robin Gibson, 'is that if we don't happen now, in *our* time, then we'll be the kind of band where suddenly a new generation of kids will pick up on us, ten years after it's all over…'

Autumn saw the release of a further 'pop single', and also another album, *The Strange Idol's Pattern & Other Stories*. 'Sunlight Bathed The Golden Glow' took a further step towards the mainstream, utilising strings and backing vocals and presenting lyrics that ran in a relatively conventional fashion (and name checked, variously, Arthur Rimbaud's prose poem *A Season In Hell* and the Egyptian *Book Of The Dead*.) It was hypnotic, 'heralding the cracking of Felt's chrysalis', according to *Melody Maker*, but the single, for all its qualities, fared no better (in fact, slightly worse) in the indie charts than the previous three.

Whilst not exactly 'weird' as such, *The Strange Idol's Pattern & Other Stories* reverted to album type, its overriding indicator, as usual, the cascading and complementing guitar parts by Maurice Deebank and Lawrence that formed a base for the cryptic and laconically delivered vocals to rest upon. The words, as ever, were impressionistic, designed to deliver an image and not meaning, as he later explained. The album revealed a new fascination, both in its cover design (which was a montage of crucifixes and pre-Columbian hieroglyphics) and in the choice of titles for the tracks ('Vasco de Gama', 'Roman Litter', 'Spanish Horse', etc). Of the ten tracks, just three were instrumentals (the wonderfully named 'Sempiternal Darkness', a Deebank contribution, 'Imprint' and 'Crucifix Heaven'). Elsewhere, the album edged towards the conventional at least in terms of the length of the songs, which, by Felt standards, were shorter. The album also benefitted from the clean and uncluttered production work of John Leckie who minimised the use of effects.

At some point in 1984, Lawrence was invited to do some demos for Blanco Y Negro, the hybrid label that had been set up the year before by Geoff Travis, Mike Alway and Michel Duval. Alas, the label declined to sign the band and so by 1985, when the band was halfway through its projected ten-year life span, Felt was no closer to the success Lawrence craved for it than had been the case in April 1980 when the group had formed. In a cruel irony, though, having been turned down by a quasi-major label, 1985 was the year when Lawrence would deliver up his most commercially successful single to date, many fan's favourite Felt song and a record that might just conceivably have crossed over into the mainstream had things turned out a little differently.

Robin Guthrie of the Cocteau Twins had long been an admirer of Felt and when the band approached him to produce an album he immediately agreed. During the recording of *Ignite The Seven Cannons & Set Sail For The Sun*, Guthrie suggested that fellow Cocteau Twin Elizabeth Fraser add some backing vocals to one of the tracks. 'Primitive Painters' was a song constructed by Deebank, with lyrics added to it by Lawrence. Lawrence found inspiration for the words in the works of primitive or naïve painters and had seen a documentary about a contemporary artist whose work had languished undiscovered until following his death, 'like Felt on the independent scene,' as Lawrence later recalled, 'battling in the darkness without acceptance.'

There is, typically, little in the actual lyric that relates to the specific subject of the song's title, save for its parting couplet where

Primitive painters are ships floating on an empty sea
Gathering in galleries were stallions of imagery

He later told *Sounds* that the song was metaphorical and that Felt represented the primitive painters of pop. In any event, no words were written for Elizabeth Fraser who simply came in and extemporized, adding a soprano glossolalia to the song that perfectly counterpointed Lawrence's deadpan delivery. Upon its release, the single, a far more baroque offering than anything previously released by Felt, quickly went to the top of the independent charts and became one of 1985's biggest selling independent releases.

In retrospect, the overall effect of the record is pleasing but slightly rupturing. Liz Fraser's sumptuous vocals undoubtedly added an element but are so melodramatic and overpowering that they threaten to emasculate the more understated sound of Felt. Releasing the song as a six-minute long 12" was Robin Guthrie's idea – Lawrence had wanted to release 'The Day The Rain Came Down', something that conformed more to his idea of the three-minute classic pop song, and, as he told Bill Prince in the *NME*, was working towards writing songs that didn't extend beyond a minute and a half, 'something only Wire have managed successfully in the last ten years'.

As a one-off collaboration, 'Primitive Painters' is a wonder, but perhaps best considered in a side context in relation to the canon of Felt. And the album remains the same. Lawrence had given Guthrie carte blanche to produce the record – 'the first time I actually let go of the reins' – and perhaps inevitably the ambience he created was not entirely dissimilar to that of a Cocteau Twins record. According to writer Ben Clancy in *Foxtrot Echo Lima Tango*, Guthrie 'buried Felt's unique sound in a gothic quagmire and lost the trademark cymbal-less drums deep in the mix. Even the sleeve looks like a terrible 4AD design.' Maurice Deebank's guitar sound – 'a golden arrow sound as elegant as the Shadows and as modern as the morning', according to writer Dave Cavanagh – was smothered in the process.

As it happened, the album marked the ending of one era and the beginning of another for Felt. Keyboard player Martin Duffy had been drafted in to play organ on the album – 'another brilliant find', as Lawrence explained to journalist Chris Heath at the time. The first 'brilliant find', of course, had been Maurice Deebank, who largely provided the melody in the Felt sound. Deebank had drifted in and out of the band on occasion, but following the release of *Ignite The Seven Cannons* left Felt for good, leaving the work of melodist to Martin Duffy whose organ sounds are all over the later period work of the band.

There was another parting of the ways, as well, as the band departed Cherry Red and signed with Creation, 'land of milk 'n' honey, of hype, myth and the best laid plans' claimed a *Melody Maker* interview with Lawrence at the time. The first fruits of the relationship appeared in May 1986 with the release of 'Ballad Of The Band'. 'It's sort of like the ballad of Felt,' Lawrence told Chris Heath at the time, 'because there's lots of stuff in there relating to when it was written, which was a pretty down time.' In praising the release to the skies, Carol Clerk summed up its essence perfectly when she commented: 'I like to imagine that if a young Bob Dylan had written "New Morning" in 1986, it might have come out sounding like this.'

In the song itself, Lawrence returned to his favourite subject – the failures of the band – and also added a lyrical dig about the departed Maurice Deebank who, in his opinion, hadn't quite had the mettle to see things out:

Where were you when I wanted to work?
You were still in bed, you're a total jerk

Lawrence reserves, of course as much criticism for himself as for Deebank when he sings, 'It's all my fault/ Yes I'm to blame/ Ain't got no money/ Ain't got no fame…'

In keeping with the 'weird'/ 'pop' modus, 'The Ballad of The Band' – the most conventionally structured single the group had released – was followed by a sixteen minute instrumental album, *Let The Snakes Crinkle Their Heads To Death*, the 'sort of thing you'd hear at a New York ice rink', according to one critic. Six of the ten tracks on the album fitted Lawrence's new ideal, running to barely more (and in some cases less) than a minute and a half in length, but sorely lacking in the expected melodic hooks or any kind of compensating texture, the album was like a diversion from the new route the band was taking with the organ-drenched 'Ballad Of The Band'. Typically, shortly after the album's release, Lawrence considered it 'the best album we've ever made' describing it as the sort of record that would be 'played at midnight by someone on their own in a darkened room'.

Maurice Deebank's departure freed up Lawrence: with the melody tethered instead to Martin Duffy's organ sound the songs are more emotionally expressive and sound less like static academic exercises. The record sleeve image to 'Ballad Of The Band', with a side-on shot of Lawrence in a straw hat, clearly pays homage to the cover of Bob Dylan's *Desire* and the same kind of rolling, episodic, free form approach infected the new songs Lawrence was writing. The lyrics became less obtuse, less fragmented and more revealing than had previously been the case, mini fables that were later 'coloured in by the band'.

Everything became thrillingly apparent on *Forever Breathes The Lonely Word*, the second-phase Felt masterpiece and the record where, for once, the 'weird' and the 'pop' happily collided. This was the epic myth territory of earlier Felt – previously best enunciated by the atmospheric, widescreen, Morricone-esque effects of Maurice Deebank's playing – put to word. Indeed, on *Forever Breathes The Lonely Word*, for the first time on a Felt album, there were *no* instrumentals. Something else had happened as well, as *NME*'s Mark Sinker pointed out in reviewing the record: 'Lawrence, who's been scrunching down a whole bunch of ancient voices into his own for a *long time* now, Reed & Dylan & Verlaine & Peter Perrett, you know the list, well, he's added himself to them this time'.

It is clear from the opening track, 'Rain Of Crystal Spires', that we are in territory of the lyrically epic, as Lawrence sings:

Seven brothers on their way from Avalon
Seven sisters shooting skyways for the sun
And Homer's *Illiad* lay burning in the fire….

The near biblical images could have dropped straight out of a Cormac McCarthy novel such as *Blood Meridian*, and the mystery and broody tension is ratcheted up by the rolling thunder sound of Martin Duffy's keyboard as it weaves in and out of the chiming guitar work of Lawrence (who plays all the guitars on the album). According to Gary Ainge, the band had been listening to *Tim Hardin 1* and *Tim Hardin 2*, where the drums are mixed very low, before recording the album. Consequently, 'on *Forever Breathes The Lonely Word* we went for a natural, quieter sound, and I mixed it up with brushes'.

The 'hero' is once more the subject in 'Grey Streets' where Lawrence returns to his signature themes of self-doubt, anguish and fame. The hero (a pop star?) is on a poster on a bedroom wall and in pictures and the song imagines him addressing a fan. Lawrence almost certainly sees himself in both these guises, as the hero responds to the unspoken criticisms that have shredded the vital connection between the adoring and the adored. 'You were so negative because once I owned the world but I gave it away,' he sings. Heroes are there ultimately to disappoint. Lawrence had met his own hero in December 1985 when Television's Tom Verlaine had stopped backstage at a London Felt gig. 'Lawrence shook Tom Verlaine's hand,' recalls Phil King, bassist with the Servants (and later Felt), 'and then asked if he could shake it again.' A decade or so later, the scales had fallen from Lawrence's eyes: 'He [ie Verlaine] blew it, didn't he?' he told Alastair Fitchett for a proposed *Plan B* magazine interview in 2005. 'I mean I wish I'd had that many chances… I'd love to know why he lost the muse.'

One of the best songs on *Forever Breathes The Lonely Word* – and a major work in the Felt songbook – is 'All The People I Like Are Those That Are Dead'. 'Maybe I should entertain/ the very fact that I'm insane,' sings Lawrence as the track gently opens with a glittering melodic guitar run before the drums, bass, organ and acoustic guitars kick in. There are no gods and no martyrs, only myths, and where myth and real life collide, myth will always win out, at least in Lawrence's world. The most revealing line occurs in the middle, when Lawrence confesses that 'it's better to be lost than to be found'.

In the interviews conducted around the release of the record, Lawrence returned to his favourite theme of fame. He had a strong feeling, he told Paul Mathur in *Melody Maker* in October 1986, that when he was 30 (he was 25 at the time) it was 'all going to start happening for me and I'm going to be really famous'. Danny Kelly, writing in the *NME*, considered that the new album *deserved* to make Lawrence famous – 'it advances Felt to the very threshold of the door marked Restricted Area: Pop Stars Only' – while the same interview saw, once again, Lawrence displaying his finely honed sense of the various gradations of fame: 'he worries constantly about how his every move will look in the book that'll one day be written about his band – "only it's not the Felt story; it's the Felt *legend*…".'

Like much of Lawrence's output, *Forever Breathes The Lonely Word* can be enjoyed for the great album that it is or as the aural equivalent of a psychiatrist's couch. But there are plenty of straightforward rock and roll moments – for instance, the wistful tale of unrequited love of 'September Lady' or the giddy rush of 'Gather Up Your Wings And Fly' where Lawrence sings, 'I was heading north on a plane that was heading south/ Whisky in my pocket, cigarette was in my mouth', a song that tears off like a motorbike in *Easy Rider*, haring across a desert road.

According to Alan McGee, writing in the *Guardian* in 2007, *Forever Breathes The Lonely Word* was 'pop perfection, a breathless rush of sensitivity and intelligence' but also a record that was 'too understated to be commercial, too art to go pop, too pop to go art'. Lawrence had been right when stating in 1986, 'We are timeless, we follow in a tradition of brilliant bands. In ten years' time people will reel us off as one of the greats.'

It was the first substantial Creation album release and for some the best independent album of the year. Where other indie albums of that year were polished and transparent, *Forever Breathes The Lonely Word* was concealing. Its splendour was all too apparent, but its mystery never fully gave itself up. At its centre was Lawrence, the ultimate enigma. Would the record have been more commercially successful if it had been released a year later when Creation was more developed and bands like the House Of Love were about to break into the mainstream charts? Perhaps Lawrence all along really did want to remain 'lost' – that was certainly the impression of some of the major label A&R men who turned up at Bay 63 in May 1986 for a showcase Felt gig only to witness a tripping Lawrence – he'd taken acid earlier in the day to 'loosen up' for the important event – disintegrating before their eyes.

Ultimately, Alan McGee's finagling with the majors would see releases by Primal Scream and the Weather Prophets funded through WEA while Felt was again passed over. Felt released a clutch of further singles and four more albums before the final one, *Me & A Monkey On The Moon*, was released in 1989 on él records, a subsidiary of Cherry Red. The release was very carefully choreographed, dressed up as the predetermined finale in a project always intended to last ten albums, ten singles and ten years. The last gig took place (appropriately enough) at Burberries in Birmingham on 19 December 1989 and Maurice Deebank turned up to give support.

From that moment on the legend of Felt was unshackled from its corporeal state and left to run free. Where previously people obsessed over the music of Felt, they began obsessing over its creator. Glossy art books, scholarly journals, endless newspaper profiles probing the man's enigma and, in 2011 a film, *Lawrence of Belgravia*, have all appeared. There have been constant whispers about biographies being prepared. One of the earliest – an 'official' book about Felt that Kevin Pearce set to work on in the early 1990s – came to nothing (perhaps fatefully so, given that part of the plan involved 'keeping the mystery caged').

Maybe fame and fortune would have answered all Lawrence's prayers, or would he, like Morrissey, have ultimately found the whole thing unbearable and shifted his neuroses elsewhere? Lawrence would be the last to agree, but sometime heroic failure is better than miserable success.

CHAPTER 19

MILLION TEARS

THERE WAS ME, THAT IS ALEX...AND MY THREE DROOGS, PETE, GEORGIE AND DIM...
AND WE SAT IN THE KOROVA MILKBAR TRYING TO MAKE UP OUR RASSOODOCKS WHAT TO
DO WITH THE EVENING....THE KOROVA MILKBAR SOLD MILK_PLUS............
MILK-PLUS VELOCET OR SYNTHEMESC OR DRENCROM..WHICH IS WHAT WE WERE DRINKING.
THIS WOULD SHARPEN YOU UP AND MAKE YOU READY FOR A BIT OF THE OLD MUSIC
DOWN AT THE UNDERGROUND CLUB...... THE UNDERGROUND CLUB..THE UNDERGROUND
CLUB.....THE UNDERGROUND CLUB....

D.J. PETE FOX.

4AD RECORDS PRESENTS..
OCTOBER...
Thur 31. XYMOX...THE WOLFGANG PRESS..DIS JUZ..£2.50.

NOVEMBER ....the dexter brothers..£2.50. ....£3.00..
Sun. 3. BUDDY CURTIS & THE GRASSHOPPERS.
WED 6. KING KURT..plus support....
Thur 7. THE CARDIACS..flowers in the dustbin..£2.50
Sun 10. SONIC YOUTH..the membranes....£2.50..
Wed 13. CHIEFS OF RELIEF..brigandige...£2.50.
THUR 14. TWENTY FLIGHT ROCKERS...max...£2.50.
Sun 17. DOCTOR & THE MEDICS.. support..£3.00 advance..£3.50 on night.
Wed 20. CREATION RECORDS PRESENTS..
MEATWHIPLASH..WEATHER PROFFITS..PRIMAL SCREAM..£2.50..
Thur 21. THE CHERRY BOMBZ..the feathers..£2.50..
Sun 24. DEEP SEA DIVERS..support..£2.50.
Wed 27. ALIEN SEX FIEND..plus support..£3.00.
DECEMBER
Wed 18. NICO & THE FACTION PLUS INTO A CIRCLE featuring
BEE AND BARRY..Ex GETTING THE FEAR..£3.00 advance
£3.50 on the night.....

UNDERGROUND CLUB
21 HIGH ST CROYDON
SURREY....
TEL:01 760 0087

ADVANCE TICKETS FROM RUTH IN THE
BOX OFFICE AND H&R CLOAKE
RECORD STORE

OPEN SUN 7pm to 11pm
TUE-SAT 9pm to 2am

ARTWORK BY THE SAUCERMAN..
SUCH A WONDERFUL ALIEN..

FEVER SURROUNDING THE JESUS & MARY Chain subsided in the early summer of 1985 as the band withdrew from public view to concentrate on the making of *Psychocandy*. The Reid brothers were living in Fulham at the time, and each day caught a cab across London to John Loder's studio in Wood Green. Recording generally took place during the civilised hours of daytime and the band forbade themselves any stimulants such as alcohol, although a small amount of speed was taken to help keep the focus at those times when exhaustion might have otherwise crept in. A typical day, according to *Barbed Wire Kisses*, would begin with a fry up in the local Wimpy bar and end post-dinner at around 9PM, at which point the band would go home. In the period between, William Reid would keep a fastidious eye on every aspect of the production: he had a very clear idea of what kind of sound he wanted and nothing was left to chance.

'My part in "Psychocandy",' recalls Geoff Travis, 'was getting the band together with John Loder at Southern Studios. John set everything up for them and then just let them get on with it on their own. That was a huge freedom. And when they needed help, John was next door in the house and they could just call him in. John had been involved with Crass and had the same independent spirit, as did the Jesus & Mary Chain, and would give them the space to make the great record that they were capable of making.'

After Bobby Gillespie had joined, the Jesus & Mary Chain had taken on a whole new complexion, most obviously in the visual shape of the band with Bobby doing his Mo Tucker bit and drumming standing up. Gillespie had managed to juggle being in his own band, Primal Scream, with his duties for the Reid Brothers. But as the Jesus & Mary Chain progressed, it became obvious that the Jesus & Mary Chain were going to need someone who was a fulltime drummer. Gillespie appears on *Psychocandy* but in spring 1986 left the group to concentrate on his own band.

Primal Scream origins go back to a local scout hut where Bobby Gillespie and his school friend Jim Beattie would pretend to be in a band, Bobby Gillespie making a noise with dustbin lids and Jim Beattie messing around with a guitar and a fuzz pedal. When they started, in 1982, they were influenced by the sounds of PIL, taking a lead also from the kind of bass lines that Peter Hook was weaving into the songs of New Order. The first gig the band played took place at the Bungalow Bar in Paisley, supporting the Laughing Apple. 'That wasn't a real gig, it was a joke,' Bobby later recalled. 'There wasn't any shape to it.'

While Primal Scream rumbled on, Bobby Gillespie also helped out Glasgow band the Wake, eventually going on to play bass with them for a short period. At the start of 1983, when the band were signed to Factory and released the album *Harmony*, Gillespie played not just bass but occasional guitar and keyboards and even wrote the lyrics for one song, 'The Old Men'. He played on the band's next single, 'Something Outside' and also during the band's first John Peel session that was aired in July 1983. He was in a band photograph when the Wake gave a lengthy interview to *Sounds* in January that same year where he commented on the lamentable state of mainstream radio.

In October 1983, Alan McGee invited Gillespie and Beattie down to London to appear at the Living Room, where Primal Scream made their London debut playing as a two-piece but assisted by a drum machine. By now, Bobby Gillespie had quit the Wake and along with Beattie had given up on his ambitions to create the kind of post-rock noise that PIL made and was developing an interest in the more jangly, 12-string guitar sounds of mid-1960s US folk rock. They did, however, leave a short audio legacy of their former sound in the shape of three tracks on a couple of cassette releases. As early as 1982 they had recorded a track called 'Thought' for the cassette release *An Hour Of Eloquent Sounds*, a compilation masterminded by Robert

King of the Scars. 'Thought' reflected the kind of industrial/ post-rock sound that Primal Scream were aiming for at the time (the sound that Bobby later said bequeathed them their name). They gave tracks to a further cassette (also compiled by Robert King) issued in early 1984 called *State Of Affairs*. That cassette bundled together a ragbag of artists that included the Passage, the Cocteau Twins, the Three Johns, Virginia Astley and Modern English and contained a brief introduction and longer end piece by Primal Scream. As John Reed noted in a detailed 1994 history of the band in *Record Collector*, the work of the other groups contributing was 'sandwiched between a short, monotonous, industrial-sounding dirge simply entitled "Intro" and a lengthy, PIL/ Throbbing Gristle experimental piece, "Circumcision", which ends with some Eastern-style yelling.'

At the start of 1984, when the Creation label was being formally launched, Primal Scream had withdrawn their proposed single, 'The Orchard', from the list of records scheduled for release. The track had been recorded with violinist Judith Boyle, who sang on the track, Gillespie suffering at the time of recording from a head cold and unwilling to commit a vocal. Gillespie later said that he didn't even know, at that time, that he *would* be Primal Scream's singer. The specific problem created was that 'The Orchard', a song *about* a girl, might have sounded odd, upon release, having a girl sing it (although the accepted precedent of such transgender interpretations extended long back, to, for instance, Ringo Starr's raucous delivery of the Shirelles' song 'Boys' on the first Beatles album, a work that in one admittedly loose sense kickstarted the whole matter of what this book is about.

In order to achieve the sound that they wanted, Gillespie and Beattie set about expanding the band, drafting it Robert Young on bass, formerly of Black Tuesday, and a drummer, Tom McGurk. They created and circulated a four-track demo containing the songs 'Crystal Crescent', 'Leaves', 'It Happens' and 'We Go Down Slowly', all classic early period Primal Scream songs carried on the winsome fragility of Bobby Gillespie's voice. The new line-up played their first 'official' gig at the Venue in Glasgow in October when the band supported the Jesus & Mary Chain: that was also the first time Gillespie played drums with the East Kilbride band.

The period between the release of the Jesus & Mary Chain's 'Upside Down' single in November 1984 and the end of spring when the Jesus & Mary Chain began recording *Psychocandy* was a busy one for Gillespie, but he still managed to get Primal Scream into the studio to record what would eventually be his group's first single. 'All Fall Down' was released in June and received a mixed reception. Some were thrown by the gentle sound, something in absolute contradiction to the name of the band which conjured up images of therapeutic howling. Jane Simon was particularly sniffy in *Sounds*, accusing Primal Scream of being 'about as primal as a chocolate pudding' and an example of 'the bottomless quagmire of waterlogged wimps where Creation Records go fishing whenever they feel the urge to sign a new band coming on'. Meanwhile, Mat Snow in the *NME* thought the problem with the song to be that it had 'everything but the sweetly unforgettable tune Primal Scream are so valiantly struggling for'. Perhaps the most prescient comment came from Drew Black in *Melody Maker* who commented that 'Primal Scream are a Sixties group with an Eighties accent but they will probably be the first indie CD band.' As it happened, the band filled their sound out further when two more were brought in to the line-up – guitarist Paul Harte and percussionist Martin 'Joogs' St. John (John Martin).

'It Happens', the B-side of the band's first release was arguably the superior track, a dry run for the kind of perfection they would strive to achieve with 'Velocity Girl', which was itself the B-side of the band's second single, 'Crystal Crescent'. 'It Happens' runs up and down the melodic register in a pleasing way even if, overall, the tune is slight and the lyrics hardly challenging (with plenty of *sha-la-la-la-la*). Both B-sides on the first two singles sound like a blueprint for something as yet, unrealised – the kind of sound that future indie would harness and develop in the next three or so years.

In Primal Scream's first mainstream music press interview, with *NME* in summer 1985, the band had complained about lack of funds holding them back in their quest for the 'classic' record. Creation pushed £3,500 their way to record 'Crystal Crescent' and this time the band produced the record. ('All Fall Down' had been a co-production with Joe Foster). They, and others, once again complained about the sound, David Swift in the *NME* moaning about 'the twiddled mix down' of the lead track and its 'tacked on horns section'. 'It's ironic, we love pop music so much,' said Bobby Gillespie at the time, 'but we can't even get the record right…'

The band had been asked to contribute to the *NME* cassette *C86* and they offered the B-side to 'Crystal Crescent', 'Velocity Girl'. The track was talked about even prior to the release of the cassette, but *C86* turned it into something that came to both define a moment and stand apart from it as the kind of 'classic' song the band aspired to. '"Velocity Girl" gave me that hit – indefinable but unmistakeable – of which only very few pieces of music are each year capable,' wrote Danny Kelly a short while after its release. 'It was proof that in all their care and craft and calculation, Primal Scream left room for that chemical thrill/ rush sought but seldom attained in 30 years of pop.'

Not content to be fronting his own band and playing in the Jesus & Mary Chain, in 1985 Bobby Gillespie also became involved with setting up a new club, helping stage a series of Splash One 'happenings' at a run-down disco club called Daddy Warbucks in the centre of Glasgow. Splash One took the novel approach of flyposting and distributing leaflets to announce its presence and from the opening night began drawing in crowds that were always in excess of 100 and often crept up towards its capacity of 450. Splash One launched with an admirable manifesto: 'INSTEAD OF NOTHING MUCH HAPPEN-ING, WHY NOT TRY A SPLASH ONE HAPPENING, RUN ONCE A MONTH ON SUNDAY EVENINGS BY EIGHT PEOPLE WE SHALL PERCEIVE AS THE GUARDIANS OF THE PSYCHEDELIC PUNK ROCK REALISM? YOU WILL BE EXPOSED TO NEAR-FATAL DOSES OF OBSCURISM AND SELF-INDULGENCE. IT WILL LAST UNTIL WE LOSE INTEREST. WE ARE ANONYMOUS. WE ARE NOT MERCENARY, NOT POLITE, BUT HONEST, ANOTHER MUSIC IN A DIFFERENT SETTING'.

Bands that played the venue included Gillespie's own band as well as the Loft, Felt, Wire, the Pastels and Sonic Youth (who, for the lucky few who where present pre-show, sound checked with 'Death Valley 69', a song they rarely played live at the time). The club took its name from a song by the Thirteenth Floor Elevators and the music, perhaps unusually, was taped onto cassettes (as opposed to being DJ'd) before being played over the PA system. It offered a mixture of (mainly) old sounds interwoven with some more recent, favoured material. On 18 May 1985, the night that Sonic Youth played, for instance, the tapes included tracks by the Seeds, Love, the Doors, Thirteenth Floor Elevators and the Velvet Underground, but also by the Shop Assistants, the Wedding Present, the Birthday Party, Wire, the Saints and the Jesus & Mary Chain.

As the Splash One tapes show, those organising the events were first and foremost fans. The same was true for Bobby Gilles-pie whose encyclopaedic knowledge of the records of key pop moments travelled from the mid-1960s through to post-punk and beyond. But it was one thing being aware of and admiring, say, the Standells' 'Dirty Water', or the Seeds' 'Pushin' Too Hard', or 'Train From Kansas City' by the Shrangri-Las, and another being able to live up to the standards set by such heroes, or at least so a number of Primal Scream's critics thought. 'Gillespie looks like he's spent his whole life indoors, listening to records in perpetual twilight,' noted Simon Reynolds in *Melody Maker* in 1987. In a theme he would return to in his later writings, Reynold's noted the 'epigonic' (or imitative) nature of the contemporary indie scene (citing Primal Scream, the Jesus & Mary Chain and the Smiths as being amongst the guilty palimpsests): 'once upon a time pop used to be a commentary on adolescent experience. Now pop is that experience… The dominant mood in Brit-pop is a nostalgia for something you never had.'

Not everyone agreed with this view – certainly Primal Scream rebutted the 'revivalist' tag at every opportunity. The fanzine community, in contrast, wasted little energy on such theories, picking up instead on the sheer thrill of the noise. The seemingly disparate nature between some of the more muscular music that Primal Scream admired and the ethereal nature of Bobbie Gillespie's stage presence was similarly of no concern. In fact, 'The contradictions make it more fun,' claimed issue 4 of *Adventure In Bereznik*. 'Sure, they play (100%) pop music…. But scratch the surface, remove a petal or two, and inside is punk rock chaos.'

Like a number who had gone before, Primal Scream was amongst those new indie bands that paid particular attention to sartorial detail when it came reimagining or interpreting the past. Gillespie stood on stage, clinging on to his microphone stand, wearing leather trousers and Chelsea boots – the personification of cool – his fringe playfully flopping about, the visual effect further enhancing the band's 'overdeveloped sense of pop's past'. The sense of cool the wearing of such outfits created was largely deemed to be timeless by those donning them – as Pete Astor of the Weather Prophets claimed when the subject came up in an interview in October, 1985: 'To me, it's like a perennial fashion. They [leather trousers] are not hip. Possibly they will become hip… It was fashionable in 1968, and that refers back to a whole line of things. That says to me, the Weather Prophets are not about 1985 *now*, things that are *only* hip now. I am saying I will remain true to things that go back a long way. There's a certain timelessness…' The contrary view (or perhaps it was the same view) was voiced by Jane Simon in *Sounds*, who argued that leather trousers were a state of mind. 'You can't put them *on*. You either *are* leather trousers or you're not.'

In 1987, both the Weather Prophets and Primal Scream were signed to Alan McGee's WEA-subsidised label, Elevation. Two Primal Scream singles were released in quick succession ('Imperial', 'Gentle Tuesday') and the band went to Rockfield Studios in Wales to record their debut album, *Sonic Flower Groove*. As had been the case before, things were nearly but not quite right. The album took six weeks to make at a cost of £40,000 and was then scrapped. By the time what little of it was later salvaged, the cost had soared to £100,000 and the band had replaced original producer Stephen Street with Mayo Thompson. During the recording process, the mood had become fraught, Bobby Gillespie and the producer at one point arguing for two hours about the merits (or otherwise) of a solitary cymbal crash on a backing track.

The singles were amongst the few fully realised tracks but elsewhere the 'classic' sound that the band was aiming for eluded them. As a consolidation of early period Primal Scream, *Sonic Flower Groove* succeeded brilliantly in theoretical terms while falling far short practically. 'The sound we tried and failed to get,' says Alan McGee, 'is the sound that a few years later the Stone Roses achieved.' Bobby Gillespie probably nailed it best when he later told *NME* that *Sonic Flower Groove* consisted of 'great songs that didn't translate into great records'. According to Roy Wilkinson in *Sounds*, it 'flounders in a kind of stylistic netherworld'. Jonh Wilde went further in *Melody Maker*, calling the album 'terribly thin entertainment' sounding like 'Sooty plays the Byrds Song-book ... blind drunk on cough syrup'.

In the end, pressure got to them. Jim Beattie retreated back to Glasgow (and formed Spirea X – named after a Primal Scream track – with Judith Boyle) and Robert Young moved across from bass to guitar. The original 12-string sound was replaced by some-thing earthier, as was illustrated on 1989's *Primal Scream* album. Referring to the earlier version of the band, Bobby Gillespie later told Michael Bonner at *Uncut*: 'There was something missing, musically or in attitude. We wanted to make *Forever Changes*, right? That was our ambition. And, of course, we never did, so we felt disappointed...'

As it turned out, Primal Scream *did* get to make their 'classic' album with 1991's *Screamadelica*, an album that for some tore up the rulebook and set those critics seeking to categorise it an impossible task. Chiming with the hedonism of the time, and anticipating the emerging Lad culture, the record blended together elements of Dub, House, Gospel, Ambient and Rock and sampled widely – from Peter Fonda in *Easy Rider* to politician Jesse Jackson's speech at the Wattstax concert in 1972. A quarter of a century on from its release, some of the record's effects and ideas inevitably sound a little more conventional than they did at the time when critics saw it as a bewildering hybrid of past, present and future. The future always borrows from the past, and *Screamadelica*, at least according to *Melody Maker*, was 'plundering the *spirit* of the past rather than its fabric to create the most revolutionary music in ages'.

Coming through the other side of the maelstrom that was the Jesus & Mary Chain, McGee switched his focus to the label, releasing a clutch of singles through the summer of 1985. One of the bands signed was the Bodines who, at the end of 1984 had sent Kevin Pearce at *Hungry Beat* a demo. Pearce passed the demo to Alan McGee along with a note saying that McGee needed to hear it. McGee listened, decided he liked what he heard and rang up the band on New Year's Eve to offer them a deal with Creation and also some gigs in London.

The band borrowed their name from a character in the American TV sitcom, the *Beverley Hillbillies*: they had been asked to play at the Hacienda after Spear of Destiny dropped out (making the Bodines, allegedly, the youngest band to ever play there) and wanted to send out a demo, both things requiring that they come up with a moniker. They went through a number of drummers before settling on a line-up that consisted of Michael Ryan on vocals/ guitar, Paul Brotherton on guitar, Tim Burwood on bass, and John Rowland on drums. Eventually, they also found a sound. The twin guitar assault of Michael Ryan and Paul Brotherton was the platform upon which Ryan's confident vocals rested. Ryan's self-assuredness and floppy fringe inevitably drew comparisons with Echo & the Bunnymen, but there was something of the more fragile grandeur of the Wild Swans about the band as well.

McGee was as good as his word and the Bodines made their central London debut in February at the tiny Three Johns pub in Islington where the Jesus & Mary Chain had famously appeared. The performance earned a write up the *NME* where it was considered that they performed like 'old masters'. The paper went on to compare their sound to that of the second wave Merseybeat bands of the late 1970s. Like those bands, the music the Bodines played was clean and sharp-cut – it had all the swagger of early Echo & The Bunnymen, but with something more contemporary added, the similar kind of drive and power presented by another beat group, the Mighty Lemon Drops. They were visually imposing and had a strong, no-nonsense attitude.

When the debut single, 'God Bless', was released in September, it didn't quite deliver on the promise of the band's live performances. The band had already rejected one version of the recording before settling on the final edit that blandly buried everything acerbic and highlighted the inadequacies of the song itself. 'I didn't even want "God Bless" to be a single,' Michael Ryan told Dave Haslam at *Debris*. 'It's a good live song but I don't think the melody is good enough for a single. [T]he first recording of it… was dreadful. They released a re-mix. They'd promised us good equipment in the studio and instead they just gave us the Jasmine Minks practising stuff which kept breaking down.'

Far more thrilling and representative was 'Therese', the follow-up single that appeared on *C86* and was released in March 1986. Ian Broudie's production shone, bringing out the power of the twin guitar assault and Michael Ryan's vocals with crystal clarity. Michael Ryan was a reluctant lyricist and often used to write down lyrical snippets and pieces of information and pull them out of a drawer as and when required in an almost cut-up way. The line in 'Therese', *It scares the health out of me*, comes from an old British film. Adrian Thrills in the *NME* called it 'a *rush* of a record, better by far than anything hyped in the real charts', a single that 'crushed magnificently any lingering notion of a "ghetto mentality" in the ranks of the oft-maligned but still vital independent upsurge'.

Adrian Thrills' comments alluded to the growing belief that independent music could meaningfully cross over into the mainstream (as happened a year or two later). The success of the Jesus & Mary Chain had cleared away some misconceptions (not least in the minds of the major labels) and shown that a move up the commercial ladder was possible, especially if the band concerned came armed with the appropriate audience, as had been the case with the the Jesus & Mary Chain. It wasn't just the bands on Creation looking for a leg-up, it was the label itself – by the end of 1985, McGee's thought horizon included a hybrid label funded by major record label money.

The Bodines released one further single ('Heard It All') before making their own major label move. 'Creation were looking to go major themselves, and were taking the Weather Prophets, Primal

Scream and initially us to a new label called Elevation,' Michael Ryan told Anthony Strutt at Penny Black website in 2014. 'But things had gone a bit sour between us, and we went with the label that offered us more money to record and promote. Frankly the Elevation deal was a bit shit.'

The Bodines did a deal with Magnet who issued a revamped version of 'Therese' in 1987 along with the further singles, 'Skankin' Queen' and 'Slip Slide', and the Ian Broudie-produced album, *Played*. The records remained faithful to the core sound of the band but failed to give them (and more importantly, Magnet) the break through they were looking for. *Played* faltered in low 90s in the national chart and the singles failed to chart at all. But it was the right move and years later Michael Ryan had no regrets: 'We recorded at Amazon in Liverpool with Ian and had a brilliant time,' he recalled. 'We remixed at Air on Tottenham Court Road and lived in the Columbia Hotel, money in our pockets, aged twenty-one, best friends making our first record and liking what we were hearing.'

The bountifulness of the Magnet deal alas came back to haunt them and the band ended up broke and touring Germany on one pound a day to pay down an Inland Revenue bill. Magnet got sold to Warner Brothers and the Bodines were dropped. They split up, since 'some members felt the whole signing back on thing beneath them and moved on to adult life'. A reconfigured version of the band reappeared briefly in 1989, releasing material on the Play Hard label, before Michael Ryan moved on, forming Medalark Eleven in 1991 and returning to Creation for a couple of well-received singles and the appropriately-titled album, *Shaped Up, Shipped Out*.

By the middle of 1985 the Jesus & Mary Chain's status (or notoriety) was rising and a concern within the Creation camp was that others might step in and exploit the situation, fatally diluting the market with imitation bands mimicking the Jesus & Mary Chain sound. With *Psychocandy* imminent, Creation came up with the ingenious idea that if any of the waters were to be muddied then Creation itself ought to be responsible.

Both Meat Whiplash's 'Don't Slip Up' and Slaughter's 'I'll Follow You Down' were part ersatz recreation of the sound the Jesus & Mary Chain pioneered, yet each was a valid work in its own right. Slaughter Joe was the deliberately-sleazy persona of Creation in-house producer Joe Foster and 'I'll Follow You Down' gave him the opportunity to underline his contribution to the Jesus & Mary Chain sound. If anything, 'I'll Follow You Down' eclipsed its inspiration – 'The first English produced piece of music I've enjoyed for a long time' was Edwin Pouncey's view, narrowly failing to make it Single of the Week in *Sounds* (soley on the grounds that to do so would swell further Joe Foster's already swollen ego). It was 'Dr Feelgood meets the Marquis de Sade, only better'. Praising it in *Jamming!*, Jonh Wilde called it 'beserk', 'a record that sounds like its done (or is doing) too much amphetamine for its own good'. Robin Gibson, also in *Sounds*, called it a 'truly great record – intelligent, belligerent and filthy raw'.

Many picked up on the Stooges feel of the single, but, as Foster pointed out, his interest in music was polymathic and not just restricted to the garage band music of the 1960s and the punk and post-punk era of indie. 'I'm a dead serious musician when I'm not involved in pop music,' he ironically told Mat Snow in the *NME*. 'The use of drones is an intonational system to build up tones, the use of feedback the same way, so that there appears to be a hell of a lot of things happening all at the same time.'

Foster claimed that triviality was the essence of rock and roll: 'As trivial as whether you've got a good jacket or not. As trivial as whether you've got a pair of leather trousers... Good haircut, good sunglasses, right sort of shoes, colour of guitar: these things are almost as important as the music in rock 'n' roll.'

The same week in September that Slaughter Joe was being interviewed by *Sounds*, Meat Whiplash's single, 'Don't Slip Up' was picking up a Single of the Week gong in the same paper. The band had been in existence since October 1984 and consisted of Paul McDermott on vocals, Stepehen McLean on guitars, Edward Connelly on bass and Michael Kerr on drums. They'd acquired a band name name after flicking through some old records by the Fire Engines. Like the Jesus & Mary Chain, Meat Whiplash grew up in East Kilbride and they had convinced the Reid brothers to produce their first single. The Jesus & Mary Chain had invited them to be on the bill on the night of the infamous North London Polytechnic gig in March 1985 when they'd first come to the attention of Alan McGee. (McGee had been irresistibly drawn to the idea of them, he later said, having been told that that they were 'the first band that actually sound like a bootleg live'.) Due to the shenanigans of the night, Meat Whiplash had barely played a note before they were canned off stage, but nonetheless McGee, typically, there and then offered a one-off deal for a single.

With its mesh of insistent guitars split perfectly by a solo bass break, 'Don't Slip Up' took more than leaf out of the hard/ soft Jesus & Mary Chain guide to making pop. But it was all their work, even if, as drummer Michael Kerr later revealed, the Reid brothers mainly 'were impressed by how bad we were'. Some *did* question who actually played on the record and others, tempting fate, wrote them off as a one-hit indie wonder. As it happens, only one single was released during the band's lifetime: a second, 'Losing Your Grip', was recorded but never released. Opening with one long distorted note over which acoustic guitar is gently laid, before a fuzz of electric guitar washes through everything, the song almost but not quite lives up to the majesty of 'Don't Slip Up', although it would be thirty years before the three tracks on the single finally saw a formal release on the *Creation Artifact* box set of 2015.

Of an undeniably more substantial nature was the debut album by the Jesus & Mary Chain, the most eagerly-awaited record of the year, bar none. The burning issue of the moment appeared to be how much feedback they (or rather their record label) would allow on to the vinyl. The singles following 'Upside Down' had given the hint as to what direction they were travelling in sonically and the latest release, 'Just Like Honey', showed them capable of motoring at more than one speed. But the album, when it arrived, was still a shock, simply because many critics were caught short by just how brilliantly accomplished it was.

Although released on a major record label, it clearly represented some sort of pinnacle for indie. The critics fought themselves in print to see who could heap the most praise upon it. 'There's no way to describe this without sounding ridiculous,' began Chris Heath in his review in *Jamming!* 'It's that good…' In *Sounds*, Jack Barron called it an 'immaculate conception of love songs, and one of the finest debut albums *ever*', noting the deliberate juxtaposition of *psycho* and *candy* in the record's title and its oxymoronic effect. Andy Gill in the *NME* – a paper that granted the release the hallowed status of a full-page review – called it 'a great citadel of beauty whose wall of noise, once scaled, offers access to endless vistas of melody and emotion'. Likening its effect to that of hearing a Velvet Underground record produced by Phil Spector, he favourably contrasted its emotions with the 'sanitised, sickly-sweet confections from groups like Wham!, Culture Club and Spandau Ballet' and noted how the 'whole fits together, how it offers up itself as salvation for rock 'n' roll, sets profound simplicity in opposition to alienating complexity, and gives the sweetest kiss-off to the status quo'.

The period that the Jesus & Mary Chain had spent out of circulation recording *Psychocandy* at Southern Studios had provided a respite for Creation as Alan McGee was able to concentrate more fully on the label's releases. Along with the Slaughter and

Meat Whiplash singles had come a further Jasmine Minks release, 'What's Happening', a short, sharp slice of combustive romantic angst that was more reflective of the sound of Belfast 1978 than Haight Ashbury 1967. There were some new additions to the label as well, including Five Go Down To The Sea: the band's 'Worm In My Brain' EP was released in September. Founded in Cork, the band was fronted by the eccentric Finbar 'Mad Dog' Donnelly, and based in Rotherhithe where they lived via the grace and favour of some builders (for whom they did the housework in return). Dinner would sometimes be six Jelly Babies on a plate. The surreal nature of their music was every bit as odd as their domestic arrangements, Finbar often extemporising lyrics to suit his mood and his various hilariously delivered political opinions.

More conventional – if slightly less colourful – was the compilation album that Creation released in September. *It's Different For Domeheads* repeated the trick of the previous year's *Wild Summer, Wow!*, offering up a selection of previously released tracks from the back catalogue. Creation '85, though, was presented as a toughened-up, more rocked out beast compared to the 1984 version, as tracks like the Pastels' 'Baby Honey' and Slaughter Joe's 'Napalm Girl' suggested. The label, as Dave Cavanagh later noted, benefitted from some 'reflected rock 'n' roll dazzle' courtesy of the Jesus & Mary Chain, and, clothed in leather, its new image suggested less 'a psychedelian's retreat' and more a 'red-blooded, no-shit-taking brotherhood of hard-drinking degenerates'.

One tune on *Different For Domeheads* that particularly stood out was the album's closing track, 'Worm In My Brain', a Pete Astor composition. The track was credited to Astor's new band, the Weather Prophets – a name that might have been lifted from a line in Henry Miller's *Tropic of Cancer* – and at the time of recording the band consisted of just Astor and fellow ex-Loft man, drummer Dave Morgan. On 'Worm In My Brain', Alan McGee helped out by playing bass. The song hinted at the broader musical palette

Astor intended to use and featured some memorable slide guitar, causing a few indie eyebrows to be raised in a world where such indulgencies were dogmatically opposed. This wasn't tangling with the mythological and hackneyed world of 'pop' as defined by indie (which extended little beyond Buzzcocks, etc) but something broader and more encompassing.

All through the summer, Pete Astor had been trying to complete the line-up of the band, at one point considering an offer from veteran journalist Nick Kent to join on guitar. In June, Astor had played a solo gig, clearing the air between the old and the new, and initially had plans to release a mini solo album as well as a double album by the Weather Prophets. The solo album, he told *Sounds* in October, would be 'intimate', 'gentle', night time listening, stylistically removed from the 'unashamedly rock band' sound of the Weather Prophets. There was no solo album, at least not immediately, but the Weather Prophets did play a gig, a low-key affair at a pub in Crouch End and became fully formed with the addition of Greenwood Goulding on bass and Oisin Little on guitar. Goulding and Astor had briefly been in a punk-era school band – in keeping with the oppositional nature of the times they had named themselves the Band With No Name – before Goulding went off to join a group of performance artists, Station House Opera. Oisin Little had also been on the scene but preferred Muddy Waters and the blues to punk.

Astor's intention with the new band, *his* band, was to inject more of a groove into his songs: 'My song writing didn't change,' he says, 'but my definition of what I wanted the band to be changed.' This could be partly achieved by having control of the reins. In the Loft, the democratic structure was such that the overall vision inevitably ended up composite. But Astor had learned a lesson following the fractious disintegration of the Loft and was careful to not paint himself into any sort of corner at the same time as recognising the band's worth. 'The thing about the band is that we don't have any kind of manifesto,' he told Brice Dessau in *Jamming!* 'I simply know that we *are* good, and come from a logical line of quality music which stretches all the way from, say, Albert Lee, through Al Green and Television. We've digested all of this, but we're not trying to *copy* anything…' Astor recognised further the truly liberating power of the great song, commenting in 1986: 'Liberation can come from the quality of the music. Some of the best escapism I've had comes from music with plenty of pain and sadness in it. You're transported by the power of those emotions.'

Astor vowed not to rush into recording and through the autumn the Weather Prophets honed their chops on the live circuit as he built up a bank of songs. It wasn't until the early summer of 1986 that the first single arrived, and then not without difficulty, since recording went badly and a Janice Long Show version of the song became the final release. Underpinned by an old rock 'n' roll/ r 'n' b riff, 'Almost Prayed' was nevertheless brilliantly realised, with understated, insinuating, chiming guitar acting as the blank manuscript upon which Astor scrawls a predictable tale of woe:

> Down by the shoreline with my back to the land
> I felt my feet sink down in the sand
> Down by the harbour, standing all alone
> I felt my heart grow heavy as stone

The record made Single of the Week in a couple of the music papers, relegating Felt's 'Ballad of the Band' to also-ran status in the *NME* which dubbed it '24-carat' and called it a song that bore 'the distinct whiff of greatness'. Creation released the single in three different formats – a total of six songs that included covers of Robert Johnson's 'Stones In My Passway' and Chuck Berry's 'Downtown Train'. One song included that has resonated with

Weather Prophets admirers ever since is 'Like Frankie Lymon', a love song – 'you make me wanna smile/ and try to sing like Frankie Lymon' – and knowing nod to the doomed '50s r 'n' b baby-faced teenage star who sang 'Why Do Fools Fall In Love' and was later found dead of a heroin dose in his grandmother's bath at the age of just twenty-five.

'Frankie Lymon had his big hit back at a time when music was just considered part of the overall "entertainment" industry,' recalls Astor. 'People of my generation were more knowing about music. Part of tapping into that knowingness appealed to me. But as a fan I was also fascinated by the whole Frankie Lymon narrative – the fucked up, tragic teenage kid who epitomised the dark paradigm of music. He made some great records and then, in the 1960s, some average records. Had he survived, I could imagine him making a record like Syd Barrett's *The Madcap Laughs*. There is irony as well in my song. I am aware that as a "non-singer" I was the complete opposite of that kind of acrobatic style of singing Lymon had in "Why Do Fools Fall In Love?".'

There was one more Creation release – the less well-received but equally as deserving ballad, 'Naked As The Day You Were Born – before the Weather Prophets moved to Elevation, along with Primal Scream. The deal was for £75,000 and Lenny Kaye (compiler of the garage rock compilation *Nuggets*, and producer more recently of James) was chosen to produce.

'We considered the move *very* carefully,' says Astor. 'We went in with our eyes open and knew what was expected of us – that we would compete with someone like Elton John in terms of record sales. We were aware also that it could all go very, very wrong and that we could fuck it up really badly. And in essence, that is what happened – we failed, I failed.'

The deal was done in autumn 1986 and two singles (one a reworking of the Loft song, 'Why Does The Rain') and the album

Mayflower followed. The themes on Mayflower cast the net wide, mythologizing, as many had done before, the fabrication of America, with its

> Buildings bigger than dinosaurs
> Seven locks on every door
> Prairies where the Greyhound Rolls
> Pilgrims in the Land of Gold

Astor began, he told *NME*'s Len Brown, with the notion of that cultural view of America as 'one big hamburger' and then proceeded to look at the country's powers to self mythologise. 'English songs never talk about going up the M62 but America is like its own myth,' he told Brown. 'The Americans draw on Route 66 the way the English draw on Greek myths. In America, the myth *is* America…'

Almost a year to the day after the Elevation deal was done, the band were dropped. 'Lenny Kaye did a terrific job and it was great fun making *Mayflower*, but we realised that we would have been better off working with Pat Collier and releasing the album on Creation. I wrote to Warner Brothers just after the album came out explaining that the next record would be produced by me and Pat Collier, saying that we'd tried it their way now let us try it mine. The option came up for renewal and they dropped us. We got the letter and sat in a pub near the record label, pretty much ecstatic. We could now do what we wanted. No more staged photographs on windy hilltops with the sun shining between our legs, no more being forced to turn the band into a kind of indie U2…'

The Weather Prophets returned to Creation but within a further year the band were no more. 'It is nearly impossible to come back from something like the experience we had with Warners – it can be done but you have to be in for the very long haul,' says Astor. 'In the end, Oisin left and I think the Weather

Prophets just reached a natural conclusion. By then, anyway, I'd begun looking at doing the kind of stuff that turned up on my *Submarine* album, which was very much a studio album rather than a recording of a band album. As ever, I was driven by artistic impulse.'

Shortly after *Different For Domeheads* was released in autumn 1985, Creation put out an album by the Membranes. *Gift of* Life remained faithful to the sonic trajectory that locked into place the year earlier with the release of 'Spike Milligan's Tape Recorder'. If anything, it ramped up the aural assault. Prior to making the album, guitarist Mark Tilton had left the band and with him floated off all hint of melody, or at least that was Alan McGee's view as told by David Cavanagh in *The Creation Records Story*: 'Tilton had a pop sensibility. Without him it was just John Robb going "I am a fish eye!" five hundred times.' There were 2000 pre-orders for the album, and a willing market for a band that, by 1985, had played over 175 gigs. The band's 'astonishing cacophony' and 'no-decibels-barred thrash' had reached a tipping point, though, with many of the critics drawn to reviewing the band's spirit rather than its music. 'I would not listen to *Gift Of Life* for fear it revealed some terrible secret to me and I went crazy bananas flip-doodle,' wrote David Quantick in the *NME*. 'MUCH COPIED, ALWAYS ADMIRED AND YET STILL SO MODEST, THE THREE PIECE POP MONSTER THUNDERED ON. HOW DARE YOU REMAIN UNMOVED?' screamed the back cover copy to the album.

In October, Creation arranged a couple of package tours. The Weather Prophets, Primal Scream, Meat Whiplash and the Bodines did a mini circuit of London, Manchester and Edinburgh, whilst the Membranes, Slaughter Joe and the Pastels appeared at a GLC-funded 'Week of Wonders' festival at Hammersmith's Riverside Studios. The London leg of the four-band tour – 'four bands for four pounds', as the tickets advertised –

passed off largely without incident, but the Riverside event was altogether different.

The Membranes had been booked to appear above Slaughter Joe on the bill, but when the bands arrived they were told that the running order would now be determined by the drawing of lots. For the Membranes who had fans taking the long journey down from Manchester, the potential was there for a catastrophe if the band went on stage too early. When the lots were drawn, the Membranes ended up having to open. 'We turned up to find McGee and Joe Foster there in their leather trousers,' John Robb told David Cavanagh. 'Now, we were all wankers. I'd turned into a wanker, McGee was wanker, and Joe Foster was a complete wanker. Our egos were out of control. We thought we were going to destroy rock 'n' roll.'

'Better known as a producer, this man is capable of anything live!' puffed the flyer for the event in reference to Foster. Disgruntled fans of the Membranes heckled Foster during his performance and a glass got thrown, at which point Foster invited certain members of the audience to 'Fuck off back up north'. 'There must have been a lot of Northerners present, wrote the *Melody Maker*'s reviewer. 'The hall visibly emptied after that.' The show was reviewed by Jon Hunter, in the following issue of *Bandits One To Five*: 'Things were afoot… Slaughter Joe's ego wouldn't fit through the front door. A local shrink helped. In order to be re-inflated Joe insists, through others, that they – Slaughter Joe – don't go on first…. Robb, John… angry man now. Pastels curse…' Over the weekend following the show, accusations flew backwards and forwards with the net result that the Membranes and the Pastels departed the label.

'Alan told me I was going on in the middle and that was that,' recalls Joe Foster. 'The whole incident was very childish and at times threatening in a way that was very uncool. We weren't into kid games and the very next day Creation dropped the Membranes and the Pastels. I thought we acted quite correctly in doing that…'

'I don't remember too much about this, or why we felt so strongly,' says Stephen Pastel. 'We had the feeling that the running order was being decided by a friendship hierarchy… There were probably plenty of other factors too, slightly under the surface but significant to us. We stood our ground, thus confirming that we were non-party line, and therefore not to be trusted when it came down to it, as it often did in those days.'

In September, prior to the fall-out, the Pastels had recorded and delivered the songs for one final Creation release. 'I'm Alright With You' appeared in December and carried on where 'Million Tears' had left off, the record 'a Pastelly cross between Maps, Ramones and Dolls – fab, well, best yet', according to Stephen Pastel writing to Paul Groovy around the time of the recording. His view has mellowed with hindsight. 'It was a reasonably good tune,' he says today. 'I remember listening back to it with Bobby Gillespie and Karen Parker, after driving to a show out in Belshill. It sounded good in the car and I thought we'd made something people would like. The mastering was terrible. I think Alan had done a deal and we used this studio off Oxford Street run by a Greek guy who had worked with Demis Roussos. He couldn't have been more patronising about our efforts. It was such a dismal experience, only made worse by the fact that George Peckham – Porky – would have been working close by, and would have made it come out as well as it possibly could.'

'I'm Alright With You' would be re-recorded for the band's new label Glass and appear in a more sanitised version on the band's debut album, 1987's *Up For A Bit With The Pastels*, an album that represented the stunning realisation of the five or so years the Pastels had put in prior to that point. Musically idiosyncratic, thematically wide ranging and adventurous, *Up For A Bit…* incorporated church bells and strings in a sound that was cleaner and more assured than anything they'd previously offered, full of space and possibility. It was, declared Dave Haslam in *NME* (in November) the year's best debut album by a British band, bar none.

There was just one other Creation record released in 1985 – the Moodists' three-track 'Justice & Money' EP that preceded the release of the Pastels single by a couple of weeks. The Australian band had been turning heads ever since the first Antipodean wave of indie had washed up bands such as the Birthday Party, the Laughing Clowns, and the Go-Betweens. 'Justice & Money Too' typified a brand of unsettling, no-nonsense, charnel-house blues, music that 'took rock into a dark alley and beat the shit out of it', as one wag observed at the time.

The Moodists' tenure at Creation was all too brief and the band were quickly moved on in what amounted to a label clear out, though, as the year came to a close. The Pastels and the Membranes had departed following the debacle that was the Week of Wonders: the Moodists followed them closely through the door, joining earlier departees that included Les Zarjaz, Five Go Down to the Sea, the X Men and Meat Whiplash. As it turned out, Joe Foster also severed his ties with Creation, moving to the Midlands to start his own label, Kaleidoscope Sound at the end of 1985, marking an end to the holy trio of McGee, Green and Foster that had sustained Creation since its formal launch in February 1984. Creation would now focus on the core roster that included Primal Scream, the Weather Prophets, the Jasmine Minks, Biff Bang Pow!, Slaughter, the Bodines and the newly-signed Felt.

1985 had started with the bang of the Jesus & Mary Chain but ended on a whimper as the label went through some necessary recalibrations. On the upside, an office had been opened (in August) and the label had been able to employ (on the Enterprise Allowance Scheme at £40 per week) the formidable talents of Jeff Barrett to take care of PR. On the downside, the somewhat disparate nature of the year's releases, alloyed with what some saw as a creeping arrogance, had caused some of the critics to turn against the label. But in 1986, Creation would be back, bigger and bolder, and more critically well-received than ever, with key releases by the Weather Prophets, Primal Scream, Biff Bang Pow!, the Jasmine Minks, the Bodines, and not least Felt whose *Forever Breathes The Lonely Word* marked the arrival of the label's first truly great album.

CHAPTER 20

FASTER! FASTER! FASTER!

AS FELT'S 'PRIMITIVE PAINTERS' ENTERED the independent charts in September 1985, steadily making its way to number one, it met the Wedding Present's single 'Go Out & Get 'Em Boy!' travelling in the opposite direction. The Wedding Present record had spent a month in the chart and skirted the top ten, no mean feat for an unknown band on the dole who had scraped together the money to produce 500 copies of their debut single by living on potatoes and crisp sandwiches.

Fame and fortune was the last thing on the Wedding Present's mind and yet, ironically, they represent a classic case study in how the independent ethic can be made to succeed. Even when the band signed to the major label RCA, following the collapse of the independent distributor Red Rhino at the end of 1988, the deal was done on terms that were wholly favourable to the ideals of the band. Written into the band's contract was the right to select its own producer and be able to release independently any single RCA rejected. Courted by every major label in town following the success of the *George Best* album, released on the band's Reception label in 1987, they resisted, according to David Gedge, the 'rather patronising pitch of most major labels that we'd done well but that they could do better' and took advantage of the muscle power of RCA whilst keeping control of what was released. Arguably, the ultimate expression of their freedom was the decision in 1992 to release a single a month for the entire year: all twelve records were released in a limited edition of 10,000 copies and all entered the national charts as the Wedding Present equalled Elvis Presley's record for the most Top Thirty hits in one year.

The singles, later collected together and issued on the *Hit Parade* compilations, reflected both David Gedge's love of the seven-inch format and his love of radio, the medium through which such music was traditionally disseminated. Growing up in Manchester (although born in Leeds) it was across the airwaves that

Gedge first came across pop music in the late 1960s and early 1970s, as he told John Robb in *Death To Trad Rock*: 'When I was off school I would quite happily sit by the stereo and listen to Radio One all day – Tony Blackburn, Jimmy Young, Dave Lee Travis, Johnny Walker, Alan Freeman – it's slightly disconcerting that I still know the running order thirty years later! Later, I got into other radio stations; Radio Luxembourg and Piccadilly Radio in Manchester… I think I kind of always knew that I would end up either making music or playing it on the radio.'

Returning to Leeds to attend university, Gedge was in a number of transient groups at the start of the 1980s, eventually forming a band called the Lost Pandas, which featured his girlfriend Janet Rigby on drums and Keith Gregory on bass. 'The Lost Pandas was a more serious proposition than the bands I'd been in and out of even going back to when I was still in Manchester,' Gedge recalls. 'Around 1983 we made a couple of demos and sent them out to record companies that we liked – companies like Rough Trade and Factory and even 4AD which was a wholly inappropriate label for the kind of music we were making. We'd visit the premises, drop off a tape with the words, "Hi, We're a band from Leeds…". Probably not the best approach, looking back on it. In time, we received a *lot* of rejection slips… Typically, we played a kind of mishmash of styles, music largely inspired by the bands we liked. There was a bit of the Chameleons in there, and the Fall, but the music wasn't going in any kind of great or unified direction.'

Gedge split up with his girlfriend and she relocated to New York, taking with her the band's guitarist Michael Duane. By necessity, a new start was called for. Peter Solowka, an old school friend of Gedge's, joined on guitar and Shaun Charman came in on drums, the piece of the jigsaw that, according to David Gedge, made the new band whole. 'The music changed substantially,' says Gedge, 'after Shaun joined. His drumming was more punk than had been the case before and the overall sound therefore naturally seemed to become more aggressive, more energetic.'

The new band scrapped the old name. For some time Gedge had been toying with the name the Wedding Present but had held back for fear of being accused of straying too close to the territory of the name of one of his favourite bands, the Birthday Party: 'But when the Birthday Party were no more it seemed that it was OK to call the band the Wedding Present. I liked the name – it sounded more like a film, or a play or a book. Over the years it has proved to be a bit impractical at times, and also odd to some, but then those are also reasons why I like it.'

The band rehearsed together, working through David Gedge's songs and picking up gigs in Leeds wherever they could, playing venues like the Royal Oak pub in Headingley and hassling landlords of other pubs, already inundated with demo tapes from bands, to put them on. The first gig played as the Wedding Present took place in the Yorkshire mining village of Allerton Bywater, in a venue opposite the pit gates, when they supported a band called Dik Dik Dimorphic. At this point, Gedge and Gregory had finished their university courses and were on the dole, Peter Solowka was a supply teacher and Shaun Charman, being a couple of years younger, was still studying. They wanted to make a record but the experience of sending out the Lost Pandas demos suggested it might not be that easy finding a label willing to help.

'The only person that we bothered sending Wedding Present demos to was John Peel, and we sent them to him in the hope that he might contact us and ask us to do a session, but we got no response,' remembers Gedge. 'We figured that rather than send out lots of demos it was better to save up and release the single on our own, which is what we did. We booked time at the Billiard Room studios in Leeds and made the record as cheaply as possible. We only did 500. I bought a National Express coach ticket and went with two suitcases to collect the records from the manufacturer in London rather than pay out for an expensive courier to bring them to us. The covers were printed locally as cheaply as possible and Keith and I sat and glued them together. *Everything* was done on a shoe string.'

'Go Out & Get 'Em Boy' may have been birthed in impoverished circumstances, but it was rich in another way. By the start of summer 1985, when the single was manufactured, independent music was only just starting to come out of the doldrums. David Gedge realised that what was needed was to *over*emphasise the band's qualities in order to gain it the attention it merited. He knew that the Wedding Present's high-velocity sound, full of trebly guitar and angular riffs offset by an underlying melody and bittersweet lyrics, would have an impact but he decided to take no chances: 'I chose which song to release carefully. I realised that because it was a debut single it didn't necessarily have to be the *best* song we had in the set, but it needed to be the one most able to leap out of the radio and grab the listener's attention. I picked "Go Out & Get 'Em Boy" because it was the most extreme of all our songs at that point.'

Asked by the *NME* in August to define his writing style, David Gedge replied, 'Faster! Faster! Faster!'. The whirlwind guitars were all present and correct on the debut single, but what immediately gripped was the song's melody, building up from the opening jangly guitar and holding its own in the face of the formidable barrage of guitars and drums. By rights, the accompanying sonic assault and the melody and plaintive vocals should have jarred, yet everything blended, and in case we misinterpreted the whole effect as one of delivery over content, the end mirrored the start as the guitars dropped off and the tale of unrequited love drew towards its sorry end as David Gedge informed us that:

… there's a whole world out there but it's shrinking fast
You want to take it all and make it last forever
Or maybe just a lifetime, maybe just a lifetime

Like that of many before, David Gedge's voice was perfectly imperfect, used more as a highly effective instrument rather than a stand-alone treat. 'I'm well aware that I don't have a particularly brilliant voice,' he later told *Q* magazine. 'I'm not one of those people who open their mouths and flowers appear on trees…'

The Wedding Present played London for the first time on 2 November 1985, appearing at the Ambulance Station as support for the June Brides who had invited them to play. By then they had recorded a second single. 'Once More' moved at a slightly less frenetic pace than its predecessor but, as Danny Kelly noted when making it Single of the Week in *NME*, was still 'FAST'. Indeed, the song's 'whirlwind whizz of guitars at times reaches *demonic* speeds', noted Kelly. Although thematically the song moved away from the romantic territory of 'Go Out & Get 'Em Boy', sound-wise, in places it was reminiscent of those other pop-noise romantics, the Undertones, and the 'sheer multiplicity of ideas present' made it 'all but irresistible'.

By the time 'Once More' entered the independent charts in February 1986, the Wedding Present were back in London, playing the Queen Mary College with the Mighty Lemon Drops. ('Great night, eh?' quipped a grumpy on-stage David Gedge. 'You've seen the Velvets supporting the Doors?') That same week the band's first John Peel session was broadcast in a set that included a cover of Orange Juice's 'Felicity'. Reviewing the Queen Mary gig in *NME*, Jane Wilkes was unimpressed by a band 'whose jangly guitars pivot uneasily between the siren grind of the Buzzcocks and ringing one-chord wonders culled, in their case, from the Postcard heyday'. The trip down indie memory lane was completed when the Mighty Lemon Drops did their take on the Teardrop Explodes' 'When I Dream'.

The four tracks on the first two singles were bundled together and released on a 12" EP, 'Don't Try & Stop Me, Mother'. The collective energy of all four songs reminded the Legend! of the Jam, when he interviewed the band in April – due to 'the determination, the *striving*; not the politics or music, or anything like that, but more the feeling' – and prompted him to answer the band's critics who foresaw a short career ahead for a band who appeared to have only one speed of music. 'Most of the best bands only possess only one song anyway (maybe two if you include the slow one),' he countered, before going on to list his favourites, which included the Ramones, the Shop Assistants and the Membranes. By David Gedge's own self-deprecating admission, it wouldn't be until after the *George Best* album that the band would properly think to mix it up a bit, adding in 'more things like texture, light and shade, fast bits, slow bits, loud bits, quiet bits, all the stuff that makes a record varied'.

In May, a Wedding Present track appeared on *C86* – the wittily titled 'This Boy Can Wait (A Little Longer)', so called because it was a longer version (and longer title) of a song with the same name that would later appear on the back of the next single, 'You Should Keep In Touch With Your Friends'. *C86* helped broaden out the Wedding Present's appeal and introduced many for the first time to the dry wit of Gedge whose songs (and song titles) were beginning to resonate strongly with the young, lovelorn and angst-driven male. As if to prove the point, 'My Favourite Dress' crept, albeit briefly, into the national charts (at number 95 for one week) at the start of 1987. The song perfectly epitomises the early Wedding Present, the home truths lyrics reminded us that 'jealousy is an essential part of the love' and the guitars burning down the song in one of the best outros ever. It certainly confirmed John Peel's later claim that David Gedge had 'written some of the best love songs of the Rock 'n' Roll era.'

1987 proved to be a landmark year for the band. The debut album *George Best* – 'a dozen little lovescapes of sometimes quite breathtaking realism, a world fuelled by desire, lust, paranoia, romance and bitterness', according to Danny Kelly – sold 60,000 copies, matching the sales of that other recent colossus, *Psychocandy*, and all achieved in its case without the aid of major label marketing money. The record was released on Reception and was a comparatively low-budget, lo-fi production job. Chris Allison who had previously worked at Sarm Studios (home of ZTT) produced the album, having been given a first break when entrusted with the production of 'My Favourite Dress'. The achievement was thrown into greater relief by the fact that a couple of months prior to the release of *George Best*, the Smiths had split up, creating a vacuum which many people were happy to see the Wedding Present fill.

'We'd always sworn to remain a "singles" band and we were pushed slightly into doing the album by our distributor, Red Rhino, who kept telling us that to succeed further we needed to start releasing albums,' says Gedge. 'By doing that we would make more money, be able to more easily play shows abroad, etc, etc. 'I'm not sure any of it was wholly true, but at the back of my mind, of course, was the idea that we *would* at some point make an album. We held off from making an album so long because I wanted to make sure that we had enough quality songs without just repackaging up the old singles.'

The Wedding Present, of course, never asked to be garlanded with the cast off mantle of the Smiths and others questioned whether their shoulders were broad enough to carry it off. Chris Roberts in *Melody Maker* had been one of the few to remain unmoved by *George Best* when he had reviewed it and later considered that the band's elevated status might only be justified 'if the world was entirely composed of polytechnic students who naughtily take an hour off revision each night to listen to John

Peel'. This was missing the point (as well as making one) and Jack Barron in *NME* made a better call when he commented that the Wedding Present 'utterly demystify the designer glamour of modern music. In its place the worst dressed band in the nation offer something far more interesting: themselves.'

The band carried on utterly demystifying the glamour of modern music and being themselves after signing with RCA at the end of 1988, refusing to compromise artistic integrity and yet ultimately delivering up 25 singles and ten albums that made it into top 75 of the mainstream charts.

Summer 1985 marked a sudden upsurge in the number of louder and faster and occasionally more dissonant guitar bands like the Wedding Present and the Shop Assistants in the UK and Butthole Surfers and Sonic Youth in America. When the Butthole Surfers had made their UK debut at the Ambulance Station on 9 October 1985 they had, claimed one observer, presented a formidably disrespecting antidote to the notion of classic rock, distorting a couple of songs by the Beatles and the Rolling Stones beyond all recognition in a performance that reeked of 'Texas Big Beat, the desert heat; drunken, slobbish bigoted rednecks; Captain Beefheart's prodigal daughters; speed-crazed, psychotic, knife-wielding punks' and 'infinitely more besides'.

But not everybody came on like a hurricane and at the centre of the squall, inevitably, was a cool stillness. This was every bit as highly-charged a place to be but those who occupied it were sometimes less obvious and more understated, bands like Miaow who were somewhat improbably regularly booked on to bills such as that at the Ambulance Station when the Butthole Surfers played. They later went on to perform a number of other 'grind-free' sets, supporting Sonic Youth, Nick Cave and others.

Miaow had formed in 1984 after journalist Cath Caroll had moved to London from Manchester. Carroll had started out writing for the Manchester fanzine, *City Fun* before moving on to the *NME* where she eventually wrote under the pen name Myrna Minkoff (a name lifted from the Jewish beatnik character in John Kennedy O'Toole's picaresque novel, *A Confederacy Of Dunces*). Whilst still in Manchester, she had become friends with Liz Naylor, with whom she 'monopolised' *City Fun* before going on in 1979 to form the band the Glass Animals. The Glass Animals who, according to Carroll, 'sounded like a very bad Fall', picked up support slots from sympathetic observers like Mark E Smith and, anxious to improve their stage presence, often performed behind a white sheet. 'Liz and I intended to eventually show ourselves,' Carroll later jokingly wrote, 'when we felt we had sufficiently incubated our mystique.'

In 1980, the Glass Animals renamed themselves the Gay Animals and then, at the start of 1984, moved to London, occupying (along with a cat called Stanley) a squat in Rotherhithe. Liz Naylor departed the band, going on to become a press officer, and the Gay Animals line-up eventually settled down to Cath Carroll on guitar and vocals, Steve McGuire on guitar, Ron Caine on bass and Chris Fenner on drums. The band heard about a free rehearsel space in the Old Kent Road but when they presented themselves they were, claimed Carroll, 'given a circumspect reception and realised now might be a good time for a name change'. They settled on calling themselves Miaow, pronounced 'm'YAAAOW', as Cath Carroll later told journalist Caroline O'Sullivan, adding that a short name was essential since it saved on Letraset when mocking up press releases.

Back in Manchester a year or two earlier Carroll had been encouraged by Richard Boon, who was then running New Hormones, to manage the art rock band Ludus, which she did for a few months, using the opportunity to squeeze the Glass Animals in on some Ludus support slots by way of compensation. When Richard Boon ended New Hormones and moved to London she kept in touch, hanging out at the favoured Malt & Hops pub in Kings Cross near the Rough Trade offices and meeting up with Boon and other Rough Traders, including Liz Naylor and her sister Pat, and also Brian O'Neill. The plan was hatched to start a record label – Venus – and release a single by Miaow.

'Belle Vue' appeared at the end of 1985, the title-track a beautifully pitched offering where Carroll's lazy vocals drift in and out of McGuire's melodic, trebly guitar lines. On the single's shorter B-side, 'Fate', an old Gay Animals song, the organ replaces the trebly guitar. The 12" version of the single came with Carroll's equally as marvellous ode to the perils of Thatcherism, 'Grocer's Devil Daughter', where we are ominously warned that 'she's gonna get you'. The cover design by Pat Naylor – 'Budgie Woman cover art' – suited the record's slightly mischievous mood perfectly. To see the record on its way, Richard Boon reviewed it in the *Catalogue*, half holding his hand up to the charge of nepotism: 'fulla references to both girly groups and '60s garage-trash. A trebly guitar, a fairground organ, a sultry voice: what more could a poor boy want? I may be biased, but as the band begins to earn a live reputation, I'm sure I'm not alone in welcoming this auspicious debut.' Mick Mercer crowned it 'almost Single of the Week' in *Melody Maker*, noting the '*Swallows And Amazons* playgroup feel. So wispy you daren't breathe lest they go home crying', before hailing it 'a charming debut'. As has been noted, the 'live reputation' was sometimes built on incongruity: Miaow had released a 'fine single', according to the admiring and teasing fanzine *Bandits One To Five*, but their somewhat static live presence made them candidates for the 'Stage Presence of Cabbages Award'.

Steve McGuire left after 'Belle Vue' and was replaced by Ron Caine (playing guitar and bass, also). Andy Winters also joined on guitar – recruited following an announcement on stage since Miaow claimed to be 'too mean to advertise', just prior to the band going into the studios to record a track for the *C86* to which they had been invited to contribute. There's more than touch of cow punk to 'Sport Most Royal', with its twangy guitar and jaunty high-jinx lyric – 'Summer days at Hampstead ponds/ Toes caught in aquatic fronds/ Drinking Red Stripe by the water/ Watching the wooing of Mrs Windsor's Swinging daughter', etc. Where Miaow might have taken this on to never became clear since 'Sport Most Royal' was the band's only release in 1986 and indeed there would be no more Venus Records either. Miaow did go into Maida Vales studios and record a John Peel session, however, which was broadcast in June and featured four new tracks, only one of which ('Did She', a tale of 'lesbian debauchery') would eventually be released on vinyl, although the other three did surface on the posthumous 2003 compilation *When It All Comes Down*, along with the four tracks recorded for a second and final Peel session broadcast in January 1987.

The same month that the band's final Peel session was aired, Miaow released a second single, this time on Factory Records. Tony Wilson had been familiar with Cath Carroll's work since the time of the Glass Animals and Cath Carroll, along with Liz Naylor, had been an early member of the Hacienda club – both were subsequently banned following an incident allegedly involving a dildo and some Gay Pride hankies. Wilson invited Miaow to record for his label and the band went on to release two singles within the space of eight or so months, a heady work rate for them. The plan was for an album to follow.

'When It All Comes Down' is undoubtedly Miaow's finest moment, refining the garage/ girl group essence on the debut single and serving it up in a far stronger song. 'Here's a boy with time on his side/ Here's a girl too stupid to hide…' begins Carroll on the promotional video, dressed in fisherman's cap and surrounded by shade-wearing mannequins, and clearly intent on having a good time. The single came with an extended seven-minute long 'Catechism' mix which benefitted from some superb soprano saxophone by Terry Edwards. Reviewing the band live at the time, David Quantick was 'paralysed with wonder' by the song. 'Describing a song is almost impossible in print,' he concluded, 'so suffice to say that the song gyrates in its own melody, scatters hooks at every turn.' The record when it was released fairly sailed into the independent top ten and stayed there for the best part of three months. The follow-up single, 'Break The Code', was every bit as hook-laden and impacting, driven by pumping bass and Cath Carroll's seductive vocal. It too made into the charts, but alas it proved to be the band's last release. Miaow played their final concert on 3 October 1987 at the Klub Foot in Hammersmith.

One month before the last show, Miaow had recorded a series of demos for a proposed album that had the working title *Priceless Innuendo*. The tracks had to wait sixteen years before seeing the light of day finally on the *When It All Comes Down* compilation where Cath Carroll threw some light in the absorbing sleeve notes on the album's aborted genesis. The title had been borrowed from a phrase uttered by Charles Hawtrey in an old *Carry On* film. The songs were made as demos but never properly recorded. The band, at that point she claimed, 'were several bands all happening at once', the sum of the total worth less than the constituent parts. '… besides,' she explained, 'how could we every truly have embodied the tawdry glamour hinted at in Mr Hawtrey's utterance?'

Cath Carroll continued her career, both as a solo artist and writer after Miaow ended, pausing only once when compiling the sleeve notes for the 2003 compilation to reflect back on her early work. She did so in typically engaging fashion, offering up fragments of information relating to the songs that illuminated but still kept the mystery intact, as in her description of 'Some Songs From Manchester' –'"Belle Vue" (1960s, same as the 1860s/ Gorton), "Fate" (1860s, same as the 1960s/ Gorton), "Did

She" (dominant partner/ Hulme)', etc –and 'Some Songs From London –"Sport Most Royal" (posh dykes/ Hampstead Women's Pond), "Grocer's Devil Daughter" (some have more boot straps than others/ Grantham), "When It All Comes Down" (obsession/ Highbury & Islington)', etc.

'The AGE OF CHANCE had to be formed. Fuelled by a burning contempt of the current musical climate – warm, glutinous, high-cholesterol chaff – we came together by spontaneous human combustion…'

So begins one of the many manifestos sent out by Age of Chance after the band's debut single 'Motor City' was unleashed on an unsuspecting public in May 1985. The manifesto, printed in the *Legend!* and other fanzine publications, didn't hide the band's light under a bushel when it came to explaining its 'PRODUCT' or 'CATACLYSMIC debut': 'MOTORCITY – a rolling juggernaut of Pop-metal, a tragic BOY-meets-GIRL-meets-CARCRASH tale of lust and corporate intrigue… CASCADIN' guitar, CAREENING vocal. A trip through A NOISE TORNADO!' The record's B-side was 'simply the greatest love story ever told'.

Age of Chance came together in August 1982 and from the start was guided more by what the band members *didn't* want to sound like than what they wanted to sound like. Although Leeds had once been an epicentre, an innovative hub of post punk music, by 1982 it was starting to become more famous as the Goth capital of the world, with bands like the Sisters of Mercy, the March Violets, and (nearby) Southern Death Cult on the rise. Carrying the flag for the *alternative* alternative was the Three Johns. 'There was nothing that really spoke to us,' remembers guitarist (power-noise generator) Neil Howson, 'either in Leeds or elsewhere, so we made our own way.'

Neil Howson teamed up with singer (mob orator) Steve E through an advert he'd read in the *NME* and together they set up a club night called Upzone that they ran out of a venue named

Belinda's. The early 1980s was a golden era for clubs, fed off a rich diet of mutant disco, discordant post-punk, experimental electronica, funk, northern soul and rudimentary hip-hop. Leeds was particularly blessed, its most famous club the Warehouse being not just one of the best in the country but also social hub and education centre for those that flocked to it, including bassist (all-nite bass frequencies), Geoff Taylor.

Taylor frequented both Upzone and the Warehouse and was looking around for some people to start a band with. 'The music ads at the time,' he recalls, 'were of the usual "No Breadheads/ No Timewasters" type and nothing was happening. Then one day, in the main music shop in town, Scheer's, I saw a more unusual-looking ad, which didn't even mention music.' Instead, the advert was a dark, photocopied picture of some people dancing with enigmatic text scrawled across the image. 'I pulled the ad off the wall, took it home and called up the number and agreed to meet the people involved, which turned out to be the two blokes from Upzone. They'd placed the ad quite a long time before – over a year – got no takers and pretty much forgotten about it.'

The three decided to join forces, first off acclimatising themselves with each of the other's tastes. 'We spent about three months just sharing music,' says Howson. 'Then we borrowed a drum machine and started writing, but we knew that using a drum machine wasn't really an option as most Leeds bands seemed to use one. For a drummer, we didn't want Phil Collins, just someone with a Motown feel...'

Geoff Taylor had been at art school and was friends with Jan Perry (beat dominator). Perry offered to have a go at 'drumming' and the band set about acquiring a rudimentary kit. In fact, the kit consisted of a snare drum, a high-hat with a tambourine over it, and a stolen 19" tom tom. Perry drummed standing up (a couple of years before the Jesus & Mary Chain had the same good idea) and the band was fully formed.

It was important to Age of Chance that they try to find new ground when it came to composing material. They took pains to avoid modelling their sound on anybody else's, at the same time as sponging up music that would lead them on to their own. The name of the band was borrowed from 'Don't Call Me Pain', a Pop Group song. 'We liked the world they created – the ambience, the threat and the energy', says Neil – but all manner of sounds fed in: Fire Engines, Suicide, Josef K, early electro, instrumental surf music, '60s girl groups, James Brown, Tamla, Stooges, Disco, Phil Spector, the Birthday Party…

Age of Chance played live for the first time 23 March 1983 when they performed a twenty-minute set on a night billed as 'Music For the Masses' at the Warehouse. Shortly after, *iD* magazine ran a feature on the music scene in Leeds. The article singled out Age of Chance and their set at the warehouse: the author of the piece was Neil Howson. 'Well, it gave us something to live up to,' he later jokingly told the *NME* around the time of the first single. The Warehouse performance – the Warehouse *itself* – amplified the post-industrial collapse that was taking place at the start of the 1980s, where money, not industry, was about to become king. Concerts were held in abandoned spaces, disused factories, ghostly mausoleums of a former age and economic culture. Age of Chance made music that deliberately reflected this, creating 'primitive soundtracks to urban life'. The age of chance, indeed.

'We played Bradford for our second gig and then slowly built up a network – bands we felt kinship with or got on with. We did gig swaps with bands like Big Flame in Manchester. In fact, we played Manchester more than Leeds at the start,' remembers Neil. Unsurprisingly for a band sophisticated and broad in taste, they were playful when it came to re-interpreting the work of others. 'In rehearsal we would play 'Diamonds, Fur Coat, Champagne' by Suicide, 'Magic's Wand' by Houdini, 'After The

Lights Go Out' by the Walker Brothers, 'This Town' by Frank Sinatra. Ironically, the band only ever performed two covers live – 'Kiss' and 'Disco Inferno',' according to Neil Howson: '"Disco Inferno" was a song we'd danced to and lyrically it fitted in with our themes. I had a riff I thought would work with the towering bass line and it came together fairly quickly. It cheesed people off we were doing a disco song…' 'Sonic Metal Disco' is how Howson described their cover of the Trammps' song at the time: 'We use fuzz guitar, fuzz bass, fuzz vocals and fuzz drums. It's our contribution to deafness in society.'

Their setup *was* rudimentary: guitar, bass and two drums, supplemented with distortion, echo and extreme treble frequencies. Having created a sound, the next task was committing it to vinyl. Age Of Chance rehearsed in Steve Elvidge's flat, which was a stone's throw from the legendary Faversham pub, performing in front of the obligatory two-bar electric fire. Part commentary on the scene they saw around them, and in particular, the goth/ grebo axis – 'hey leather for brains' – 'Motor City' was chosen as being the most representative of the band's ideas at the time. The band recorded 'Motor City' (and also the B-side 'Everlasting Yeah') at Box Studios in the small, Yorkshire town of Heckmondwike (in a studio owned by the guitar player in George Hamilton IV's band). Hamilton's guitar player wasn't overly keen on distortion so the record came out sounding cleaner than the band had hoped for but still made an impressive statement.

Age of Chance pressed up 1,000 copies (at a cost of £645) and Geoff Taylor took care of the artwork, creating the star eye logo that would go on to be used for the next couple of singles. The record came with an insert and liberally sprinkled between that and the punky yellow covers was a series of quotes, some lifted from the words of the late satirist, Lenny Bruce. 'Moral: Wash Your Hair And Die', read one (possibly informed by Big Flame); 'Too Sexy For Television', another. Everything hit its mark, Mick

Mercer in *Melody Maker* making 'Motorcity' Single of the Week – 'such a great record, you'll never want to go home' – and running a half page picture of the cover. Interviewing Age of Chance shortly after, Mercer nailed the single's essence, calling it a 'syndrome wrecker. Put against the lumbering sloths of the rock 'n' roll brotherhood you'll find true pace – big, bold, beautiful scenarios of clashing zest.' As the band's manifesto claimed, 'Motor City' was a spontaneous combustion, reminiscent in its power of early Subway Sect and layered through with confidence and wit as Steve Elvidge sang:

> If you will give me my wall of sound
> I will marry you

Word spread quickly, John Peel picking up on the single with particular enthusiasm: 'Neil and I used to live in the same street and David Gedge from the Wedding Present lived in the street behind,' recalls Geoff Taylor. 'David wrote a fanzine called *Blood From A Stone* and came around one night to interview us – we were the only band interviewed in it. I had the radio on in the background and 'Motorcity' came on the John Peel show as we were talking.' As Taylor later recounted, at the moment when Peel began enthusing about the single 'the room fell silent, the pathway to glory was laid out before us.' Or something like that…

Age of Chance followed up 'Motor City' with another seven-inch gem, once again released on the band's own Riot Bible label. 'Bible of The Beats' took the Tamla/ T Rex template and moved it on some, delivering its sonic rant through a static-racked loud hailer. 'By that time we had a better idea of sound and depth,' says Neil. 'The record was a mix of early Garage/ Glenn Branca and featured the first use of synth on our tracks.' It came also with a warning: 'Contains extreme sonic frequencies. Must not be played in the presence of pre-teens…' Once again, the Geoff Taylor cover reprised the collage effect, this time presented in shocking pink. It too offered up a series of 'Commandments': 'Be L-Louder', 'Be More Beautiful', 'Be Unreasonable', 'Worship Screech', etc. It signed off, 'From Now On, This Will Be Your God'.

The last commandment turned up as the title of the track Age of Chance contributed to *C86*, where once again a different approach was adopted: 'We thought we'd do something more nuanced than just a "single" and try the layering and crescendo dynamics,' says Neil Howson. 'The drums were a nod to "Wipe Out" by Z'ev and the bass was Geoff in Moroder mode. Steve's lyrics reflected the US foreign policy of the time...' The release of the tape was celebrated with the ICA Rock Week of July, when the band made their first performance in London. The night was dogged by power cuts – Age of Chance's sonic assault in a moment reduced to an acoustic whisper halfway through the song 'How The West Was Won'.

By the time of the ICA gig the band had swopped their bright jumpers for a fashion statement that was altogether more arresting as they began appearing in the racy cuts and bold lines of cycling gear. At a photo shoot for a music paper earlier, Jan Perry had turned up in a black and white cycling top and gradually the band worked the style into their image, picking up outfits from Paolo Garbini, a cycling emporium in the west end run by a family of competitive cyclists.

'We wanted something distinctive and unifying also to reflect our music,' recalls Neil Howson. 'We loved Mondrian, El Lizzitsky and Warhol, and consumerism was a big influence, so the fact that cycling clothes had adverts and brands and logos really worked with our, er, aesthetic. We then used that on our sleeves and visuals.'

By autumn 1986, Age of Chance were coming to the attention of a number of major labels but before signing with Virgin hooked up with Sheffield's FON (or Fuck Off Nazis, a label and studio set up with advance money the band Chakk had received) to release a controversial cover version of Prince's 'Kiss'. The intention, Geoff Taylor later said, had been to record '1999', the Prince song that Age of Chance had entered the stage to on the occasion of their first gig at the warehouse back in 1983. But '1999' was a track that Big Audio Dynamite had incorporated into their live set, so Age of Chance plumped for 'Kiss' instead.

There wasn't any intention to release 'Kiss' as a single when the band covered it for their second John Peel Session in autumn 1986, but the audience response to the song when the session was broadcast made them choose it for their next single. It was all part of parcel of the band broadening their sound, not least because the exposure to the FON studios provided a world of new equipment, including an Akai S900 sampler and a DMX drum machine. The experimentation led not just to 'Kiss' but also to 'Crush Collision' and the supressed 'Kisspower'. Single of the Week in *NME*, 'Kiss' showed the band to have 'sprouted teeth and eaten royalty for breakfast' the paper said and ended up one of the biggest-selling independent records of all time, notching up total sales of around 110,000.

At the end of 1986, Age of Chance quickly switched from FON to Virgin, taking their 'lure of noise and passion for pop' to the major label for 1987's 'Who's Afraid Of The Big Bad Noise' and 'Don't Get Mad Get Even' and the debut album *One Thousand Years Of Trouble*. The records may have been better liveried but still addressed the themes the band had started out with, providing the soundtrack for the space between the inner city industrial estates and the suburbs, 'capturing,' as the band noted at the time, '*that* sound of driving through cities, past factories with the echoing rows…'

One Thousand Years Of Trouble showcased the band's 'crush collision' approach, sampling gospel choirs, the Clash, House music, Van Halen and much more, grinding everything into power pop chords, rumbling bass, frenetic drumming and the chanting assault of Steve Elvidge, whose beef covered everything from militarism to Reaganomics to inner city blight and the evils of Thatcherism. Sadly, it proved to be the band's swansong, as Steve Elvidge departed in the middle of 1988. The band recruited a new singer and limped on before finally calling it a day in 1991.

Gone but not forgotten, they inspired a legion of imitators but no equals.

CHAPTER 21

RED SLEEPING BEAUTIES

1985 WAS DESIGNATED INTERNATIONAL YOUTH Year. In October 1984, a UK launch took place and Paul Weller was elected as President. The official aim for the forthcoming year, according to the United Nations, was threefold: to encourage young people to participate more in the affairs that affected them and 'strike out against apathy'; to crush poverty; and to encourage peace. Weller hoped also that young people would 'stand up and have their say in their lives and hopes and fears'.

The then three main political parties (Conservatives, Labour, Liberals) were condescending and out of touch when it came to dealing with youth concerns. The various Government youth schemes were seen for what they were – sham exploitative, and a largely unregulated threat to life by 1985 when the number of those killed on them had risen to 31. Bereaved families received a one-off, token death grant (of around £29). No wonder then that on the part of some young people there was open hostility towards a government that appeared to disdain them, and general indifference towards politics, which all but ignored them.

International Youth Year forced the parties to address their failings. Unsurprisingly, the Conservative Government felt it was doing enough already (and planned instead to scrap previously in place wage protections for young people, who would no longer be allowed to take grievances to the Wages Council). The SDP (the Socialist Democratic Party that had formed when a number of Labour MPs had defected) took a more proactive line, although typified the remoteness of politicians when they announced that the solution to getting youth more of a voice was to employ on a part-time basis the head of the games department at the Virgin Megastore in Oxford Street to help them 'contact anybody, especially celebrities' who might want to join their cause.

The most welcoming initiative, however, came from Labour when it joined forces with Billy Bragg to launch a 'Jobs For Youth' campaign. 'We either build together or go down together,'

Labour leader Neil Kinnock told the *NME* in February 1985, adding that the party had recognised that it potentially had the lion's share of youth votes if it could find a way of making young people vote. Bragg toured, taking in eight venues, all sponsored by the Labour Party. A number of Labour MPs attend the shows and answered questions from the floor. (Hitching his star to the cause further taxed the already over-burdened Bragg who was concurrently playing benefit gigs for both CND and the miners.) Kinnock was well-briefed at the campaign's launch (which took place in the Shadow Cabinet rooms at Westminster), conceding that 'Youngsters are asking a lot of questions about jobs, the economy, the bomb, the environment, racism, housing and the future.' The *NME*, for its part, applauded the move whilst raising the age-old concern that politics and pop music didn't mix, not least in the current climate. 'Mr Kinnock's theories might contradict the undercurrent of Toryism that runs through a lot of modern music,' observed Adrian Thrills who claimed that 'images of glamour and success through capitalism' permeated most current chart pop.

Labour followed up the initiative with an official Charter For Youth that set out some rights it would enshrine when it got into power – these included the right to negotiate a wage if between 16 and 17, the right to receive £27 per week if in full time education and the right to better job opportunities and training if unemployed. These noble but largely toothless promises were undermined by Government treatment of the young unemployed: single homeless people, for instance, were forced to move from temporary accommodation (hostels, etc) every few weeks in order to keep claiming and many just gave up and slept on the streets.

One Government measure that had an indirect but very real effect on young people was the policy of rate capping whereby a number of local authorities around the country (all Labour run) had their powers curtailed to restrict spending, which the

Government considered to be getting out of hand. Many local authorities traditionally supported worthwhile projects such as setting up recording studios for young people, creating drop-in centres for the unemployed and subsidising local venues like the Leadmill in Sheffield. In some areas of Liverpool, youth unemployment at the end of 1985 was 100%. The fact that 50,000 people marched through the centre of Liverpool protesting against the rate capping measures in 1984 had caused delay but ultimately the Government got its way.

Billy Bragg showed himself to be a sophisticated songwriter of considerable quality whose more political numbers in his repertoire were generally (but not always) miles apart from the more tub-thumping, sloganeering approach of some of his contemporaries. And whilst there had been bands that delivered up a political message in a subtle way – the Specials immediately spring to mind – the lead generally was taken from the work of the Clash whose messages of urban and racial frustration tended to be splenetic, in keeping with the general timbre of the punk era.

But there was another approach. In the summer of 1985, around about the time that Neil Kinnock was launching his Jobs For Youth policy, a band from Billy Bragg's hometown of Barking was scratching around to raise funds to self-finance 456 copies of their debut single. Coincidentally, three members of McCarthy had attended the same secondary school as Billy Bragg (the grandly-named Barking Abbey Comprehensive) and between them felt a similar kind of anger at the way the country was being governed. They too voiced their despair at the political status quo, flagging up inequality and corruption in an apple they saw rotten to the core, but they delivered their message (as Bragg often did his) with beauty not bombast: Nicky Wire of the Manic Street Preachers later spoke of them as 'the great lost band of the 1980s', one that 'redesigned' his idea of politics and pop. 'It could be intelligent; it could be beautiful. They were frail, tragic, romantic idealists.'

The first clue was in the name – McCarthy, so chosen with a healthy dose of irony after the Communist-baiting 1950s US senator, Joe McCarthy. McCarthy wasn't the first name the band christened itself with – for years it existed as the somewhat cryptically-named Underground Bus. As a left wing band playing music that was both melodic and lyrically poetic, the name McCarthy went beyond irony, deliberately chosen to confuse those who approached the band with a preconceived idea of what it was about.

The song titles were more obvious, as was the case with the debut single, 'In Purgatory', a three track seven-inch that also contained 'Something Wrong Somewhere' and a track called 'The Comrade Era', with its lyric:

Comrade now
Comrade now and forever!
Citizen
You're not the only one

The lyric might well have tumbled fully formed out of the Communist Manifesto but, like all three tracks on 'In Purgatory', it came dressed in a melodic pop rhythm, with ringing guitar and purposeful, strident drumming, a present to unwrap that was both arresting *and* alluring. Malcolm Eden's vocals avoided any hint of preachiness.

The sound hadn't always been like that. Malcolm Eden (vocals/guitar), Tim Gane (guitar) and John Williamson (bass) had been in bands together since 1978 and the time of their school days, initially inspired by punk and the sounds of the bands they emulated, such as Buzzcocks and the Undertones. A succession of drummers led them in 1984 to Gary Baker – the 'best musician in the band', according to Eden – and his input immediately changed the way the band sounded.

They found their sound – and they also found their subject. The social and political discord and friction of the period led lyricist Malcolm Eden ever closer to his quarry, a study that wasn't limited to but included the moral zealots, fraudulent bankers, idle royals, corrupt officers of the law and sleazy media hacks who all propped up, in the words of one of their songs, the procession of popular capitalism.

'Margaret Thatcher was obviously a very divisive figure, who was deeply unpopular in many ways yet still managed to win three elections in a row,' recalls Eden today. 'I was already vaguely interested in politics before she came to power, but I think the challenge Thatcher presented to the left really made me start to think about politics more seriously. I started writing political lyrics around 1984 and suddenly found it was much easier than it had been to write and find things to say. Before that, I had mostly been playing with words.' Eden wanted to avoid sloganeering, believing 'that even in a three-minute pop song you could provoke some thought, challenge people in some way. We weren't keen to preach to people or only address those who had similar ideas.'

Prior to releasing 'In Purgatory', McCarthy had sent demo tapes out but received no joy. Like the Wedding Present and others bands at the time in a similar position they reasoned that the best way forward was to self-produce their single, although they didn't bother sorting out a distributor and simply sent the single to a few music press journalists, some independent record labels they thought might be interested, and some DJs, including John Peel. The record was recorded and mixed in one day, the monotone cover printed cheaply and the basic white labels used on the record's middle individually scrawled on by hand.

According to Malcolm Eden the only positive response the band got was from Pink Records: Paul Sutton contacted them and arranged to go and meet them at the clubhouse of East Ham Football Club, where the band rehearsed. Liking what he heard, he offered to arrange some gigs for the band and invited them to record a single for the label. The track McCarthy chose was a song called 'Red Sleeping Beauty', an early number already in the locker. 'Tim had written this in about 1983, I think,' says Eden. 'Gary added the drums and I added the lyric. Tim had written a few songs before, and they weren't bad, but were nothing compared to this. It was a great leap forward, so to speak. The demo was very dream-like, hence, I suppose, the idea of a lyric about someone who is asleep.'

Malcolm Eden's lyric clearly alludes to Charles Perrault's classic fairy tale but transplants the narcoleptic aspect to the nightmare of living in mid-'80s Britain where the evil fairy is, of course, Margaret Thatcher. The juxtaposition is worthy of the work of Angela Carter and the hypnotically beautiful music created by Tim Gane adds a further disturbing twist to the whole.

> I've been sound asleep for twenty years
> If I'm sound asleep for a hundred years
> She won't wake me…

But, as in every respectable fairy tale, good *has to* triumph over evil and the narrator is fortified by his beliefs:

> While there's still a world to win
> My Red dream is everything….

The subtlety of the song rests in the way that neither the politics nor the art cancels each other out. For many listeners it was just a beautiful pop single, although Malcolm Eden made clear in a *Sounds* interview with Ron Rom what had motivated the writing of the song: 'The first part [of the song] is saying that I won't be distracted from my convictions, and its also about the fact that there's no revolutionary party or option at the moment. There's the Labour Party, but I can't see them doing anything whatsoever. I think, eventually, like in *Sleeping Beauty*, where the sleeping princess is woken up by the prince, that there will be a revolutionary party in this country… It may not be now, it may not be in twenty years, but it will happen one day.'

Prior to McCarthy making records, Malcolm Eden had briefly been a member of the Revolutionary Communist Party – 'I definitely regarded myself a Marxist during all the McCarthy period', he says – but discovered that he was a better lyricist than party member, as he told *Cloudbase* fanzine in 1987: 'I had to choose in the end between the two. I think that what I am doing now is quite useful… I think it is contributing in a small way to building a revolutionary movement.'

Eden's approach complemented that of Tim Gane, whose own revolutionary interests favoured the surreal over the dogmatic. Gane admired the Situationists, and also the Dada art movement of Berlin at the turn of the Twentieth Century. Forget the orthodoxy, revolutionising your own life was the way forward, as he told *Cloudbase* in the same interview with the band, adding, 'revolution and innovation go together, really attacking the bourgeoisie view of life, politics, art and culture.' Both Gane and Eden were 'keen on the Weimar period in terms of art', remembers Eden. 'We both liked George Grosz, Otto Dix and John Heartfield, for example. At that time, Stalin hadn't yet taken control of the Communist movement, and there were more opportunities for creative expression. I think these artists struck the right balance between political and artistic innovation.'

Yet none of this shared philosophy interfered in a pretentious way with the music that McCarthy delivered. Any statements as such were contained in the song titles, while the songs *per se* left the listeners to do the thinking for themselves. Once the audience got beyond the titles, the songs worked on two levels, and for those less interested or even unaware of the more submerged meaning, the music itself – 'beautiful, captivating and poetic', in the words of *Sounds* at the time – was lure enough.

McCarthy appeared on *C86*, offering up 'Celestial City', a song that John Williamson told the Penny Black website the band considered to be its best to date. 'When we finished it we thought it sounded great, easily our best recorded song to that point,' he told the site. 'We soon had also recorded 'Red Sleeping Beauty' and realised we were totally wrong. I actually can't remember if we knew before or after we submitted it to the *NME* that we could have given them something so much better, but boy, we really could have.' This is Malcolm Eden's view, as well: 'We used to record demos of our songs on Tim's Fostex 4-track tape recorder, just the guitar parts and bass, and a guitar playing the melody. Some of these demos were really good, and 'Celestial City' was one of them. Unfortunately, when we came to record it in the studio, it was nowhere near as good. I always found it a bit leaden and dull, to be frank…'

In March 1987, McCarthy released their third single, the much more substantial 'Frans Hals'. With its signature jangling guitars and crisp drum part, it was yet another offering of astonishing beauty. This time Eden found inspiration for the lyrics from John Berger's classic art treatise, *Ways Of Seeing*, where the author describes how the Dutch Golden Age artist memorialised in the song painted his *Regents of the Old Men's Alms House* (in Haarlem) as a subtle form of revenge for his impoverished state.

There was a further single in the autumn, by which time Pink had folded and Paul Sutton had re-launched the label as September Records. McCarthy by then was also in the process of recording a debut album, *I Am A Wallet*. It was released a couple of months later in November and borrowed a painting (*The Funeral*) by of one of the band's heroes, George Grosz, for its cover art. As ever, the song titles were explicit labels of the content contained within – 'An MP Speaks', 'Charles Windsor', 'The Vision of Peregrine Worsthorne', 'In The Dark Times',

'The Procession of Popular Capitalism', etc… And as ever the songs were delivered via 'the reedy, choirboy voice of Malcolm Eden which is vulnerable and wise but never hectoring,' according to Jack Barron, reviewing the album for the *NME*. 'Bad news on the home front has seldom sounded so wistfully camouflaged, delivered like cyanide pellets among the tea and crumpets.'

Inevitably, Margaret Thatcher was the muse for *I Am A Wallet* (and would continue to serve the band in that role) but Malcolm Eden's lyrics were informed as much by literary technique. He'd worked in a bookshop briefly and around the age of sixteen had started reading a lot of poetry. 'I used to pore over poetry into the night,' he told the Louder Than War website in 2014. 'I particularly liked William Blake, Keats, Shelley, Gerard Manley Hopkins and TS Eliot. I always liked the sound of the words in their poetry, perhaps even more than the meaning.' McCarthy lyrics often eschew rhyme, sometime favouring alliteration, as in 'Up and down the Strand I strolled…' ('A Child Soon In Chains') and he has used Brecht's Alienation Effect, which distances the audience from emotional involvement in a work by deliberately stressing the artificiality of the performance itself. All of this makes what might otherwise on the surface appear to be straight-forward three-minute pop songs unusual.

Four more singles followed and an EP, and by the time that McCarthy ended the band played the same number of BBC radio sessions (three for John Peel and one for Janice Long) and recorded two further albums, *The Enraged Will Inherit The Earth* and *Banking, Violence & The Inner Life Today*. Once again, the song titles on the later releases crisply tell the tale – 'Should The Bible Be Banned?', 'The Home Secretary Briefs The Forces Of Law & Order', 'And Tomorrow The Stock Exchange Will Be The Human Race', 'The Drinking Song Of The Merchant Bankers', and so on. By the time of the third album, in 1989, Laetitia Sadier had joined on vocals, helping reinvigorate the band.

McCarthy played a final gig at the London School of Economics in 1990 before Malcolm Eden quit, apparently feeling that the band had reached its zenith. Tim Gane and Laetitia Sadier went on to form Stereolab whilst Malcolm Eden formed Herzfield, with Nathalie Joly and Philippe Lavergne. Gary Baker went off to become a journalist and John Williamson became a music publisher.

'Towards the end, I really wanted to make music that made a comment on the lyrics,' says Malcolm Eden. 'So, for example, there would be a statement in the lyrics that was "contradicted" or "commented on" by the music. It would have been hard to achieve, but it made me feel dissatisfied with what we were doing, or at least made me think we couldn't do very much better, so I prefered to call it a day.'

After they had signed the band, Pink Records had introduced McCarthy to another label band, the Wolfhounds. David Callahan went to see McCarthy live at the Enterprise pub in Camden in late 1985 and the two bands struck up a friendship. When it came time for McCarthy to record 'Red Sleeping Beauty', Callahan (who has a production credit on the record) was present in the studio. 'The Wolfhounds had already made a decent-sounding disc with 'Cut The Cake' and so, as a mate and a fan, I was asked to come in and offer my opinions and keep an eye on proceedings. I didn't do an awful lot, just tried to make sure the record sounded reasonably powerful and balanced and reinforced the band's wishes to avoid bland, '80s-style effects in the face of an engineer who was used to recording bland AOR rock bands. I got them to put down two bass tracks which was unconventional, but really the record is the band's live sound sharpened up a bit, and it mostly came from them.'

The Wolfhounds weren't only friends but close neighbours, based just down the road from Barking in Romford. They too had a history that went back reasonably far – David Callahan (vocals) and Paul Clark (guitar) had been at school together just after punk and began playing together in 1980. Callahan had three guitar lessons before stopping, and Clark was a southpaw that spun his right-handed guitar upside down and began playing that way. 'All our early rehearsals ended with our fingers covered in blood,' recalls Callahan. 'We didn't know you were meant to use plectrums.'

Having left school in 1982, Callahan went off to college for a year, but it didn't agree with him – 'I was really out of sorts there. It was full of spoilt kids and I didn't like it all. At the same time, there didn't seem to be any obvious cultural way out of the situation we were in, so the most obvious thing for both Paul and I seemed to be to carry on playing in bands. I was fortunate in that I had got into punk at a really early age – I was twelve or thirteen, the only kid in my group into that music – and so ended up hanging around with older kids, some of whom were eighteen and nineteen. I sort of became their mascot. Some of them went on to be in the Purple Hearts and Department S, so I was shown an example of how you could do something from scratch and yet suddenly become well-known for it. And that set something off in the back of my head somewhere that there was some kind of way out of normal life, or out of the drudgery of it.'

The Purple Hearts had ridden the tails of the Mod revival but singer Bob Manton and drummer Simon Stebbing haboured a secret passion for playing '60s garage rock and needed a below-radar outlet for it. They roped in Callahan and Clark who ended up backing Manton and Stebbing as they ploughed their way through songs by bands such as the Thirteenth Floor Elevators, the Seeds and Love. 'They were playing similar stuff to that being played by bands like thee Milkshakes and the Sting-Rays,' says Callahan. 'Mike Spenser from the Cannibals organised his club, the Garage, and sometimes hosted it at the Clarendon Hotel in Hammersmith. He took us under his wing and let us play gigs there quite a lot. We were called the Changelings. Things went well, but then, around 1983, Simon and Bob sort of gave up on us, although we were already starting to write our own stuff anyway. That was when we decided to call our band the Wolfhounds.'

The Wolfhounds rumbled on, but got a lot more serious about the band in 1984 when Andy Golding joined as second guitarist. The line-up was David Callahan, Andy Golding, and Paul Clark, together with Andy Bolton on bass and Frank Stebbing, Simon Stebbing's fifteen-year-old brother (who often needed sneaking into gigs), on drums. 'We had equipment, but it was all cheap and some of it was nicked and some of it stuff borrowed and never returned,' says Callahan. 'Paul got his equipment, along with a battered bass, from a German woman who lived in the same council block. Her son had beaten her up, so in revenge she took all his musical equipment and gave it to Paul.'

Also in 1984, the Rezz Club in Romford opened. It was run by a friend of David Callahan's called Chris French who began semi-managing the Wolfhounds and let them play the club on a regular basis. The Rezz attracted a host of indie bands, such as the Membranes, the Three Johns and others and a steady stream of musicians passed through giving the fledgling Wolfhounds the chance to start making a few contacts. After a while, French realised that if he was going to take managing the band seriously he needed to get them some gigs other than at the Rezz and the Clarendon and he began calling up London clubs like the Marquee and hassling them for support slots. 'We got supports with old punk bands like Chelsea and New Psychedelia bands like the Playn Jayn, none of them we liked very much, but the gigs worked. We stuck out like a sore thumb – young and naïve and dressed in nothing but second-hand clothes and playing really cheap gear.'

The Wolfhounds played squats, dingy bars, basements, colleges, and anywhere that would have them. According to Callahan, they were on the circuit for a long time before they even met another band listening to the kind of music they listened to, let alone one that shared the same ideas. Influences feeding in included post punk records on Rough Trade and Postcard and similar labels and the more obscure stuff gleaned from Julian Cope's *Tales From The Drug Attic*. They were listening to jazz from the 1950s and 1960s and the work of pastoral singer songwriters like Nick Drake. 'All this,' admits Callahan, 'while still being barely able to master three chords...'

Playing supports to all and sundry hardly put the band on the fast track to indie success but did lead to a succession of mentions in the live reviews sections of the music press, and often the reviewer favoured the Wolfhounds over the lead act. The Wolfhounds supported Turkey Bones & the Wild Dogs at the start of 1985 and were rewarded with a well-observed mention from Mat Snow in the *NME* who called them (rightly) 'five badly-dressed youthniks... reversing into 1985 via the Fall and, strange but true, the Seeds'. The band's sound teetered on 'the very edge of rock 'n' roll's ledge' and was a 'throbbing, hysterical garage rumble framing weird atonal guitarisms and Dave Callahan's psych-out preachifying – the Wolfhounds, a band not to be ignored.' Six months later, in *Sounds*, Robin Gibson was also picking up on their youthfulness when the band played the Clarendon – 'they look like they've just come from school' – but also praising their 'upside-down, Sixties-tinged pop dynamics that could manage a happy marriage of the Voidoids and Dusty Springfield.' The gig at the Clarendon had taken place on 17 May, the same Friday night that the Rain Parade (on their first, eagerly-awaited visit to the UK) played the upstairs room of the venue. Fearing that the Wolfhounds gig would be all but deserted and picking up on the growing dissatisfaction with the infatuation the music press seemed to have with the Paisley Underground (which was undeniably detrimental to both new UK *and* US bands who missed out on coverage), Callahan took matters into his own hands, leafleting the snaking Rain Parade queue with a samizdat flyer that read: 'FED UP WITH TENTH-RATE PSYCHEDELIA? COME AND SEE THE WOLFHOUNDS DOWNSTAIRS TONIGHT. CHEAPER, MORE EXCITING, NASTIER. DEPORT NEW-WAVE HIPPIES.'

Good reviews helped but the band was no closer to signing a record contract of any sort. At the end of 1984, the Wolfhounds had gone into a studio and made a four-track demo at a cost of £65. None of the tracks saw the light of day (although one, 'Skullface', was reworked and issued thirty years later). They'd posted tape copies off to EMI and CBS and awaited the rejection letters that arrived a month or so later. 'I had absolutely no idea what to do next,' says Callahan. He filled in time by going out to lots of gigs, discovering the events being put on by Leigh Goorney at Thames Polytechnic and being introduced for the first time to the sounds of bands like Big Flame and Bog-Shed whose waywardness and enthusiasm he immediately liked. Appraising the competition was part of the learning curve.

'I saw Sonic Youth for the first time at Thames Poly, and I remember being really excited but also really disappointed,' remembers Callahan. 'At home I'd taken one of my Woolworths guitars and tuned all the strings to the same note, copying Lou Reed's 'ostrich guitar'. We thought that nobody else was doing that and then realised that Sonic Youth was way ahead of us. As soon as we knew that someone else was covering the territory we looked for somewhere else to go. All of the time, you looked to other bands as competition, but that at least made for a creative environment.'

By the middle of 1985 David Callahan's band was being reviewed in the music press regularly. Callahan had come into contact with a number of indie bands in passing but knew only two people involved in the scene. One was John Robb, the other, journalist Ron Rom who one day suggested to Callahan that he should go and see a band called the June Brides. Ron Rom favourably compared the music the June Brides played to that of Josef K. 'He told me that they had a trumpet player and that piqued my interest,' remembers Callahan. 'He also told me to make sure that I brought a tape along to the gig he was suggesting we go to because he knew that there was going to be someone there from the June Brides' record label. On the night I just gave the tape to Simon Down from Pink and didn't say a word. I settled down to watch the June Brides and loved what I saw. Second-hand suits, crappy cheap haircuts and, what I *really* liked, the music they played was off-key beat music. I could see out of the corner of my eye that this was a tribe I could belong to, but I was still a bit cynical…'

A couple of days after the show, Simon Down called Callahan and told him that he wanted to make a record with the Wolf-hounds on the strength of the £65 demo that Callahan had given him. Down had been impressed with a track called 'Sand Castles' that featured the unusual addition of slide guitar. The demo, however, was ten months old and, taking a more forward-looking approach, the Wolfhounds decided instead to release the four newest songs that they had.

The four tracks on 'Cut The Cake' were recorded in November 1985 at Scarf studios in Bow. The studio was tiny, barely big enough to contain a drum kit and nestled into a space next to the owner's living room, yet compared to the studio where the demo had been recorded was richly appointed, complete with a 24-track desk. The engineer on the record had previously been in novelty band the Tweets, setting up a precedent of sorts for the Wolfhounds went on to rehearse in a studio owned by the Rubettes.

'"LA Juice" was a record with a guitar sound that divided people,' recalls Callahan. 'This wasn't a sound like the feedback backwash effect of the Jesus & Mary Chain but something that was right in your face. So we knew that had to go on the record.

We knew it was a standout number that would separate us from a lot of the wishy-washy bands that we were starting to hear around then. "Cut The Cake" was like a psychedelic pop song, so we also knew that needed to be included. I don't know why we added "Deadthink", a sort of belated homage to the Birthday Party. I really wish we hadn't included that. The final track was "Another Hazy Day on The Lazy 'A'", which was just weird. I'm not sure where that came from'.

The critics more or less agreed with him, generally favouring three of the four tracks and viewing 'Deadthink' as more of an anachronism ('as deflatable as the sum of its influences', according to *NME*). The twin guitar attack (also favoured also by bands such as the Nightingales) hit a target, Bruce Dessau noting at the time how 'Cut The Cake' was 'almost drowned in cross currents of melody and malady, slickness and sickness, as one guitar churns out a relentless white noise and t'other picks out a spindly, chilling tune'. Richard Boon writing in the *Catalogue* thought that there was nothing that quite compared with the sound of the Wolfhounds, which was 'full of big, reverbed, trebly guitars, swamp-blues vocals, repetitive riffs and a heartfelt yearning', even if, on occasion, the band was 'a little too determined to put the "rage" into "garage"'. The record made Single of the Week in *Sounds*. 'Everything you've read about this band is true,' declared Mick Mercer in *Melody Maker*.

The Wolfhounds had found their pack but were still uncomfortable: 'We could be aloof, and we would always try to blow any band off stage that we were playing with no matter how much we liked them. I guess that by the time that we found some like-minded people we'd developed a bit of a chip on our shoulder. We certainly felt that we hadn't received the advantages of some other bands and it made us feel isolated and see ourselves at the time very much as underdogs. The bands we played with tended to have better gear than us, they had better clothes, and they all seemed to get on – they'd been to the same college or whatever. It was like that for a long time. So, when we fell in with the new indie crowd we were naïvely intimate but at the same time mistrustful of them…'

One band the Wolfhounds did form a close bond with was McCarthy. McCarthy weren't just label mates but close east end neighbours and the two bands quickly became close, playing a number gigs together before McCarthy went into Scarf studios to record 'Red Sleeping Beauty'. 'Malcolm Eden, in particular, was a witty and intelligent person,' recalls Callahan. 'McCarthy were more of an out and out pop band than us and very politicised. Malcolm had been part of the RCP and knew about the various strands of socialism and could talk about avant-garde literature and Brecht, an author he admired – all of which we were ignorant of back then. We *were* political, in the sense that the punk phrase *No Future* had certainly come true for us and what I was trying to do in my writing was reflect the situation we were in back through what felt like a fractured mirror.…

'I ended up on so many Government schemes and community programmes and what jobs we ever had we tended to lose because it was impossible to turn up on time in the morning if a gig had gone on late or taken place far from home. I'd worked at Our Price for a bit and then at the DHSS, but I quit that after the bassist rang up and left a message with my boss to pass on to me to say that we'd got a John Peel session booked – I'd kept that I was in a band quiet – and I was asked to choose, band or job. I was still able to claim dole immediately, though, since back then you just went and signed on in another borough. We made a choice for things to be that way, but we needed some income since we didn't make any money on the gigs. The songs very much reflected what I saw around me, a decaying society, one drained and corrupt it seemed, and one that only worked for the top percentile. This may sound familiar right now…'

The obvious chip on the shoulder and the sheer force with which they presented themselves led many to view the band as making political statements – the second single, for instance, 'Anti-Midas Touch' some regarded as Marxist in tone, although David Callahan's lyrics tend to the impressionistic rather than the explicit. This is politics with a small 'p' and an eye turned on the topography and the chancers and no-hopers of the east end where Callahan lived. It's there sometimes in the song titles – 'Boy Racers, RM1', 'Disgusted, E7', 'Public Footpath Blues' – and also in the words. In 'Goodbye Laughter 'the streets are sheened with last night's sweat'; in 'Public Footpath Blues' a beggar is crashed out on the pavement 'but innocent passers-by never look underneath'; and in 'Disgusted, E7' itself, Callahan sings:

> I rode to Aldgate on the 225
> And the crowd shook me alive
> And I swear by the dirt in my nails
> And by the will that always fails
> These are the streets where nothing grows…

'Trashland, USA, Romford-style, guitars singing and spitting out their fury' is how the Legend! described the Wolfhounds' music in their first *NME* interview in March 1986, but by the time of the second single eight months later it was the band's more melodic side that shone through. Between the two singles the band had contributed a track to *C86* – something 'knocked out quickly' ('Feeling So Strange Again') for a tape that would be yesterday's news before the year was out. 'The *NME* would pay for studio time for a day,' Andy Golding told John Robb in *Death To Trad Rock*, 'so we thought that if we got the song for their tape out of the way quickly then we could record some demos as well… No one wanted to give away good songs to a tape that would only be available via mail order in a music paper, as no-one really knew how it would be received, or how they would promote it… What were we all thinking?' The contribution fell far short of the splendour that was 'Anti-Midas Touch'.

As is the case with so many tracks by the Wolfhounds, there's quietly controlled emotion – part rage, part wonder, and part astonishment – bubbling just beneath the surface of 'The Anti-Midas Touch'. David Callahan's vocals sore and swoop – 'you pray to the sun and worship the dirt', and the underscoring guitar riff is simply magnificent. The song predates Nirvana by a few years but Kurt Cobain must surely have been listening to the riff when he wrote 'Smells Like Teen Spirit'. Callahan's (lifelong) interest in paleontology and wildlife helped add a nice subliminal touch when coming up with the cover design that mirrors the song's theme: 'The covers of both versions of the single feature birds – a pelican and an Hawaiian O'o – that are extinct, they've failed.'

'The Anti-Midas Touch' was a firm favourite when the band played live (and a blistering recorded version had already delighted listeners when the band's first – of two – John Peel session was aired in March 1986). The song had originally been written back in 1984 but, says Callahan, the addition of some impressive guitar input by Andy Golding once he'd joined made it an altogether superior number. It was the only old track that the band chose to record when they went into Scarf studios again in the early autumn to start recording their debut album.

'We kind of did a stupid and naïve thing when it came to choosing what to record for *Unseen Ripples From A Pebble (Become Tidal Waves On A Shore)*,' remembers Callahan. 'Up until mid-1986 we were still playing a lot of noisy, discordant music that sat more at the garage end of things. Whether or not we were influenced by the approach of Wire, who always seemed to move on after each record, we decided to just record new tracks for the album and consequently dumped quite a lot of good songs, something I later came to regret. We had little experience in the studio as well and fell into that trap of mixing everything high (which can make the recording sound artificially powerful), when we should have listened to it at normal hearing level. To me, it came out sounding tinny and thin…' The album received good – albeit brief – reviews but sold less well, shifting around 6,000 of the 10,000 hoped for.

'By the time we got around to recording our first album we were musically scizophrenic,' Andy Golding told John Robb. 'My heart wanted me to be in AC/DC, my head told me that the Smiths sold loads of records. We were listening to the Fire Engines, Captain Beefheart and Wire but the music press had gone pop-friendly… I was really into Johnny Marr's playing, as was [Paul] Clarkie, and we mistakenly believed that if we made a "clean" pop album then we would get to number one, become famous and could all retire. Distorted guitars were not in vogue and we turned ours down just at the point when we should have been turning the amps up to eleven.'

'We'd moved on, even by the time *Unseen Ripples* came out and we had wanted to extend our palette,' says Callahan. 'We didn't like the way a lot of independent bands were becoming more and more jangly in their sound and deliberately trying to be commercial, and all that bowl haircut and stripy jumper pose was an anathema to us. We started bringing more of our influences to bear – everything from the Pop Group and John Coltrane to hip-hop – and the press anyway had written off *C86*, which we were lumped in with, in a last-year's-thing kind of way.'

The Wolfhounds toured with My Bloody Valentine and took note of the range of guitar sounds Kevin Shields was conjuring up with the aid of effects. This was assimilated when the Wolfhounds went in to the studios to record a mini-album in 1989. *Blown Away* was recorded live, an approach the band hadn't taken since 1985's debut single. In spite of a generally purist approach, the album was made using some of the guitar effects that many bands were starting to favour. A new element to the sound was introduced with vocalist Mary Hansen, who went on to work with Stereolab, adding some fitting extra melody to counterpoint the general noise of the sound elsewhere.

'The album came out but we struggled to get reviews or any kind of publicity,' recalls Callahan. 'A few stood by us, including Bob Stanley who absolutely raved about the record. But nobody was listening, and I think the album sold only around 900 copies all done.' The record, being neither an album proper nor a single was ineligible for both the singles and the album charts.

There was a final album, *Attitude*. It was almost a contractual obligation album, yet one that still maintained the band's high standards even if it suffered the usual fate of positive reviews matched by negative sales. The strain on the band began to show and although the Wolfhounds toured to promote the new album's release – including a couple of sell-out dates at the Falcon in Camden, and what would turn out to be a final gig in Brighton – they quickly bowed to the inevitable.

'By 1990, we'd knackered ourselves out touring,' says Callahan. 'We were still rehearsing in our front rooms or bedrooms and we were broke, still on the dole. We could barely afford to eat. We called it a day.'

Back at the start of 1986, a new dawn beckoned as a genuine effort was made to engage young people in the politics of their day-to-day life. International Youth Year had ended on a positive note, with the setting up of Red Wedge. Although launched in conjunction with the Labour Party, Red Wedge was, as the *NME* noted in breaking the story in its 30 November 1985 issue, 'a drive to mobilise the vote for the next election' and was only 'loosely affiliated' to the Labour Party. Its broad aim at the outset was, perhaps, somewhat similar to that of the Rock Against Racism movement that had risen up following the racist killing of factory machinist

Altab Ali in Whitechapel in 1978. One of RAR's early pioneers, David Widgery, later described how people 'outside conventional politics, inspired by a mixture of socialism, punk rock and common humanity, got together and organised to change things'.

Red Wedge (Labour officials worried that Fleet Street would have a field day with the use of the word *Red*) took its name from the Russian constructivist artist El Lissitzky's painting *Beat The Whites With The Red Wedge*. Billy Bragg, the movement's most visible driving engine, had also been inspired by the concerts he had done supporting the work of the beleaguered GLC, where leaflets and paraphernalia were handed out and dialogue and debate could take place. This would be the case with a Red Wedge tour planned to start in Manchester on 25 January.

Post the Red Wedge announcement and prior to the tour, *Melody Maker* organised a debate where a number of those involved or deemed to have an interest offered views as to the viability of the organisation. Billy Bragg, Jerry Dammers, Paul Weller and the Labour MP Clare Short were all involved with Red Wedge, whilst Chris Dean of the Redskins, a member of the SWP, offered the doubter's view. Greg Knight, Conservative MP for Derby North (and owner of a recording studio) was against the movement, as was Stewart Copeland, former member of rock band the Police and avowed 'raving capitalist'.

A week earlier, in announcing Red Wedge to its paper's readers, *Melody Maker* had cruelly put its finger on what it saw as a problem that plagued both camps: 'The campaign trail starts with punters listening to Billy singing "It Says Here", which leads them to "New England", which leads them to AJP Taylor, which leads them to Ramsay MacDonald, which leads them to socialism, which leads them to Kinnock, which leads them up the garden path.'

Neither side trusted the politicians, and neither side trusted the media, Billy Bragg commenting that that the last election 'was fought on Michael Foot's duffle coat'. The plan, initially, was to 'run ideas up a flagpole for people to see whether they want to join'. Chris Dean's aversion to Red Wedge was ideological – the Labour Party was bad enough, but a Labour Party in power would inevitably shift to the right. Music, noted the equable Bragg, had 'always been a good vehicle for socialism'. It was also, thought Stewart Copeland, 'the best possible flag for capitalism. The thing about socialism is that it's great for writing songs about – you have intense emotive issues.' But socialism didn't work practically. Money was love. Capitalism just wasn't romantic. 'There's a blinkered view of socialism that comes from the right wing that says that socialism is going to drag everyone down to the sewer level,' countered Paul Weller. 'But the idea of socialism… is to raise people up.' People would go to the Red Wedge concerts primarily, thought Greg Knight, 'because they liked the music not because they agreed with the politics.'

Many musicians joined Bragg in Red Wedge, including Paul Weller, Strawberry Switchblade, Kirsty McCall and Jimmy Somerville. Those who lent support for tours included the Style Council, the Communards, Junior Giscombe, Jerry Dammers, Madness, and Lloyd Cole & The Commotions. Robert Wyatt, an avowed Trotskyist, also supported the socialist group, maintaining at the time that Billy Bragg's sharpness would force Neil Kinnock and the right wing of the Labour party to match up.

The inaugural tour went well, with many unadvertised guests showing up to lend support, including the Smiths and Prefab Sprout and the reviews from the London-based media elite were reassuringly positive, John Gill in *Time Out* making the point that 'out of London and away from the brutish consumerism promoted by the likes of the *Face*, the Red Wedge tour developed a momentum that surprised its most cautious supporters'.

Making Red Wedge work was a tough ask. Certain old school labour strongholds were wary of the organisation's motives, suspecting a connection with Militant (a Trotskyist faction that had grown out of the paper of the same name), or else just stuck in their ways where youth wasn't considered. According to Andrew Collins' biography of Bragg, *Still Suitable For Miners*, the local party in Derby told the singer: 'Don't bother coming here, we haven't got any young people.' Some people generally were sympathetic but objected to the name – Elvis Costello, for one (although he did by default play one gig on behalf of Red Wedge). Then there was the Militant faction itself, who, according at least to Bragg and others involved, did everything they could to sabotage Red Wedge's efforts, including falsely advertising Paul Weller as playing at a gig, a disaster partly salvaged when Elvis Costello offered to step in and play the gig.

One of the biggest obstacles Red Wedge had to overcome, however, was the cynicism of some of those it targeted, some of whom saw the involvement of name musicians as just another example of celebrities easing their consciences a la Live Aid. Others criticised a perceived trendiness. Getting *Face* designer Neville Brody to come up with the logo didn't help. 'Isn't Red Wedge just another accessory to match the stitching on Robert Elm's 501s?' wrote one worried reader in the *Gasbag* column of *NME*, a point made more forcefully by Julie Burchill in *Time Out* who worried that Red Wedge was 'in danger of becoming the Saatchi & Saatchi of socialism'. Matters for some weren't helped when Red Wedge's co-ordinator, Paul Bower (an activist and former editor of the excellent punk fanzine *Gun Rubber*) flippantly told the *NME* that Red Wedge 'wasn't a bunch of bores in flared jeans and raincoats trying to sell some dull paper' thus alienating a fair few who gave up their Saturday mornings selling political papers outside factories. In 2015, comedian Phil Jupitus, who appeared on the Red Wedge tour as Porky the Poet, told the spiritofmarckarlin blog: 'The reason I got involved was 20% because I believed in the cause, 30% because I loved Billy Bragg, and 50% because I wanted to meet Paul Weller.'

Red Wedge was not a political movement but, to use its own words, 'a broad Left alliance' yet it illustrated the difficulty of tethering pop and politics together. Asked by the *NME* what he thought of Red Wedge shortly after it came into being, Tony – 'Red Wedgie', as the paper jokingly dubbed him – Benn told Quentin McDermott that he doubted very much that you could 'replace politics with pop music' (and presumably vice-versa). 'I think you've got to distinguish very clearly,' he added, 'between what I would call political music, which is the music of the people, and for the people, and is part of the struggle – and a public relations view of the role that music might play – like the Pied Piper of Hamelin, where you *collect* a lot of people and guide them in by indirect means. I think you've always got to keep an eye out for the use of any art-form as a come-on to the people.'

According to Andrew Collins in *Still Suitable For Miners*, Red Wedge *did* help in that it 'apparently increased Labour's vote among eighteen to 24 year olds' (although he doesn't quote statistics and the overall turnout in the election was in any event slightly up). The 'cool-looking manifesto', *Move On Up*, that Red Wedge produced ('all woodcuts and Style Council typography') was ultimately all to no avail, though, when on 11 June 1987, the Conservatives were once more returned to power. A robust economy and lower taxes were two of the main planks of the Conservative campaign, but also a firm commitment to defence, leading the SDP's Dr David Owen to comment – obliquely referring to Neil Kinnock's abrasive style – that the British public had overwhelmingly shown that they 'preferred sandbags to windbags'.

But this is to leap forward, and there were further battles to be fought in the first half of 1986. It wasn't just regional local councils that came under fire and the Greater London Council received the long expected mortal blow from Margaret Thatcher's government and was dissolved at the end of March, waving goodbye to the various free festivals and support structures that had been put in place for the benefit of young people. The benefits had been spectacular – as anyone who witnessed the 1985 Jobs For Change Festival in Battersea Park (where an estimated 500,000 spectators showed up and Billy Bragg, Aswad, the Pogues and others played) could testify. The threat of nuclear annihilation also swam back into focus following the Chernobyl Nuclear Reactor disaster in April creating bitter arguments about the then safety of nuclear power: at Seascale, the village closest to the British nuclear plant Sellafield, cancer rates were ten times higher than the national average. The government ran a very pro-nuclear initiative, offering day trips to Sellafield (a site guarded by armed police where customers exited through the gift shop which had an array of souvenirs on sale, such as 'I'VE BEEN TO SEL-LAFIELD!' badges and carrier bags boldly proclaiming 'CLICK ON TO NUCLEAR ENERGY!). The anti-nuclear protest took in also the Peace Convoy – 'a hundred vehicles, 400 people and a million dogs', according to journalist Steven Wells – a group of travellers who travelled in convoy between various CND sites and various free festivals. Targeted by the Government, police and right-wing media as particularly insidious vermin, the worst skirmish took place on 1 June 1985 during the so-called Battle of Beanfield, when 600 people fought Wiltshire Police in an attempt to set up the 'cancelled' Stonehenge Free Festival. The 'medieval brigands' (in the words of one tabloid newspaper) later won damages from an over zealous force, one that resorted in their frenzy to even clubbing pregnant women with children, according to the *Observer*. Over 500 people were detained in one of the largest mass arrests in English history.

CHAPTER 22

'SWIRLING 'ROUND THE GARDEN'

THE SOUP DRAGONS' FLEXI DISC, 'If You Were The Only Girl In The World' made Single of the Week in the *NME* at the end of 1985. A split release obtainable only via the *Legend!* fanzine or *Pure Popcorn* fanzine, it was the first time a national music paper had garlanded such an obscure item with the grand status. A thousand copies of the flexi had been printed up at a cost of £70. In the scheme of things, the *Legend!* was one of the more prestigious organs of indie, but *Pure Popcorn* (published in the Glasgow suburb of Bearsdan and hand-written), was more remote, reflecting (as did the *NME* review) a kind of suburban response to the metropolitan elite.

Alan McGee's comment that when he first met the Jesus & Mary Chain they 'looked like punks by accident', like 'a small town version of a movement', wasn't being critical but stating fact. Glasgow did for independent music what Seattle later did for Grunge, but in a pre-internet/ social media age cultural interpretation was a hit-and-miss thing. Instinct, rather than the weighing up of instantly-available cultural poses shaped expression.

Sushil Dade edited *Pure Popcorn* and was also a member of the Soup Dragons. The Soup Dragons were a band from Belshill, a Glasgow suburb not too far from the new town the Jesus & Mary Chain came from. Belshill became a seed-bed of indie activity in 1985, even if, being thirteen miles from the centre of Glasgow, its isolation meant that those involved needed to be more imaginative. 'You had to suss people out,' recalls Sean Dickson, who founded the band. 'When I was fourteen or so, I met this boy called Norman who used to wear tartan trousers and lived around the corner from me. For some reason, I just knew that he was going to be the same kind of person as I was, I knew that I was going to like him, be able to hang out with him.'

It turned out that Norman Blake was every bit as obsessive about music as Dickson was. By the time that he met Blake, Dickson already had quite a musical history. He'd been pressganged into taking classical guitar lessons by his parents between the ages of seven and thirteen, but had then rebelled, acquiring a Roland synthesizer and drum machine and compiling in 1982 his first 'album', an electronic extravaganza influenced by a love of the so-called 'Sheffield Sound' of the time. Recorded using two mono tape recorders, *Silent Industry* featured a cover version of the Human League's 'Crow And The Baby' and some primitive dub achieved by pressing the record button on the machines on and off in rapid succession. It wasn't available to the wider world.

Dickson then began hearing records by the Pastels and the early Jesus & Mary Chain and his loyalties swung back to the guitar: 'Norman's parents were newsagents and the house they lived in was next door to the shop. While they were working we had the run of the house and set up guitars and synthesizers and messed about. I guess we were making the equivalent of about one album's worth of material a week. At some point we decided that we'd start busking in Glasgow, not to make money, but simply for the fun of freaking people out…'

Joining Dickson and Blake was school friend Duglas T Stewart. The three would set up their busking pitch and then bewilder the Saturday afternoon shoppers with Throbbing Gristle songs played acoustically, or Velvet Underground numbers, or, on one memorable occasion, a version of Talking Head's 'Psycho Killer', delivered in appropriately psychotic fashion, by Stewart. The three also formed a band, led by Stewart, called the Pretty Flowers, and played the local Hattonrith Hotel, mainly to annoy the substantial band of anarchist punks who all lived in the local caravan park. One day, sitting in the kitchen and watching a movie on television, Stewart told Dickson that he was packing in the Pretty Flowers and Dickson told him to start a new band. But what would it be called? asked Stewart. 'We were watching the film BMX Bandits,' remembers Dickson, 'and I suggested that BMX Bandits would probably be the worst name ever for a group, why not go with it…?'

By that point, the Soup Dragons had formed. Guitarist Jim McCulloch was a fellow busker, and an accomplished musician to boot: through seeing each other around, Dickson, Dade and McCulloch somehow got together, recruiting guitarist Ross Sinclair from a band called Gods For All Occasions to play drums. Sinclair's debut attempt at drumming took place the first time the Soup Dragons played live, supporting Primal Scream at Splash One on 14 July 1985. Such was the ramshackle nature of the band that the gig was also the first time that Dickson had ever sung into a microphone.

Shortly after the flexi disc was reviewed in *NME*, Dickson received a phone call from John Peel inviting the band to come to London to record a Peel session. 'We had absolutely no money to get to London. Peel said to meet him the following day after the phone call at Queen Margaret's College where he was appearing. He pulled out £150 in cash from his pocket and asked me if that would be enough to get the band to London. Right up until the day he died, I been trying to pay him back but he'd never take the money…'

A demo tape circulating ('You Have Some Too') summed up the infectious nature of the band's sound – 'always, we wanted to play as fast and loud as we could,' recalls Sean – which was part garage band thrash and part pure pop essence. 'The greatest contribution we could make,' Sean Dickson told the *NME* at the time, 'has nothing to do with music and everything to do with enjoying ourselves.' The band seemed able to bottle enthusiasm in a way few of the competitors could equal. Inevitably, references to Buzzcocks abounded, but something more primal was at work: Ross Sinclair, for instance, had to go out and buy a copy of *Singles Going Steady* (a Buzzcocks compilation) to make sense of the comparisons since he'd never previously heard the Manchester band. A bigger influence on the Soup Dragons had been, argu-ably, Wire – another band who, in the words of Dickson, 'played pop songs with distorted guitars and a bit of life in them'.

One of the band's key admirers, Stephen Pastel, sent a copy of the band's demo tape to Martin Whitehead at Subway Organ-isation. In December, the Soup Dragons went into Pier Head Studios in Glasgow to begin recording a four-track EP, 'The Sun Is In The Sky'. The results were mixed and something of a ragbag – from the atmospheric 'Quite Content', with its quintessential early Soup Dragons sound, to 'Fair's Fair', which employs a Sui-cide-style electronic drum rhythm and rips off Metal Urbaine's 'Paris Maquis' ('Ross insisted on playing some drums, so we let him bang a snare, a bit like the Shop Assistants'). The intrigu-ing 'Not For Humbert' took inspiration from Nabakov's *Lolita*, and delivered up a prophetic line, 'All good stories have a happy ending.' In the end, the EP was scrapped, the band preferring to launch its career with the altogether more accomplished 'Whole Wide World' single that appeared in spring 1986, a ninety-sec-ond blast of feral guitar and feverish vocal that leapt into the independent chart and was only kept off the number one slot by the Mission.

The Soup Dragons session for John Peel was broadcast in February and shortly after that they made their London debut, supporting the Shop Assistants at the Room At The Top. They signed a management deal with Jaz Summers (ex manager of Wham) and set up their own RAW TV record label, releasing the 'Hang Ten' single in October. Both 'Whole Wide World' and 'Hang Ten' made it into Peel's Festive Fifty for the year (at number 17 and 25 respectively) and the band had a further Peel session broadcast just before Christmas.

One of the earliest *C86* generation bands to begin having chart hits, by the time the band's debut album, *This Is Our Art* came out on Sire in 1988, the four singles released on Raw TV had already entered the mainstream Top 100. As the band became more competent at playing their instruments, and technology advanced, the sound of the band shifted but never strayed from elements that had always been present: when Sean Dickson had graduated from his early dub experiments with mono tape recorders to attempting to nail the perfect two-minute pop song, experimentation was never far away. Back in 1986 when a horrified German promoter informed them that their ten-song, twenty-minute set needed to be stretched to an hour and a half to satisfy the paying customers, they adapted, setting up various beats on the drum machine and introducing the individual instruments dub-style, turning their two minute songs into ten-minute freak outs.

Duglas T Stewart and Norman Blake were hardly left behind by the success of the Soup Dragons, Stewart forming BMX Bandits (with Dickson) and signing with 53rd & 3rd for a debut single, 'E102'. The earlier incarnation of the band, the Pretty Flowers had also at one point contained Frances McKee, later of the Vaselines. Norman Blake formed his own band, the Boy Hairdressers, lifting its moniker from the title of a Joe Orton novel (*Lord Cucumber And The Boy Hairdresser*) at the same time as helping Duglas out with the BMX Bandits. In time, the Boy Hairdressers became Teenage Fanclub.

But Belshill wasn't the only satellite area of Glasgow to be conjuring up indie pop groups. A thriving post-punk scene had existed in Paisley ever since the late 1970s when bands like Defiant Pose and fanzines like *It Ticked And Exploded* (featuring the early writing of Robin Gibson) came into being. One of the very best early-to-mid-1980s fanzines also hailed from Paisley, the short-lived but impassioned *Ferocious Apache* that was edited by Andrew Burnett and Stewart McFadyen. By 1985, *Ferocious Apache* had served its purpose and McFadyen and Burnett were ready for a new challenge, setting up the Close Lobsters.

The Close Lobsters originally started out as a four piece, with Burnett and McFayden, Bob Burnett on bass (later replaced by Paul Bennett) and Graeme Wilmington on guitar. They played locally before adding Tom Donnelly as an extra guitarist, at which point the Close Lobsters began getting the makings of a sound – the music of fast guitars and clean melodies, often served up with an edge that spilled over into the provocative, Andrew Burnett occasionally stalking the stage playing an imaginary guitar. 'I would travel many miles to be able to smile at guitars just so,' claimed the Legend! in an early *NME* review. The band was more than the sum of their influences and the influences were far ranging, from Hendrix through Stump, via the Go-Betweens, Swell Maps, the Fall, the Wedding Present and in particular, the Only Ones.

The band received some early, crucial help from the admiring June Brides. Through the interconnecting world of fanzine swapping, Jon Hunter and the Close Lobsters had been in touch, *Ferocious Apache* reviewing a gig by the June Brides – 'they were like our Buzzcocks,' recalls Andrew Burnett, 'all painted shirts and fast pop.' The June Brides reciprocated by inviting the Close Lobsters to play on a bill with them in London and Hunter wrote about the group in *Bandits One To Five*. Andrew Burnett even joined the fanzine's editorial team, contributing an occasional *Letter From Glasgow* column that he signed off, A. Ogilvie. When the June Brides declined to appear on *C86*, they put forward the name of the Close Lobsters.

Close Lobsters songs were short in length and taut in texture –early live favourites included the ringing, emphatic 'Just Too Bloody Stupid', where Andrew Burnett would howl into the microphone, and 'Firestation Towers', the track that appeared on *C86*, which is ostensibly a love song, but more an ode to the declining fortunes of Paisley's symbolic fire station towers building. 'The song is a sort of tale of unrequited love "underneath the fire station towers",' recalls Andrew Burnett. 'The towers had been derelict for some time but left standing, a completely symbolic reminder of the post-industrial decline of the whole area, of the whole of western Scotland even.'

The band's method of song writing was unusual: snippets of lyrics, fragments of ideas and melodies and breaks were pushed through through the rigours of a live performance: only after the performance would the song then assume its final shape. If musically they shared an affinity with golden guitar bands such as the Wedding Present (with whom they toured, and later gifted a song that the Leeds band recorded for a B-side, 'Let's Make Some Plans'), then intellectually they looked towards more overtly political bands like McCarthy. An early Close Lobsters song, 'Deutschland Democratic Republic Intelligence Network' was inspired by the wrongful imprisonment of the somewhat colourful character Paddy Mehan (who boasted of having helped the British agent and Soviet mole George Blake escape from jail): a singles compilation was given the title *Forever, Until Victory!* – Che Guevara's last farewell to Fidel Castro.

Fire Records signed the Close Lobsters and in November 1986 released 'Going To Heaven To See If It Rains', a credible if somewhat tame debut that was quickly followed by the altogether more mature 'Never Seen Before'. The band's debut album, *Foxheads Stalk This Land*, came out in November, followed, belatedly and somewhat incongruously, by the single chosen to help promote it, 'Let's Make Some Plans', a song complete with 'a guitar figure to make you weep, a hefty noise but God it's joyous' according to Bob Stanley (who later released a single by the band on his Caff label) in the *NME*.

Foxheads pulled off the trick of meshing the melodic beauty of the Close Lobsters overall sound into the anarchic observations of Andrew Burnett who provided cryptic accompanying notes to each of the songs on the album's back cover. The splendour of

'A Prophecy', with its jubilant and ringing guitars, was 'a shadow cast before (ha)nd… "There will be more calamities, more death, more despair"…' The majestic 'I Kiss The Flower In Bloom' was the tale of a narrator 'who woke up on the wrong side of the world'. 'Foxheads' itself was of slightly more prosaic derivation: 'It was meant to be *Fuckheads Stalk This Land*,' says Andrew Burnett, 'but we didn't know if we would get away with using foul language.'

The Close Lobsters juxtaposed language and ideas and a gritty style that was often misinterpreted by those who saw in their name (and therefore nature) something twee. 'It was "Close", as in passageway, out of the general malaise,' claims Andrew Burnett. 'It was "Lob-sters", as in those who would throw things at the powers-that-be.'

The approach was wilfully situ, added Burnett, and summed up by a piece of graffiti from May 1968: 'In a society that has abolished every kind of adventure, the only adventure is to abolish the society.'

The Close Lobsters weren't the only band with a magpie eye that took in subject matter as esoteric as the nuances of eastern bloc culture. Birkenhead band Half Man Half Biscuit had a song called 'All I Want For Christmas Is A Dukla Prague Away Kit', partly inspired by the Czechoslovakian football team but informed also by the nostalgic recollection of growing up in the 1960s in an age of malfunctioning Christmas presents, Scalextric cars and Subutteo football games. The band's work was a synthesis of dole life and pop culture, particularly that experienced through the narrow confines of 1980s television. John Peel called the band a national treasure, one he was quite happy to be buried with.

Half Man Half Biscuit announced themselves in spectacular fashion with 1985's mini-album, *Back In The DHSS*. Recorded for £40 at the studio where songwriter Nigel Blackwell worked as a caretaker, the record referenced a bewildering array of char-acters and scenarios, imagining drug rackets in Trumpton (the fictional town of the children's TV series of the same name) and Haliborange vitamin tablet overdoses and lampooning a whole host of cultural icons and minor British celebrities (including magician Ali Bongo, snooker referee Len Ganley and comedic sidekick Bob Todd). Early on, Blackwell modestly described the songs as 'just pub conversations put to music really'.

Blackwell lived in a flat without a ready supply of heating and, up until the band became popular, signed on. The mini album's title referenced both the Department of Health & Social Security and the Beatles song, 'Back In The USSR'. *Melody Maker* went up to interview the band, and found that in Birkenhead, an area of unusually high unemployment, 'every house we passed on every estate appeared to be occupied despite the fact that it was just after three o'clock on a Wednesday afternoon and every TV set in every house was on'. Yet in spite of the circumstances, Half Man Half Biscuit songs deliberately shied away from preaching on the ills of Thatcherism. Indeed, in one of the band's earliest interviews, Blackwell expressed his intention to spoil his ballot card at the next General Election by scrawling the words Hamilton Bland (the name of an obscure swimming commentator) across it.

Even if the songs weren't political, they were a breath of fresh air for many whose circumstances were challenged and for whom unadorned humour was just what the doctor ordered. Blackwell valued the power of laughter to transfigure and interestingly, like Morrissey, admired George Formby – 'probably the first work-ing-class humourist'. Formby's tragicomic tales mirrored those made by Blackwell, where sadness also had its role to play.

But the songs were generally played for laughs, and possibly the satisfaction of picking up the endless stream of cultural ref-erences that sometimes collided in the most surreal of circum-stances.

> Times flies by when you're the driver of a train
> Speeding out of Trumpton with a cargo of cocaine

sings Blackwell in 'Times Flies By', before adding a little touch of detail that chimed with the psychedelically savvy:

> Under bridges, over bridges, to our destination
> Careful with that spliff, Eugene, it causes condensation…

Although only 1000 copies of *Back In The DHSS* were initially pressed, there were many represses and it quickly climbed to the top of the indie charts and even scraped into the national charts, as did the 'Trumpton Riots' EP released just at the start of 1986. The band was in demand, although in typical fashion, when they arrived in Bristol for a show and were confronted by a queue that snaked around the corner they assumed the people were queuing for the disco (as a journalist reported at the time). Live shows could be strangely monotonous, on occasions the four other band members coming across as a listless pub backing band scared to distract from the primary business of Blackwell's ode finding its muse. Reviewing the band on the home turf of the Liverpool System Club, early champion John McCready noted in the *NME*: 'Such is their commitment to the visual aspect of their performance, they make the Cocteau Twins seem like the Jackson Five'.

'I Hate Nerys Hughes (From The Heart)', a song where the dead rise up and descend on the social security offices before engaging in a spot of supermarket looting, appeared on *C86*, followed by a second single, 'Dickie Davies Eyes', a work that punctured the pretentiousness of its narrator's former lover, and, along the way, mused on the *Lord Of The Rings*, Michael Moorcock, the graphic art of Roger Dean, the pornographic nature of old Cadbury's Flake TV adverts and the shape of football commentator Brian Moore's head (which from above resembled the London Planetarium, apparently).

'Dickie Davies Eyes' gave Half Man Half Biscuit a third indie number one in a row but the band quit shortly after its release, citing 'musical similarities' as the reason for its demise. *Back Again In The DHSS* was a posthumous release (although the band later reformed), gathering up Peel sessions and unreleased tracks. Once more, it reflected the fact that the band had possessed a much harder edge than usually given credit for – at one point, mid-song, the question is asked, 'Is this the bit where we're supposed to make guitars collide?' Half Man Half Biscuit were perfect for those who found Morrissey's lyrics psuedo and the agitations of the more sloganeering bands absurd, creating in the songs instantly recognisable characters who were (in the words of Paul Du Noyer) 'too educated to be on the dole but too luckless or lazy to be anywhere else'.

Ted Chippington never played it straight for laughs but he got the laughs anyway. If anyone could be said to have played jester at the court of indie in the mid-1980s, then Chippington was that person, delivering up witticisms with a deadpan delivery on the wings of flat, Midland vowels. He wasn't a comedian but an *anti-comedian* and on any of the bills he played, guaranteed to be the most subversive of the acts, twisting the notion of stand-up out of all recognisable shape. Like Les Dawson's piano playing, or Tommy Cooper's magic tricks, his was light entertainment of a high order and confusing for those slow on the uptake, who sometimes asked, 'Is he *meant* to be funny?' In truth, he was meant to be *annoying…*

Ted Chippington's first gig, he told John Robb in *Death To Trad Rock*, was 'in a pub in Bristol, to no-one. The second was in a blizzard in Malvern.' His third was in the Malt 'n' Hops public house in Stafford, where he was billed as Eddie Chippington. A tape exists of a legendary gig on HMS Ark Royal, where Chippington played the mess to an almost silent audience. Jumping forward a couple of years to 1984, Chippington supported the Fall in Birmingham. The set was recorded and released in 1985 by Vindaloo as a 7" EP, 'Non-Stop Party Hits Of The '50s, '60s & '70s'. John Peel gave the record a spin and Chippington was on his way.

'Ted used to perform on a bill with a band called Here & Now,' remembers Rob Lloyd. 'He was always a fan of that kind of space/ prog rock stuff like Gong and he used to get up on stage really just to roil the audience. He then started appearing with a Birmingham band called the Dangerous Girls – another slightly hippyish, free festival type of outfit – and at some point the Nightingales played with them and that was how I got to know Ted and how Ted began playing supports for us.

'Ted always records himself with a sort of Dictaphone type thing he has. One time we were in my flat listening to his performance with the Fall and I just suggested to him that we ought to put the thing out, which is how the EP came about.'

In the very early 1980s, off-kilter comedy clubs were something of a rarity and opportunities for alternative stand-up were few and far between. Transported from the antiseptic environment of the conventional comedy club into the more volatile environment of the rock circus, Chippington's antagonistic act fitted perfectly. His trail of discord stretched right back, to vagabonds and poets such as Attila The Stockbroker and Seething Wells (who regularly boasted of the occasion he 'blew New Order off stage' at the Leeds F Club), frontiersmen with choice repertoires that often earned them the honour of being canned and bottled off stage. Chippington took a particular delight in standing up for himself. 'Who the fucking hell are you?' a drunken Liverpool crowd chanted on one occasion. 'Ted Chippington' came the lugubrious reply, three times in succession.

Ted Chippington had two drapes (one green, one blue) and even fewer 'jokes'. How do you sell a blind man a dog? You ask him if he wants to buy one, he's not deaf. Do you want some LSD? ('No thanks mate. Gone decimal. No use for pounds, shillings and pence…') Etc, etc. Occasionally, he'd offer to tell a joke about any subject. 'Sellotape!' shouted out one member of the audience once. 'Done that one before, mate,' quickly came the reply. Some people got it, some people didn't. Steven Wells considered him to be 'funnier than Lenny Bruce, sharper than Tony Hancock' but others were baffled: 'Something called Ted Chippingden (sic) came on while we waited for Yeah Yeah Noh,' wrote Dave Thompson in *Melody Maker* in March 1986. 'Looking like a cross between Howard Devoto and an oil derrick, he told a joke about Shergah, sang a song about a disco and had the well-lubricated audience rolling about helplessly with little more than a deadpan voice and a monotonous routine.' Steve Sutherland in the same paper called him 'shite, a Kevin Turvey rip-off who told the same non-joke endlessly in the hope it would acquire the stature of satire'. At least he recognised the 'non joke'…

The Man In A Suitcase album appeared in March 1986 – the title referred to the battered case Chippington used to carry with him from gig to gig – and a single lifted from it, a cover of the Beatles' 'She Loves You', caught the ear of daytime Radio One DJ, Steve Wright, who began playing the record on his afternoon show, sending it (on re-release through Warners) into the lower reaches of the national charts. For a short period, Chippington fever was afoot, with a book of cartoons in the pipeline and a video. Asked by *NME*'s Terry Staunton what the video would be like, he responded: 'A cross between *On The Buses* and *A Hard Day's Night*, a bit like the *Magical Mystery Tour* only with some laughs…'

Chippington famously claimed that the deal with Warner Brothers earned him 'a £1000 and a nice curry'. In fact, the deal, brokered by Bill Drummond who worked at the time for the label, was inextricably linked with both Ted's label Vindaloo and with the Nightingales and We've Got A Fuzbox and We're

Gonna Use It. By 1986, Vindaloo, the label started by Rob Lloyd in 1979 to release a single by his band the Prefects, was enjoying something of an Indian summer. The success of Ted Chippington had motivated Lloyd to reanimate the label, and along with *Man In A Suitcase* and 'She Loves You' he released an album by the re-energised (and reconstructed) Nightingales, *In The Good Old Country Way*, and a single by Bob & Vi (where Lloyd teamed up with Vi Subversa), 'Keep Lying, I Love It'. It was Fuzzbox, however, that caused all the fuss.

When We've Got A Fuzzbox And We're Gonna Use It formed in 1985, three of the girls were still at school and only band member Maggie Dunne worked for a living (employed at the local dole office). It was Dunne who came up with the name of the band after the group had gone out to buy a distortion pedal and she had commented: 'We've got a fuzzbox and we're gonna use it!' On their first gig, the girls supported (as a joke) local band the Bang Brothers at Birmingham's Barrel Organ. They played three songs – hyperventilated versions of the old classics 'Fever' and 'Spirit In The Sky', and a fumbling rendition of 'Console Me', a song Victoria Perks (Vix) later claimed to have written at the age of eight. They were shambolic, but shambolic in a way that absolutely exuded enthusiasm.

Word got around the grapevine and Robert Lloyd turned up for the band's second gig with a mind half set on poaching some of the girls for his own band, the Nightingales. A combination of the band's artlessness and naivety, though, thoroughly floored him, as did the band's visual presence that rested somewhere between the chic of punk and the cheerful rebelliousness of St Trinians. Lloyd asked the band to make a record for him instead.

'I thought they were right good fun,' remembers Robert Lloyd. 'We'd just made Ted's album and things were selling well back then, well enough for Rough Trade to be happy with me to keep putting stuff out. At first, the girls thought that I was taking the piss, but they agreed instantly to let me make a record. It was a bit weird because the recordings had to be done at night since during the day three of the girls had to be at school. They'd each tell their parents that they were staying at the home of one of the others so that they'd be allowed out. They did their bits in the studio and then they'd catch a bit of sleep under the mixing desk before it was up in the morning for school.'

Four tracks were recorded – 'XX Sex', 'Rules And Regulations', 'Do I Want To?' and 'She' – and when the record was finished Lloyd travelled to London to visit Rough Trade where label manager Simon Edwards suggested that the record be released as a 'limited edition' in coloured vinyl, a ruse that might help shift some copies in view of the fact that the band was completely unknown. The girls decided on a lurid purple for the pressing and 1000 copies were pressed. 'Within days, Simon rang me to say the pressing had sold out and that since we hadn't actually said how many copies the release was limited to it was legitimate to go on and repress it,' remembers Lloyd. 'He asked what colour we wanted this time and I think we picked lime green. This process went on for weeks and weeks, the pressings increasing to batches of 3-5000. In the end we ran out of colours and just pressed it up in black. We made a video that was shot in the back garden and got shown on the Chart Show and the record ended up in the Top 50.'

The press had a field day with Fuzzbox – interpreting their music in a way that embraced feminism and made Year Zero amateurism laudable again. There was a fuzzbox, mainly used to treat the bass, and the band's line-up – Maggie on keyboards and guitar. Vix on vocals and violin, Jo on bass, guitar, drums and piano, and Tina on percussion and saxophone – caused a bit of havoc with engineers used to conventional line-ups. The girls often switched instruments, and, as the Legend! pointed out, their live set was 'equal parts bluff, tunes and charisma... closer to Kleenex than the Slits…' 'It's amusing when a review says we are really amateurish,' the band told another journalist at the time, 'because we *are*, we *know* we are and we're *glad* we are…'

Around about the same time that Warner Brothers contacted Vindaloo about Ted Chippington, the company was also in touch about Fuzzbox. Fuzzbox, through their manager Patsy Winkelman, were keen to stand by Lloyd and Vindaloo and so a multi-component deal was reached whereby Warners signed Fuzzbox and Ted Chippington but also supported a Vindaloo compilation album called *A Baker's Dozen* (where Bob & Vi and Bumbites joined in the fun), funded a 'Vindaloo Summer Special' EP release and backed a Vindaloo Summer Special package tour featuring all three artists. The tour went out under the banner 'Rockin' With Rita' and sticks of Vindaloo rock were available to purchase in the auditorium foyers. Fuzzbox had supported the Nightingales previously but for the tour the roles were reversed, Fuzzbox headlining, with Chippington and his suitcase carrying up the rear.

The 'Vindaloo Summer Special' EP featured all three artists vamping up Chippington's 'Rockin' With Rita' and was backed with a Nightingales track ('Let's Surf') and a 'Fuzzy Faves' medley by Fuzzbox, the girls getting to grips with 'Sitting In The Backseat', 'Itsy Bitsy Teeny Weeny Yellow Polka Dot Bikini' and 'Kookie Kookie'. On the tour, Fuzzbox worked their way through a number of classics, including an a cappella version of 'Tutti Frutti' (occasionally delivered in a camp style with the song's original gender kept as written) and a bastardised version of 'Da Doo Ron Ron' where the lyrics were sometimes amended at the expense of Sigue Sigue Sputnik. Chippington also took on the classics, 'Hound Dog' going down particularly well, not least with a couple of fans who trailed the entire tour, throwing on to stage fluffy rabbits each time Ted deliberately mis-delivered a line – 'You ain't never *killed* a rabbit and you ain't no friend of mine…'

Once the buckets and spades were put away and the deck chairs folded orderly, life resumed some sort of normality. Fuzzbox carried on with Warners and released a debut album in the winter. In truth, the structure couldn't for long support the 'multi-coloured buoyancy' that was the band at its fragile best, but it was fun while it lasted. Chippington also carried on, delivering a fine if predictably warped version of Dion's 'The Wanderer', in which he pleaded, 'I'm not the wanderer…. Not too keen on roaming around and around.' In time, both he and the Nightingales returned to Vindaloo HQ and their misfit lives of old.

'The absolute fucking blast,' as Rob Lloyd describes it, 'was over.'

EPILOGUE

C86 AND
ALL THAT

ON 3 MAY 1986 THE *NME* announced the next two cassettes to be issued in its long-running tape series – a Billy Holiday compilation called *Holiday Romance* and a compilation of contemporary and largely unknown indie bands, *C86*. In February, *Pogo A Go Go* (a punk compilation) and *Feet Start Dancing* (a soul one) had appeared, bringing the total number of *NME* cassettes up to twenty-two since the series had launched in 1981. Reader's collected up coupons (usually four were needed out of a six-week period) and sent them in to the paper with a postal order or cheque to cover postage and packing. In return they received a tape.

The *NME* had launched its tape series in a golden age when grass roots taping culture was at its height and all the major music papers reviewed cassettes in columns with names like Garageland (*NME*), Playback (*Melody Maker*) and Cassette Pets (*Sounds*). There was even tape formatted magazines – including *SFX*, *Tapezine*, *Fast Forward* and the curiously named *Morrocci Klung* – and also tape fanzines (fanzines that just reviewed tapes), the best being *Stick It In Your Ear*. The most obvious criticism of *C81*, the debut and landmark *NME* cassette that featured Scritti Politti, Cabaret Voltaire, Josef K, Orange Juice, Robert Wyatt, the Raincoats and others was that it did little for street-level tape culture.

C86, although well-intenioned, was, ultimately, a similar marketing device. Twenty-two acts were chosen for inclusion: Primal Scream, the Mighty Lemon Drops, the Soup Dragons, the Wolfhounds, the Bodines, Mighty Mighty, Stump, Boghsed, A Witness, the Pastels, Age of Chance, the Shop Assistants, the Close Lobsters, Miaow, Half Man Half Biscuit, the Servants, MacKenzies, Big Flame, We've Got A Fuzzbox And We're Gonna Use It, McCarthy, the Shrubs and the Wedding Present. Sales of the tape were expected to at least match those of others in the series (which peaked at around 4000) but with luck, *C86* might go on and emulate the success of *C81* (released at a time when the *NME*'s circulation was double what it was in 1986). That had sold an impressive 25,000 copies. Over a period of time, *C86* outsold all of the non-charity *NME* tapes but its life initially was intentionally circumscribed – the paper did around six to eight tapes a year and the next was already in the pipeline: *We Have Come For Your Children*, a 'psychedelic punk trash, garage band' tape of '60s underground tracks that was to include such gems as the Barbarians' 'Are You A Boy Or A Girl?', Count Five's 'Psychotic Reaction', and the Loolipop Shoppe's 'You Must Be A Witch'.

Filleting up and metaphorically wrapping in chip paper cult and underground classics was a relatively risk-free operation (then, as now). But with *C86*, the paper really put its neck on the line (as it had done with *C81*), 'strenuously supporting new bands rather than sneering at them', as it later said, and recognising, as it saw it, that 'around a big four that comprised of the Smiths, New Order, Depeche Mode and the Cocteau Twins, the independent chart of the early '80s was more than a stagnant scrapyard'. For some bands, being invited to appear on the tape meant the first time they had ever stepped into a professional recording studio. Some declined to be on the tape and some who should have been on it weren't asked to be. Some offered up exemplary work – as has been noted, Primal Scream's 'Velocity Girl' was a blueprint for a whole indie sound that would follow – whilst a great number thought they would be shrewd, taking the *NME*'s shilling but keeping the good stuff back and not squandering it on a here-today-gone-tomorrow opportunity.

By early June, *C86* was dropping through the letterboxes of *NME* readers and the ICA announced a rock week at the end of July to celebrate it. Sixteen bands appeared on the bill, which ran Monday through Friday. A measure of the tape's immediate cultural impact is the fact that 'The Sonic Skyscraper', a saboteur promoter, attempted to organise a week of counter shows, flyers pressed up promoting a 'Fuck The ICA Rock Week' event to be held upstairs at the Enterprise in Chalk Farm. Proposed bands on that bill included Chesterf!elds, BMX Bandits, Razorcuts, Hobgoblins, Talulah Gosh, A Riot of Colour and My Bloody Valentine, but the event never happened.

Already, the controversy that would dog the tape in its early days rose up. While many took the tape at face value, including the weekly listings magazines, others viewed it with suspicion, some as an attempt to create a genre where none had previously existed. *Melody Maker*, the *NME*'s IPC stable mate, and bitter rival, fiercely took against the tape, sending a troupe of reporters to the ICA but never once in its pages of reviews mentioning the tape's title or its sister paper, reviewing instead an event that it claimed was called 'Cool In The Spool' (the strapline the *NME* used when announcing the tape). The three-line whip meant that the reviewers did everything possible to reduce the acts while paradoxically giving them a huge amount of publicity. David Stubbs' review of Tuesday night's proceedings scored a double-hit since one of the band's he insulted contained the *NME* journalist Cath Carroll. '*Miaow*! How sweet. Who'd kick a little kitten?' his review tittered, adding, 'By the end of the set every song is like a Morris Minor proceeding at a gentle 30mph.' Stubbs also reviewed the Rough Trade vinyl edition of *C86* that appeared in September, maintaining the sixth-form wit in calling the album's participants 'fanatics for whom Camberwick Green is a sort of Palestine'.

The right wing liberal view treats rock music like an Olympic sport, with the annointed at the top and the lowliest, designated inept at the bottom. It is important that everyone knows their place, or they'll jolly well be told it. Such a pinched approach ran contrary to the spirit of *C86*, which was wayward, unfocussed, inept even, but summed up, surely, one of the purposes of youth, which is to have fun regardless and to be allowed expression. It was obvious even at the time that the exuberance of *C86* would win out over those for whom the business of having fun was far too serious a matter to be left in the hands of those enjoying themselves.

David Stubbs' reference to the children's television programme Camberwick Green was carefully placed, and not intended merely to put a smile on the face of Half Man Half Biscuit's Nigel Blackwell (although it would have undoubtedly done that). A couple of articles had appeared – also in *Melody Maker* – attempting to assess, from a quasi-sociological point of view, the meaning of the new indie. 'Examine indie pop closely,' wrote Simon Reynolds in a June 1986 article entitled 'Younger Than Yesterday', 'and you'll see that at every step it defines itself as pop's opposite.'

Reynolds argued that the very names of the bands – the Soup Dragons, Close Lobsters, the June Brides, etc – reflected a retreat into childhood, and that the music itself lived in 'the interstices of *possibility*', unlike 'pop' music that had in manly fashion accepted its responsibilities and for better or worse was grown-up (or, put another way, it might be argued, had willingly conformed in a Thatcherite way to the realities of the market).

The idea of indie pop as some sort of deliberately-regressed nirvana was followed up in a more specific article, 'Ladybirds And Start-Rite Kids', where, amongst other things, the asexual nature of the indie scene was examined. Hopelessly trapped souls reflected the order of the day – girls caught in a sexual netherworld, the pale and pasty boys the opposite of 'the mainstream image of a desirable body – vigorous, healthy, bronzed muscles for men, curves for women'. In places, the article reads like parody: 'Some hardcore activists go all the way, and sport a satchel or a quaint duffle bag –and then they really look like Start-Rite kids….' At the end of the article, a group of indie kids assess their 'cutie' style in a fashion worthy of a Blue Peter badge.

The articles needed to be taken with a rather heavy pinch of academic salt and did far more in attempting to invent largely non-existent labels than *C86* ever did – carefully offering up some appropriate tags such as 'Cutie', the pre-cursor to the more ghastly 'Twee' that lurked just around the corner. Adrian Thrills, writing in the *NME* at the end of the year questioned the validity of such 'shambling sociologists' and referred specifically to the 'psuedo intellectual tract' that was 'making a ludicrous link between the rise of the baggy anorak as a fashion extra with a disdain for the hedonistic pleasures of the flesh. Did anyone concerned check out the opening line of the *C86* cassette? It concerned a certain velocity girl: "here she comes again, got vodka in her veins…" Yeah, very cute.'

The bands were oblivious to all this, short of arguing that they were or weren't part of something that was or wasn't happening: most, as Simon Reynolds had pointed out, directed their ire towards the world of big, bad pop while others just got on with things. Some bands – whose work demands further analysis elsewhere – emerged right on the cusp of *C86* and moved the aesthetic forward, taking what suited them and discarding the rest. They include Talulah Gosh (wilfully 'cutie', FUN, theoretical), Pop Will Itself (self-explanatory, proto Grebo, songs so brief 'they make the Ramones look like the Alan Parsons Project' (NME)), Razor-cuts (the quest for the perfect *moment*), the Primitives (fuzzbox), the Chesterfields (BIG pop), Mighty Mighty (perfect pop), and the Sea Urchins (transient) all of whom began making their mark in the post-*C86* world of indie. Some others were in the process of recalibrating their sound for the future order, bands such as the Stone Roses, Spacemen 3 and My Bloody Valentine.

It is too easy to lay all the ills of the sanitised and branded future 'Indie' at the door of *C86*, but 1986 was a transitional year anyway. The *NME*, for the first time, took on a fully designated marketeer, charged with protecting/ exploiting the paper's 'brand'. Meanwhile, in the wider world, the deregulating of the City of London opened up the way for the casino culture approach to global fiscal management that surprisingly took until 2008 to come home to roost. The CD – 'perfect sound that lasts forever', as the early ads proclaimed – began its aggressive rise, in tandem with the emergence of heritage culture/ Dad Rock music magazines like *Q* (launched with the express intention of appealing to the CD buyer in an age when rock would become one long re-mastering project, as it has largely become, or so say some). In music journalism, the shift from critical function to extension of PR had already began, at least that was the view of observers Fred and Judy Vermorel, who in May were noting what they called a 'consensus terrorism – the process whereby writers, artists, management, etc, work together as a team in order to conscript emotions as part of … huge worldwide marketing strategies'. It is hard to argue with this conclusion.

Eventually, the market *did* take its toll, as always it will. Many of the labels that had started up to service the new indie music folded, almost as quickly as they had started. The hard-luck stories mounted up as the banks moved in, repossessed homes, sequestered stock, and sent the entrepreneurs back to the biscuit factories and clerks' offices, or, in some cases, into academia and the professions. Acid House and Rave culture was just around the corner, even closer if you were in the know, as Danny Rampling opened his Schoom Club at the end of 1987. The lads' magazines would follow on shortly. The old music looked out of step.

Hedonism was the coming thing. Some of the original bands, record company owners, and journalists embraced the new scene, which was far more successful in terms of crossing over into the mainstream and having 'real' chart hits. Coming out the other side, there would no biscuit factories or clerks' offices waiting for them, just rehab.

For a period, the music of *C86* went underground, but it never disappeared. Like the cool universe – the dark matter the astronomers tell us floats between the stars and is the most interesting, dynamic and volatile part of the night sky – it was always out there, if not always visible to the naked eye.

ACKNOWLEDGEMENTS

THE STORY OF THE MUSIC of this book is detailed in the pages of the weekly music press for the period, sometimes in day by day detail, and also in the array of extraordinary fanzines produced during the period. This primary source material forms the basis for the book. I did, however, conduct a small number of interviews and would like to thank Gina Hartman, Jowe Head, Paul Groovy, Jed Dmochowski, Alan McGee, Dave Evans, Ken Popple, Jerry Thackray, Simon Down, Geoff Stoddart, Adam Sanderson, Pete Astor, Bruce Dessau, David Callahan, Sean Dickson, Tim Naylor, Andrew Burnett, John Robb, John Hyatt, Rob Lloyd, Simon Crab, Ron, Phil Wilson, Jon Hunter, Greg Keeffe, Derek Hammond, John Grayland, Joe Foster, Stephen Pastel, Geoff Travis, Pete Flanagan, Edwin Pouncey, Philip King, David Westlake, Martin Whitehead, Mike Bryson, Nic Beales, Dave Parsons, David Gedge, Geoff Taylor, Neil Howson, Malcolm Eden, Simon Reynolds, Dave Haslam, Jim Kavanagh, Simon Murphy and, last but not least, Kevin Pearce. The list of fanzines sourced includes, but is not limited to: *Born To Lose, Kings Road, Nag Nag Nog, Jamming!, Fumes, Communication Blur*, the *Legend!, Juniper Beri Beri, Airstrip One, Noise Annoys, Bucketfull of Brains, Grim Humour, Artificial Life, Blackpool Rox* (later *Rox*), *Groovy Black Shades, Slow Dazzle, Simply Thrilled, Class War, Hungry Beat, Trout Fishing In Leytonstone, Adventure In Bereznik, To Hell With Poverty, Ferocious Apache, Bandits One To Five, Attack On Bzag, Debris, Monitor, Underground, Rouska, Alphabet Soup, Pure Popcorn, Printhead*, the *Bumper Book of Yeah Yeah Noh*, and *Cloudbase*. I also made extensive use of material printed in the *Catalogue*, the Rough Trade-funded publication that represented the King James bible (not least in the quality of its reviews) 'for the independent music trade'. I quote the following manifestos and thank the authors of them: Big Flame

Manifesto, Age of Chance Manifesto, Splash One Manifesto. The Felt journal, *Foxtrot Echo Lima Tango* (2010) was invaluable, as was Michael Hann's exceptionally good online history, *The Paisley Underground: Los Angeles's 1980s Psychedelic Explosion* (*Guardian*, 16 May 2013). The following were also a mine of information: *Brochure* (1981), *Bandzine* (1981), the Television Personalities *Fan Club Newsletter* (issues 1 and 2, 1985). Stephen Pastel and Paul Groovy allowed me to quote from letters between them and Paul Groovy gave me acces to his formidable archive of material from the time. I also briefly quote from letters between Paul Groovy and David Keegan, and Paul Groovy and Alan McGee. Chapter One quotes from Alex's Ogg's excellent sleevenotes to the deluxe edition of *Pillows & Prayers* (2007): a number of Mike Alway quotes are taken from there (and also from a *Guardian* interview at the time). Chapter Three owes a small debt to *The Groovy Movie*, Chapter Five to Michael Moorcock's 'Positive Punk' television article (*South of Watford*, 1983), Chapter Nine to *Stop the City 83-84*, the film made by Mick Duffield and Andy Palmer, and Chapter Nineteen to Jim Demuth's *The Outsiders*. 'Ron', who was part of the organising group, gave me access to his private diaries at the time of the Stop the City marches. The following books were also sourced: *Bedsit Disco Queen: How I Grew Up & Tried To Be A Popstar*, Tracey Thorn (Virago, 2013), *Alan McGee & The Story of Creation Records: The Ecstacy Romance Cannot Last*, Paolo Hewitt (Mainstream, 2000), *The Creation Records Story: My Magpie Eyes Are Hungry For The Prize*, Dave Cavanagh (Virgin, 2000), *Creation Stories: Riots, Raves & Running A Label*, Alan McGee (Sidgwick & Jackson, 2013), *New Romantics: The Look*, Dave Rimmer (Omnibus, 2013), *Rip It Up & Start Again*, Simon Reynolds (Faber & Faber, 2005), *A Pretty Smart Way To Catch A Lobster*, Christian Paris (Completely Novel, 2011), *Digging The Seam: Popular Cultures of the 1984/5 Miners' Strike*, ed. Simon Popple & Ian W Macdonald (Cambridge Scholars Publishing, 2012), *Bash The Rich: True Life Confessions Of An Anarchist*

In The UK, Ian Bone (Naked Guides Limited, 2016), *Document & Eyewitness: An Intimate History of Rough Trade*, Neil Taylor (Orion, 2010), *Autobiography*, Morrissey (Pengin Classics, 2013), *Death To Trad Rock*, John Robb (Cherry Red, 2009), *Still Suitable For Miners: Billy Bragg, the Official Biography*, Andrew Collins (Virgin, 1998). Finally, more general thanks are owed to the following: Karen Walter (as ever), Karen Morgan, Megan Sheer, Simon Williams, Ian Wells, Bruce Dessau, Derrick Louden, Ian Preece, Dave Watkins, Richard Fletcher, Alison Taylor and Roy Carr.

C86 & All That: The Creation Of Indie In Difficult Times, covering the years 1983-86, is the first volume in a projected trilogy. The second volume, *The Revolution That Took Place Before Tea-Time*, will move the story on from 1986 up to 1989 and introduce a new cast. A final volume will cover the years 1989 to 1992. Curiosly, and surely not coincidentally, the rise of the independent sector more or less ran parallel to the rise (and fall) of Margaret Thatcher, seriously gaining traction at the end of the 1970s as a loose conglomerate of like-minded individuals help bring into being the Cartel. By the time of Thatcher's fall in 1991, the indie sector itself was in trouble, Rough Trade collapsing the same year and Factory following suit a year later. What came after was something different.